FEMINISMS AND PEDAGOGIES
OF EVERYDAY LIFE

FEMINISMS AND PEDAGOGIES OF EVERYDAY LIFE

edited by
Carmen Luke

STATE UNIVERSITY OF NEW YORK PRESS

Versions of three chapters in this book were originally published elsewhere:

Bartky, Sandra Lee. "Shame and gender," in Bartky, S. L. *Femininity and domination.* © 1990. By permission of the publisher, Routledge, New York.

Bordo, Susan. *Unbearable weight: Feminism, Western culture, and the body,* pages 99–134. © 1993, The Regents of the University of California. Reprinted with permission of the publisher.

Eisenstein, Zillah R. *The female body and the law,* pages 42–69 and 222–24. © 1988, The Regents of the University of California. Reprinted with permission of the publisher.

Published by
State University of New York Press, Albany

© 1996 State University of New York

For information, address State University of New York Press,
State University Plaza, Albany, N.Y., 12246

Production by Marilyn P. Semerad
Marketing by Dana E. Yanulavich

Library of Congress Cataloging-in-Publication Data

Feminisms and pedagogies of everyday life / edited by Carmen Luke.
    p.   cm.
    Includes bibliographical references and index.
    ISBN 0-7914-2965-2 (alk. paper). — ISBN 0-7914-2966-0 (pbk. :
alk. paper)
    1. Feminism and education. 2. Critical pedagogy. 3. Social
learning. 4. Women—Socialization. 5. Sex role. I. Luke, Carmen.
LC197.F466 1996
370.19'345—dc20   96-1356
                                                                              CIP

10 9 8 7 6 5 4 3 2 1

CONTENTS

ACKNOWLEDGMENTS

Editing an anthology always constructs new social and intellectual relationships around the collaborative production of knowledge. It is nearly three years now since I first started developing the ideas for this anthology. My special thanks and gratitude go to all the women and the sole male contributor in this volume for their rich and varied contributions which refocus issues of pedagogy in new and interdisciplinary directions. I have learned much from having worked with such a diverse group of scholars. Although their work does not appear here, I would like to thank Cheris Kramarae, Andrea Press, Liz Stanley, and Sue Wise who contributed valuable dialogue. Special thanks also go to Dianne Cooper who held the project together during my sabbatical. For enduring friendship and support, always ready to listen to my ideas and give me ideas and encouragement, my thanks go to Rhonda Hammer. Allan and Haida, of course, are always my core team.

Versions of three chapters in this book were originally published elsewhere:

Bartky, Sandra Lee. Shame and gender. In Bartky, S. L. *Femininity and domination*. © 1990. By permission of the publisher, Routledge, New York.

Bordo, Susan. *Unbearable weight: Feminism, Western culture, and the body*, pages 99–134. © 1993, The Regents of the University of California. Reprinted with permission of the publisher.

Eisenstein, Zillah R. *The female body and the law*, pages 42–69 and 222–24. © 1988, The Regents of the University of California. Reprinted with permission of the publisher.

INTRODUCTION

Carmen Luke

Readers of this anthology might believe that because its title bears the terms "feminisms" and "pedagogy," that the issues addressed here are exclusively about gender and teaching. This is not the case. Feminist theory and research have expanded exponentially in recent years both in diversity of inquiry and theorizing. That work, it seems to me, has made it abundantly clear that gender identity and relations cannot be apprehended or theorized on their own abstracted terms. That is, sex, gender, or femininity needs to be studied and theorized in its constitutive relationship to other sociocultural significations, economic and political histories, hierarchies, and discourses.

I use the term feminisms, therefore, to signify a collective orientation, albeit diverse theoretical positions, among this group of authors exploring issues of pedagogy. In that regard, each of the essays here provides only a partial take on aspects of identity politics in relation to parts of the pedagogical project of everyday life. Similarly, 'pedagogy' cannot be conceived of as an isolated intersubjective event since it too is fundamentally defined by and a product of a network of historical, political, sociocultural, and knowledge relations. Let me begin, then, with an anecdote to illustrate how concepts and meanings, in this case of pedagogy, are products of historically and culturally situated social formations.

On a visit in the summer of 1994 to the Institute of Pedagogics at the University of Ljubljana in Slovenia, I was invited by Valerija Vendramin and Eva Bahovic to give seminars on feminist pedagogy. In the many informal and formal discussions that followed my presentations, I was certainly prepared for debate about my own assumptions, those underlying feminisms, and feminist pedagogical models more generally. However, what I had not anticipated was a reluctance, among academic staff and students at the institute, to use the term pedagogy, particularly its use to name any distintinctly Slovenian, post-independence educational model. We came to that particular intellectual and cultural encounter from very different sociohistorical political contexts. Our conceptual assumptions and visions of political practice—whether through feminisms or models of education—were grounded in radically different experiences. For Slovenian academic educators, the term "pedagogy" was tied to two historical educational models, both of which remain affiliated with ideologically rigid mechanistic transmission models of education. The first was modeled on nineteenth-century Prussian didacticism under Austro-Hungarian rule and the second under Tito's communism. Generations of Slovenians have been subject to *pedagoski*—a centralized national curriculum and pedagogy of indoctrination, via nineteenth-century Prussian and twentieth-century communist models, which many Slovenian educators and intellectuals in Slovenia wanted to change in the public mind and all educational theory and practice. One way to achieve this transformation, they believe, is to rename education, to refuse reference to the term "pedagogy" in public and scholarly educational discourse in order to begin theorizing and implementing educational practice, to articulate a new vocabulary untainted by the traces of a colonial and authoritarian educational system.

But this particular aversion to the term should not suggest that what we in the West have called pedagogy—at the levels of institutional education in schools and universities, and of mass education through media and popular culture—are not hotly debated and central to visions of "the new order." For instance, a then-recent billboard ad in the city center of Ljubljana, featured close-up shots of five female posteriors clad only in a g-string thong. As a sign of "new times," it generated academic and public debates about the political and moral ramifications of such public pedagogies—lessons in mass-media advertising, consumption, and the objectification of women. Dealing with these new issues of representation in newly emergent, hybrid, and local discourses of capitalism clearly raised many questions and contradictory solutions about reeducating the public.

Wary of terms such as pedagogy or critical pedagogy, the phrase of choice among my Slovenenian colleagues was "democratic education." This, they argued, characterized new ways of thinking about education in a post-independence age. While we struggled over meaning, so to speak, of terms such as culture, feminism, and pedagogy, we had lengthy debates over the implications of calling any educational practice "democratic." In my view, liberal democratic education has always managed to construct itself as egalitarian, inclusive, and as valuing and rewarding individual ability within what many feminist and educational scholars consider a rigged and discriminatory meritocracy. Throughout this and the last century, democratic principles enshrined in the meritocratic ethos of competitive schooling, selective curriculum, and standardized testing, have managed to maintain and legitimate themselves through the mechanism of credentialing, rigid class, gender, and race divisions. Arguably, in the United States, Great Britain, Canada, and Australia, no other public institution has managed to do so as effectively. Under the liberal rhetoric of democratic participation, schools have long functioned as a selection and certification mechanism whereby the politics of exclusion and inclusion are institutionalized under the guise of equal access (to unequal competititon) and measurable merit based on individual potential and achievement.

The discourse of democratic schooling claims that individual difference of intellectual ability, processed through allegedly fair and equal access and participation in the competitive game of schooling, will "logically" produce unequal outcomes. How the cultural, gender, and class bias of curriculum texts and tests, pedagogy, and policy, work to tranform the discourses of equal access and equal participation into unequal material outcomes and the reproduction of class, gender, and race divisions is not part of the official promise and ethos of democratic education.

So, as an educator, I skirt the term 'democratic' as cautiously as my Slovenian colleagues skirt the term 'pedagogy'. For them, the term democracy promises genuinely new potential: both discursively and in the political agendas they now set themselves in establishing a new nation-state. After four decades of communist rule, preceded by Austro-Hungarian colonialism, democracy is a new, unknown entity and a conceptual and political possibility. As a "naming," it does not carry the same historical baggage as is the case in North American and other Anglo-liberal democracies. Our debates about feminism(s) shared similar but different concerns over meaning.

But what this account illustrates so clearly, and what feminist and cultural studies scholars have long argued, is that meaning is never guaranteed, fixed, or unproblematically shared among social agents. Terms such as pedagogy, on first glance, might appear to mean more or less the same thing to most people involved in the educational enterprise. Yet because they are embedded in substantively diverse cultural and historical contexts and experiences, appeals to a common meaning become problematic, debatable, if not altogether impossible.

Why Pedagogy?

My own life-long experiences of having been object and agent of pedagogical practices have led me to conceptualize pedagogy in very different ways than those commonly forwarded by educational theory. I have chosen pedagogy as the operant term for this volume for several reasons, all of which are tied to the fact that I engage in, construct knowledge and relations around, and am myself constructed by pedagogical encounters. But this choice is not based on the exclusivity of my own personal experience. Rather, the many personal and professional relationships I have formed in the process of becoming an educator and writer, have repeatedly taught me about shared educational experiences among women of all ages and from different cultural backgrounds, working in diverse disciplinary areas and countries. These shared experiences have revealed patterns of how we were taught to become girls, then women; how we learned to become academic women; how we learned to teach students and teach colleagues about ourselves as scholars and women. These have been long apprenticeships, often both difficult and rewarding. Yet they have profoundly influenced how we teach, what our research, theoretical, and methodological choices are, how we manage our institutional relationships, and how we negotiate our political agendas through diverse community activisms, scholarly networking, the university bureaucracy, and the building of professional and personal friendships with other academic women.

At the core of all this, is our labor as academic teachers, and "common" histories of having been objects of countless pedagogical regimes. These common histories do not imply identically shared experience but acknowledge that we have been formed in socially and culturally unique ways through the common experiences of schooling, growing up with television, learning from our mothers, "othermothers," childhood and professional peers, partners, and friends. It is this expanded sense of the term pedagogy that I have used to frame this volume. I wanted to put together a book that would reflect the many pedagogical dimensions of everyday life implicated in the constructions of gendered differences and identities.

Pedagogy in strict educational theoretical terms variously refers to the "art" or "science" of teaching, the processes and practices of imparting knowledge to learners and validating students' knowledge through evaluation and assessments. Within that definition, pedagogy refers to both intentional teaching and measurable learning, both of which are assumed to take place in formally named educational institutions. However, conventional definitions have generally failed to acknowledge the power/knowledge politics at the center of all pedagogical relations and practice:

> pedagogy refers to culture-specific ways of organising formal teaching and learning in institutional sites such as the school. In contemporary educational theory, pedagogy typically is divided into curriculum, instruction and evaluation: referring respectively to cultural knowledge and content, classroom interaction, and the evaluation of student performance. . . . Pedagogy entails a 'selective tradition' of practices and conventions . . . [and] insofar as such selections serve the interests of particular classes and social relations, decisions about . . . pedagogy are ultimately ideological and political (Luke & Luke, 1994, 566).

My own experiences as a girl in schools and a woman in university have taught me well both the selective tradition and the politics of selection. As girls in schools during the 1950s and 1960s, we didn't see ourselves in the curriculum other than in silly and stereotypical roles. Ten years at university completing three degrees also taught me quite clearly about which authors and what kinds of knowledges are ruled in and which are outside the canon of what Elizabeth Grosz (1988) calls "phallogocentrism." The gendered politics of classroom encounters—at school and university—have taught me and so many other women about the politics of voice and silence, even though we didn't always have terms or theory to talk about how pedagogy can function as a silencing device.

I have worked in the field of sociology of education for the past decade, and so my own academic and intellectual labor is centrally focused on questions of pedagogy and the sociology of knowledge. And, not insignificantly, the common experience of academic feminists—in fact, all academics—is that we all teach or at least have taught at some point in our careers. Yet for the most part, the politics of authority and knowledge which structure pedagogical relations and workplace culture of the academy have not received much theoretical or analytic attention in feminist theorising other than by feminist educators. Questions of curriculum, pedagogy, evaluation, and assessment have been addressed primarily by academic feminists in the discipline of education which, in my view, limits the theoretical scope and possibilities of rethinking pedagogical and knowledge relations from different disciplinary and subject positions.

Feminist practice in the academy takes many forms: women combat sexist, patriarchal, and phallocentric knowledges at many different institutional levels and sites (Luke & Gore, 1992). Yet we all teach in one way or another: whether it is in the form of research training and supervision, writing for publication, or delivering lectures and conference papers. But how our labor is contextualized in the specificity of diverse institutional settings, the particularity of our student composition, and the disciplinary areas in which we work, profoundly influences how and what we select to teach, how we teach, and how we locate and construct ourselves in the subject position we occupy as the signifier 'teacher'.

I believe that our labor as teachers exerts critical influences on our institutional and personal identities, on scholarship, theoretical choices, and how we interpret and enact the pedagogical project of teaching to enable learning. And since what we teach we have ourselves learned, we are by no means, to use Gayatri Spivak's phrase, "outside in the teaching machine." We read books and journals, deliver conference papers, exchange and debate ideas, all in efforts to learn so that we can engage in the academic business of institutionalized scholarship: the (re)construction and (re)production of knowledge. The same process holds for teaching: we learn in order to teach and thereby are doubly located in the knowledge production and reproduction equation.

Academic labor requires that we select and develop curriculum, teach it, and assess student learning. We not only teach the scholarly word in print, but we teach with and about the world which scholarly work attempts to theorize. We interpret through instruction the course readings and related materials and, finally, appeal to certain criteria to assess what we determined as learning outcomes. Selection, interpretation, and evaluation of knowledge are the core relations of exchange between teacher and student, and these are fundamentally embedded in intersubjective—but institutionally constrained—relations of authority, desire, power, and control.

For feminists, these relations often entail substantial moral and ethical dilemmas because "feminist pedagogy" has long claimed that it refuses traditional authority and power in teacher-student relations and, instead, claims to construct pedagogical encounters characterized by cooperation, sharing, nurturing, giving voice to the silenced (e.g., Culley & Portuges, 1985; Grumet, 1988; Pagano, 1990). The feminist classroom, as Jennifer Gore (1993, 88) puts it, is marked by "the rhetoric of freedom, not control." In these alleged spaces of freedom, teacher authority is often disavowed and the sexual politics of institutionally authorized feminine authority and power are generally not debated or questioned (Gallop, 1994; Gallop, Hirsch, & Miller, 1990; Luke, in press, 1996; Matthews, 1994).

For feminist academic educators across the disciplines, these are issues of considerable theoretical and practical significance in relation to the still important feminist agenda of a politics of transformation. For all of us, regardless of our diverse subject positions, identities, historical trajectories, or disciplinary locations, pedagogy is fundamental to our everyday work in academia, much as it has been a central feature of all our lives in the shaping of our knowledge and identities.

Teaching/learning encounters begin in infancy, and range from learning letters and numbers from "Sesame Street," concepts of home and family from the 1980s "Roseanne" or "Family Ties," 1970s "Brady Bunch," or 1950s "Father Knows Best," concepts of femininity from *Seventeen* or *Glamour*. They include "things my mother taught me," culturally different protocols we learned at our friends' homes, and years of lessons in what counts as knowledge derived from decades of schooling and, for many, college or university education. Informal pedagogies begin with toilet training, the instructional toys parents buy for their children, parental lessons about hot stoves, crossing the street, or how to ride a bike and tie one's shoes.

What girls learn about femininity and sexuality from their mothers, other girls, and magazines, boys learn from other boys in the playground and locker-room. Lessons in manhood, as David Morgan (chapter 4) explains, are constructed in ways significantly different from how girls learn and relate over issues of identity, sexuality, and gender relations. Morgan writes of growing up male in England in the late 1940s and early 1950s. In that particular historical and cultural context, he recalls how boyhood and consequently manhood was constructed through models of male heroes in popular culture, and through male bonding in the "rhetoric of [sexual] experience." Having taught at university for over three decades, his enounter with feminisms in the 1980s has led him to reconceptualize his own boyhood and adolescent experiences of learning to become a masculine subject. Morgan's chapter speaks to the pedagogical project of reconstructing one's theoretical position on the basis of new learnings (feminisms) which led to a reconceptualization and, importantly, "rewriting" of parts of his own historical trajectory into discourses of masculinity.

PUBLIC PEDAGOGIES OF EVERYDAY LIFE

Learning and teaching, in my estimation, *are* the very intersubjective core relations of everyday life. They exist beyond the classroom, are always gendered and intercultural. I have taught and been taught in many different kinds of educational institutions on several continents. As a girl, I was taught in Sunday school, Saturday-afternoon German-language school, English in a special school for immigrant kids, and so on. My domestic education entailed relatively formal lessons from my German mother and grandmother (sewing, gardening, and cooking "German"), my Canadian girlfriends' mothers (cooking "Canadian"), and my Chinese-American mother-in-law (cooking "Chinese"). I have learned from and have been taught by popular culture, peers, parents, and teachers, as a girl and as a woman. It is this broader (cross)cultural and social dimension of pedagogical practices—of teaching and learning the "doing" of gender—which shaped the focus of this book. That is to say, it is about the teaching and learning of feminine identities as they are variously constructed in potentially transgressive as well as normative models in a variety of public discourses, and as they are variously taken up by women.

Pedagogical regimes of subject formation begin in infancy. Before an infant is even born, most Western working-class and middle-class women consult not only other women, but pregnancy, birthing, and infant care books and magazines, teaching themselves about the ABCs of early childcare (Phoenix, Woollett, & Lloyd, 1993). Most parents attempt to teach young children the fundamentals of literacy, even if that literacy comes in the form of alphabet fridge magnets or playdough letters. In Western culture, parents induct the young into the sociocultural order and teach them culturally relevant moral lessons from folk and (often gruesome) fairytales in storybooks. Parents who can afford it, buy developmentally appropriate instructional toys in order to enhance their children's motor-skill, perceptual, and cognitive development.

As I show in my own chapter on children's popular culture as public pedagogies, computer games teach, and so do comic books, magazines, billboards, television, Barbie's Malibu Fun House, Voltron, Transformers, or the "multicultural" Power Rangers. Theories of play historically have been premised on the assumption that hands-on experience with manipulable objects are the basis for all learning. Yet psychological descriptions of play and pedagogy have tended to treat the sites, practices, and objects of play as individuated and nonideological. Children's toys and popular culture market not only desires and consumer behaviors, but cultural discourses, meanings, and values. Miniature tea-sets, little ironing boards and stoves, kiddie make-up sets, baby dolls, little cribs, and mini-strollers were the foundations of girls' play, learning, and "doing" femininity among the girls I grew up with and, as research continues to demonstrate, this discourse has changed little (Kline, 1994; Willis, 1992).

The social relationships generated around children's popular culture are centered on teaching and learning skills and values, and larger sociocultural and political lessons about class, gender, ethnicity, social power, family, good vs. evil. So, for instance, playing "house" or Barbie enables gender-specific social relations among girls and, of course, between individual girls and their toy objects. Boys' toys enable similar gender-specific relations among boys, and it is through these early gendered commodity discourses of play that kids are taught and actively learn about social power and relations, gender and race-identity formation. However, this is not to say that all children acquiesce to the play strategies and social relations implicitly prescribed by gendered toy commodities (see chapter 5). There is no simple and unmediated correspondence between, for instance, the lessons of children's popular culture, girls' or women's magazines, or even the more explicitly didactic lessons of schooling, and the formation of subjectivities and social identities. As most of the authors in part II argue, contrary to traditional social theory, culture industries do not produce a seamless hegemonic discourse which construct identically "duped" and experientially impoverished social subjects. Yet it would be equally naive to suggest that popular cultural texts and practices, or mass schooling, enable a boundless deferral to difference in the politics of meaning, reading positions, and identity formation.

The lessons of life are always simultaneously hegemonic, contradictory, and enabling of difference and diversity. But such tensions and contradictions can be particularly complex for children from dual-culture households who can experience diverse and often ideologically conflicting sources of formal and informal pedagogies that often add both a special burden and a unique complexion to identity formation (Luke, 1995; Reddy, 1994). As young parents, we made endless searches in toystores and bookstores for culturally inclusive books or toys which would teach our child about interracial families and cultural diversity. Much as my parents went to inordinate lengths to teach me about my cultural heritage, and to counterteach against the anti-Semitism and anti-German sentiment which was somewhat rampant in small-town Canada in the early 1950s, I too as a parent in an interracial family ended up having to learn how to teach my own child about bicultural identity, and to counterteach so much of the racism and sexism that came home from school and peers.

As a six-year-old immigrant girl, I spent hours in front of the television at my friend's house trying to learn English pronunciation and for years during my childhood, my parents sat me down almost weekly to learn and practice reading and writing German. In addition to language and literacy instruction at home, I was sent to Sunday school and Saturday-afternoon German school. Many of the Asian and European migrant kids I grew up with had to endure the same kinds of extra schooling we all hated. But what became more difficult as we grew older, was coming to terms with the tensions and contradictions between the cultural lessons of home and those we learned at school, from peers and popular culture about gender relations, career aspirations, and feminine identity. The lessons in *Seventeen* magazine were a lot more important than the lessons on femininity I was taught by my mother, the church group, or the girls' guidance teacher at school. Then, as today, girls studied teen magazines intently, wanting to learn everything we could about boys, dating, sexuality, how to be a young woman, how to cope with parents, and so forth. And, as Kerry Carrington and Anna Bennett argue in chapter 6, much of what has been condemned by first-wave feminist analyses as politically suspect and hegemonic constructs of normative femininity in such magazines, can in fact provide positive counter-discourses to traditional concepts of femininity.

Cultural clash and dissonance, cultural difference and cultural diversity is a lived reality for millions of bicultural children and adults. It was the texture of everyday experience for me and for the kids I grew up with in the many neighbourhoods where migrants invariably start out from (cf. Tizard & Phoenix, 1993). My generation was a product of postwar modernist schooling, the first to grow up with television and mass-media culture, yet a generation marked in large part by our generation of parents who themselves grew up before World War II in a radically different cultural sphere. Moreover, many of that generation were dislocated and relocated as a consequence of World War II, just as many of the previous generation drifted to the "new world" as a consequence of World War I. In fact, what is now widely conceptualized as the 'postmodern subject'—one constituted by multiple discourses and local sites, and continually reshaped through travel along and across life trajectories and cultural zones—is a condition of subjectivity not that uncommon to entire generations of mobilized groups following high modernist events such as industrialization, "hot" and "cold" wars, or the breakup of empires. Growing up mobile, crossing boundaries, straddling cultures, learning the "old" and the "new," profoundly shape a lived sense of gendered bicultural identity, ways of knowing multiplicity, diversity, difference, and a provisional sense of place. And it is this struggle for place, identity, and, indeed, survival—this learning to make the self in relation to the overlapping, sometimes congruent and often contradictory discourses that variously combine to constrain and enable subject positions and identities—that is the very substance of everyday life for most people in what are now called postmodern conditions.

Relations of learning and teaching, then, are endemic to all social relations, and are a particularly crucial dimension of parent-child relations. The authors in this volume argue that pedagogy is fundamental to all public/private life and all communicative exchanges, from the nursery to the playground, classroom to the courtroom. Social agency in the world is about learning from and reacting to multiple information sources, cues and symbol systems. In chapter 2, for instance, Elisabeth Porter develops an analysis of women's friendships. She makes the case that learning about others' desires, life narratives, needs, and goals is a prerequisite of identification with a concrete other in order that one may reciprocate with appropriate care, respect, and responsibility in the building and maintenance of women's friendships. We learn from others and we teach others about ourselves, our viewpoints, and our understandings. This volume, then, is an attempt to explicate the experiential and representational texture and political parameters of some of those everyday sites where gender identities and relations are taught and learned.

Thematic Framework

Most collections like this begin with an idea. That idea quickly turns into an intellectual and social project as one maps the initial idea onto existing and related areas of debate and inquiry, and then goes about contacting scholars in efforts to secure contributions. The intellectual debate over a project that ensues with potential contributors also produces social relationships which form a writing community of sorts. In the three-year course of this project, I have formed fax, e-mail, phone, and writing relationships with people I have never met. That in itself is a dimension of sociality and intellectual work which both requires and generates certain kinds of pedagogical skills as well as a politics of identity claims and positionings. Let me elaborate on this.

My case for a volume such as this had to be argued in order to convince potential contributors of the merit of taking the concept of pedagogy out of its traditional semantic field and connect it more directly to issues of identity. Papers had to be edited and arguments provided to justify those edits; in many ways, that kind of textual work is similar to the teaching function inherent in marking student papers. Through this negotiation over knowledge, I have learned much about the lives of the women in this volume. Many who started out committed to this project three years ago have had to drop out, mostly for work-related and a variety of personal and health-related reasons. Moves to a new job and all the institutional and social pressures that accompany taking on a new position—particularly in the case of academic women who are also single mothers—also took its toll. Events such as the birth of a child, or serious illnesses, call for a very different kind of social and writing engagement between editor and author(s) alongside the usual business of editorial work. Repeatedly, the dimensions of these relationships illustrated Elisabeth Porter's argument in her essay on women's friendships.

This volume consists of thirteen essays organized into three parts. Part I addresses questions of identity formation, part II focuses on the public pedagogies of popular culture, and part III examines pedagogical agendas and politics in academic and legal discourse. I thought it conceptually and politically important to begin the book with the politics of identity formation, and believe that chapter 1 makes a powerful contribution to debates about the complexity of gender and cultural intersections that impact on women of color. In "Learning Identities and Differences," Patricia Dudgeon, Darlene Oxenham, and Glenis Grogan talk about the identity politics of being Aboriginal women.

All three women come from diverse personal, disciplinary, and community backgrounds, but all claim a strong sense of self as Aboriginal women, and a shared commitment to advance the academic achievements of their people. Much has been written in Australia about Aboriginal identity—importantly, the reclaiming of lost identities. The three women here speak of a particular inflection of that struggle for identity: being Aboriginal, female, high-achieving, and working in academia. In this country where indigenous rights, standards of health care and housing, education and employment rates are far behind those achieved in many communities in developing countries, being Aboriginal, female, and in academic leadership positions, is a powerful accomplishment. One of the many difficult issues to come to terms with, they claim, is dealing with racisms from the white community and with their sense of difference wihin their own communities. Their stories tell parts of each woman's life experience. This approach—the telling of stories to each other—reflects the Aboriginal tradition of story telling which defines individuals' sense of place and belonging. From these stories emerge in sharp relief the impact their experiences have had upon the development of the philosophy of the Centre for Aboriginal Studies at Curtin University, where Darlene Oxenham and Glenis Grogan are centre coordinators and Pat Dudgeon is the head of the centre. Unlike the history of African-American Studies Centers, universities, and colleges in the United States, Aboriginal academic centers of study are relatively new in Australia. In that regard, the institutional positions the women occupy are testimony to their political and pedagogical commitments, tenacity and perserverance of purpose in a society and institutional context which has only recently let go of European, pastoral, and missionary models of Aboriginal welfare and education.

In the second chapter, "Women and Friendships: Pedagogies of Care and Relationality," Elisabeth Porter analyzes the moral dimension of women's friendships. She argues that women's friendships are characterized by learning about others' desires, life narratives, needs, and goals. Learning about others is a prerequisite for identification with a concrete other in order to reciprocate with appropriate care, respect, and responsibility. What differentiates women's friendships from men's disconnected sense of self and other, are shared intimacies, mutual supportiveness that emerge from concrete everyday lives, and a concerned partiality for and responsiveness to particular others, relations, and contexts. This orientation to particular others, not to an abstract generalized other, underpins women's relational caring. The social and ethical differences between women and men's orientation to self and other, Porter argues, are the consequences of pedagogic differences in early gender socialization and identity formation which are taught from birth and reinforced by social structures. Importantly, Porter argues for a feminist concept of friendship which is built on a dialogics of caring relationality and requires strong ideas and practices of the self: self-trust, self-love, and self-respect.

In "Motherhood as Pedagogy: Developmental Psychology and the Accounts of Mothers of Young Children," Anne Woollett and Ann Phoenix examine developmental psychology textbooks and use transcripts from interviews with mothers to identify constructs of motherhood and childrearing pedagogies. Their analysis supports Porter's argument about the early socialization of relationality among girls, and ties in with my own chapter in part II on the textual construction of childhood and parenting. But because undergraduate developmental psychology texts are not popular cultural texts per se, I thought it conceputally appropriate to include Woollett and Phoenix's essay in this first part of the book on identities and differences. Their transcripts demonstrate that mothers actively teach their children about sex-appropriate gender behaviors, values, and identities. These women identified more with their daughters than sons, and saw their relationships with their daughters in relational terms. Woollett and Phoenix show that developmental psychology constructs parenting as mothering, and idealized mothering is based on assumptions of white middle-class and heterosexual nuclear families. Class or cultural differences are ignored in these texts other than when "problem" families and mothering are discussed in terms of deviation and deficit.

Mothers' pedagogical functions, the authors claim, tend to be concretely based on, for instance, the children's ages, the number of children, and the contexts of women's everyday lives. Women's home pedagogies of childrearing and the construction of their identities do not follow the decontextualized lessons of "good" mothering promoted in developmental texts. Rather, the identity politics and power struggles within mother-child relations are mixed: women feel both good and ambivalent about motherhood; the alleged middle-class ethos of reciprocity, mutuality, and ("elaborated code") reasoning is riddled with mother-child conflict and tensions, battles of will, and power struggles. The image of ideal motherhood in developmental psychology theory, then, is an inadequate and unrealistic image of women-as-mothers. The perpetuation of this model to undergraduate students, many of whom will work in the public sector as social workers, counsellors or teachers, is politically naive and dangerous in an age when more and more women claim social identities which this discourse condemns: "working mothers," "young mothers," "single mothers," "lesbian mothers."

The last chapter in this part, "Learning to be a Man: Dilemmas and Contradictions of Masculine Experience" by David Morgan, examines the construction of masculinity. Given the relative paucity of scholarship by men on the construction of masculinities, I thought it important to include a contribution on pedagogic regimes that shape masculine identity formation. Morgan's essay, therefore, provides an historically interesting, class- and cultural-specific account of early lessons in masculinity, particularly lessons in male bonding over issues of sexuality. What Morgan describes are practices that are significantly different from girls' learnings and relations over issues of identity, sexuality, and gender relations. The relationships among boys that Morgan describes are often confrontational and hierarchical. Bullying is one such early boyhood experience through which boys learn "how to take it," and learn to be a man.

Morgan writes of growing up male in England in the 1940s. In that particular historical and cultural context, he recalls how boyhood and consequently manhood were constructed through models of male heroes in popular culture, and through male bonding in the "rhetoric of [sexual] experience" which, he argues, interects with what is commonly claimed as the dominant mode of masculinity—"the rhetoric of reason." Morgan counters the argument that divisions identified between women and men, femininities and masculinities, are usually mapped onto splits between emotion and reason. He claims that this differentiation "also maps out differences among men or styles of masculinity." Reason and experience combine in different ways to form masculine knowledge and identities, and are used in different ways by men within systems of patriarchal dominance. Masculinine identity formation, then, is not a unified experience among men and is never wholly experienced and constructed on one side of the experience/reason dualism.

How popular culture functions as public pedagogies is taken up in part II. This section begins with an excerpt from Susan Bordo's important book *Unbearable Weight* (1993), nominated for a Pulitzer Prize and selected by the *New York Times* as one of the "Notable Books of 1993." In "Hunger as Ideology," Bordo examines the politics of the gendered discourse of food in media representations. Food ads targeted at men often equate eating with sexual appetites, whereas women are positioned in a much more restrained, but no less eroticized, relation to food. The sexualization of desire and gratification, coded onto women's and men's relationships with food, is particularly evident in dessert, candy, and snack food ads. Food ads, however, do more than push to sell products: they teach consumer, gender, and cultural behaviors and values. Bordo points out that women's historical relationship to food has been to prepare and serve food to men and children, often foregoing her own portions in places and times where food was scarce. For women, the preparation and serving of food is the socio-cultural conduit through which she expresses her care, love, and devotion to kin through the giving of (oral) sustenance at the price of self-denial. Representations of gender in food ads are often ambivalent and contradictory, but mostly hegemonic. Women claim to "crave," "obsess," or "dive into" those scrumptuous deserts, yet compared to men's voracious appetitites and the generous portions they consume in food ads, women eat restrained and then only "tiny scoops" and "bite-size pieces." Busy career women (and, more recently, men) prepare and serve quick meals for the family, but a woman's "self-feeding" is almost always a solitary, "private, secretive, and illicit" affair in isolation behind closed doors.

The lesson for women is straightforward. In public she denies her hunger but in private, she obsesses, indulges, and fills herself with tiny bonbons, a few potato chips, or phallic ice cream bars. Bordo argues that the representation of women in Western media food ads "offer a virtual blueprint for disordered relations to food and hunger," and functions as a Foucauldian social discipline "that trains female bodies in the knowledge of their limits and possibilities." These texts and imageries do teach powerful lessons about what and how women should eat, how they should feel about food, and what foods they should be publicly seen with. The huge financial resources invested in the Madison Avenue vision of sex-food-gender, the billion-dollar diet industry, and the statistical evidence of women's many eating disorders, are testimony to the power of these images from which women do learn how to discipline their hunger, bodies, and identities.

Kerry Carrington and Anna Bennett also analyze textual imageries of femininity in "'Girls' Mags' and the Pedagogical Formation of the Girl," which provides an important counter-argument to scholarly critiques of sexist ideology in girls' magazines. Unlike the hegemonic gendered imagery in the more specialized discourse of food ads examined by Bordo, Carrington and Bennett argue that girls' magazines provide both hegemonic and "productive" images of femininity, and that there is no simple correspondence between textual form and content, and "the pedagogical formation of adolescent femininity." A close textual analysis of the four most popular Australian teen magazines (*Girlfriend, Dolly, Cleo, Cosmopolitan*) reveal that much of the imagery and textual content is in fact positive, productive, and enabling. They argue that there is not just a patriarchal plot, not just a hegemonic "culture of femininity," nor just a single stupifying discourse of "romantic individualism" at work in these magazines. Instead, girls are provided with a range of instructions, devices, and techniques for transgressing normative constructs of femininity. Ads and editorial texts provide lessons on how to manage menstruation, address common concerns about tampons, provide guidelines for safe sex and information on HIV, AIDS, and sexually transmitted disease, nutrition and health, contraception, eating disorders, lesbian and gay relationships, dating, make-up and make-over strategies with which to reinvent, remake, and "play" with sexual identity. Question and answer sections address a remarkably broad range of issues of pressing concern to teenage girls which many parents or school counselors probably do not deal with.

These magazines comprise one form of what Foucault called "governmentality" for the formation of feminine identity. However, these texts are no more than a cultural resource in the bricolage of everyday life in which we all make and remake ourselves *in relation* to a range of other discourses which are sometimes commensurate and hegemonic, other times contradictory and transgressive, but never static. Millions of girls today and in the past have learned how "to do femininity" from these magazines, and yet waves of generations did not grow up identically stupified and duped into *Stepford Wives* bliss. In Carrington and

Bennett's view, these magazines "are transgressive texts which expose femininity as a prop, a put-on, a make-up and make-over."

In my own chapter, "Childhood and Parenting: Constructs of Race and Gender in Children's Popular Culture and Childcare Magazines," I look at how race and gender are written into constructs of childhood, parenthood, motherhood in children's popular culture and parenting magazines. In contrast to the "productive" and "transgressive" constructs of femininity found by Carrington and Bennett in adolescent teen magazines, constructs of gender in children's popular culture and childcare magazines are decidedly reproductive of traditional gender divisions. The big money-spinning toy, videogame, and mass-media hits remain anchored in gender stereotypes, and parental self-help texts such as parenting magazines, do little to alter traditional perceptions of mothering or the family.

A content analysis of visual imagery in Australian, American, and British parenting magazines found that parents and children of color are virtually absent, as are gay and lesbian parents, and men in active parenting roles. Men function as professional experts, celebrity endorsements, or as cartoon features. Mothering, as Woollett and Phoenix also note in their essay, is represented as an isolated, indoor, and somewhat lonely activity centered solely on the care of an infant. The visual and textual representation of women in these magazines suggests that she has sole responsibility for the social and moral development of the young which, in turn, positions her as prime target for the kind "mother-blaming" perpetuated in developmental psychology and media pop-psychology discourse. The commodification of childhood, evident in the huge success of national and international retail toystore chains, is a central part of the instructional discourse of childcare magazines. "Good mothering" is based on assumptions of heterosexual and affluent nuclear families and on a woman's product expertise necessary for addressing children's innumerable developmental requirements which the commodity discourse claims to enhance and cater for. The commodification and marketing of childhood has segmented childhood into increasingly finer developmental stages, and mothers are continually exhorted to assume the moral and pedagogical responsibility of being knowledgeable of these developmental and corresponding commodity differences in order to make the right product choice. Thus, the articulation of finer-grained developmental categories, distinctions, and stages has become a way of constructing niche markets. Parenting, then, is a seductive but disciplining discourse embedded in fantasies of idealized normative femininity, exclusively white, middle-class, and heterosexual.

Susan Willis, in "Play for Profit," also looks at childhood as market
with a focus on the commodification and changing public space of play.
She argues that children's imaginative play is social and cultural practice through which gender stereotypes are variously combined, reproduced, and transgressed. Children's play, unfettered by high-tech gad-
getry, is fluid and malleable, drawing on and combining multiple
story-plots, characters, social relations, rules, and strategies. The play of
children's commercial culture, however, is contained within a controlled
environment of menued choices, much like schooling contains children
in a site of negotiated but nonetheless disciplinary regimes and within
similarly "menued"—categorized and boundaried—knowledges.
Amusement parks such as Disney World provide another site for what
may appear like a cultural domain for children's play, imagination, and
amusement. Yet here too experience is programmed, ordered, and
orderly, tightly "meshed with the economics of consumption as a value
system." The trend in the last decade towards the commercialization of
children's play zones, in Willis' view, aids and abets the encroachment
of capitalist logic into one of the last "free" spaces of children's play.
Pay-by-the-hour play areas in shopping malls, the identical colorful
and plastic play zones at McDonald's (free play if you eat), and "Discovery Zone" in the United States are regimented and supervised
spaces of play which promote a uniformity of "pretend" and play possibilities. Discovery Zone is a high-tech space replicating a Nintendo-
like game format. Structured activities confine kids to specific experiences (sliding through tubing or into ball vats, scaling mountains), and
to specific utterances. Much like fast-food chains only enable menued
dialogue between customer and attendant ("small fries, large coke . . . ,"
etc.), so do places like Discovery Zone limit dialogue to shouts of "Let's
do that again" or "Hey, follow me." Creative play, social interaction,
complex discourse structures, and intercultural play experiences are
increasingly limited.

Willis notes that because public parks and playgrounds are
becoming increasingly unsafe, the middle-class white flight to paid and
supervised play areas leaves public spaces to the poor, often black,
immigrant, and inner-city kids and their families. In the United States,
massive cutbacks in spending on public infrastructure and social services have hit public education particularly hard. As a consequence, a
private enterprise like Burger King "now runs ten high schools in the
West and Mid-west." Commercial television already has made substantial inroads into curriculum and pedagogy of the U.S. public school
system. Children's culture, their play and learning is undergoing radical change, and what this shift from free play to play for profit signals is

a shift to, in Willis' words, "technologically programmed definitions of play" which "fits the needs of managerial capitalism" (cf. Kenway, Bigum, & Fitzclarence, 1993).

The last chapter in this part, "Women in the Holocene: Ethnicity, Fantasy and the Film *The Joy Luck Club*," examines two cinematic texts as cultural pedagogy. Rey Chow's provocative analysis of the film *The Joy Luck Club* suggests a very different reading than the commentaries I have read or heard from viewers. She argues that the "ethnic film," a relatively new and burgeoning genre in Western cinema, is constructed in ways that white films and film-makers are not. The ethnic film has a double pedagogical functions in that it purportedly functions as a recovery of origins for ethnic groups, but serves also as cultural lessons for whites about others: their history, identity, social relationships, and experiences. Certainly the most recent collection of ethnic films focus precisely on those issues (e.g., *The Wedding Banquet; Like Water for Chocolate; Eat, Drink, Man, Woman; The Scent of Green Papayas*). Chow argues that these films function much like Foucault's "confessional," and "repressive hypothesis" by exposing to the normative gaze, and bringing "to light" the repressed histories and dark continent(s) of others. *The Joy Luck Club* reveals that otherness, the "secret" of Chinese identity and history, through the autobiographical narratives of the lives of four mothers—all from another time and place—through the eyes of their American daughters. However, the narrative and cinematic conventions used to symbolize "Chineseness" construct a pastiche of cultural stereotypes which, in turn, construct an "orientalist" reading.

In the second part of the chapter, Chow takes a different and unexpected turn by arguing that *The Joy Luck Club*, much like *Jurassic Park*, is part of the same moment of postmodern delegitimation of (traditional) knowledges, knowledge boundaries, and genres. By juxtaposing both films against Lyotard's notion of the delegitimation of knowledge, the science-fiction film and ethnic film fiction are ultimately legends of fantasy, fantasies of history with equal claims to narrative "truths" about our diversely constituted collective culture. Rather than reading *The Joy Luck Club* as subcultural, separate, and other, Chow reads it as functioning concurrently and at the same epistemological level as *Jurassic Park* in the postmodern partial and perspectival revisioning of knowledge about our multiple selves, ancestries, and origins. Ultimately, Chow argues, the scar on the neck of one of the mothers functions both as narrative hinge and metaphor which enables the narrative unfolding of mother-daughter continuities, and signifies woman as marked yet able to heal and recover (herself). But, importantly, the scar also signifies "the mark of a representational ambivalence and inexhaustibility—in this case, the ambivalence and inexhaustibility of the so-called 'ethnic film,' which participates in our cultural politics not simply as the other, the alien, but also as us, as part of our ongoing fantasy production."

Part III consists of four essays which consider the pedagogical functions and consequences for women of pedagogic and legal discourses and practices. The first essay by Sandra Lee Bartky, "The Pedagogy of Shame," is a revised excerpt from her influential book *Femininity and Domination* (1990). Here she articulates what, I believe, many feminist educators have witnessed in their own classrooms. For many but certainly not all women, academic discourse and the gendered politics of classroom encounters, can be a profoundly humbling and threatening experience. Women's sense of intellectual inadequacy, Bartky argues, reveals itself in both bodily habitus and speech. Self-denigrating comments about their work, excessive qualifiers which preface their comments, and the use of tag questions characterize "women's language" in the classroom. Female students are often apologetic for their work, and often interact with teachers in physically diminutive ways, whether that is standing back from the group, heads lowered, eyes down, "chest hollowed and shoulders hunched." Silence, hiding, concealment, a subtle cringe and tentative speech, a sense of self as inadequate, defective, or diminished—these are the hallmarks of shame that many women students embody.

Bartky speculates that women's habitus may be a counter-pose to men's competitive, verbally and physically assertive self-representations. But given the male-defined tenor of many university classrooms, silence can be a safe space for women, particularly since women's assertiveness or disputations are not always affirmed as valued intellectual contributions. However, if we look at the research on girls and schooling, which Bartky does in the last half of her essay, the evidence is clear that women enter university with a life-time of socialization behind them in learning to take second place. Whether through classroom speech or pedagogy, teacher attention, verbal questioning, praise or explanation, boys get more and girls get less. Although girls' achievement levels across the curriculum, in Australia at least, slightly exceed those of boys, girls learn to learn in a different mode, one marked by restraint, silence and, for many, an enacted sense of inadequacy.

Efforts to reverse girls' and women's socialized learning styles have been the focus in recent years of feminist and "critical" pedagogy models which seek to empower girls and women, and other silenced culturally marginalized groups. A key pedagogical and political strategy of emancipatory pedagogy is to give voice to the diversity of student experiences through inclusive curricular content and classroom dialogue in place of exclusive curriculum, and monologic transmission models of pedagogy. Anneliese Kramer-Dahl's chapter, "Reconsidering Notions of Voice and Experience in Critical Pedagogy," explores some of these tensions and contradictions that can emerge from the imperatives of institutionalized equity agendas in the university, and the politics of emancipatory agendas of critical pedagogy.

Speaking from her experience of teaching introductory composition courses, the tensions Kramer-Dahl analyzes are located in debates about equity, standards, il/literacy, culturally diverse students, and the institutional place of introductory writing courses. "Free and authentic expression," critical pedagogy advocates claim, helps "inexperienced writers gain confidence and overcome their fear using their own opinions." Yet, according to Kramer-Dahl, to allow students their own modes of expression in an effort to encourage their confidence and develop academic literacy skills, does little more than legitimate their "remedial" status and "reproduce their own commonsense." To enable them to voice and value their own experiences and points of view can further divisions between already privileged students and those enrolled in university writing courses in order to overcome their various social, cultural, and educational disadvantages. Kramer-Dahl's efforts to implement a critical pedagogy, a "language of critique," and inclusive minority-authored curriculum content that would bring cultural diversity from the "margins to the center," had several disempowering consequences, not least of which was students' resistance to the "ban" on white authors. Her students did not want to dwell on their "othered" status but wanted to be taught those texts, genres, and writing skills that would lead them to authoritative academic discourse and literacy skills. Furthermore, providing forums for "authentic voices" did not always generate dialogic encounters among culturally diverse women whose complex and conflicting histories of racial and gender oppression generated what Dianne Fuss (1989) calls a "hierarchy of oppressions" that so easily slip into identity-based pedagogical encounters.

Importantly, Kramer-Dahl points out that teachers' marking and evaluation of student writing of personal experience reproduces a kind of (student) confessional and (teacher) voyeurism which can function as yet another ideological and cultural controlling mechanism. Pedagogies, then, offerered in the name of relevance, empowerment, or liberation can easily turn into disempowering practices that potentially reproduce disadvantage, exacerbate divisions between minority and white students, between minority men and women, and even among minority women. I suspect that many of the classroom encounters Kramer-Dahl recounts here are reminiscent of similar scenarios and dilemmas feminist educators have faced in their various university teaching experiences. In that regard, this chapter is instructive for all of us by urging caution of some of our taken-for-granted assumptions about our own pedagogical choices and the lessons those choices teach students.

In "Legal Pedagogy as Authorized Silences(s)," Zillah Eisenstein theorizes legal discourse as a "pedagogy of privilege and sex/race discrimination." This essay is a revised chapter from her book *The Female Body and the Law* (1988), where she undertakes a wide-ranging theoretical critique of how the law's putative neutrality conceals a contradictory treatment of the female body. Here Eisenstein explicates some of the political and legal contradictions embedded in law's "objective" treatment of feminine embodiment as variously equal to and yet also sexually different from the male standard. Some laws in the United States (as in Australia) have been based on sexual differentiation, denying women access to military combat, to tending bar, working in underground mines, or flying commercial aircraft (this ban has only recently been lifted in Australia). On the other hand, in contested child-custody cases for instance, "the best interests of the child" are now a common legal axiom which reflects sex-neutral assumptions about men/fathers and women/mothers as "equally situated." However, in these instances, past care of the child (usually a mother) is minimized, and economic resources and lifestyle are invoked as criteria for future custody which clearly disadvantages women who, by and large, cannot always match the economic resources of men. Yet, if a woman can match a male's economic and lifestyle resources, she is likely to work full-time and thus may be considered "not like a woman, a good parent, because a mother who works in the labor force doesn't have the time to be a good mother."

In law, equal protection applies to persons assumed to be similarly situated. Yet women are not always equally situated to men, in which case the law can treat women differently from men. Pregnancy is a case in point of a class of persons, namely women, who are differently situated. An inalienable "real," natural, or biological difference such as the pregnant body, justifies different treatment of women. Whether women are treated the same as or different from men, under the guise of impartiality and neutrality, the phallus remains the standard of en-gendered law. Discrimination, therefore, remains concealed since different treatment can be justified on the grounds of women's "real," natural differences from men. Conversely, equal treatment can mask discrimination because the normative standard of sameness, remains male. Eisenstein argues that sex-neutral law is contradictory: positioning women "the same as men challenges the phallocratic structure of law from the inside but also upholds the core of meaning that makes law's normative standard the 'rational man'."

We are all subjects-in-law, bound by the language, power, and symbols of laws that we invoke to secure our rights and responsibilities, and which govern our everyday public and private lives. Laws and the law are thus intimately structured into all social experience and relations. Yet the engendered character of law teaches us that feminine embodiment can be used to deny women equality regardless of whether women are conceptualized the same as or different from men.

Terry Threadgold interrogates both the law and the academy in the last chapter, "Everday Life in the Academy: Postmodernist Feminisms, Generic Seductions, Rewriting, and Being Heard." Through a close textual reading of several "postmodernist" and "deconstructionist" articles in critical legal studies, Threadgold describes the authors' claims for law's indeterminacy, for its intrinsically interpretive function and procedures. Legal argument and interpretation, so the rhetoric goes, is already deconstructive practice, a continual rereading and rewriting of law's indeterminacy. Yet she argues that their claims of law's deconstructive and "already feminized" character conceal and in fact restore the logic of liberal humanism under the guise of postmodern deconstruction. Postmodernism's linguistic turn has enabled critical legal theorists to incorporate the most recent theoretical and political challenges of postmodernism and feminism, by co-opting their strategic practices into legal discourse and practice. Indeed, deconstruction is often claimed as foundational to the American "social system whose very 'constitution' depends on the reading and rereading/rewriting of a written text (the Constitution . . .)." As Threadgold sees it, "the system reasserts itself and deconstruction, embraced and incorporated into the body of the law, is effectively feminised, seduced, and disempowered." This stance silences all theoretical and political challenges, while enabling a perpetual restoration of inequalities.

In the second part of the chapter, Threadgold engages the work of *political* postmodernist and poststructuralist feminists to argue that politically motivated feminist deconstruction can effect change systemically and discursively through what Drucilla Cornell terms "habit-change." She uses three examples of legal texts (one from an aborginal authored novel; another from a Supreme Court appeal transcript; the third from an academic legal paper) to illustrate such habit-change through an exposition of the textual politics of recuperation and contestation. Threadgold highlights instances of habit-change in legal textual practices and speech events by teasing out from the transcripts: Who gets access to talk in the genre of the cross-examination? How are

social identities and action "rewritten" in the genre of the judge's judgment? How are "unruly private stories," sexuality, or eye-witness
accounts rearticulated and rewritten into the norms of public, legal,
white, male, and middle-class discourse? All three examples are
instances of an actualized politics of contestation directed toward transformed practice. They illustrate a politicized postmodern, distinctly
feminist intervention involving strategies of subversion and habit-
change. These strategies recognize the limits of modernity, and challenge the powerful restorative tactics—achieved through text, talk,
(re)reading, and (re)writing—that underpin stances posturing as dis-
passionate postmodern critique and deconstruction.

Ultimately, Threadgold argues, how we envision going about
changing the social relations of law is pedagogic work: work that is
crucially dependent upon "how we go about teaching, reading, writing,
and what sorts of things we teach that texts are, as well as how we theorise and go about the teaching." Feminist commitments to the possibility of doing things differently by rewriting patriarchal grand narratives—whether in the courtroom or the classroom—are fundamentally
concerned with reading/writing practices which, as Foucault taught
us, raise questions about the disciplining and making of social subjects,
the relation between body and consciousness, power-knowledge relations that constitute regimes of truth, the making of literate bodies, and
practices of pedagogy.

POSTSCRIPT

Books, which Foucault called "manifest discourse," constitute a
textual unity, a textual archive, a set of knowledge truth-claims and
narratives that circulate through and are authorized by discourse communities as authoritative units of knowledge. Anthologies, in particular,
usually claim that the individually authored narratives are bound
together by some common vision, shared epistemic standpoint, or topic
of inquiry. They are somewhat like postmodern families—social hybrids
and eclectic, provisional and strategic alliances. I do not wish to impose
any such unity on the diversity of subject positions, research interests,
and theoretical orientations here. Rather, I take the position that each
discursive event is a unique formation and interplay of differences
which are never reducible to a seamless unifying principle, despite the
fact that "commentary" or critique is always contained, and thus unified, by the inevitable repetition and reappearance of its referent—that
is, its object of critique. I would defend, therefore, the openness of this

text, its theoretical divergence, standpoint and subject differences, and multiplicity of commentary on its reference point, that of pedagogy: the disciplining and normalizing regimes that write the possibilities of the subject, the social, and the relations of difference among them.

Looking back over the volume, two thematic referents among the diverse voices in this volume are those of difference and textuality. I suspect that it is indicative of feminism's current historical and theoretical juncture that questions of gender regimes, sexual politics, and identity no longer hold analytic center-stage. Instead, as nearly all the chapters illustrate, engagement with various intersections of gender/race/ethnicity/sexuality is emblematic of the making of a new kind of gendered subject. Another shared focus among all the chapters, and one not elicited by me, is the textual turn. Almost all the preceding chapters have begun from or focused exclusively on textual analysis in one form or another in order to expose how social subjects and groups are subjected in and by textual regimes.

Yet textuality and pedagogy, in Western contexts at least, are analogous. Thus, how law, media, (post)colonial policy, or educational theory conceptualize and shape hierarchies of difference, the normative subject and social relations, is fundamentally an educative process in text-based power-knowledge regimes, enacted across a network of diffuse events of social and self-disciplining. I would like to close with some comments by Foucault (1972) of the pedagogical function of all discourse, mindful that he was speaking of and for a social order and epistemology rooted in Western, print-based logocentrism. Of education, he writes (p. 127):

> What is an educational system, after all, if not a ritualisation of the word; if not a qualification of some fixing of roles for speakers; if not the constitution of a (diffuse) doctrinal group; if not a distribution and appropriation of discourse, with all its learning and powers? What is 'writing' . . . if not a similar form of subjection, perhaps taking different forms, but nonethless analogous? May we not also say that the judicial system, as well as institutionalised medicine, constitute similar systems for the subjection of discourse?

The will to knowledge and the will to "truth" historically have been invested in pedagogical institutions and relations, and are as "foundational" to patriarchy as to feminism. And this will to knowledge, this struggle and tension between the truths of modernist discourses and feminism's project of destabilizing those truths, "relies on institutional support; it is both reinforced and accompanied by a whole strata of practices such as pedagogy—naturally—the book-system [and media], publishing, libraries [and electronic networks], . . . and laboratories today" (p. 219). Foucault talked about the will to knowledge in the "great mutations of science" throughout the modern age. We are now undergoing similarly profound and radical mutations in knowledge, technology, political and social organization, modes of inquiry, inquirers, and the objects of inquiry (i.e., cultural "others," women, cyberspace). At the same time, we are repositioning the will to knowledge in historically different institutional sites and relations: in popular culture, media, new age counseling and therapy, in emergent electronic information and social networks, in bedrooms and courtrooms, in boardrooms and on the streets.

The feminist project of writing and teaching difference, of contesting universalisms and hierarchy, of deconstructing the legacy of women's collective but uniquely shaped subjection, occurs on new and established frontiers, on old institutional grounds (such as the university classroom), and in newly formed social or electronic collectives, newly formulated hybrid genres and narratives of dissent, assertion, and subject formation. This anthology is part of the feminist project of revealing the powerfully insistent hegemony of public discourse in maintaining hierarchy and inequality, and of contesting identities of the same and rewriting difference, albeit from the old institutional ground of the "the book-system, publishing." Insofar as the teaching machine of institutionalized scholarship is still the primary venue for differentiating, qualifying and authorizing speakers to speak authoritatively within and of a discourse, this book—this unit of discourse—is part of the "habit-change" or ways of thinking things differently within established ground. It emerges from those gaps, endemic to all discourse, which are neither stable, constant, nor absolute.

References

Culley, M. & Portuges, C. (Eds.) (1986). *Gendered subjects: The dynamics of feminist teaching*. New York: Routledge.

Foucault, M. (1972). *The archeology of knowledge and the discourse on language*. (A. M. Sheridan, Trans.). New York: Pantheon.

Gallop, J. (1994). The teacher's breasts. In J. J. Matthews (Ed.), *Jane Gallop Seminar Papers* (pp. 1–12). Humanities Research Centre Monograph Series No. 7. Canberra, Australia: The Australian National University.

Gallop, J., Hirsch, M., & Miller, N. K. (1990). Criticizing feminist criticism. In M. Hirsch & E. Fox Keller (Eds.), *Conflicts in feminism* (pp. 349-69). New York: Routledge.

Gore, J. (1993). *The struggle for pedagogies: Critical and feminist discourses as regimes of truth.* New York: Routledge.

Grosz, E. (1988). The in(ter)vention of feminist knowledges. In B. Caine, E. Grosz, & M. de Lepervanche (Eds.), *Crossing boundaries: Feminisms and the critique of knowledges* (pp. 92–106). Sydney: Allen & Unwin.

Grumet, M. R. (1988). *Bitter milk.* Amherst, MA: The University of Massachusetts Press.

Kenway, J. with Bigum, C., & Fitzclarence, J. (1993). Marketing education in the post-modern age. *Journal of Education Policy,* 8(2), 105–123.

Kline, S. (1993). *Out of the garden: Toys and children's culture in the age of TV marketing.* Toronto: Garamond Press.

Luke, A. & Luke, C. (1994). Pedagogy. In R. E. Asher & J. M. Simpson (Eds.), *The encyclopedia of language and linguistics* (pp. 566–68). Tarrytown, NY: Elsevier Science/Pergamon.

Luke, C. (1995). White women in interracial families: Reflections on hybridization, feminine identities, and racialized othering. *Feminist Issues,* 14(2), 49-72.

———. (1996). Feminist pedagogy theory: Reflections on power and authority. *Educational Theory,* in press.

Luke, C. & Gore, J. (1992). *Feminisms and critical pedagogy.* New York: Routledge.

Matthews, J. J. (Ed.) (1994). *Jane Gallop Seminar Papers.* Humanities Research Centre Mongraph Series No. 7. Canberra, Australia: The Australian National University.

Pagano, J. (1990). *Exiles and communities: Teaching in the patriarchal wilderness.* Albany, NY: SUNY Press.

Phoenix, A., Woollett, A., & Lloyd, E. (Eds.) (1993). *Motherhood: Meanings, practices and ideologies.* London: Sage.

Reddy, M. (1994). *Crossing the color line: Race, parenting, and culture.* New York: Routledge.

Tizard, B. & Phoenix, A. (1993). *Race and racism in the lives of young people of mixed parentage.* London/New York: Routledge.

Willis, S. (1991). *A primer for daily life.* New York: Routledge.

PART I

Learning Identities and Differences

CHAPTER 1

LEARNING IDENTITIES AND DIFFERENCES

Patricia Dudgeon
Darlene Oxenham
Glenis Grogan

INTRODUCTION

The Centre for Aboriginal Studies at Curtin University in Perth, Western Australia, is a unique building. It is circular in design with a central lobby or meeting area. There is a sense of light and openness throughout the building due to the many window and doors in every area. Earth colours, terracotta, ochre, and wood predominate and great jarrah tree logs surround the lobby. There is a sense of peaceful stillness in the Centre, which stands on land that was once the turtle-hunting grounds for the Nyoongar people centuries ago. Both in the lobby and outside the building the flag owned by Australian Indigenous people proudly flies. The three colours of the flag are vivid against the background earth tones of the building. The flag consists of a black rectangle representing the people, and a red rectangle representing the earth and blood that has been shed. In the centre is a golden circle that depicts life and hope.

This introductory word picture of the Centre is created to portray the scene of where we work and from where this story emerged. It is about how we came together to create the Centre's unique environment and more importantly, how we developed the programs we now offer from the Centre.

Rather than present information within a theoretical framework to portray the educational programs and the dynamics of its development, we decided to refer to the ideology and principles that underpinned our professional operation from the personal. This allows a story in true Aboriginal tradition to be told of real humans beings who think, feel, and work in an educational context, yet within an Aboriginal cultural heritage. This fits in with the notion of us as human beings operating in a holistic reality that is professional, personal, and societal. The past and future is also tightly woven around individuals in the here and now. Therefore, we are also women endowed with legacies of past people, and thus the actions we take will cause consequences that will ripple into the future.

Against this introductory background the format of this chapter can best be appreciated. It is a personal reflection of three Australian indigenous women working in a higher education setting. As explained before, a personal approach was preferred as it allowed us to examine education from a broader perspective yet keeping intact the personal, social, and rich cultural influences that had a part to play in shaping the Centre's developments.

In this way we seek to minimise the influence of the "master narratives"—the theories and perspectives of non-Aboriginal academics—which tend to dominate writing in books such as this. We claim the right to speak in our own voice, to have that voice accepted as legitimate and authentic, and, in the process, to minimise the likelihood that our experience will be colonised by other interpretations of our own experience. Stringer (1993) contends that that right is legitimated within the academic world itself by many postmodern theorists, including Foucault (1972), Huyssens (1984), Derrida (1976, 1978), Lyotard (1984), and West (1989). Accordingly, the diversity and quality of educational programs in which we are involved have been developed and implemented because of the specific ideologies held by us and the others who work with us.

To place the present circumstances of Australia's indigenous peoples into context, it is necessary to provide some information about the past. Berndt and Berndt (1980) have undertaken considerable research on the traditional lifestyles of Aboriginal people and hold that, prior to colonisation, the original inhabitants occupied and travelled within what is now known as Australia for many thousands of years. The level of resource management was considerable, with a viable hunting-and-gathering subsistence pattern of living. Seasonal exploitation of regional resources and the maintenance of sociocultural ties and religious practices ensured the continuation of Aboriginal people and their cultural integrity. Everything that existed, whether living or nonliving, had meaning and was integrated in a world that constituted the present, but which also included continuation of that which was before, the past, and even the future. There was nothing to conquer in the land because the people belonged to the land: people, animals, flora, and land were one. The people's power and sense of being came from the land. Pride and esteem emanated from celebrating the land, which included the cosmos and the intricate interaction of spiritual beings, whose continuing action gave meaning, purpose, and strength to all living and nonliving things.

Into this intelligently balanced material and spiritual world came the British colonisers with their perceived superiority and ethnocentric views that lead to the subsequent denial of the rights of the indigenous people. Still today Australia refuses to acknowledge prior ownership of the land to its original inhabitants. Aboriginal people were regarded as "without property" and consequently without authority and status to contest British imposition. From the colonisers' perspective, domestic agriculture and pastoral endeavours were the only proper purpose for land useage. Aboriginal people obviously did not use the land as it should be used, therefore they did not have a legitimate claim to land.

It was from such opposing views that the competition for land began and with this a history of misunderstanding and conflict, resulting in massacres, discrimination, and oppression that has left the original inhabitants of Australia as the most socially and economically deprived group in what is a multicultural society. From an Aboriginal perspective, dispossession of land involved severe dislocation not only from cultural and social links which give meaning and purpose of life, but also from access to traditional subsistence technology such as bush foods and medicine, which prior to the occupation of the land had been a natural and plentiful source for health and preventative care. As the competition for land intensified, it was not only the technologically superior instruments such as rifles held by the British that led to the eventual control and subjection of Aboriginal people, but also the introduction of new diseases such as smallpox, measles, tuberculosis, influenza, and venereal diseases, to which Aboriginal people had little immunity.

Furthermore, oppressive legislation and policies towards Aboriginal people were imposed over time that denied them all rights. Haebich (1992) and others have documented the development and implementation of such policies and outlined how these ensured that a process of disempowerment and destabilisation was set in motion as settlement took root.

The fact that there was only a small ratio of women initially in the non-Aboriginal population encouraged the exploitation of Aboriginal women for sexual services, resulting in increasing numbers of "mixed descent" children. Concern about the increasing numbers of children described by non-Aboriginal people as "half caste" led to policies and actions of removing Aboriginal children from their natural mothers and institutionalising them. The practice of forcibly removing children from their families became legalised by policies influenced by notions of Social Darwinism. This "scientific theory" that portrayed Aboriginal people as creatures of the lowest order is evident in inhumane legislation and policies that ultimately left Aboriginal people prisoners in their own land.

In the nineteenth century, Aboriginal reserves were created throughout Australia. These were to have a profound effect on Aboriginal people. On the one hand, the reserves provided some protection against the increasing violence of the Europeans. However, on the other hand, the reserves created a total institution. In line with the then current ethnocentric attitudes, Aboriginal people were viewed as "children" whose lives must be constantly supervised. Every aspect of life was regulated, from the food they ate, the employment that was permitted, the money they spent, and even the most intimate aspects of their lives, such as whom they could marry.

Under the policies of what was considered protection, the people were not given a choice as to whether they should live on these reserves. Legislation prevented them from entering the towns unless for employment and, even then, curfews were strictly enforced. Absconding from the reserves was largely unsuccessful and would result in capture and punishment.

For the children on most of the reserves, education opportunities were extremely limited. They were either excluded from the schools in town or subjected to a lower form of education from an untrained, unqualified person such as the reserve manager's wife. For those children removed from their families and placed in other institutions such as homes or with white families, the belief was that this was "for their own good"; they needed to be de-Aboriginalised and civilised. This was deliberate assimilation. Aboriginal people did not have citizenship.

For Australian indigenous people it has been a history of genocide and dispossession. It was not until 1967, during a historic referendum, that the non-Aboriginal population of Australia voted in favour of counting Aboriginal people in the census and deeming them to be citizens. This was a turning point in Aboriginal affairs. At this time the federal government made a commitment to address Aboriginal issues with real resources. This enabled the establishment of community-driven organisations, specifically developed to meet Aboriginal needs. Some of these organisations included land councils, medical services, legal services, and other bodies.

Since then, major policies and subsequent funding aimed at improving the circumstances of Aboriginal people have changed their focus from assimilation to self-determination and self-management. However, the legacies of the past are still evident today. Across the board, Aboriginal people are significantly impoverished socially—in education, health, housing, levels of income, employment, and the law.

Over the last decade, outstanding new initiatives have been initiated such as the Royal Commission into Aboriginal Deaths in Custody, from which a host of recommendations were drawn up across all areas of Aboriginal and non-Aboriginal spheres. These also required government and other institutions to implement and respond to the relevant recommendations. Other such initiatives include the Native Title legislation and the Reconciliation process.

This is the heritage and history that we three Aboriginal women at the Centre have in common with each other and all Aboriginal people. Our story begins when we came to know each other approximately six years ago. From that time we have established a close working relationship as well as a close friendship with each other. The three of us, Pat Dudgeon, Glenis Grogan and Darlene Oxenham, hold academic and administrative responsibilities at the Centre. Pat Dudgeon is the head of the Centre for Aboriginal Studies. Glenis Grogan is the coordinator of the Aboriginal Health Unit, and Darlene Oxenham is the coordinator of the Aboriginal Community Management and Development Program. The latter are two units within the Centre for Aboriginal Studies. Together we form part of the senior management at the Centre for Aboriginal Studies at Curtin University of Technology, Perth, Western Australia.

Our common values, experiences, and principles have greatly enhanced the ways in which we work together, and provide the foundation of our professional and personal interaction. We openly acknowledge that each of us complements the others' style of operation so that, on another level, our differences blend to create a singular strength. What appears as a weakness in one is considered a strength in another. We have developed a way of working that provides a balance in the enactment of the Centre's activities.

The principles that we hold and by which the Centre operates are highlighted in the intent and processes of naming the central lobby in the Centre's new building. After considerable consultations with the Aboriginal community, it was decided to name the lobby after Midgegooroo, an Aboriginal resistance fighter to European settlement. The plaque commemorates the memory of Midgegooroo and reads as follows:

Midgegooroo Meeting Place

This area is dedicated to the memory of the Nyoongar elder, Midgegooroo. Together with his son Yagan and other Aboriginal warriors, he fought and died in resisting the invasion of Nyoongar territory by British colonialists. He was executed by firing squad at Perth, WA in 1833.

Midgegooroo's struggle symbolises the fierce spirit of resistance to oppression. This spirit has motivated people throughout the ages, to fight for their human rights.

The striving for freedom and equality embodied in the life and death of Midgegooroo, Yagan and other Aboriginal resistance leaders epitomises the struggles of all oppressed cultures across time.

This history, like that of other oppressed peoples and nations, has until recently gone unrecognised. This is the beginning of a new era where the truths of the past will be acknowledged and become part of our global heritage.

The legacy of Midgegooroo lives on in the consciousness of Aboriginal people and inspires us, with the people of all nations to continue to work towards a vision of a world where all persons are free and equal on their own terms.

Our story unfolds in three parts which are separate but interrelated to form a composite whole. We begin with Pat's recollections.

EARLY INFLUENCES—PAT DUDGEON

When I was twelve years old I dreamed of being an astronaut, but when I was fifteen I ran away from home and was seen as the girl most likely to end up in a "bad way." That meant, either going to prison, becoming a drug addict, or ending up as a welfare mother and so on. With such preconceived ideas, I nearly went to prison when I was young. I was a welfare mother. Yet it was the experience of motherhood that began a process of centering for me as I grappled with being a person in my family.

If one looks back over life and the personality snapshots taken at different intervals, it would be difficult to be convinced that the first snapshot was that of the same person in the last. In essence, the person would be the same, but during life's journey and the positive and/or negative experiences the same clay is moulded into quite different shapes.

My perceptions of things that happened in my life and how they have shaped the person I have come to be, as in the latest snapshot of my life, is now presented. My racial identity is Australian Aboriginal. My mother's people came from the Kimberley region, which is in the upper area of Western Australia. We came from a coastal people called the Nyul Nyul people. My grandmother must have had a very hard life. Yet when I asked her about her upbringing, she could only recall the good things that had happened to her. The more I begin to understand about my people, the more I am convinced that grandmother's life must have been hard. I read the Department of Native Welfare's records about her and my great-grandmother. Those reports portrayed my foremothers with great injustice. These women were seen as less than human, and as sexually promiscuous. They labelled them as the "original mothers of sin" and as such they were denied the right to marry whom they desired, as well as the right to move to another town for employment.

My grandmother was never bitter when she spoke about her past, nor was my mother. I have taken on the luxury of bitterness and resentment on their behalf, as I am in the situation in history with the view and the position that enables me to do so. I see the same histories of oppression in all my people. Bitterness and outrage, sadness and respect about all that has been and should be, channelled into a positive force that works toward shaping a better future for all of us.

Although my grandmother had nine children, she didn't raise any one of them. Government officials and missionaries pressured her into giving up her children to the missionaries. My mother and her sister were sent to the Beagle Bay Mission. Although Nanna said she worked hard in various domestic and menial jobs to send money and clothes to her children, there was a feeling that nothing was passed on to the children. My mother and her sister had no direct contact with my grandmother, and accordingly the seeds of discontent and abandonment were sown in the hearts of these sisters. I can only imagine the great yearning and feeling of loss that stayed with my mother all her life.

There was a great rift between my mother and grandmother that was only finally resolved at my grandmother's deathbed. Despite the separations, the spiritual link between my grandmother and her children was strong. Strong enough for her to stave off death until all the children came home to her from all over the country.

In Nanna's time there was no support in place to enable her to keep her children, and little had changed when my mother had two children. My mother knew the pain of growing up without her mother and strived hard to ensure that she would not be separated from her children. Despite the adversity, and times of hardship my mother, with help from family and friends, managed to keep her family together. My mother is a small woman in stature but she has the heart of a lion. She left the mission, when she was eighteen years old, in the back of a provisions truck. She was young, knew nothing of outside life, but had the courage and conviction that she could make a better life for herself somewhere else in the world.

My mother was a mother figure to all around her. There were and are always extra people in her household, such as adopted children for whom she cared. Even now in her late fifties she has chosen to commence a career as an Aboriginal Liaison Officer with the schools. Her love for children is one of her strongest characteristics and she firmly believes that if children are given enough love, care, and guidance, the world will be a better place.

My mother married a white man. It was after the days when cohabitation was illegal and interracial marriages were socially unacceptable. They loved each other and made a life together in spite of the then existing nontolerance of mixed marriages. Even though mixed marriages were not tolerated, covert sexual liaisons were accepted and even encouraged. The government officials who labeled my foremothers as "mothers of sin" and had such power over their lives under the Aboriginal Protection Policy, probably chased "black velvet" under the cover of night. Many prominent white families in both urban and rural areas have unacknowledged indigenous family branches.

Socially it was a white man's perogative to satisfy his lust with Aboriginal women, whether it was through rape, by mutual attraction, or tribally given. This resulted in a different group of Aboriginal people termed coloured or half-castes. Since the portion of white blood made them more "human," government policies were put into place that, among other issues, legislated for the removal of non-full-blood children. These children were taken to missions and homes to be trained to be useful menial workers for the new country. The government of the day devised many categories to determine the percentage of Aboriginal blood of a person. The people were still Aboriginal in reality, still rejected by white society, and still largely accepted by the Aboriginal family despite any percentages of Aboriginal blood. So my father married my mother at a time when he couldn't be jailed for cohabitation but the attitude was that you "did not marry them."

I am always grateful that I grew up in Darwin, Northern Territory. During my childhood there seemed to be a relative ease between Aboriginal people or coloureds and whites. At that time there were three racial groups, whites, coloureds, and Aboriginals. Looking at other people in other areas I used to think that my hometown was relatively free from racism, that it was a racial "melting pot." I see now that the racism was covert. It was subtle and more deadly than the blatant racism of other areas. There was always a sense of waiting for the coloured person to fail, to revert back to their so called native ways.

The experience of living through various government attitudes and actions toward Aboriginal people has left a legacy that will take generations to heal. As well as blatant racism, there is an internalised racism where some of our people have come to share the oppressors' values and negative attitudes towards themselves and each other. I was always aware that I was an Aboriginal person. Like many other people of oppressed minorities, my first realisation of difference was a negative one. It was at primary school when a friend said they couldn't be my friend anymore because I was "too black." Around that time my family went on holiday to visit my father's family in Melbourne, Victoria. The paternal side were told that my mother was Malaysian. They might not have been able to accept us without that "white lie."

Contact with the Aboriginal side of my family was not as intense as I would have wished. We never went to my mother's country and only knew those members who came to Darwin. Whilst my father did not deny our Aboriginal family, a distancing was maintained. Still, my mother held an affinity for other Aboriginal people within the local community and even with the traditional people of remote communities. When we were relocated for two years because of my father's work in a remote, semitraditional Aboriginal community, I will always remember my mother sneaking out from the "white side" of the settlement to play cards and socialise at the "blacks'" camp.

Many changes occurred when I was between thirteen and fifteen years old. My parents divorced, I became a delinquent, and I left home and school at that time. My father then decided to send me to an upper-middle-class girls school in Adelaide, South Australia. This was a generous attempt to remove me from the bad influences and to give me a chance to succeed in a mainstream way. Having been forced away from my family and friends, however, proved that it was too late to turn me from the path I had chosen. I was in an environment where I felt alienated both by race and class. This could only have had one inevitable conclusion—I was expelled after two terms.

After my return to Darwin and increased levels of wild activities, the Children's Court decided to banish me to Beagle Bay Mission rather than place me into an institution. Too late again to veer from the path, after a few weeks I came back again. At the age of eighteen I was a mother.

Education and Training

I worked in a range of jobs, mainly waitressing and bartending. With my partner and son I travelled this vast and wonderful country. Yet during this time there was always a sense that somehow there should be more to life. I had undertaken studies (matriculation) for university entrance with psychology as a study objective. It was years afterward when I felt that the time was right for me to pack my belongings and make a move. Travelling with my son and partner we drove to Perth from Darwin. My partner had decided to come along.

Throughout my life I have always been interested in people. I wanted to know why people did what they did and why some responded differently to others. Above all I wanted to help people. In order to do so effectively I enrolled in a psychology degree at the university. The experience of learning was a profound one for me. A whole new world was opened up for me. In those years I lost myself and found myself again in a renewed sense as a woman, an Aboriginal person, and as a human being. I clung to other Aboriginal students at the university. Without my indigenous peer group, I would not have survived in this new educational environment. The first year was hardest in terms of overcoming the intense feelings of not belonging and feeling I had no right to belong. No one in my family had ever been to university. Although my family was proud of my achievements, they did not know what it was really all about. This experience was totally out of their worldview and certainly was not a part of anyone's envisagement of my future.

At the university the pieces of my life seemed to come together for me. I began to understand where I stood, how things were, or could be according to the theory I used. This was not attributed to formal education alone but to the sharing that we did as Aboriginal students isolated on campus, and engaged in an experience that was alien to most of our families. During my student days I became more involved in social action activities. I was the first female chair of our indigenous student organisation and race relations officer for the student guild.

Through social action activities I learned precious lessons about politics and life. I learned never to compromise one's integrity, to risk everything for a just cause and, more importantly, to respect the ultimate power of a group. I was fortunate that these same convictions were shared by my Aboriginal student peers. This was because we held the same principles and ideologies, shared similar struggles that helped consolidate our outlook on life.

EARLY INFLUENCES—GLENIS GROGAN

I have a bond of steel with my family, of which I consider myself fortunate to be a member. My mother is of Aboriginal and Malay descent, my father, Aboriginal and Irish. Despite the other influences in my racial heritage, my identity as an Aboriginal person of Australia is such that it can never be taken from me. Being proud of who you are and where you come from was positively affirmed in many ways throughout my childhood. Apart from the influences of my immediate family, the extended family also played a huge role in the shaping of me as Glenis Grogan.

My maternal grandfather, the son of a full-blood Aboriginal woman and a Malayan labourer, was raised in the Malay town of Innisfail in northern Australia. This town was a collection of shanties housing people of Malaysian and mixed Aboriginal-Malaysian descent. His impoverished upbringing led him to embrace the ideals and principles of communism. This gave him the zest to actively seek social justice and equality for minority groups. After his wife died, he was converted to Christianity at the age of forty and followed the tenets of the Seventh Day Adventist Church. This intensified his approach for equity issues and his quest to change the status quo of the Aboriginal people.

My paternal grandfather too was of mixed decent. He was the son of a full-blood Aboriginal woman and an Irish station owner from the Queensland Gulf of Carpentaria. Being raised on the station, he acquired many work skills such as that of a Black tracker, bullock-team driver, blacksmith, wheelwright, and policeman. In addition, he was a skilled horseman and fluent in seven different Aboriginal languages. When he met and married my paternal grandmother from the Mona Mona Mission, he forfeited his so called "exemption" to move freely outside of an Aboriginal reserve. It also meant that his children would be considered as "wards of the state" according to the Native Protection Act of Queensland. Years later he applied to the Native Welfare Department to move out of the mission and to gain employment at Kuranda. His determination and strength of character in adverse times enabled him to provide the best he could for his five sons and four daughters. Such a role model was not lost on the generations to come. My paternal grandmother, a recipient of the then government's assimilation policies, was as a child removed from her traditional Aboriginal family and taken to reside at Mona Mona Mission. Even so, in true Aboriginal tradition, she cared for her own nine and several other Aboriginal children. As a midwife, she delivered and cared for the women at the mission.

My parents married in the late 1940s and lived with their extended family in Kuranda, where my father was employed as a timber cutter. His job often took him away from home for periods of time. The household of nine children plus the many relations was left in the capable hands of my mother. I am the third eldest of two boys and seven girls. I remember my father most for his giving nature. In his spare time he could often be found with the elders conversing, carting water, or collecting firewood. He pursued equality for the Aboriginal people and became politically active in social justice issues. In such an environment, I became aware of social discrimination early in life. I remember such remarks as the "impending black invasion" prior to Mona Mona being closed in 1964. This awakened in me a feeling of what it meant to be different, but the extent of my knowledge of Aboriginal people was limited to family and local community. It was not until I was sixteen years of age and traveling in New Zealand that I realised that I knew very little about the Aboriginal people of Australia. I was so embarrassed when questioned that I resolved to redress the glaring gap.

Education and Training

Nearing my seventeenth birthday I commenced a nurse training program in the Innisfail District Hospital. During my training I did not have to deal with issues of being a black woman in the work force. This was because nursing was and continues to be predominantly a woman's domain and other Aboriginals were employed at the hospital for many years before me. My training was disrupted in the second year as I became a single mother.

My carefree and partly undisciplined life ended with the arrival of my child. I informed my parents that they had a grandson a week after he was born. To keep him I travelled to Melbourne, as I suspected that if I returned home relatives rather than I would raise him. My son and I stayed in Melbourne until he was three months old. I wanted to work and sought registration in Victoria as an enrolled nurse on the basis of previous studies. This option was possible but, after thinking carefully, I decided that if I was to continue nursing and contribute to the improvement of Aboriginal health, I would do so as a nursing sister or not at all. I returned to the Innisfail District Hospital, completed my third year and was one of the last midwives to be trained at that hospital. In 1976 I completed both my general and midwifery nursing and prepared mentally for the wider work force.

My first position as a qualified nurse was at a hospital in the Gulf of Carpentaria. This was a segregated hospital with an identified section to accommodate Aboriginals only. During the term of employment there I observed the conditions of local Aboriginal people, the majority of whom were relatives from my grandfather's side. I noted the appalling conditions under which they were forced to live. This heightened my awareness of the gross injustices handed out to Aboriginal people and strengthened my resolve to participate in change. Feeling helpless and unable to change the conditions that surrounded me, I resigned and return home. I then contacted the Medical Director of the Central Australian Aborigines Congress. The Congress, which still operates today, is an independent, Aboriginal-controlled health and medical service. I was employed by this service as a nursing sister.

As well as taking on normal nursing duties, I was part of a team who regularly visited the traditional lands of the Pitjantjatjara and Ngaanyatjatjarra people. Their area spans over a huge tract of land where the three states of South Australia, Northern Territory, and Western Australia meet. On these visits we would provide medical and nursing intervention and collect health data. This was used as a basis to apply for funds to establish a community-controlled Aboriginal Medical Service located in the outback.

I was constantly being confronted with issues and explicit discrimination against Aboriginals from several directions. This was mentally, physically, and emotionally draining. What I was seeing, feeling, and experiencing was out of the normal boundaries of my understanding. For example, I was sent to do an assessment analysis of Aboriginal people's needs after their dwelling and belongings were washed away in a flash flood, when the Todd River in Alice Springs became a raging torrent. The end result was my sitting on the river banks crying with the people affected. In addition to the alien environment and the increased expectations placed upon me as a black nurse, I again felt inadequate about not being able to solve any problems for Aboriginal people. I went into deep culture shock and self-loathing for feeling this way. I returned in a hurry to Queensland, needing to be in familiar surrounding.

After a rest I worked a short time with the National Eye Health and Trachoma Team Programme, coordinating the screening of Aboriginal people living in the North Queensland Tablelands area, then joined the team as a nursing sister going to the Torres Strait to conduct screening on Thursday Island and several other nearby islands. When the Pitjanjatjarra Homelands Health Service in the northwest corner of South Australia was finally established, I decided to return and assist in its further development.

After two years I assumed the role of executive officer of the health service, which was developing at a rapid pace. These were times when I felt that I was an instrument in the further destruction of a culture on its road toward assimilation. I agonised over this matter until I came to the realisation that all cultures change and we were similar to other groups in transition. At this point in time we lived in a colonised country, with a predominantly white population, with new diseases and other impinging factors just as any other group. Aboriginal people could adopt, for example, "the easier way to hunt over sparse desert lands, with a rifle in a four-wheel-drive vehicle, [rather than walking] for days with a spear acquiring food to feed a family." I finally concluded that the need was for Aboriginal people to maintain a cultural identity whilst on their terms change what it is they wish to change.

Like a homing pigeon I returned again to Queensland for sustenance and to reflect on my future direction. Physically and emotionally burnt out, vowing never to get to this point of distress again, I resigned from the Pitjantjatjara Homelands Health Service in early 1981. Furthermore, my son needed to enrol in a primary school. At seven years of age his early Western education had been a hit-or-miss affair. I justifiably considered that the education gained in his many travels would benefit him in the future especially in the area of social skills.

These experiences in the area of Aboriginal health and the increased awareness of Aboriginal culture, developed in me a conviction to contribute within limits and to the best of my ability. I led a normal life at the same time, bringing up my son. I questioned my abilities in this department, as I would often feel that I was dragging him from pillar to post across the country. My family gave lots of support and would look after him when necessary. I would never be able to repay their generosity particularly as, while I trained, he would be cared by them for ten days and I would have him for the other four days. Until he was nearly four, he spent more time with my parents than he did with me. Today I am so proud of him, of who he is, and what he is doing.

I further assisted in the setting up of the clinical aspect of the establishing Wu Chopperen Aboriginal Medical Service in Cairns and a Halfway House for malnourished Aboriginal children in the same location. I worked on several community projects, in various state and community hospitals. For four years I was employed as a community nurse for the Queensland State Health Department.

Between 1981 to 1988 I married and separated. The circumstances of marital separation led me to seeking refuge in Western Australia. My fourteen-year-old son and I drove from Queensland to Perth and had we had enough money on arrival, we would have returned to Queensland. I took on a position east of Kalgoorlie in the Aboriginal community clinic at Coonana. I was employed by the Health Department of West Australia. I only intended to be in Western Australia for twelve months to "get my head together." After eight months, however, my son and I were homesick, so I decided to find a job in Perth.

I began looking for employment in Perth and subsequently applied for a position advertised at the Centre for Aboriginal studies. By the time I received a response to my application, I had changed my mind on the grounds that teaching Aboriginal Studies to unaware non-Aboriginal people was not my desire. It was only after I was told that I was to develop award courses in Aboriginal Health for Aboriginal people that I wanted the job.

Coming from a hospital-based nurse-training background, I faced a steep learning curve in the world of academia. My community experience assisted in what was to be achieved in the development of a culturally focused award course in Aboriginal health as is offered by Curtin University today.

Following extensive consultation with the Western Australian Aboriginal Medical Services, we received approval to develop a course which would explicitly meet the needs of West Australian Aboriginal people. A two-year statewide, action-based research program was conducted, with the outcomes forming the basis of a competency-based curriculum. The development of this curriculum involved a number of Aboriginal people, academics, and allied health professionals. The final curriculum reflected a culturally appropriate and community-based academic program.

What I have described so far in these course developments does not illustrate the sheer trauma, struggles, heartache, and, yes, the achievements that took place over a period of six years. Many times I wanted to resign and felt like I was hitting my head against a brick wall. In my teaching, I portrayed powerful health and medical professions as "the wall." In addition to the health and medical professions, Aboriginal people influenced by Western styles proved to be one of the major obstacles to overcome.

There were times when I felt that as woman in a managerial position I was not taken seriously. My co-developers were non-Aboriginal men and it was to these people that many of the referrals were made rather than directly to me. These referrals were primarily evident in a non-Aboriginal setting. I attributed this to people who knew who I was and what position I held within the Centre for Aboriginal Studies.

Despite the obstacles in developing the programs, the environment of the Centre with its underlying principles of empowerment and social change helped the Centre succeed, together with the overall support of the Aboriginal people both within the community and in the Centre, without whom the task would never have been possible. The final result is that Western Australian Aboriginal people own, control, and were part of curriculum development and delivery of programs which reflect Aboriginal cultural values and beliefs whilst maintaining academic standards.

When joining the Centre for the first time, I personally felt that I was able to participate in bringing about realistic, long-term, and lasting measures to address Aboriginal health. Today I feel pleased that along with the Aboriginal community, twenty strongly committed staff members of the health unit and unquestionable support of the Centre, we are training the future Aboriginal change agents.

In conclusion, it is my perception that as the Centre intensified its developments over the past years, it was on the grounds of necessity that Pat Dudgeon, Darlene Oxenham, and I needed to act as a formidable team of women managers. Sometimes with ignorance of the finer details about the operational realities of non-Aboriginal bureaucracies and processes, it was with great trepidation that we would carry out our endeavour to achieve our objectives. Our tenacity came from our commitment to our principles.

EARLY INFLUENCES—DARLENE OXENHAM

Reflecting on my life to date, I would summarise it as a journey towards becoming actualised as an Aboriginal and politicised as an individual. My life experiences to date have led me to a point whereby my goals and ambitions are directed towards achieving social change for Aboriginal people.

Many of my early life experiences, which have resulted in increasing my awareness of Aboriginal issues, were negative experiences. This, I believe, is the case for many Aboriginal people. Our cultural differences are often reinforced through racist encounters. These encounters have two effects—they can be destructive and disheartening to the individual, whilst also strengthening our resolve to achieve equality, self-determination, and self-management for our people.

I was born in the small coastal town of Denham (Shark Bay) in Western Australia. The main industry in the town was fishing. My grandfather fished to support his family of twelve.

I am part of a large extended family which continues to maintain close links. As is common in many Aboriginal families when a child is unable to be raised by its mother, other family members take responsibility for raising the child. Although I have always had close contact with my mother, I was raised by my uncle (mother's brother) and aunt. I have three brothers and five sisters, of which I am the eldest. My family have greatly influenced many of the values and attitudes I hold. Each of the women in my family are strong outspoken characters. As role models they taught me to stand up for my beliefs and to make sure I had my say on different matters. Although, never overtly stated or enforced, there is a trend in my family for children to take the mother's family name. This makes a great deal of sense to me as it provides me with a sense of belonging and connectedness. Giving the children the mother's name clearly demonstrates the tie between siblings, irrespective of the father(s) of these children.

The majority of my family now reside in Carnarvon and have been there for many years, and as such are very much a part of the Aboriginal community residing there.

With my uncle and aunt, I moved to Carnarvon at the age of six. It was during my primary school years (approximately ten years old) that I first realised that Aboriginal people were perceived differently. In this instance it was the children from the mission. I realised that other children at the school treated the Aboriginal children from the mission with contempt and pity. The children from the mission were generally perceived in a negative light. They were stereotyped as smelly, dirty, and dumb. Unfortunate as it was, the mission children were easily identifiable by two specific items, the standard issue of shoes they wore and the sandwiches they were provided with for lunch, which were always contained in brown paper bags. To me there appeared to be a hierarchy at school based on racial classifications and typical stereotypes. This consisted of white kids being at the top of the hierarchy, and town-based Aboriginal kids next. I assume this was due to the fact that town-based Aboriginal families lived in a similar style to the whites. At the bottom of the ladder came the kids from the mission. I fitted into this hierarchy as a town-based Aboriginal kid, and so was in a relatively luxurious position of being more readily accepted by the white kids. On reflection, this blatant racism suffered by the mission children did not really impact on me or appear unusual to me, rather this was our reality at the time.

The first time that I was directly effected by racism was in high school and served to highlight the racial difference between myself and my non-Aboriginal friends. This situation arose when my non-Aboriginal friends began to describe Aboriginal people as "boongs," "niggers," "coons," and "abos." I now realise that the usage of racist terminology is a generally accepted component of speech by many people in

Carnarvon. As such it becomes obvious that through the processes of socialisation many young children will begin to use such terminology to describe groups different from their own. When I heard my friends use these terms, I challenged them and questioned as to what that made me? The response to this was often "but you are not like them." This explanation allowed my friends to maintain their own prejudices by isolating me from the group as different or unique. On a personal level I was left with the question of who was this vague "them." I questioned my own identity as an Aboriginal person and how I then related to other Aboriginal people in the community—what made me different and apparently more acceptable? Besides the anger I felt at the usage of these terms, I remember being very shocked and disappointed that my friends were unable to see the hypocrisy, unfairness, and blatant untruths in the situation. In response to this incident, I effected change within myself to ensure that my own values and principles were consistent to my beliefs and actions. Thus, since my adolescence and early adulthood I have chosen not to use any racist terminology to describe any ethnic or cultural group. I firmly believe that by doing so, I am not perpetuating the usage of such terms and thereby giving the terms a greater level of acceptability in everyday speech.

A growing awareness of being different also made me realise that Aboriginal people in Carnarvon were broadly categorised into four groups. These were the town-based Aboriginal people, the Mission people (now I realise that these may have been children separated from their families by the government, perhaps from more traditionally oriented backgrounds), the Aboriginal people who lived at Bore Street (generally negatively perceived as similar to a shanty town), and Aboriginal people who lived on the reserve (these people may have come from traditional backgrounds but moved into reserves which were established by the government to house Aboriginal people). Generally the living conditions at Bore Street and the reserve were terrible. It has been the case in Australia that often as towns grew, the reserves were moved to ensure they fell outside of the town's expanding boundaries. This was an attempt to keep the "Aboriginal problem" hidden. In Carnarvon, for individuals within these categories also came certain expectations. In short, individuals from the mission, the reserve, and Bore Street were not expected to achieve. The town-based people were viewed more respectably.

As I have matured I have realised that if you wish to contribute to social change, you need to choose the battles you are to fight. It is pointless to deal with some people who are not open to any new ideas or perspectives. It also means you are able to conserve your energies to fight those battles that will really make a difference. Without sounding too idealistic, the battle is against racism and inequality generally and, specifically, that which is directed towards Aboriginal people. I guess to make the assumption that victory will be achieved is to believe in the fundamental goodness of people. This in itself generates much discussion particularly in light of the many atrocities that have and continue to be committed on the premise of racial superiority and inferiority.

Many Aboriginal people, myself included, feel that we are often placed in a position where we must continually attempt to educate people. This can occur in any setting (professional and social), as all Australians appear to have an opinion on Aboriginal people and issues. Once some individuals find out that you are Aboriginal, they feel they have the unquestionable right to express their opinions to you, irrespective of the nature of their opinions. I now accept that being Aboriginal means accepting that many components of everyday life take on a political meaning.

The foundation of my beliefs and values were formulated and influenced by my family. From my mother I have learnt the joys of giving to others, and to be protective and loyal to the family. From my uncle I have been taught a very strong sense of fair play, to work hard and do well at your job, and to take pride in all that I do. From my aunt I have learnt to always accept responsibility for my actions, and to face whatever consequences may result from those actions. My aunt also taught me to look for the best in people and attempt not to prejudge individuals. From my grandfather I learnt of the dignity of people and life. Those valuable gifts of family inheritance shaped my character and served as a resource sustaining me on life's journey.

Education and Training

I am unsure why I decided to go to the university, all I know is that I did not image myself staying in Carnarvon like so many of my friends. This was not because I disliked the town, but rather that it could not offer me what I wanted. I enjoyed and demonstrated an aptitude for learning. One logical option, therefore, was for me to continue learning. I was lucky enough to be offered a place at the university. I was the first of my family to undertake a university course and this generated mixed feelings in my family. Overall, I believe my family were very proud and supportive of my undertaking higher education.

In order to attend university I was required to move to Perth. Carnarvon is approximately 960 kilometres from Perth (around 10 hours drive by car). This meant a total change in my life. I was now

independent, totally responsible for my own actions. It took me approximately twelve months to settle into Perth. I was not used to being in a
situation where my family were not around. I initially disliked the
city—it was far too big and anonymous. On top of this I had to adapt to
university life, which I found to be initially very alienating. Whereas in
Carnarvon a status quo has been achieved between Aboriginal and
non-Aboriginal people based on familial knowledge and history, where
individuals knew each other and their place in the world, this was not
the case in Perth. Perth is a city in which many non-Aboriginal people
have had no direct contact with Aboriginal people. Within the university system, as the numbers of Aboriginal students was low, other Aboriginal students and I stood out like sore thumbs. Also adding to this
feeling of alienation was the fact that I came from a small country town
in the northwest of Western Australia. Consequently, I had not established relationships with other students as was the case with many of
the university (Perth-based) students. I was in a sense a small fish in a
big sea. I had to continually fight shyness in an attempt to establish
friendships. I eventually found a niche when I met and made close
friendships with other Aboriginal students on campus.

Throughout my studies (primarily anthropology and sociology) I
was taught to appreciate the pursuit of knowledge, to think analytically,
to become more conscious of issues and the different approaches/per-
spectives bought to bear on particular societal institutions, structures,
and people. This, by virtue of its academic nature, was very theoretical.
I took this new-found knowledge and ways of thinking and applied it to
my life situation. I used this knowledge for self-exploration as well as a
personal analysis of Aboriginal people, culture, and society. This was
invaluable as it provided me with a basis from which to explore and
analyse those questions and issues that I had previously asked and
observed as an adolescent. This questioning and analysis was further
clarified during dialogue with other Aboriginal students. From these
discussions an interesting tension arose in relation to the requirements of
academic work (e.g., based on empirical data) and our indigenous realities. This tension was demonstrated when I co-authored a paper with
Pat Dudgeon soon after the completion of our studies. This paper
focused on Aboriginal identity. In the paper we wrote about the feelings,
attitudes, and values of Aboriginal people as we saw it and as it was
expressed to us by others. The major criticism we received came from
white academics who claimed that the paper was not academic enough,
we had not conducted enough research, nor did we have enough statistical data to "prove" our assertions. From our perspective it was not our
intention to write an academic paper, rather we wished to explore con-

cepts, feelings, and Aboriginal realities about Aboriginal identity and present it in a way that many Aboriginal people could relate to and understand. In short, this was an attempt for us to record what we perceived as our Aboriginal reality.

As I have already shown, prior to my entering university I grappled with questions of identity and my place in Aboriginal society. Looking back I realise that even though I may not have held the same feelings or views of non-Aboriginal people, I had, to a certain extent, accepted them as a natural part of the world. Through academic study and the sharing of my experiences and reality with other Aboriginal people, I learnt a whole new history of Aboriginal Australians. A history, for all intents and purposes, that had been hidden from me prior to this time. I learnt of the atrocities committed. I learnt of the taking away of land and the granting it to the squattocracy. I learnt of the rounding up of Aboriginal people and forcing them onto reserves, the taking away of children and placing them in missions to Christianise them. I learnt of the enforced dependency on government handouts and money. I learnt of the resistance of Aboriginal people, of the battles that took place. I learnt of the enormous untruths that had justified an invasion of an allegedly "Terra Nulius." These are facts that many Australians may be unaware or have a limited awareness of. In their ignorance many Australians blame the victims; that is, they blame Aboriginal people for things which we had until recently no power to control. Over generations we have been taught to be ashamed of our heritage and taught to be dependant on the government for financial assistance and, to a certain degree, to let others control our lives and existence.

I will forever be grateful for whatever took me in this direction, as it was during my time at the university that I became actualised as an Aboriginal and politicised as an individual. This cannot just be attributed to the academic learning within the university to which I was exposed. A large part of this growing awareness was due to the friendships I established with certain other Aboriginal students on campus. During this time I redefined and reclaimed my Aboriginality with pride and validity. Further, I learnt that this had to be a public declaration of identity as it demonstrated to many people that diversity exists within Aboriginal culture. My attempts to share this growing awareness with family and friends in Carnarvon met with limited success. I felt that many people viewed my new realisations and opinions as strange and slightly weird. Upon reflection, this is understandable as our lives were diverging and moving along different paths.

With the choices that we make in life as we mature and as we accept more responsibility, we become actualised as individuals.

Accordingly, we seek our place in the world as we follow our chosen directions. At times the life paths we follow cross over and merge with others close to us, even though those others may have chosen to take a different path. We may in fact find, as I have, that we reach the same desired end point. For members of my family, social, personal and political awareness has come through other means, such as, their participation in Aboriginal organisations and Aboriginal politics in the local environment. The path that I have chosen has differed to others in my family, but somehow we were led to the same end points and goals.

I can see that with life's choices come life regrets. For myself, because of the choice I made to leave Carnarvon at a relatively young age, I missed out on certain things. For example, I do not have the same intimate knowledge of the community and community members as others who remained in Carnarvon. I feel a sense of loss at this. I hope that with time, I will gain such knowledge. Learning should never cease for any individual, it is a lifelong experience.

A Shared Vision and Hope

Our lives moved into another stage when each of us chose to work for the Centre for Aboriginal Studies. Pat Dudgeon was the first to begin working for the Centre. Upon graduation Pat was presented with many job offers. An Aboriginal person with a degree is a very marketable product. Pat chose to work for the Centre as she felt this provided a good opportunity to engage in her chosen profession of counselling in a way that would benefit Aboriginal people. The position that Pat assumed was titled trainee lecturer/counsellor.

A couple of years later Darlene began working for the Aboriginal Community Management & Development Program (ACMDP) at the Centre for Aboriginal Studies as a tutor. Darlene was one of two Aboriginal staff within this program. Glenis, coming from a wide and diverse community background as a general nurse, joined the Centre to coordinate the development and implementation of the Aboriginal health programs.

In time, Pat assumed the position as head of the Centre for Aboriginal Studies. Darlene participated in an Aboriginalisation process which enabled her to take on the coordinator's position in the ACMDP. Within a very short period of time Glenis assumed full responsibility for the development and implementation of the Aboriginal health program.

On reflection we have come to realise that the dominant influences from our childhood and early professional life had prepared us to challenge existing structures and perceptions of the role and purpose of higher education. Our experiences have always been outside the mainstream and we have seen the inequities around us. Further, our educational experiences have shown that Aboriginal realities and values are not truly reflected in the content and delivery of mainstream programs. We have bought this experience to bear in the development of the Centre's programs, management processes, and structures. We have always maintained that the Centre serves two masters: the academic world and the Aboriginal community. This Centre's operations epitomises our direction and should any conflict arise between the Aboriginal and institutional demands, we will be obliged to give precedent to the Aboriginal community. This is a liberating position because our reference group provides a strength of purpose. The enactment of our principles are validated by the reference group enabling clear strategies for future actions. We take on this enactment with confidence and courage.

Although we three women came from different personal and professional backgrounds, we have shared a vision and hope to bring the Centre to maturity. The realisation of a vision does not come alone from merely desiring it, there are other elements that come into play. We have established a mode of operation which was sustained by mutual support, respect and honesty. This, in turn, enabled us to remain focused and motivated through the many conflicts and struggles undertaken in the stages leading to this point. The solidarity we have shared has contributed to the ongoing development of the Centre by providing a sound and stable management foundation. This means that the Centre, at times, is required to take a position on particular issues that impact on Aboriginal people.

There is a perception that academic institutions are in the community and yet apart from it; they appear to float above the "real world" and all too easily can remain a thing apart. The Centre for Aboriginal Studies by its very existence as an Aboriginal organisation, cannot be separate from the community, neither can it be politically neutral or passive.

The path forward has not been an easy one. One of the obstacles facing us in the provision of educational options has been a scepticism of the Centre's academic validity. We have also had to contend with the notion of apartheid and the development of apartheid systems, as perceived by individuals external to the Centre. In addition, at a university level we are often measured against Western yardsticks and found to be falling short, as ethnocentrism still prevails. Even when successful there is, in some cases, a resentment rather than respect. Furthermore, by nature of our Aboriginality, equal performance is often not enough: we are required to perform above average.

The previous section touched on the politics of race in the academic setting, but what must also be addressed is the politics of gender. For we three, as can be seen from our stories, our primary concerns and issues have been in relation to Aboriginal/non-Aboriginal relations rather than gender issues. All three of us have experienced racism and sexism although, in this higher educational setting, we believe that racism is the focal point. It is sometimes difficult for us to separate racism and sexism. We believe we hold a comparatively unique position as individuals and as a group in the Centre for Aboriginal Studies. In some ways we have been fortunate, but for a lot of Aboriginal women this is not the case and, depending upon the setting, they may face a double yoke of oppression. It has been acknowledged by many Aboriginal women that the feminist movement has not always been of full benefit to them as it can be seen to undermine Aboriginal men's role and place in Aboriginal culture.

From our perception, the Aboriginal woman (and man) who moves into the professional arena, has all too commonly been seen as the protégé of their white colleagues. This allows limited or no credence to prior experiences or knowledge that individuals bring to their positions. As empowered Aboriginal woman, we lay claim to leadership and accept that on occasions we may need to be forward in making this known.

In conclusion, we three women at various times in our lives have had to come to terms with and accept our differences. The strengths that emerged from this process have enabled us to embrace these differences and to create a learning environment that truly operates from an Aboriginal reality rather than from a modified non-Aboriginal construct.

REFERENCES

Berndt, R. M. & Berndt, C. H. (Eds.) (1980). *Aborigines of the West: Their past and present.* Perth: University of Western Australian Press.

Derrida, J. (1976). *Of grammatology.* Baltimore: Johns Hopkins University Press.

――― (1978). *Writing and difference.* Chicago: University of Chicago Press.

Foucault, M. (1972). *The archaeology of knowledge.* New York: Random House.

Haebich, A. (1992). *For their own good.* Perth: University of Western Australian Press.

Huyssens, A. (1986). *After the great divide: Modernism, mass culture, postmodernism.* Bloomington: Indian University Press.

Lyotard, J.-F. (1984). *The postmodern condition: A report on knowledge.* Minneapolis: University of Minnesota Press.

Stringer, E. (1993). Socially responsive educational research: Linking theory and practice. In D. Flinders, and G. Mills (Eds.), *Theory and concepts in qualitative research perpsectives from the field.* New York: Teachers College Press.

West, C. (1989). *The American evasion of philosophy.* Madison: University of Wisconsin Press.

CHAPTER 2

WOMEN AND FRIENDSHIPS: PEDAGOGIES OF CARE AND RELATIONALITY

Elisabeth Porter

Friendships between women have often been viewed historically as a substitute for erotic love, or a preparation for it. "Once women have tasted love," La Rochefoucauld declared, "most of them will find friendship boring" (in Enright & Rawlinson, 1991, 96). This declaration is far from the truth. As Jane Austen writes in *Northanger Abbey*, "the men think us incapable of real friendship you know, and I am determined to show them the difference" (in Enright & Rawlinson, 1991, 107). In support of Austen, this chapter makes five major points.

First, an understanding of a classical Greek notion of friendship explains women's exclusion from philosophic ideals of love, yet provides some important insights into the nature of quality friendships. Secondly, any distinctiveness of women and men's friendships can be explained partially by traditional gender developmental differences in early self-identity formation which are reinforced through social structures. Consequently, my third point demonstrates why men's friendships are typically characterized by comradeship, shared activities, an achievement orientation, and an emotional toughness, factors standing as obstacles to men's intimacy with each other. In contrast, my fourth claim argues that women's friendships typically are characterized by shared intimacies, mutual support, and a concerned responsiveness to particular special relations. Feminine subjectivity is constructed in ways that encourage women to place a high value on friendship, and enable the learning of necessary skills of sensitive relationality. Fifthly, I argue the benefits in viewing a friend as "another self." Friendship thus requires not only strong notions of relationality, but of individuality, notions which require self-trust as a basis for trusting relationships between women, between men, and between women and men.

1. UNDERSTANDING THE NATURE OF FRIENDSHIP

Aristotle's views on friendship remain influential. He writes, "without friends no one would choose to live" (in McKeon, 1973, bk. 8, chap. 1, 509). Friends are indispensable to our everyday well-being. Aristotle distinguishes between the objects of friendship in terms of utility, pleasure, and goodness. Some friends are useful to us, they comfort, support, and encourage us. Other friends give us pleasure, they are fun to be with, we enjoy their company, and we share mutual delights. With other friends, beside utility and pleasure, the chief object is a shared happiness of those who mutually do good to each other and affirm selfhood. It is this type of friendship that this chapter examines.

Friendship is crucial for good living, for our happiness necessarily includes the happiness of others. This shared happiness entails a joint promotion of common ends. Friendship for Aristotle includes reciprocal goodwill, familiarity, mutual love, a similarity of age, a common upbringing, a sharing of common property, equality, and time spent sharing in discussion and thought. Mutual friends seek to do good for each other. Attachment to others is thus crucial to the individual expression of a virtuous life, for friendship cements good living as the condition of educational thought, and the basis of citizenship. In this tradition of classical friendship, women, judged to be incapable of rationality, public worldliness, and citizen goodness, are excluded, because "perfect friendship is the friendship of men who are good, and alike in virtue" (in KcKeon, 1973, bk. 8, chap. 3, 513). Women's inclusion into full citizenship removes traditional philosophic barriers to considering women as "good friends."

Over time, the Greek ideal of friendship diversified to include anyone with whom you were intimately connected via marriage, national identification, personal pleasures, shared political beliefs, or values. This diversification includes references to friends as "like family" and affirms the intensity of connection, belonging, continuity, and security. Indeed in family situations where abuse, violence, or discord is the norm, people value friends for their acceptance, and what good friends affirm—"trust, honesty, respect, commitment, safety, support, generosity, loyalty, mutuality, constancy, understanding" (Rubin,

1985, 7). Ties of close friendship are a precious form of communion. Yet, whereas with "the Ancients, friendship seemed the happiest and most fully human of all loves, the crown of life and the school of virtue, the modern world in comparison ignores it" (Lewis, 1963, 55). We still value friendship, but the nature of friendship has changed, from its basis in community and public citizenship, to those people we retreat to in our private relations.

In modern times, friendship has been so emptied of its fuller meaning that we "speak of home cleaning products as a woman's 'best friend'" (Raymond, 1987, 161). Indeed, "interested persons would be hard pressed to find discussions of friendships or intimacy in the literature of modern moral philosophy" (Bishop, 1987, 16), and, I add, they are scarce in feminist journals. As I shall progressively explain, morality has concentrated on formal duties and rights and has understated the way that moral relations are characterized by connectedness. To the question, "how am I to meet the other morally?," Nel Noddings answers, "one must meet the other as one-caring" (1984, 201). This chapter examines how women understand their relatedness and the moral priority many give to care, specifically the care of their friends. My first main point is that the nature of friendships is best understood to involve bonds of deep moral significance. I will explore these bonds further in sections 4 and 5, but first we must ascertain whether socialization affects girls' and boys' friendships.

2. DIFFERENTIAL GENDER DEVELOPMENT

Research seems unequivocal in showing that at every life stage, "women have more friendships . . . than men, and the differences in the content and quality of their friendships are marked and unmistakable" (Rubin, 1985, 60). Why is this so? Gender-based developmental differences in traditional childhood socialization give some clues. I want to situate my discussion of these differences in the theories of relationality that have emerged around Carol Gilligan's articulation of the "ethic of care" (1983, 1987). To summarize Gilligan's work briefly, she builds on earlier theorists like Jean Baker Miller (1976), who documented ways in which women's sense of self frequently focuses on their connections with others, so that a disrupted relationship amounts to a threatened self. Gilligan also builds on Nancy Chodorow's work (1978), which suggests that whereas boys typically define themselves in opposition to their prime caretaker, usually a mother, by an autonomous distancing and view intimacy as a threat to identity, girls' relational tendencies emerge from their interaction with their mothers, and this gives them the necessary mothering skills to nurture others, and to define themselves in connection with others.

Gilligan refuses to see these ideas of nurture, connection, and relationality as inferior to, or deviant from, norms of identity formation derived from traditional masculine standards which prioritize autonomous emotional distancing. Gilligan's interest lies in the interaction of experience, thought, and dialogue. In listening to what people say about themselves, what is significant to them, and what connections to others are made, she discovered a "different voice," a contrast to traditional masculine forms of thought, interpretation, and judgment. But she added that this is "*not* a generalization about either sex" (Gilligan, 1983, 2). I agree with Barbara Houston that what is important is articulating "a coherent formulation of an ethics of care, not the empirical question of whether there are sex differences in the use of this morality" (1989, 85). Nevertheless, Gilligan's findings relate to a general tendency of women to use a different moral perspective that pivots around conflicts between the self and others. The ethic of care and relationality is thus defined thematically, suggesting that more women than men are regularly engaged in practices of childcare, care of the aged, disabled and ill, emotional nurture, and employment in service industries. All of these are practices that depend on context, content, social responsibilities, and concrete relations. In valuing care, relationships connote responsiveness, engagement, and a resilience of connection, symbolized by networks. Moral concerns focus on problems of detachment, disconnection, abandonment, and indifference (Gilligan, 1988, xvii). For many women, and for some men, a morally mature subjectivity values the interconnection between self and others, rather than prizing a self defined by separation from others. This priority given to care lays a firm foundation for friendships.

To understand how women typically learn such care and relationality, it is helpful to contrast this "care perspective" with the "justice perspective." The latter is dominant in liberal individualistic, contract, and rights-based theories. The justice perspective is characterized by abstract, ideal, universal, impartial, formal, generalized principles, the care perspective by contextualized, particular, informal, concrete practices. Between these perspectives, there are three main conflicts of priorities: a formal abstraction and a contextualized content; individual rights and social responsibilities; the generalized other and the concrete other. I shall summarize these contrasts briefly. First, formal abstractions stand in tension with the way morality figures in our life, since there is always a content to moral dilemmas, like the messy, muddled confusion with the friend we have disagreed with. Feminist theory draws our attention to the considerations of the personal, arguing that the contexts in which our prime moral experiences occur make a difference to the way we construct moralities. For example, women often exchange confidences of common experiences related to pregnancies, births, childcare, and household concerns. Our experiences of growing up as a girl, and as a woman with specific subjective variations, influences the way we approach moral relations like friendships. Friendships emerge in contexts. Our past experiences, including our gender socialization, affects what we bring to the contexts and to the friendships, and this of course applies equally to men.

The second contrast is between rights and responsibilities. A morality of rights, based on equality and justice, is geared to rational resolutions. Its concern is to balance individual competing claims, like my right to my new friend's time, energy, and possessions, over her closer friend's claims. A morality of responsibilities, based on the principle of connection to others, is a morality tied to experiences of relationships. The chief concern is to include those who need care. It takes into account issues of equity and differences in need, such as, why one desperately upset friend needs my time tonight in contrast to my friend who wants to celebrate her new job. Morality is perceived as a problem of inclusion of those requiring care which may produce a conflict of responsibilities, and which I try to resolve, for example, by phoning my joyous friend, and visiting my upset friend.

The third contrast centres on how we view others. As Seyla Benhabib expresses it, when we consider others as a "generalized other" we view each individual "as a rational being entitled to the same rights and duties we would want to ascribe to ourselves" (1987, 163). These relations are governed by equal reciprocity, the moral requirements of which are rights, obligations, entitlements, and the responses those of respect, duty, dignity, worthiness. This means we would view all our friends in generalized, formal terms of rights and duties. With the "concrete other" we identify each individual in her historic, specific contexts. Identification here requires that "I confirm not only your humanity but your human individuality" (1987, 164). Benhabib identifies the moral categories associated with a concrete individuality as those of responsibilities, bonding, and sharing, and the corresponding moral feelings as those of love, care, sympathy, and solidarity. This means we need to know a lot about the specific life narratives, needs, desires, and goals of our friends to respond with appropriate care. In summary, the justice and care perspectives contrast different priorities. A priority given to the care perspective means that good friends take context, social responsibilities, and concrete relations seriou_

Early perceptions of justice and care can influenc_
adolescent identity and friendship formation. For examp_
relations with their parents and friends show how early g_
ization becomes ingrained on their patterns of behavior. J_
and Jacqueline Smollar (1985) summarize adolescent perc_
fathers as authority figures, or as administrators of just pr_ of
providing advice on practical matters and guidelines for behavi_
often engage with fathers on practical problems and recreationa_
suits, but both daughters and sons typically view fathers as provi_
advisers, problem-solvers, and arbiters of serious disputes who call
impartial principles. Mother-daughter relationships are complex, com_
bining an authority tempered by intimacy and thus equality. "Daughters feel free to confide in their mothers, as well as to fight with them
and to disobey them" (1985, 70). Sons usually perceive mothers as caring and concerned although intrusive. Both daughters and sons describe
their mothers as disciplinarians, conversational partners, carers for their
needs, and solvers of personal problems. They acknowledge mothers'
willingness to listen to their self-revelations.

In terms of adolescent friendships, "a pattern of same-sex affiliation is found so consistently in all cultures that this tendency may be a
universal character of human social behaviour" (Gottman, 1986, 140).
John Gottman suggests three reasons why this is so: perceived similarity to self enhances interpersonal attraction; adult reinforcement; sex-
role stereotypes in the peer group. Boys' friendship groups tend to be
large, collective, built around outdoor sport games, away from adult
supervision, over a large physical space. Girls' friendships involve
smaller exclusive networks, close to adults, frequently confined to a
bedroom. Girls often "just talk." A study of 400 adolescents by Youniss
and Smollar found that whereas the majority of close friendships with
girls were characterized by "shared activities; mutual intimacy; mutual
understanding; acceptance of and respect for differences of opinions; a
wide range of topics for discussion; and a perception of self as relaxed,
open, natural, outgoing, accepted and accepting" (1985, 109), this characterized only 45 percent of boys' friendships. For another 30 percent of
boys, shared activity but a guardedness in communication existed. For
25 percent mutual intimacy and understanding were not at all relevant
to boys' friendships. Gilligan also argues that girls' resistance to detachment underscores ethical complexities that orthodox accounts of relationships obscures, that attachment indicates a "struggle to find an
inclusive solution to the problem of conflicting loyalties" (Gilligan,
1988, 13). Her point is that dependence is not a weakness, but is part o_

condition, part of the chain of interdependence, of mutual comfort, listening, understanding, and paying attention to each needs. Evidence seems to suggest that girls learn the impor- of interdependency more readily than boys.

My house is often full with children. My sons use the phone mentally to make arrangements with their friends who race in out to swap sports cards, skateboard, cycle, play computer games, kick or throw a ball. They have a wide range of friends. My daughter sits talking for hours on the phone. Her friends who visit sit on her bed talking about appearance, other girl friends, boys, personal problems, parents. It is crucial for her to have several "best friends." She has an extended wardrobe, her girl friends lend and borrow clothes with intimate ease. There seems to be a real distinctiveness in the way girls and boys value friendships, a difference created by differential gender socialization and reinforced so strongly through social structures like education, role models, and the media, that even children socialized in nonstereotypical ways are still affected. How do these gender differences translate into adult friendships?

3. MEN'S FRIENDSHIPS

"All the bullshit about mates. I've got mates but no friends" (Colling, 1992, 55). It is interesting that increasing numbers of men writing on friendships confirm the shallowness of many male relations. They write of mateship and comradeship which develops through hardship, or the unique sharing of experiences, like sailors on a long sea voyage, teenage boys in a summer resort, and particularly soldiers in a trench, wartime buddies who share deeply personal matters in quite abnormal circumstances and hence form unique bonds that may persist after war ends. Yet comrades are "bound to one another as generalized others" (Strikwerda & May, 1992, 113), for here there is an impartial respect for the fellow soldier, compatriot, co-worker that may involve an emotional distancing.

Men's relationships with other men are marked typically by shared activities, like going to the pub, or a sports game, or playing sport together, mending, repairing or building objects together. Discussions often concentrate on sports, sharing expertise, work, and sexual conquests. These common activities revolve around a typical masculine socialization into an achievement orientation. Achievement and competitive relations bond a football team, but in interpersonal relations, it "makes men reluctant to reveal things about themselves that would make them vulnerable" (Strikwerda & May, 1992, 118). Kicking a ball, achieving a pay rise, having a pretty girlfriend are tangible achievements, affirming masculinity. Admitting you are a scared, worried, lonely, confused man to another man does not seem to come easily, although men often reveal these concerns to women. "Being doers by training, they will devalue being, seeing it as incidental to a friendship" (Colling, 1992, 93). An important component of this activity orientation and suppression of emotional disclosure is that frequently sex is men's only act of tenderness, but it also symbolizes a "substitute for expression of most other emotions; fear, anxiety, hurt, loss, disappointment" (Colling, 1992, 67), and this means that sex also can be an act of violence, power, and control.

The chief obstacle to achieving intimacy in men's friendships with other men lies in the male cult of toughness, whereby the ideologies surrounding masculinity that idealize aggression, self-sufficiency, and an abstraction from context are buttressed by an emotionally distanced objectifying autonomy. Take, for example, life in an elite boarding school, where the cohesion of the dormitory is achieved by a pack mentality, victimizing any boy who appears weak, odd, awkward, or gentle. The school culture of everyday violence, where boys' pushing, shoving, crude swearing is accepted as normal, means generations of boys grow up associating physical aggression and the suppression of emotions with masculinity, and reason and emotion are dislocated. David Jackson summarizes his school experiences poignantly. It is "difficult to count the emotional and social costs of that time of having to 'act hard and talk tough'" (1990, 205), and where boys are deprived of affectionate tenderness.

A further obstacle to men developing intimacy is the association of emotive expressivity with femininity, and thus the frequent masculine denial of the existence or legitimacy of one's feelings. Where this occurs, it is difficult for self-disclosure to be anything other than superficial. It prevents men from talking with other men about how they still grieve for the loss of their stillborn baby, or the aborted foetuses of past lovers, or their mother's handmade doll collection sold by their father immediately after her death. Homophobic overtones also obstruct men's friendships with other men, particularly when men's emotional responses are focused singularly in sexual expressions. Nonsexual touching threatens some heterosexual men. Many homosexual men, for whom emotional vulnerability is unproblematic, have greater freedom to explore deep relationships with other men, including men who are not their sexual partners. There is a strong connection between social structures and men's friendships. As definitions and expectations of masculinity change, friendships between men are positively enhanced (Nardi, 1992). Men can learn to become intimate with each other through close engagement, talking about themselves, and self-disclosure. An essential part of deconstructing masculinity is to accept that "the time has come to value mateship for its contribution to our survival and development but to replace it with friendship" (Colling, 1992, 159).

4. WOMEN'S FRIENDSHIPS

What typically makes women's friendships with other women qualitatively different from men's friendships with other men? I want to point to three significant factors. First, women's friendships historically have hinged on a unique supportiveness that emerges from concrete everyday lives, particularly the lives of women as mothers. Secondly, a real affection for other women affirms vital shared aspects of feminine subjectivity. Thirdly, intimate friendship requires a concerned partiality for particular others, a skill women seem to have developed more acutely than men. Before elaborating on these factors, I want to make an important qualification regarding the rhetoric of "sisterhood" which is an important political device, but does not lead necessarily to friendship.

The expression of female friendship involves more than emotivism. It involves the shared participation in a common world, a merging of personal and political aspects of life that gives women's friendship its strength. "Sisterhood" differs. Much of the second-wave feminism relied on a victim mentality, that all women are oppressed by all men, and therefore supposed that in women banding together a collective resistance and a protective bonding would emerge. But the nature of shared participation for heterosexual women is often the men in their lives, and for some lesbian women it comes through the move to a separatist disassociation from the masculinist world. A superficial sisterhood short-circuits feminist politics. A communion of resistance alone is not enough to bind women beyond the struggle, but actually naturalizes and sentimentalizes female friendship.

Yet there were clear strategies in advocating separatism and in representing the feminist political community as a familial group of sisters. Claudia Card explains how separatism is not isolationism, but "a severing of certain *bonds* to men and to male-serving practices" (1988, 127). Kathleen Jones suggests that when affective ties replace functional ones, there is a creative development of personality rather than instrumental goals, a shared sense of community rather than competitive norms. She remarks that to define "the citizen in the feminist polity as . . . a friend transforms the characteristics of citizenship" (1990, 807). It presupposes nurture, and the development of solidarity. Yet, practically, expectations of "politically correct" behavior and promises of nurturance have led to guilt and ostracization for women who do not conform. I am agreeing with Raymond that feminist "political activity consists in more than just conflict and struggle with men and male supremacy. Its end is to bring women together with our Selves and with each other" (1987, 174). Reiterating the Greek ideal of friendship, the feminist politics that proceeds from a shared friendship affirms similar values and attractions that make connections to the everyday world of personal relations, such as family life, work, leisure, dreams, and despairs. This type of friendship ensures an intrinsic vitality in women coming together to confirm a world held in common with some other women.

With these qualifications in mind, I look now to the three main qualities typical of women's friendships—unique supportiveness, genuine affection, a responsive particularity. First, the supportiveness is a distinct feature of female friendship. In the past, particularly in the working classes where everyday life was a struggle, the traditions of female friendship relied on relatives and neighbours who became friends through the sharing of domestic burdens. Women took it in turns to care for the children, the old, the invalids; they attended confinements, assuaged the grieving. There was a "wifely conviviality" (Limb, 1989, 54) in industrial towns with terraced houses that was the lifeline for many women, a factor urban redevelopers do not sufficiently take into account. As de Beauvoir expresses it, the value to these relations is the "moral ingenuity" and the "truthfulness" whereby "women help one another, discuss their social problems, each creating for the others a kind of protecting nest" (1975, 55). The mutuality of support enabled women to admit to each other when they were too tired, too sick, too poor, too exhausted through countless pregnancies to continue. Mutual support led to friendships grounded in everyday worldliness.

Now urban redevelopment, larger fenced houses, mobile societies, segregation from kin networks, divorce, and separation, have created social dislocation and altered the nature of many of these supportive relationships. Precisely because of these changes, friendship is increasingly valued as the bedrock of society, as a way to sustain women in the manifold decisions women must make concerning men, partnerships, children, jobs. Girls learn this supportiveness early through the alibi, "I was at Holly's place," a cover-up for a secret tryst, an attempt to avoid hurting the parents, and reported in detail afterwards to bosom chums. Sue Limb (1989) refers to a "spaciousness" in female friendship, which permits the "subversive" and the "satirical," the flirtatious and the fantastical. The shared intimacy of heart-to-heart discussions provides the relationship with a depth of supportive self-knowledge.

The second major distinctiveness of women's friendship lies in the depth of affection. Janice Raymond in her *A Passion for Friends* posits a strong argument, which I extend in section 5, that "friendship begins with the affinity a woman has with her vital Self" (1986, 5). To talk of a friend as "another self" presupposes a self-love. This is important, for women who are devoted to the service of others often lose their sense of self in the care of others. Raymond uses the term *Gyn/affection* to express an all embracing "*continuum* of female friendship" (1986, 15). The continuum gives an idea of movement, of personal growth and development. Her language is strong, it is of "the power of female friendship . . . drawing forth a dynamic response . . . that sets free and enhances movement of all kinds. To attract is to cause a movement toward" (1986, 41). This is an attraction where "women affect, move, stir, and arouse each other to full power" (1986, 9, 229). This vital passion is a fascination for the company of those who bring us out of ourselves when we are low, who help us to realize our full potential, who tap into the deep wells of our selfhood. This friendship ideal extends beyond social chit-chat, to the space "in which the female Self is allowed to grow" (1986, 9). Raymond's vision of female friendship does not rely on an essential feminine naturalized relational ontology, since this would represent a romanticism of sisterhood, but rather, it looks in history to institutions that nurtured and empowered women, like European convents prior to enclosure restrictions, and to Chinese spinster houses created by women who did not marry. Her vision of women's friendship crystallizes ordinary everyday lives which are anchored in cultural and material bonds created with other women.

A supportive passionate affection for other women requires a third distinctive feature of many women's lives, that is, a sensitivity to "the domain of particular others" where the self is "closely entwined in relations with others" and the others are "not something one can universalize" (Held, 1987, 118). Friendship involves partiality. This partiality is not exclusive to women. Most of us would not hesitate to give preference to our drowning friend over the stranger drowning. There are moral explanations for this that have to do with the particularity of intimate relationships. In explaining the nature of this particularity, I want to make three claims that draw further attention to the priority many women give to caring friendship relationships. First, special relations are moral relations, but literature does not give relatedness the due moral weight it deserves. Secondly, there are substantial differences in appropriate modes of interaction between relations in the impersonal impartial public realm, and the personal private world of close relations. Thirdly, close relations prompt particular commitments to unique, irreplaceable persons. Let us explore these interrelated claims more fully.

First, friendship is a special moral relation. For Iris Murdoch (1970), the central task of the moral agent involves a loving perception of another individual. Her view is that morality requires a "concerned responsiveness," a "loving attention" to particular others, a particularity irreducible to universality. In Murdoch's writings, she makes it clear that our morality emerges in our personal relationships. For example, loving attention to our friends involves understanding particular needs so that we can relate meaningfully to them. The moral task is not just to find universal principles that govern friendship, but to attend to the individuality of our friends. Special relations like friendships are often overlooked in ethical theories which see other concerns like justice or impartiality as constituting the central moral values. What feminists and communitarian theorists stress is the way that relatedness requires sustained moral attention.

Friendship as a relationship of partial particularity is no less a moral relation than are the relations by efficient bureaucrats working with impartial universal procedures of equal opportunity policies. As outlined in section 2, herein lies a core tension between justice and care perspectives. Impartiality is seen as essential to mature justice reasoning. With friendship relations, we are implicated ourselves in the roles we assume and we cannot stand off as impartial observers. Women often immerse themselves in their relationships. It is not that women cannot be impartial, but that in trying to determine what is right and wrong, what is just and unfair, they often recognize that genuine identification with others regards abstraction and impartiality as inappropriate to real human crises. This recognition frequently arises from childcare demands to attend meaningfully to hungry, tired, cold, sick, upset children. Similarly, when our friend is low in spirit or grieves her loss after a miscarriage, we identify lovingly with the needs of our friend. As noted in section 3, men writers on friendship concede that a limitation of typical men's friendships is that they rarely know each other intimately enough to respond to specific needs. Friendship is an important moral relationship.

Secondly, impartial and partial relations are moral, but there are differences between the requirements, expectations, and norms of each.

Norms of impartiality require that we treat people in abstract, generalized ways. While there are universal traits belonging to the general
character "friends," we respond to the actual traits our friends possess.
It is particular friends we love—Sally, Helen, Carol. We love specific
things about our friends' spontaneity, clear logic, musical talents, wit,
joyous laughter. "The legitimacy of acting from such personal reasons is
connected with our personal autonomy" (Blum, 1986, 345), an issue I
will develop shortly. Our selfhood is bound with this priority given to
friendships. Yet partiality does not preclude impartiality. Marcia Baron
argues that impartiality is often needed for close relations. Her example
is that it would be wrong to favour one grandchild and give nothing to
her little brother. "Because the demands for impartiality are so highly
contextual, considerable reflection and sensitivity are needed for the
agent to judge that treating So-and-So as special . . . is permissable"
(1991, 837, 838). As Baron maintains, while we have different behaviors and expectations for close friends than for casual acquaintances,
moral principles like respect for privacy and autonomy still apply. We
need to be careful when we borrow friends' possessions, but there may
be latitude with our close friends, requiring contextualized judgments.
Hence, as Michael Stocker argues, we do rank our responsibilities
toward different friends, so moral education, sensitivity, and contextu-
alism, are needed for duty and for friendship (1987, 60). Stocker's point
is that rights and responsibilities, duties, and friendships are intimately
related.

    In agreement, I argue that tensions between justice and care
remain in most friendships, but that there is a dialectical interplay
(Porter, 1991). Justice, presumed to be appropriate to the public, formal world of social relations, plays an explicit role in our everyday life.
As Neera Kapur Badhwar points out, when lovers or friends break up,
their common complaints are "that they were manipulated, used,
attributed wrong motives, wrongly neglected . . . that they were unfairly
treated" (1985, 123). It is concepts and practices of justice that support
dispositions needed for just treatment of friends. It is only when we
view love and friendship as moral concerns, as important components
of the moral life that we recognize the moral worth of friendship and
that justice is a fundamental virtue of friendship. The moral dimensions of these relationships generate rationales for how we act. How
we care for a new friend, an old friend, our best friend, a hurt friend differs. The more experienced we are in sensitive, reflective, contextualized
judgment, the better our care.

    Consequently, my third claim is that close friendships require
particular committed responsibilities. As Friedman argues, intimacy

social responsibilities, and concrete relations seriously.

Early perceptions of justice and care can influence childhood and adolescent identity and friendship formation. For example, adolescents' relations with their parents and friends show how early gender socialization becomes ingrained on their patterns of behavior. James Youniss and Jacqueline Smollar (1985) summarize adolescent perceptions of fathers as authority figures, or as administrators of just procedures, providing advice on practical matters and guidelines for behavior. Sons often engage with fathers on practical problems and recreational pursuits, but both daughters and sons typically view fathers as providers, advisers, problem-solvers, and arbiters of serious disputes who call on impartial principles. Mother-daughter relationships are complex, combining an authority tempered by intimacy and thus equality. "Daughters feel free to confide in their mothers, as well as to fight with them and to disobey them" (1985, 70). Sons usually perceive mothers as caring and concerned although intrusive. Both daughters and sons describe their mothers as disciplinarians, conversational partners, carers for their needs, and solvers of personal problems. They acknowledge mothers' willingness to listen to their self-revelations.

In terms of adolescent friendships, "a pattern of same-sex affiliation is found so consistently in all cultures that this tendency may be a universal character of human social behaviour" (Gottman, 1986, 140). John Gottman suggests three reasons why this is so: perceived similarity to self enhances interpersonal attraction; adult reinforcement; sex-role stereotypes in the peer group. Boys' friendship groups tend to be large, collective, built around outdoor sport games, away from adult supervision, over a large physical space. Girls' friendships involve smaller exclusive networks, close to adults, frequently confined to a bedroom. Girls often "just talk." A study of 400 adolescents by Youniss and Smollar found that whereas the majority of close friendships with girls were characterized by "shared activities; mutual intimacy; mutual understanding; acceptance of and respect for differences of opinions; a wide range of topics for discussion; and a perception of self as relaxed, open, natural, outgoing, accepted and accepting" (1985, 109), this characterized only 45 percent of boys' friendships. For another 30 percent of boys, shared activity but a guardedness in communication existed. For 25 percent mutual intimacy and understanding were not at all relevant to boys' friendships. Gilligan also argues that girls' resistance to detachment underscores ethical complexities that orthodox accounts of relationships obscures, that attachment indicates a "struggle to find an inclusive solution to the problem of conflicting loyalties" (Gilligan, 1988, 13). Her point is that dependence is not a weakness, but is part of the human condition, part of the chain of interdependence, of mutual reliance, comfort, listening, understanding, and paying attention to each other's needs. Evidence seems to suggest that girls learn the importance of interdependency more readily than boys.

My house is often full with children. My sons use the phone instrumentally to make arrangements with their friends who race in and out to swap sports cards, skateboard, cycle, play computer games, hit, kick or throw a ball. They have a wide range of friends. My daughter sits talking for hours on the phone. Her friends who visit sit on her bed talking about appearance, other girl friends, boys, personal problems, parents. It is crucial for her to have several "best friends." She has an extended wardrobe, her girl friends lend and borrow clothes with intimate ease. There seems to be a real distinctiveness in the way girls and boys value friendships, a difference created by differential gender socialization and reinforced so strongly through social structures like education, role models, and the media, that even children socialized in nonstereotypical ways are still affected. How do these gender differences translate into adult friendships?

3. MEN'S FRIENDSHIPS

"All the bullshit about mates. I've got mates but no friends" (Colling, 1992, 55). It is interesting that increasing numbers of men writing on friendships confirm the shallowness of many male relations. They write of mateship and comradeship which develops through hardship, or the unique sharing of experiences, like sailors on a long sea voyage, teenage boys in a summer resort, and particularly soldiers in a trench, wartime buddies who share deeply personal matters in quite abnormal circumstances and hence form unique bonds that may persist after war ends. Yet comrades are "bound to one another as generalized others" (Strikwerda & May, 1992, 113), for here there is an impartial respect for the fellow soldier, compatriot, co-worker that may involve an emotional distancing.

Men's relationships with other men are marked typically by shared activities, like going to the pub, or a sports game, or playing sport together, mending, repairing or building objects together. Discussions often concentrate on sports, sharing expertise, work, and sexual conquests. These common activities revolve around a typical masculine socialization into an achievement orientation. Achievement and competitive relations bond a football team, but in interpersonal relations, it "makes men reluctant to reveal things about themselves that emerge from their interaction with their mothers, and this gives them the necessary mothering skills to nurture others, and to define themselves in connection with others.

Gilligan refuses to see these ideas of nurture, connection, and relationality as inferior to, or deviant from, norms of identity formation derived from traditional masculine standards which prioritize autonomous emotional distancing. Gilligan's interest lies in the interaction of experience, thought, and dialogue. In listening to what people say about themselves, what is significant to them, and what connections to others are made, she discovered a "different voice," a contrast to traditional masculine forms of thought, interpretation, and judgment. But she added that this is "*not* a generalization about either sex" (Gilligan, 1983, 2). I agree with Barbara Houston that what is important is articulating "a coherent formulation of an ethics of care, not the empirical question of whether there are sex differences in the use of this morality" (1989, 85). Nevertheless, Gilligan's findings relate to a general tendency of women to use a different moral perspective that pivots around conflicts between the self and others. The ethic of care and relationality is thus defined thematically, suggesting that more women than men are regularly engaged in practices of childcare, care of the aged, disabled and ill, emotional nurture, and employment in service industries. All of these are practices that depend on context, content, social responsibilities, and concrete relations. In valuing care, relationships connote responsiveness, engagement, and a resilience of connection, symbolized by networks. Moral concerns focus on problems of detachment, disconnection, abandonment, and indifference (Gilligan, 1988, xvii). For many women, and for some men, a morally mature subjectivity values the interconnection between self and others, rather than prizing a self defined by separation from others. This priority given to care lays a firm foundation for friendships.

To understand how women typically learn such care and relationality, it is helpful to contrast this "care perspective" with the "justice perspective." The latter is dominant in liberal individualistic, contract, and rights-based theories. The justice perspective is characterized by abstract, ideal, universal, impartial, formal, generalized principles, the care perspective by contextualized, particular, informal, concrete practices. Between these perspectives, there are three main conflicts of priorities: a formal abstraction and a contextualized content; individual rights and social responsibilities; the generalized other and the concrete other. I shall summarize these contrasts briefly. First, formal abstractions stand in tension with the way morality figures in our life, since there is always a content to moral dilemmas, like the messy, muddled confusion with the friend we have disagreed with. Feminist theory draws our attention to the considerations of the personal, arguing that the contexts in which our prime moral experiences occur make a difference to the way we construct moralities. For example, women often exchange confidences of common experiences related to pregnancies, births, childcare, and household concerns. Our experiences of growing up as a girl, and as a woman with specific subjective variations, influences the way we approach moral relations like friendships. Friendships emerge in contexts. Our past experiences, including our gender socialization, affects what we bring to the contexts and to the friendships, and this of course applies equally to men.

The second contrast is between rights and responsibilities. A morality of rights, based on equality and justice, is geared to rational resolutions. Its concern is to balance individual competing claims, like my right to my new friend's time, energy, and possessions, over her closer friend's claims. A morality of responsibilities, based on the principle of connection to others, is a morality tied to experiences of relationships. The chief concern is to include those who need care. It takes into account issues of equity and differences in need, such as, why one desperately upset friend needs my time tonight in contrast to my friend who wants to celebrate her new job. Morality is perceived as a problem of inclusion of those requiring care which may produce a conflict of responsibilities, and which I try to resolve, for example, by phoning my joyous friend, and visiting my upset friend.

The third contrast centres on how we view others. As Seyla Benhabib expresses it, when we consider others as a "generalized other" we view each individual "as a rational being entitled to the same rights and duties we would want to ascribe to ourselves" (1987, 163). These relations are governed by equal reciprocity, the moral requirements of which are rights, obligations, entitlements, and the responses those of respect, duty, dignity, worthiness. This means we would view all our friends in generalized, formal terms of rights and duties. With the "concrete other" we identify each individual in her historic, specific contexts. Identification here requires that "I confirm not only your humanity but your human individuality" (1987, 164). Benhabib identifies the moral categories associated with a concrete individuality as those of responsibilities, bonding, and sharing, and the corresponding moral feelings as those of love, care, sympathy, and solidarity. This means we need to know a lot about the specific life narratives, needs, desires, and goals of our friends to respond with appropriate care. In summary, the justice and care perspectives contrast different priorities. A priority given to the care perspective means that good friends take context, requires partiality, special attentiveness, responsiveness and favoritism (1991, 818). Being a friend involves being committed to and trusting our friend. The primary focus is "the needs, wants, attitudes, judgments, behaviors, and overall way of being of a particular person" (Friedman, 1989b, 4). A friend is unique, so partiality requires us to respond specifically to who she is, someone we love for the qualities she has, and not the qualities we wish she had. Kapur Badhwar (1987) differentiates these unique qualities. If I love a person unconditionally, the individual qualities are not conspicuous. If I love a friend instrumentally for some benefit I derive from particular qualities, my friend's value depends on my desires and she can be dispensable when I have fulfilled my desire. If my object of love is a specific friend with a concrete individuality, this involves the whole constellation of moral, psychological, aesthetic, intellectual qualities she possesses and she is irreplaceable. "Loving and delighting in her are not completely commensurate with loving and delighting in another . . . the loss of the old friend is a distinct loss, the gain of the new friendship, a distinct gain" (Badhwar, 1987, 14). My committed responsibility thus requires an intimate knowledge of how best to fulfil my duties of friendship, to care, be responsive, listen, be honest, and be good to my friend. The priorities many women place on care and relationality translate readily into friendships, where supportiveness, affection and a partial particularity abound.

5. SELF-TRUST AND FRIENDSHIP

Before elaborating further on a feminist understanding of friendship, I want to clarify that the general conditions of friendship overlap for women and men, but my argument is that women's experience in caring relationships often qualitatively distinguish their friendships. In terms of these general conditions, both women and men recognize friendship as an act of goodwill. Goodwill in itself does not constitute friendship, since we are friendly toward neighbors and strangers. Friends are defined by the goodness they do for the sake of their friends. Intimate friends are "persons toward whom and with whom one can most fully and continuously express one's goodness" (Sherman, 1987, 595). As I have stressed, friendship is a principled relationship. Mary Wollstonecraft, in *A Vindication of the Rights of Women* (1792) writes, "friendship is a serious affection; the most sublime of all affections, because it is founded on principle, and cemented in time" (in Enright & Rawlinson, 1991, 151). Friendship is durable, it lasts "whatever the vagaries of fate and irrespective of separations in time and space" (Armstrong, 1985, 212). Past behaviors, understandings, shared experiences, and proven loyalties create special bonds. The care, concern, and sympathy within a friendship is built upon a knowledge base of past trust and intimacy (Blum, 1980, 69). We trust out friends to be honest with us, to be fair, to consider what is best for us, and similarly, we treat our friends well, for friendship produces special expectations and duties. Where there is a mutuality of trust, affectionate care, and intimate self-disclosure, this is usually built over time, and "this mutuality is the basis of special responsibilities" (Annis, 1987, 352). We accept each other's views, listen, keep promises and confidences, lend possessions, and give emotional support.

For Aristotle, friends constitute the "greatest" and "most necessary" of external goods. Here I return to the idea that "in choosing a character friend, we select 'another self' who shares a sense of our commitments and ends, and a sense of what we take to be ultimate 'good and pleasant' in living" (Sherman, 1987, 597). With friends we take on a shared conception of "good living," through mutual choices that express shared commitments to goals in life, goals that may encompass cooperative, communal, harmonious ways of living. I weep with my friend's grief, I rejoice with her pleasure. Her happiness affects my happiness. The more I know about my friend's character and needs, the greater my attachment, and the more I can identify with her joys and sorrows. The origin of character friendship is another self, and the origin is located in self-love. To choose another on the basis of stable character presupposes a self-trust and a self-knowledge. This self-trust is valid for women and for men, but because many women still see the nurture of others to be more important that their own self-regard, particular attention must be paid to women's sense of self. I want to conclude this chapter by arguing that a feminist concept of friendship builds on caring relationality and requires strong ideas and practices of self-trust.

First I need to qualify the idea of a friend as "another self." In locating the origin of friendship in self-love, Aristotle takes for granted that friends are of the same sex and are necessarily male. C. S. Lewis, in extension, writes, "the sexes will have met one another in Affection and Eros but not in friendship. For they will seldom have had with each other the companionship in common activities which is the matrix of friendship" (1963, 105). Robert Armstrong agrees with Lewis that "Eros tends to take priority over friendship in relationships between men and women . . . human beings are either friends or lovers, but rarely both" (1985, 212–13). This is changing, particularly as women move into the workforce and mix with male colleagues whose company they enjoy. To see a friend as "another self" is not to say that our friend must be the same sex, nor is it to obliterate difference. If I am white, European, unemployed, and married with children, my best friend may be black, Afro-American, single, and careerist. I want to argue that a friend as "another self" affirms shared interests and goals, and knows how to tap into inner resources. As Friedman aptly summarizes it, "'a passion for friends' is also a passion for one's *Self*, and a woman's affectionate *Self*-regard is, at the same time, the realization of Gyn/affection" (1988, 136). Self-knowledge is crucial to friendship. Thus we need to explore three factors: the role of self-trust in friendship; the contribution of friendship to pedagogical moral growth; and the need for strong concepts of autonomy.

First, self-respect implies a personal valuing of our unique capacities, abilities, choices, interests, and ends that underscores that we are persons of dignity and worth with something to offer others. This is important to women who often feel devalued and describe themselves as being "just a housewife" or "just a mother." Women who are in the care of others continually make important moral choices, such as which child or friend gets what, when, and why. As reflective moral beings, we deliberate on options, choose on the basis of our judgments, trusting our decision-making abilities, but accepting the possibility that we may choose wrongly. For example, we believed Sally to be our friend, until she continued to lie to us. Self-trust provides us with an inner strength, a positive sense of our motives, competency, and integrity. Self-trust enables us to function as cognitive agents responsible for, among other things, the type of friends we are, and our commitments to friendships with others. It is not easy to let Sally know our hurt at her betrayal. "The self of self-trust is the everyday self" (Govier, 1993, 116), the embodied self located in particular social contexts with this friend, that possible friend, that person you wanted as a friend, but cannot get close to. This "self is the I of relation and dialogue as well as the I of self-understanding and independent action. . . . The self is the I that listens and speaks, that wonders, feels and responds—that accepts or rejects, confirms or disconfirms, persists or desists" (1993, 117). In this context we can trust a friend not to harm us, to act with integrity toward us, to be reliable and dependable, and to act toward us as a good person. Strengthening this self-trust is important, especially given the exclusion of women from classical ideals of friendship.

De Beauvoir writes, "women's fellow feeling rarely rises to genuine friendship. . . . Their relations are not founded on their individualities" (1975, 558). I disagree. The sort of happiness and female friendships that I am advocating are grounded on strong notions of thought-ful individuality and emerge with ethical meaning in the search for self-integrity. Thus I explore further Raymond's idea of the rationality and the self-trust involved in friendship. She writes that there can be no genuine friendship between women that "does not come from a strong Self" (1986, 162). The normative dimensions to this individuality diverge from individualism, for selves are understood in their contexts of relationships with particular others. To realise what we share in com-mon with other women depends on knowing what we believe, think, desire. This does not foreclose the possibility of confusion or uncer-tainty, or the prospect of someone stirring our imagination to new heights, but it does rely on a healthy self-regard. Through thinking we discover what our real self might be like. "This is the awakening of female friendship in which the search for others like my Self begins" (Friedman, 1988, 132).

The context in which this self-regard develops is through acknowl-edging the fragility of intimate friendships that must be nurtured sen-sitively. Raymond refers personally to the power of female friendship in convents, which "must be allied to other forms of emotional, intellec-tual, social and spiritual life" (1986, 112) to survive. That is, close friends long to know the truth of each other—their upbringing, education, work experiences, lovers, families, hopes, and fears. Developing this knowl-edge requires privacy, time, reflection, and what Alice Walker calls the "rigours of discernment," an important means of self-regard, that "over-comes a sentimentalizing attitude . . . that feminism makes all women friends" (Friedman, 1988, 133). The conditions of friendship require a thoughtfulness, a considerateness of care, a concern for others, an atten-tiveness to others' needs, and careful reasoned thinking. As noted, in the classical tradition women are judged to be without the character traits indispensable to good friendship—rationality, passionate individual-ity, virtuous friendship. Paul Lauritzen (1989) denies that an ethic of care is a new form of Romanticism by emphasizing the way it draws on *intellectual* and emotional skills required particularly of good mothering. Sara Ruddick too draws attention to distinctive ways of thinking that emerge when there is a "priority of keeping over acquiring, of conserv-ing the fragile" (1982, 80). An affectionate self-regard that cares deeply for particular friends requires thoughtful passions.

Friedman (1989b) calls attention to a second factor of self-trust, an important, often neglected good made possible by friendship, the good of moral growth. Our first values and moral rules are learnt in pri-mary socialization, usually in the family. Familial attachment and inter-dependence are primary experiences which tie "the psychology of love to the representation of moral growth and self-development" (Gilligan, 1988, 5). The moral growth Friedman points to is when we start to grasp our experiences in new lights, in different terms, when we open them up to the voice of "the other." Friendship gives us new standpoints, new insights into ranges of experience beyond our personal boundaries. Among friends, there is a mutual sharing of stories, of experiences, of disagreements and uncertainties, and of alternative ways to approach moral dilemmas that enable us to grow through a broadening of our theoretical and practical base. The point I have stressed is that personal experience makes an epistemological contribution to the way we construct morality, subjectivity, and our relationships with others.

For example, where there is trust and self-disclosure, we come to know intimately what is happening to a good friend. Where this intimacy has been built over time, our friend sees us when we are vulnerable and can advise whether our actions make sense—that is, that they are true to who we are. Imagine I am a happily married woman with healthy children. My best friend has devoted her energy to her career, and has not found it easy to have committed love relationships. The man she has shared a house with for two years left her when he found out she wanted children. Her experiences live for me "with narrative specificity and richness" (Friedman, 1989b, 8). I cannot be of much use to my distraught friend if I do not know what she considers important, what upsets her, what gives her hope, what makes her laugh, why she suddenly wants children. "Through intimate knowledge of one's friends, one participates vicariously in the living which *embodies and realises* her divergent values" (1989b, 9). Friends expand the opportunity for growth in moral knowledge, contributing both to a plurality of standpoints that influences our choices, values and principles, and to the development of our characters. Through friendship our lives are enriched.

I am suggesting that feminists need to continue the project of reconceptualizing the third factor of self-trust, which I shall call *caring autonomy*. In orthodox liberal individualist accounts of the self, autonomy is the state of being radically independent, unencumbered by attachment to others, free to be self-reliant, detached, impartial. The critique of this atomistic, self-made individual emerges in communitarian writings as well as in feminist theory. For example, as Charles Taylor explains, our understanding of who we are is shaped by recognition from others, and in its absence "grievous wounds" are inflicted. Where there is affirmed recognition, we can discover an individualized identity. This identity has a "fundamentally *dialogical* character" (1992, 32), negotiated through interaction with others. For example, "if some of the things I value most are accessible to me only in relation to the person I love, then she becomes part of my identity" (1992, 34). There is a profound richness to the mutual understanding that situates a valuable friendship. Taylor's point is that it is on the intimate plane that we realise self-discovery and self-affirmation. The problem both communitarian and feminist traditions share is how to manage the importance of autonomous self-determination with the constitutiveness of social relations.

Feminists in their talk of "self-in-relations" articulate "the inseparability of the self and context" (Porter, 1991, 170) and make a clear statement about the way the self is constructed in relation with others. But the relational dimensions of women's identity and friendships are often stressed by feminists over the importance of the self, hence the need for a reconceptualisation of autonomy. Lorraine Code (1991) is one philosopher who reflects on the epistemic significance of knowing others, suggesting that the autonomous reasoner learns not just through detached, impartial self-reliance, but through attachments to parents, teachers, friends. The dilemma lies in achieving a realistic balance between "self" and "relations," between "autonomy" and "care." Women often struggle to preserve a sense of themselves as individuals with specific feelings, capacities, values, identities, in contexts where this often disappears into relational identities (Govier, 1993, 104). Women's experience of embeddedness in relations have often been oppressive in submerging their autonomy. Friedman (1989a, 286), retaining communitarian insights, critically reflects on the moral particularities within communities that might encourage nonoppressive relations, and where our ties to others are integral to our self-identity. Black women writers also stress the complex significance of relationships in the family and community, among women, and between men and women. Patricia Hill Collins (1990) speaks of the centrality of women in the Afro-American communities—of woman-centred networks of organised, resilient, bloodmothers and othermothers, grandmothers, sisters, aunts, cousins. This strong notion of self in relationships emerges in the everyday taken for granted situated knowledge of nurturing children in black extended family networks. This nurture "stimulates a more generalized ethic of caring and personal accountability among Afro-American women who often feel accountable to all the Black community's children" (1990, 129). What I have tried to show in this chapter is that a *caring autonomy* grants moral significance to special emotional bonds by affirming human connectedness.

As Diane Meyers points out, a caring autonomous woman is not a woman who submerges her self-interest, but this woman embraces the dual injunction to be true to one's own needs while caring for others. Meyers develops her ideas on the importance of autonomy to subjectivity more fully when she articulates a notion of "autonomous competency." This is a delving into one's "repertory of coordinating skills," including introspective, communicative, reasoning, imaginative, and volitional skills (1989, 79). Through exercising these skills, we grasp *who* we are, what constrains, limits, or excites us and how we can give expression to our autonomous skills. Relying on our critical reflection and judgment requires a sense of our self-competence and worth. We need to ask important questions about what we really value and then act accordingly. We learn through doing, hence Meyers urges societies to support autonomous modes of living, so that children's education, and social, political, and economic institutions are responsive to the autonomous desires of participants (1992, 129). Feminist theory requires strong concepts of subjectivity. Indeed, "until the Self is another friend, it is often difficult for women" to have confidence in their power of making and sustaining friends" (Raymond, 1986, 222). I have argued that a feminist understanding of friendship requires first, considerations of self-trust, secondly, that this contributes to moral growth, and thirdly, that a synthesis of care and autonomy confirms active friendship.

To conclude, *caring autonomy* brings together concerns of "others" and of "self." Friendship fosters "other-regarding" dispositions of benevolence, so we can be generous in good times, helpful in bad times, forgiving in the face of injury, acting justly, not causing injury, hurt or judging harshly, and friendship fosters the "self-regarding" disposition of autonomy, acting on one's own self-determination and integrity, being true to ourself (Kapur, 1991, 484). These dispositions develop over time through our relationships with relatives, loved ones, teachers, colleagues, friends, where we learn to negotiate self-other conflicts, and acquire the skills of caring autonomy. For children, dependency on parents is a necessary foundation for their autonomy and yet something which if in excess, can undermine autonomy. For both children and adults, powerlessness is destructive of autonomy, for as we have seen, autonomy requires a sense of self-power, which is possible only in structures of relationships genuinely conducive to autonomy. Our dependence on others, when mutually reciprocated is not "the antithesis of autonomy, but a literal precondition of autonomy, and interdependence a constant component of autonomy" (Nedelsky, 1989, 225). In prioritizing caring, Noddings rejects an ontological otherness, inviting those of us who are teachers and/or parents to teach our children to care, for "a relational ontology posits the fundamental role of relation" (Noddings, 1990, 124). I have suggested that this relationality is not a losing of the self, but it is an affirming of self through our caring connections. Let us practice our caring autonomy. As good friends, supportive, affectionate, and responsive to the particularity of each other, let us grow together in friendship.

REFERENCES

Annis, D. (1987). The meaning, value and duties of friendship. *American Philosophical Quarterly*, 24(4), 349–355.

Armstrong, R. (1985). Friendship. *The Journal of Value Inquiry*, 19, 211–216.

Badhwar, N. Kapur (1985). Friendship, justice & superogation. *American Philosophical Quarterly*, 22(2), 123–131.

——— (1987). Friends as ends in themselves. *Philosophy & Phenomenological Research*, 48(1), 1–23.

Baron, M. (1991). Impartiality and friendship. *Ethics*, 101(4), 836–857.

Benhabib, S. (1987). The generalized and the concrete other: The Kohlberg-Gilligan controversy and moral theory. In E. Feder Kittay & D. T. Meyers (Eds.), *Women and Moral Theory* (pp. 154-177). Totowa, New Jersey: Rowman & Littlefield.

Bishop, S. (1987). Connections and guilt. *Hypatia* 2(1), 7–23.

Blum, L. (1980). *Friendship, altruism and morality*. London: Routledge & Kegan Paul.

——— (1986). Iris Murdoch and the domain of the moral. *Philosophical Studies*, 50, 343–367.

Card, C. (1988). Female friendship: Separations and continua. *Hypatia*, 3(2), 123–130.

Chodorow, N. (1978). *The reproduction of mothering: Psychoanalysis and the sociology of gender*. Berkeley: University of California Press.

Code, L. (1991). *What can she know? Feminist theory and the construction of knowledge*. Ithaca, NY: Cornell University Press.

Colling, T. (1992). *Beyond mateship: Understanding Australian men*. Sydney: Simon & Schuster.

Collins, P. Hill (1990). *Black feminist thought: Knowledge, consciousness, and the politics of empowerment*. Boston: Unwin Hyman.

De Beauvoir (1975). *The second sex* (trans. H. M. Parshley). Harmondsworth: Penguin Books.

Enright, D. J. & Rawlinson, D. (Eds.) (1991). *The Oxford book of friendship*. Oxford: Oxford University Press.

Friedman, M. (1988). Individuality without individualism: Review of Janice Raymond's *A passion for friends*. *Hypatia*, 3(2), 131–137.

―――― (1989a). Feminism and modern friendship: Dislocating the community. *Ethics*, 99, 275–290.

―――― (1989b). Friendship and moral growth. *The Journal of Value Inquiry*, 23(4), 3–13.

―――― (1991). The practice of partiality. *Ethics*, 101(4), 818–835.

Gilligan, C. (1983). *In a different voice: Psychological theory and women's development*. Cambridge, MA: Harvard University Press.

―――― (1987). Moral orientation and moral development. In E. Feder Kittay & D. T. Meyers (Eds.), *Women and moral theory* (pp. 19–33). Totowa, New Jersey: Rowman & Littlefield.

Gilligan, C., Ward, I. V. & Taylor, J. McLean (Eds.) (1988). *Mapping the moral domain. A contribution of women's thinking to psychological theory and education*. Cambridge, MA: Harvard University Press.

Gottman, J. (1986). The world of corordinated play: Same-sex and cross-sex friendship in young children. In J. M. Gottman & J. G. Parker (Eds.), *Conversations of friends: Speculations on affective development* (pp. 139–191). Cambridge: Cambridge University Press.

Govier, T. (1993). Self-trust, autonomy, & self-esteem. *Hypatia*, 8(1), 99–120.

Held, V. (1987). Feminism and moral theory. In E. Feder Kittay & D. T. Meyers (Eds.), *Women and moral theory* (pp. 111–128). Totowa, New Jersey: Rowman & Littlefield.

Houston, B. (1989). Prolegomena to future caring. In M. M. Brabeck, (Ed.), *Who cares? Theory, research and educational implications of the ethic of care* (pp. 84–100). New York: Praeger.

Jackson, D. (1990). *Unmasking masculinity: A critical autobiography*. London: Unwin Hyman.

Jones, K. B. (1990). Citizenship in a woman-friendly polity. *Signs*, 15(4), 781–812.

Kapur, N. Badhwar (1991). Why it is wrong to be always guided by the best: Consequentialism and friendship. *Ethics*, 101(3), 483–504.

Lauritzen, P. (1989). A feminist ethic and the new romanticism—Mothering as a model of moral relations. *Hypatia*, 4(2), 29–43.

Lewis, C. S. (1963). *The four loves.* London: Fontana Books.

Limb, S. (1989). Female friendship. In R. Porter & S. Tomaselli (Eds.), *The dialectics of friendship.* London and New York: Routledge.

McKeon, R. (1973). *Introduction to Aristotle.* Chicago: University of Chicago Press.

Meyers, D. T. (1987). The socialized individual and individual autonomy: An intersection between philosophy and psychology. In E. Feder Kittay & D. T. Meyers (Eds.), *Women and moral theory* (pp. 139–153). Totowa, New Jersey: Rowman & Littlefield.

——— (1989). *Self, society and personal choice.* New York: Columbia University Press.

——— (1992). Personal autonomy or the deconstructed subject? A reply to Hekman. *Hypatia,* 7(1), 124–132.

Miller, J. Baker. (1976). *Toward a new psychology of women.* Boston: Beacon Press.

Murdoch, I. (1970). *The sovereignty of good.* London: Routledge & Kegan Paul.

Nardi, P. M. (Ed.), (1992). *Men's friendships.* London: Sage Publications.

Nedelsky, J. (1989). Reconstructing autonomy: Sources, thoughts and possibilities. In A. C. Hutchinson & L. Green (Eds.), *Law and the community: The end of individualism?* (pp. 219–252). Toronto: Carswell.

Noddings, N. (1984). *Caring: A feminine approach to ethics and moral education.* Berkeley: University of California Press.

——— (1990). A response. *Hypatia,* 5(1), 120–126.

Porter, E. J. (1991). *Women and moral identity.* Sydney: Allen & Unwin.

Raymond, J. (1986). *A passion for friends: Toward a philosophy of female affection.* London: Women's Press.

——— (1987). Female friendship and feminist ethics. In B. Hilkert Andolsen (Ed.), *Women's consciousness, women's conscience: A reader in feminist ethics* (pp. 161–174). San Francisco: Harper & Row.

Rubin, L. B. (1985). *Just friends: The role of friendship in our lives.* New York: Harper & Row.

Ruddick, S. (1983). Maternal thinking. In B. Thorne & M. Yalom (Eds.), *Rethinking the family: Some feminist questions* (pp. 76–94). New York: Longman.

Sherman, N. (1987). Aristotle on friendship and the shared life. *Philosophy & Phenomenological Research,* 47(4), 589–613.

Stocker, M. (1987). Duty and friendship: Toward a synthesis of Gilligan's contrastive moral concepts. In E. Feder Kittay & D. T. Meyers (Eds.), *Women and moral theory* (pp. 56–68). Totowa, New Jersey: Rowman & Littlefield.

Strikwerda, R. & May, L. (1992). Male friendship and intimacy. *Hypatia,* 7(3), 110–123.

Taylor, C. (1992). *Multiculturalism and "the politics of recognition."* Princeton: Princeton University Press.

Youniss, J. & Smollar, J. (1985). *Adolescent relations with mothers, fathers, and friends.* Chicago: University of Chicago Press.

CHAPTER 3

MOTHERHOOD AS PEDAGOGY: DEVELOPMENTAL PSYCHOLOGY AND THE ACCOUNTS OF MOTHERS OF YOUNG CHILDREN

Anne Woollett
Ann Phoenix

INTRODUCTION

Traditionally, developmental psychology has been concerned with understanding how children develop and how their development may best be fostered. It has not generally been concerned with questioning the values and assumptions which lie behind the establishment of the "facts" of children's development and the cultural and historical context in which research is conducted (e.g., Burman, 1991; 1993; Morss, 1994). Mothers are consistently constructed as the major sources of influence in their children's development, as responsible for both childcare and the ways in which children develop. Their main roles with regard to their children is that of pedagogues, creating both the context for children's development and the sources of children's developmental problems as identified in childcare manuals (Marshall, 1991; Woollett & Phoenix, 1991). More recently, issues of gender equality encouraged by feminism has led to a reconsideration of the extent of maternal responsibility and acknowledgment that fathers should ideally share responsibility for their children and that other people also play a part in children's lives. However, even though mothers are constructed as central to their children's development, their experiences as mothers and their accounts of how they bring up children and foster their development is rarely examined. This contrasts with feminist analyses where women's experiences as mothers are examined in their own right (Phoenix & Woollett,

1991; Oakley, 1979; Boulton, 1983; Walkerdine & Lucey, 1989; Richardson, 1992).

This chapter examines some of the ways in which developmental psychology articulates pedagogy for mothers as evidenced in three recent and popular texts for undergraduate courses in developmental psychology. These texts have been chosen because, in many ways, they are progressive and enlightened. The ideas articulated in the texts will be compared with the findings of some observational studies of mothers and young children and the accounts of mothers bringing up young children. As we show, mothers share some of the values and prescriptions articulated in the texts. But while they acknowledge their influence in their children's lives and development, they view pedagogy as only one part of their childrearing tasks. We argue for the necessity of examining the implications of prescriptions in developmental psychology texts for women, for mothers, for children, and for feminist accounts of motherhood.

MOTHERHOOD AS PEDAGOGY: AN OVERARCHING THEME

Implicit within many developmental psychology texts (the majority of which are written for the U.S. market) is the conviction that there is a particular goal to childcare and child development which is the production of responsible, well-educated children. This goal is culturally and class specific but its specificity is not addressed in the texts. The following extract illustrates what are considered to be positive qualities in childhood by contrasting them with the negative ones popularly associated with 'only' children (i.e., children without brothers and sisters):

> What is the only child like? The popular conception of the only child is a "spoiled brat" with such undesirable characteristics as dependency, lack of self-control, and self-centered behavior. But researchers present a more positive portrayal of the only child, who often is achievement-oriented and displays a desirable personality, especially in comparison to later-borns and children from large families. (Santrock, 1992, 343)

Parental responsibilities, as outlined in developmental psychology texts, lie in the fostering of the development of achievement-oriented, independent, self-regulated, and unselfish children. Parents then are constructed as the major explanatory/independent variable with regard to their children's development. The term 'parents' is intended to convey the recognition that both mothers and fathers are responsible for children (Phoenix & Woollett, 1991). However, contrary to the egalitarian gender ideology suggested by the use of the term 'parent', the texts suggests that it is mothers, not fathers, who are responsible for their children's development:

> I have used the word "parents" in the discussion so far, but most of the research I have talked about has involved studies of mothers. Still, many of the same principles seem to hold for fathers as well. (Bee, 1992, 417)

> Unfortunately, some of those *parent*-infant dyads that fail to achieve early interactive synchrony also fail to develop secure infant-*parent* attachment later. *Maternal* responsiveness to infant signals can play an important role in the emergence of attachment. (Hetherington & Parke, 1993, 224, our emphases)

The apparent gender-blindness in the use of the word 'parent' appears therefore to be disingenuous and serves to maintain traditional gendered divisions of labour between mothers and fathers.

> Parents want to develop a strong attachment with their infant, but they still want to maintain strong attachments to their spouse and friends, and *possibly* continue their careers. (Santrock, 1992, 188, our emphasis)

In order to produce independent and cognitively competent children, mothers (or parents) are required to behave in such a way that independence and intellect are fostered. Thus, effective or ideal mothering is presented as a mix of (mainly) indirect pedagogy and of diligence in the provision of the circumstances (emotional and physical) which encourage children's learning and acquiring of these characteristics. This, of course, assumes that it is indisputably clear that these qualities are desirable and how they are to be achieved.

DEFINING THE NORMAL

Many developmental psychology texts are written in the style of "objective" presentation of the latest psychological knowledge about human development, as in the following extract:

My reading of the rich array of research . . . has led me to the following list of five general characteristics of families whose children achieve higher IQ scores:

1. *They provide an interesting and complex physical environment* for the child. . . .
2. They are *emotionally responsive* to and *involved* with their child. . . .
3. *They talk to their child*, using language that is descriptively rich and accurate.
4. They *avoid excessive restrictiveness*, punitiveness or control, instead giving the child room to explore. . . .
5. They *expect* their child to do well and to develop rapidly. They emphasize and press for school achievement. (Bee, 1992, 226–27)

Part of the claim to authority of developmental texts lies in the differentiation of their expertise from the lay experience of parents. Parents tend to be presented as inadequate, partial sources of information about their children (although, of course, some parents are also developmental psychologists) and other, more "objective" sources of data are preferred.

Parents often are asked to provide reports of their own or their children's behaviour. However, such measures are criticized for being inaccurate, unreliable and open to distortions. (Hetherington & Parke, 1993, 54)

There is, however, occasional reference to the fact that even though parents are not trained in objective measures (such as experimentation and observation) which are the hallmark of developmental psychology, parental interpretations of what their children are doing may provide valuable data and insights for psychologists and observers. The second part of this chapter demonstrates that mothers are often extremely observant of, and reflective about what their children do.

The definition of mothers as inexpert observers of their children allows writers of developmental psychology texts to take a double step. First, they describe maternal behaviour and then use their decontextualised accounts as the basis for prescribing ideal "mothering." The example of mother-infant synchrony, argued repeatedly to be a prerequisite for children's acquisition of cognitive and social competence, demonstrates how what is observed as "natural" in mother-infant interaction is often reflected back as ideal behaviour for all mothers with no account being taken of the fact that it is middle-class, white mothers who are generally observed in very specific contexts (Woollett & Phoenix, 1991). The first step, of describing spontaneously occurring maternal behaviour, is demonstrated in this account of mother-child synchrony:

> The interaction of mothers and their infants is symbolized as a dance or a dialogue in which successive actions of the partners are closely co-ordinated. (Santrock, 1992, 189)

"Motherese" provides an example of the way in which claims of "normality" are set up on the basis of findings from a limited sample. "Motherese" is a term often used to refer to a special register of language which adults use to speak with infants (with higher than usual pitch, simplified content, repetitions, and slowed-down delivery) (Snow and Ferguson, 1977), which it is claimed is both natural and involuntary:

> It is hard to talk in motherese when not in the presence of a baby. But as soon as you start talking to a baby you immediately shift into motherese. (Santrock, 1992, 180)

However, as research in other cultures on mother-child relations and children's development makes clear, motherese is neither inevitable, nor essential to the language development of babies and young children. Indeed, as Schieffelin and Ochs (1983) argue:

> The specific features of caregiver speech behavior that have been described as simplified register are neither universal nor necessary for language to be acquired. White middle-class and Kaluli children, become speakers of their languages within the normal range of development and yet their caregivers use language quite differently in their presence. (Schieffelin & Ochs, 1983, reprinted 1991, 226)

Thus, the second step common in developmental texts, prescription to all mothers from observation of a few, is in itself problematic. The texts do recognise that social contexts vary and that there is cultural diversity. Indeed, Hetherington and Parke (1993) cite Schiefflin and Ochs. However, recognition of diversity has not led to fundamental changes in the approach taken to developmental psychology or to questioning the ways in which research is used to imply that white, two parent, middle-class families provide a "better" context for development than other kinds of families. The very fact that developmental psychology manages to encompass new research evidence and new theoretical developments within its existing frameworks may be seen as strengthening the discipline, but its eclecticism does not open it to a fundamental rethinking of its parameters or to a questioning of the range of contradictory theories routinely described in developmental texts. (See Henriques et al., 1984, for a discussion of how irreconcilable theoretical frameworks can be presented in one text.)

FROM DESCRIPTION TO PRESCRIPTION: MOTHER BLAMING

So, by assigning mothers responsibility for supporting their children's development through the use of concepts such as scaffolding, synchrony, and motherese, what began life as description of the "natural" becomes transformed into prescriptions for pedagogy in which mothers are held responsible for how their children turn out. Even when the texts speak of "parents" and other "influences" on children, it becomes clear that it is mothers who are meant (as in the examples in the previous section on motherhood as pedagogy).

The message that children's development is produced by their parents and that "ideal" mothering is "natural" leads easily to "mother blaming" when children's development does not match the optimal as defined by the developmental psychology texts and children do not turn out well (Urwin, 1985). Walkerdine and Lucey (1989) make it clear that the pedagogical imperatives mothers are expected to pursue are much more likely to lead to failure than to success:

> The mother is often held responsible for the educational success of her children. By producing the correct early environment, she is to allow them to "separate" from her. This separation then paves the way for independence and autonomy which is taken to lead to educational success. . . . Their mothers are set up as guarantors of a certainty which, in practice, it is impossible for them to produce. (Walkerdine & Lucey, 1989, 173)

When texts engage in mother blaming, they often make explicit values about who makes good parents which are implicit in many discussions about good or normal mothering. But they also make explicit the ways in which parents are invoked to produce self-regulating children in such a way that the children are beguiled into believing that their behaviour is the result of their free choice.

> If parents are consistent in their discipline, use the minimum amount of pressure necessary to change the child's behavior, and encourage the child to view this compliance as self-initiated, children are more likely to cooperate and to adopt or internalise the standards of the parents. (Hetherington & Parke, 1993, 429)

This lends confirmation to the concerns of Walkerdine and Lucey (1989) that the regulatory function mothers are expected to take in relation to their children is an oppressive one. It contradicts the emphasis on "coregulation" and "mutual socialization" in developmental texts by deliberately advocating that parents should dissemble when imposing their power over their children in the interests of pedagogy.

MAINTENANCE OF THE STATUS QUO

In spite of their inclusion of new and apparently more progressive themes such as diversity in family composition and life styles and cultural practices, the developmental psychology texts are deeply conservative in their assumptions about the situations and contexts which provide "normal" and "ideal" pedagogy. Issues of cultural diversity and maternal employment, for example, tend to be dealt with as add-on chapters rather than as mainstream ones.

The texts identify a number of ways in which maternal failure can occur (although texts vary in the extent to which they consider factors identified as causative to be deterministic). For example, mothers can come from the wrong backgrounds, have experienced poor parenting themselves, be the wrong age (although some texts, e.g., Hetherington and Parke, 1993, now recognise that it is not young or older age per se which are responsible for poor child outcomes), live in inappropriate circumstances, either when they give birth or through later divorce, use inappropriate strategies of stimulation and control or even mother "too much."

The consequences of providing the "wrong" kind of parenting are dire.

> It is not just that children with disengaged parents are socially incompetent, irresponsible, immature, and alienated from their families. They also show disruptions in peer relations and in cognitive development, achievement, and school performance. . . . [I]t is this "double whammy" of not having the skills to be able to

gain gratification in either social or academic pursuits that frequently leads to delinquency in children with neglecting parents. . . . Parental involvement plays an important role in the development of both social and cognitive competence in children. (Hetherington & Parke, 1993, 433)

Conservative assumptions can also be seen in the treatment of gender relations and social class. Despite the use of the gender neutral term 'parent', the texts help to maintain implicit gender inequalities. As we have indicated, not only is the word 'parent' often used to signify "mother," but expectations of what mothers' and fathers' responsibilities and feelings should be is highly traditional. Thus, even though it is acknowledged that these may create strains for mothers and fathers, there is still a focus on traditional gender roles.

Most women usually enjoy tending to the needs of their loved ones and keeping the family going, even if they do not find the activities enjoyable and fulfilling. Women experience both positive and negative family work conditions. They are unsupervised and rarely criticized, they plan and control their own work, and they have only their own standards to meet. However, women's family work is often worrisome, tiresome, menial, repetitive, isolating, unfinished, inescapable, and often unappreciated. (Santrock, 1992, 501)

Expectations of traditional gender roles can also be seen in discussions of the employment of mothers outside their households. The impact of social changes brought about by the widespread employment of women outside the home is recognised but it is assumed that it is mothers who do the combining of "career and family" and that fathers do not have this double role. Maternal employment is viewed with approval on a number of levels, as meeting parental needs, providing good role-models for children of both sexes and because technological advances have made it possible for women to be employed, do household chores, and still have time for their children. However, the context in which maternal employment is discussed is one in which the status quo with regard to gender relations remains unchanged and unchallenged. This can be seen in the tone of the debate and the way in which uncertainty about the consequences for children of maternal employment are used to raise questions about the advisability of maternal employment as well as in the lack of consideration of what the costs might be for mothers of forgoing employment:

> However, the effects of maternal employment can be evaluated
> only in relation to other factors, such as the reason why the mother
> is working, the mother's satisfaction with her role, the demands
> placed on other family members, the attitudes of the other family
> members toward the mother's employment, and the quality of
> substitute care and supervision provided for the children. (Hether-
> ington & Parke, 1993, 453)

> But even if one agrees . . . that the conclusions are not clear (which
> I do), what do we say to parents who ask us whether the baby
> will be okay if *Mom* [our emphasis] goes back to work before the
> child is a year old? I find myself in agreement here with Alan
> Sroufe who argues that precisely *because* we are not sure, the more
> cautious advice to parents is that one of them should care for the
> child for the first year. (Bee, 1992, 512)

Another way in which developmental texts serve to maintain the status
quo is with respect to power relations within society. While the texts
take an apparently egalitarian approach to social class, culture, and ethnicity, and the diversity of family organisation, the concept of good or
ideal mothering is mainly derived from the practices of middle-class
mothers married to their children's fathers:

> The student should keep in mind that although parental behaviors
> and characteristics are related to intelligence and achievement in
> children, other factors such as *social class, education and social oppor-*
> *tunities set important limits* on the attainments of children. (Het-
> herington & Parke, 1993, 391, our emphases)

Social class differences are not discussed in chapters on mother-child
relations and mothers' influence on children's development but come
into play only when the focus is on atypical development or problems
in development when little consideration is given to the differing physical circumstances in which mothers bring up children. Instead, diversity is often dealt with quickly, superficially, and simplistically, and
hence has the effect of stereotyping, trivialising, and essentialising the
working classes and members of minority groups. They are further
stereotyped and trivialised when assumptions are made that the members of any minority ethnic groups will share the same characteristics, as
in the following extract:

> Ethnic-minority families differ from White American families in
> their size, structure, and composition, their reliance on kinship

networks, and their levels of income and education. . . . Large and extended families are more common among ethnic-minority groups than White Americans. (Santrock, 1992, 259)

This superficial handling of social class and ethnicity is further illustrated by reference to both as little more than "social addresses," with no examination of the reasons for any reported differences, such as the impact of living in small and cluttered homes for the strategies parents can adopt for keeping children safe. Whether mothers are "restrictive" or not, and how much time they spend in "child-centred" play may relate, for example, more to whether they have safety gates for stairs and can keep windows safely closed, or to the means to wash and dry dirty clothes than to their preferences about styles of childrearing (Mayall, 1986; Newson & Newson, 1968).

It is when "problematic" families and mothers are being discussed that the class partiality in the texts is most obvious. Working-class mothers are much more likely to be considered problematic in terms of not giving children sufficient resources of time, language, education, space, toys, and other goods. Thus, even in "progressive" texts, we see the normalised absence/pathologised presence couplet for working-class mothers and children and those from minority ethnic groups together with failure to consider the differential impact of prescriptions around motherhood for the working classes and the middle classes (Walkerdine & Lucey, 1989).

> Not only are there social class differences in childrearing values but also in parenting behaviors. Middle-class parents are more likely to explain something, use verbal praise, use reasoning to accompany their discipline, and ask their children questions. By contrast, parents in low-income and working-class households are more likely to discipline their children with physical punishment and criticize their children more. (Santrock, 1992, 261)

MOTHERS' PEDAGOGICAL ROLE

The findings of studies of mothers' behaviour with their young children and mothers' accounts of their experiences of motherhood do indicate a pedagogical role (for example, Tizard & Hughes, 1984). The following extracts taken from conversations between a young child and her white, middle-class mother at different points in the child's second year provide examples of pedagogical exchanges. In the first, shortly after the child's second birthday, the mother encouraged her child's use of colour terms:

Mother: What did you go in?
Child: Daddy car.
Mother: What colour is it?
Child: Blue.
Mother: Blue, that's right.
Child: Mummy car.
Mother: My car isn't blue, is it? What colour is Mummy's car?
Child: Blue.
Mother: No, it isn't. Can't you remember?
Child: Grey.
Mother: Grey, that's right.
Child: Daddy blue.
Mother: Yes, Daddy's is blue. What colour is Hazel's?

And in the second, about the time of the child's third birthday, the mother taught the child about shapes:

Child: Triangles.
Mother: Get the triangles out then. That's a triangle. How do you know it's a triangle?
Child: Because that isn't it.
Mother: It is, yes.
Child: That isn't a diamond, is it?
Mother: No, it's not a diamond.
Child: It's a square.
Mother: No, it's a triangle. It's got three sides, one, two, three. . . .
Child: That is, isn't it?
Mother: No, that's not a triangle. How many sides has it got? Can you count them?
Child: One, two, three. That's a triangle. That one is too.
Mother: It is, yes.

Women's accounts of their experiences as mothers, here illustrated by two Asian women bringing up young children in East London, also indicate their commitment to fostering children's development through play:

We do all enjoy playing with her. The time passes by so quickly when you play with your children. We play with toys, games, we talk to her and things like that. It's important to play with your children even if it's for a short while. I believe that the more time you spend with your children, the more they'll feel wanted and loved and it's good I think to do that from the very beginning.

Taking them to interesting places like the zoo. They probably know about animals but it's good for them to see what an animal looks like. I would like to take them to other people's houses so they know what good behaviour means. We've started doing that. Just being with them and telling them everything you know. Spending lots of time with them. Even when they get to the talking stage there are so many questions, they keep on and on, I think you've got to be patient and answer them.

The mothers quoted point to the costs as well as the benefits for mothers of maintaining a pedagogical role. One cost is time. The first mother's reference to "even if for a short time" indicates that she was aware that it takes time to engage in pedagogy. A second cost arises from the prescription to be child-centred and sensitive to children's needs and activities, expressed here as the need to be patient in the face of incessant questions. In the name of being a "good" mother, women have to set aside their own needs and interests. These costs are not usually observed in their most pressing form by developmental psychologists, who do not generally observe mothers when they feel frantic through lack of time or at the end of their tethers. This provides one explanation for the inadequacy of the prescriptions in the developmental psychology texts. They provide a partial picture of mother-child interaction but with little indication of the extent of the partiality or of the ways in which the picture is restricted. The commitment of the two women quoted here to being "good" mothers, whatever the costs, is reflected in the negative ways in which they talk about mothers who are employed outside the home because they are not always available for their children:

The more time you spend with them, the better they'll be. (Interviewer: In what ways better?) Well, good manners, they'll be quick to learn new things. There are some women like my sister-in-law who goes out to work and leaves the kids with the mother-in-law. She didn't spend too much time at home. I don't like leaving the kids at home from a very young age.

Implicit Pedagogy

Much of the pedagogy in which these mothers engaged was implicit rather than explicit, with mothers teaching through example and supporting children's activities and attempts to understand the world around them. Often, mothers' pedagogical agenda does not match closely those in developmental psychology texts. They rarely refer explicitly to the terms used in the developmental psychology texts such as intellectual skills, language, or emotional development (Tizard & Hughes, 1984).

Instead, mothers were more interested in children's acquisition of information, knowledge, and rules, especially domestic and household knowledge about family members and family relationships, baby care, and development (Tizard & Hughes, 1984). Mothers often talk to children about social rules and how children should behave in social situations. Their pedagogy is thus often related to the real-life issues with which mothers and children are continuously engaged (Dunn, 1988). General principles emerge from their conversations and play as can be seen in the following extract in which the mother tries to make her two-and-one-half-year-old daughter understand that she should not wake her sister during the night. This is related to her elder sister's tiredness the next morning when it is time to go to school:

Mother: Who came to see us last night? Who came into my bed?
Child: Me.
Mother: Yes. Why did you do that?
Child: 'Cos I woke Nunu up.
Mother: You woke Nunu up, did you?
Child: Um.
Mother: Poor Nunu, she was very tired this morning.
Child: She felt sick. She felt sick.
Mother: Nunu felt sick this morning, yes. I think it was because she felt so tired because you woke her up. Wasn't good, was it?
Child: No.
Mother: Next time you wake, perhaps you'd better wake Mummy up, not Nunu.
Child: Not Nunu.
Mother: No, not Nunu, because Nunu has to go to school and we don't want her to feel tired and sick at school, do we?

These extracts give a sense of the extent to which mothers balance the interests and concerns of each of their children and other members of the family. Much of their pedagogy derives from and is embedded in everyday family events (Newson & Newson, 1968; 1976). Mothers' concern with such issues relates to their desire that children are accepted and liked by others, to the smooth running of households, fairness to other children/family members, and also to their awareness that these are criteria on which their effectiveness as mothers is assessed by those outside the household.

Gendered Identities

Developmental texts are concerned with understanding the ways in which children acquire their gendered identities and this has also been a major concern for feminists. Developmental psychologists tend to consider that inborn or genetic factors have a part to play in the development of gender-appropriate behaviour, but like feminists, they also consider that mothers play a major role in encouraging and reinforcing gender appropriate behaviour. Many mothers do differentiate between boys and girls in terms of dress (thereby ensuring that everyone knows whether a child is a boy or a girl) and through the toys which they (and others) often buy for children. They also talk about children in gender-differentiated ways, as about a girl in the first and a boy in the second extract from McGuire (1991):

> She has a very happy temperament. She's lovely and she's a pleasure to be with, a happy little girl. She's not aggressive, she's sociable, and she loves people and children. She's very affectionate, gentle, and loving. (149)

> My beautiful son, he's loving and nice. He picks you flowers and kisses you better. He's very, very boy, manly, a boyish boy, a good boy, not really naughty, mischievous in a nice way. (151)

Ideas about gendered identities can also be found in mothers' conversations with their children. In the following extracts hoovering [vacuuming] and mending bikes are presented as gendered activities to young children. In the first extract David, aged two years, who has fixed the vacuum, wants to use it, but it is unable to do so because his three-year-old sister Megan is using it. He complains to his mother:

> *David to Mother:* I wanted to do it [vacuuming]. Because I fixed it up. And made it work.
> *Mother to David:* Well, you'll have to wait your turn.
> *Mother to Megan:* Are you going to let David have a turn.

Megan to Mother: I have to do it. Ladies do it.
Mother to Megan: Yes, ladies do it. Yes, and men do it sometimes. Daddy sometimes does the hoovering, doesn't he? (Dunn, 1988, 57)

In the second extract a four-year-old girl, Kelly, and her mother dispute about Kelly's broken bicycle:

Kelly: It's not fixed. It's still tipping over. Fix it.
Mother (annoyed):   Well, you let the big boys ride it, don't you?
Kelly: It's broken. (Moans.)
Mother (angry):   Go on, it won't hurt you. O God, you drive me nuts. You let them ride it. So what do you expect? It gets broken and Daddy says he is not going to mend it again. I'm not going to keep paying the price for you Kelly. I tell you not to let the big boys ride it, and what do you do?
Kelly: Joan [a friend] did.
Mother: Joan's not too big. Colin and David are. Colin and David are far too long for your bike and they break the stabilizers on it. Now you've got to ask your Daddy to mend it tonight. I bet you he moans. You ask him. I'm not asking him. I did yesterday. You'll have to be good for him tonight and he might do it.
Kelly (seeing younger sister on another bike): Mummy, let me have a go. (The wrangling continues.) (Tizard & Hughes, 1984, 91)

Some mothers also see their relationships with children in gendered terms. They talk in terms of similarities and companionship between themselves and their daughters. By middle childhood, girls tend to be more home-based than boys and are less likely to be allowed to play away from home (Petrie & Logan, 1986), making mothers' behaviour more salient to their daughters and providing more opportunities for interactions and shared interests between mothers and daughters than between mothers and sons, as the following mother of a seven-year-old suggests:

I think a girl is more with her mother, you know; if ever I want to go into town, it's useless trying to take these [two boys], but with

> Moira she'll trudge around with me for hours and not complain. I
> think, um, you've got more of a companion with a girl—a mother
> has, anyway. (Newson & Newson, 1976, 281)

Some mothers expressed their closeness to daughters in terms of identification:

> She's adult enough to have a grown-up, almost, conversation with
> me and she's a real friend, and I can see myself in her, and know
> almost exactly her thoughts—it's rather charming, and I'll say,
> "You're thinking such-and-such," and she'll say, "How did you
> know?" and I say, "You're recalling to me how I was at your
> age" . . . a nice comfortable feeling we have together. (Newson &
> Newson, 1976, 288)

This closeness and identification with daughters is also associated with greater tension and more confrontations between mothers
and daughters than between mothers and sons (McGuire, 1991). In contrast, mothers tend to distance themselves from sons and encourage
their independence through, for example, mothers' fostering of sons'
relationships with their fathers, and by reference to fathers in their
absence when playing "masculine" games (McGuire, 1991; Newson &
Newson, 1986).

POWER, CONTROL AND CONFLICT

The fostering of appropriate gendered identities is a part of some
mothers' pedagogy, a process taken for granted in developmental texts.
Approaches to mothering and mother-child relations articulated in
developmental texts emphasise sensitivity and child-centredness and
relate these to mothers' positive feelings about mothering and the mutuality of mothers' relations with their children. This view of mother-
child relations is perpetuated by the popularity of one-off observational
studies in which mothers find it relatively easy to act out their expectations of the "good mother" role and remain sensitive and child-centred
(Bradley, 1989). However, these snapshots avoid the complexity of
mother-child relations and the power relations which underlie them. In
longitudinal studies where families are revisited the conflicts inherent in
family life are more frequently reported (e.g., Dunn, 1988; Tizard &
Hughes, 1984), as in the following extract between a white middle-class
mother and her two-and-one-half-year-old:

Mother: What do we need to put under the easel? What do we
        have to put on the floor? Don't paint yet. What do we
        have on the floor?
Child: Paper.
Mother: Paper, that's right. Now, just a minute. Chloe, would you
        wait, please, until I've got the paper on the floor. I'll get
        cross. I don't want you to be naughty.
Child: I'm not naughty. I'm not a cheeky girl. I'm not naughty.
Mother: Yes, you are. Now, come and sit down.

Power, control, and the ways in which parents deal with conflict
between their own and their children's interests are major concerns in
parents' accounts of their childrearing (Newson & Newson, 1968; 1976;
Boulton, 1983; Walkerdine & Lucey, 1989; White & Woollett, 1992;
Woollett & Phoenix, 1991). These studies provide only limited support
for the idea that mother-child relations, even in white, two-parent, middle-class families, are characterised by reciprocity and that mothers use
reasoning as a means of controlling children. Rather, they indicate the
powerful emotions and battles of will that characterise many mother-
child interactions and provide children with opportunities to learn in a
highly charged emotional setting about power and control (Bradley,
1989; Walkerdine & Lucey, 1989). Children, being unaware of the prescriptions of the developmental psychology texts, are less constrained
than mothers, undermining still further the viability of notions of mutuality and reciprocity and the assumption that what is good for children
is necessarily good—and enjoyable—for mothers, as Walkerdine and
Lucey (1989) argue:

> The children's expression of violent emotions in these transcripts
> is most commonly displayed in attempts to control and regulate
> their mothers: they want to make their mothers do what they want
> them to do, to regulate the mother as they are regulated. (Walker-
> dine & Lucey, 1989, 121)

By ignoring conflict and power relations in families and children's resistance to mothers' attempts to "socialise" them, key aspects of children's
development and contexts in which that development takes place are
ignored in developmental texts.
    The emphasis on mutuality and reciprocity in mother-child rela-
tions also fails to take into account women's ambivalent feelings about
motherhood. Mothers often experience tensions between their own
needs and those of young children and the constraints childcare places

upon their ability to engage in other activities (Walkerdine & Lucey, 1989; Boulton, 1983; Prendergast & Prout, 1980; Oakley, 1979). The constraints and the hard work of childcare are illustrated in the following extract:

> If you have your baby in the first year of marriage, you become so busy that you can't go anywhere because you're so tied down with the baby. After marriage and having a baby your life is no longer how it used to be when you didn't have a baby. You spend all your time looking after it and if you want to go anywhere you have trouble taking it with you. So some wait and spend time with each other and enjoy themselves.

Women also acknowledge their feelings of irritation and annoyance, as in the following extract, when children cry a great deal:

> No, she doesn't cry as much as the others used to. When she does cry it's because she wants something like food or to be played with. I do get upset when babies cry so much. I can't understand why they cry so much. Sometimes I get annoyed when I can't find out what's wrong with her. You do get children who have a habit of crying all the time. I don't like that, that would really irritate me I think.

The ambivalence some women feel also relates to the context in which mothers bring up children. The assumption in the developmental texts that mothers ought to be available to spend time facilitating their children's development ignores the varieties of women's circumstances and their other responsibilities. Women's accounts indicate how their other responsibilities reduce their ability to behave in sensitive and child-centred ways and how facilitating children's development is only part of a wider set of responsibilities (Riley, 1983; New & David, 1985; Boulton, 1983; Singer, 1992). For example, housework vies with childcare for mothers' attention and energies and finding a balance between their different responsibilities is a major concern for many women:

> Just that I can't cope with him a lot. I get depressed and things like that easily. I do manage to get my work done but it's all day you know, it takes all day. I can't finish in the morning or afternoon. . . . When there's a lot of work to do I get down and think, "How am I going to get it done? How the time's gone."

This approach also ignores the pressures on the majority of mothers who have to balance the needs of two or more children. Observational studies are almost always of one mother interacting with one child at a time and many studies of women's experiences of motherhood examine the experiences of first-time mothers only. However, "only" children are the exception rather than the rule and when there are two or more children in a family, siblings become an important part of one another's lives (White & Woollett, 1992). Mothers' experiences and their agenda around childcare change when they have second and subsequent children: keeping the peace and managing the interactions between their two children become major concerns and extend the pedagogy provided for children (Munn, 1991), as the woman quoted here illustrates:

> It's hard work, it's not easy to bring up children. You've always got to worry whether you are hurting one while you are seeing to the first. They are all different. Who do you see to? That's a great problem with me having four. She'll say, "You don't say that to her, why do you say it to me?" "Why are you being horrible to me?" You get a lot of that and you have to sit and explain and talk and say, "it's your mood, you know, it's not how you really feel but it's just the way your moods are at the moment." My eldest is ten. I need to help her a great deal with school work and I can't because of the other children.

CONCLUSIONS

Developmental texts create a view of "normal" mothering in which mothers are constructed as sensitive and child-centred and taking their own needs into account is selfish and "unmotherly." This view of mothering is limited in its approach and inappropriate to the context of most women's lives as mothers. By "normalising" a limited range of experiences of a small proportion of mothers, the texts marginalise the feelings and experiences of many women and define them as "deviant." These deviant forms of motherhood form the basis of accounts of "problems of development" or "atypical development." Deviance is defined in terms of women's feelings and responses to motherhood (e.g., as depressed or abusive mothers, Nicolson, 1986) or through the circumstances of their lives (as "working mothers," "young mothers," or "single mothers," Phoenix & Woollett, 1991). Women who do not conform to prescriptions for "ideal" mothers are seen as providing their children with inadequate environments for their healthy and successful development and are constructed outside normative discourses of motherhood.

While mothers are treated in developmental psychology as all-powerful in the lives of their children and the main force in their development, even those mothers who are constructed in the developmental texts as "ideal" (white, middle-class, married mothers) often experience themselves as powerless as they recognise the limitations on their abilities to ensure their children's development in the ways outlined in the developmental texts and observational studies (Chodorow & Contratto, 1982). Their power is also limited by the other sources of influence on children and their development which are often ignored or underestimated in developmental accounts (such as fathers, the wider family, school, neighbourhood, media) as well as by the power of the child exercised through resistance or violence (see Walkerdine & Lucey, 1989). Developmental psychology thus provides a limited account of motherhood and mothers' pedagogical responsibilities, particularly since its main focus continues to be infancy and early childhood. In doing so, developmental psychology serves to maintain the status quo with regard to gender relations, social class, "race," and ethnicity and is thus antithetical to feminist aims of changing existing power relations.

Furthermore, while mothers do have some pedagogical intentions towards their children, their pedagogy often does not coincide with the prescriptions of developmental psychology. Rather than setting out to teach the decontextualised lessons identified as ideal in developmental texts, as we have shown, mothers' agenda arise from the ways in which they are positioned, and hence vary with their children's age, are designed for specific purposes within the context of their daily lives and are concerned with the facilitatation of good social relationships as much as cognitive understandings. Mothers' desires to ensure smooth, familial relationships may well be partly responsible for the findings of Walkerdine and Lucey (1989), that middle-class mothers tend to fit their children for living in a liberal democratic society where self-control and the denial of aggression are highly valued. In contrast, feminist analyses of motherhood and pedagogy acknowledge that motherhood is differentiated and hence are able to move beyond the limitations of the overinclusive approaches within developmental psychology to further understandings of motherhood, pedagogy, and the relationship between them.

REFERENCES

Bee, H. (1992). *The developing child*. 6th ed. New York: HarperCollins.

Boulton, G. M. (1983). *On being a mother: A study of women with preschool children*. London: Tavistock.

Bradley, B. S. (1989). *Visions of infancy*. Cambridge: Polity Press.

Burman, E. (1991). Power, gender and developmental psychology. *Feminism and Psychology*, 1, 141–153.

———— (1993). Review of P. Mitchell, *The psychology of child development. Feminism and Psychology*, 3, 389–395.

Chodorow, N. & Contratto, S. (1982). The fantasy of the perfect mother. In B. Thorne & M. Yalom (Eds.), *Rethinking the family*. London: Longman.

Dunn, J. (1988). *The beginnings of social understanding*. Oxford: Basil Blackwell.

Henriques, J., Hollway, W., Urwin, C., Venn, C., & Walkerdine, V. (1984). *Changing the subject: Psychology, social regulation and subjectivity*. London: Methuen.

Hetherington, E. M., & Parke, R. D. (1993). *Child psychology: A contemporary viewpoint*. 4th ed. New York: McGraw-Hill.

Marshall, H. (1991). The social construction of motherhood: An analysis of childcare and parenting manuals. In A. Phoenix, A. Woollett, & E. Lloyd (Eds.), *Motherhood: Meanings, practices and ideologies*. London: Sage.

Mayall, B. (1986). *Keeping children healthy*. London: Unwin.

McGuire, J. (1991). Sons and daughters. In A. Phoenix, A. Woollett, & E. Lloyd (Eds.), *Motherhood: Meanings, practices and ideologies*. London: Sage.

Morss, J. (1994). Making waves: Deconstruction and developmental psychology. *Theory and Psychology*, 2, 445–465.

Munn, P. (1991). Mothering more than one child. In A. Phoenix, A. Woollett, & E. Lloyd (Eds.), *Motherhood: Meanings, practices and ideologies*. London: Sage.

New, C. & David, M. (1985). *For the children's sake: Making childcare more than women's business*. Harmondsworth: Penguin.

Newson, J. & Newson, E. (1968). *Four years old in an urban community*. Harmondsworth: Penguin.

———— (1976). *Seven years old in the home environment*. Harmondsworth: Penguin.

———— (1986). Family and sex roles in middle childhood. In D. J. Hargreaves & A. M. Colley (1986). *The psychology of sex roles*. London: Harper & Row.

Nicolson, P. (1986). Developing a feminist approach to depression following childbirth. In S. Wilkinson (Ed.), *Feminist social psychology*. Milton Keynes: Open University Press.

Oakley, A. (1979). *From here to maternity: Becoming a mother*. Harmondsworth: Penguin.

Petrie, P. & Logan, P. (1986). *After school and in the holidays: The responsibility for looking after school children*. TCRU Working Paper No. 2. London: Thomas Coram Research Unit.

Phoenix, A. & Woollett, A. (1991). Motherhood: Social construction, politics and psychology. In A. Phoenix, A. Woollett, & E. Lloyd (Eds.), *Motherhood: Meanings, practices and ideologies*. London: Sage.

Prendergast, S. & Prout, A. (1980). What will I do? Teenage girls and the construction of motherhood. *Sociological Review*, 28, 517–535.

Richardson, D. (1992). *Women, motherhood and child rearing*. London: Macmillan.

Riley, D. (1983). *War in the nursery: Theories of the child and the mother*. London: Virago.

Santrock, J. W. (1992). *Life-span development*. 4th ed. Dubuque, IA: Wm. C. Brown.

Schieffelin, B. B. & Ochs, E. (1983). A cultural perspective on the transition from prelinguistic to linguistic communication. Reprinted in M. Woodhead, R. Carr, & P. Light (Eds.), *Child development in social context 1: Becoming a person*. London: Routledge, 1991.

Singer, E. (1992). *Child-care and the psychology of development*. London: Routledge.

Snow, C. & Feguson, C. (Eds.) (1977). *Talking to children: Language input and acquisition*. Cambridge: Cambridge University Press.

Tizard, B. & Hughes, M. (1984). *Young children learning: Talking and thinking at home and at school*. London: Fontana.

Urwin, C. (1985). Constructing motherhood: The persuasion of normal development. In C. Steadman, C. Urwin, & V. Walkerdine (Eds.), *Language, gender and childhood*. London: Routledge & Kegan Paul.

Walkerdine V. & Lucey, H. (1989). *Democracy in the kitchen: Regulating mothers and socialising daughters*. London: Virago.

White, D. & Woollett, A. (1992). *Families: A context for development*. Basingstoke: Falmer Press.

Woollett, A. & Phoenix, A. (1991). Psychological views of mothering. In A. Phoenix, A. Woollett, & E. Lloyd (Eds.), *Motherhood: Meanings, practices and ideologies*. London: Sage.

CHAPTER 4

LEARNING TO BE A MAN: DILEMMAS AND CONTRADICTIONS OF MASCULINE EXPERIENCE

David Morgan

In this chapter I wish to explore the various claims which men make to the ownership of knowledge of various kinds and the ways in which these claims derive from and construct masculinities. When people make various statements about the world, they are simultaneously laying claim to the ownership of that knowledge, of their right to deploy or to use it on the occasion when it is being used. Excluding charismatic claims for the present, I make a distinction between the rhetoric of experience and the rhetoric of reason.

I use the word 'rhetoric' here to indicate that I am concerned with techniques of persuasion, not always overt or recognised by the parties concerned, that are woven into statements about the world. I am talking about claims to the rightful ownership and use of the words which are uttered, claims which need to be recognised in everyday human encounters. In other words, whether or not we agree with what is being said we recognise that the other has some kind of legitimate claim over his or her words. Thus, in contemporary societies at least, we often discount the utterances of children, drunks, "madmen," or poets in that the words seem loosely anchored to the person uttering them. In mixed-sex encounters, the utterances of women may be treated in similar ways.

In talking about the rhetoric of experience, I am talking about claims which are made upon the basis of some kind of present or past being in the world. "I have been there. Trust me. I know what I am talking about." It has affinities with traditional authority in that it is often based upon some kind of particularistic membership, a tribe, a club, a caste of some invisible freemasonry. In talking about the rhetoric of reason, I am talking about claims which are made on the basis of seemingly universal criteria, something which the speaker has grasped and understood but which does not, in any exclusive sense, belong to the speaker. "Looking at the matter logically. Having considered all the evidence. After careful examination." These everyday claims clearly have affinities with Weber's model of rational-legal authority (Weber, 1947, 130–32).

I wish to explore these two rhetorics, separately and in combination, and their relevance for the examination of masculinities in contemporary Western society. I shall go on to continue these explorations through the examination of some key features in the lives of young men: sexual knowledge and experience, bullying, and popular heroes. In doing so I shall, in part, draw upon some of my own experiences that add a personal layer of complexity to the analysis.

THE RHETORIC OF REASON

If we do not speak as often as we might about the rhetoric of reason this may be because it is so often disguised. We understand reason as speaking for itself, as requiring no rhetoric. However, it is not enough that someone provide a reasonable argument; the argument must be seen and presented as being reasonable. Thus we may say, "let's be reasonable about this," "we must try to look at the matter rationally," and these requests often are accompanied by open-handed gestures signifying reasonableness.

Vic Seidler (1994) has identified the centrality accorded to reason and rationality in modern society as having historical origins and, more significantly for our purposes, as being a covert story about gender. There are deep historical roots linking reason and masculinity although these connections are obscured through claims of universality:

> In part, the workings of masculinity within modernity have remained invisible as dominant men have learned to speak in the impartial voice of reason. This has been part of an Enlightenment tradition and is deeply embodied in western inherited forms of philosophy and social theory. So a man's voice assumes a pitch of objectivity and impartiality as it becomes an *impersonalised* voice, a voice that has "authority" because it belongs to no one in particular while claiming at the same time to respect all. (Seidler, 1994, 109, original emphasis)

Thus splits between men and women become mapped onto splits between reason and emotion: the one division reinforcing the other.

One interesting feature of Seidler's discussion is the way in which he explores the unreasonable side of reason. This is manifested in a variety of ways. First, the claims of reason are often asserted, unreasonably, against the claims of experience. Second, the rhetoric of reason may sometimes sound louder than the actual arguments themselves. The person who says, "let's be reasonable about this" may be staking a claim to reasonableness that is weakly based.

Weber noted the irrational or unreasonable component within rationality itself (Weber, 1947). He contrasted a rationality which entailed the weighing and balancing of a whole range of means and ends with a rationality that sought to achieve one particular goal by the best means available without calling into question the reasonableness of the goal itself. Weber described how rationality was becoming a dominant theme in modern society, marginalising any alternative modes of understanding. He was aware that individuals develop vested interests in ideas and that these vested interests could be, under certain circumstances, as powerful as more material interests. What was perhaps muted in Weber's account was a recognition that the historical development of rationality was, in part, also a gendered story (Bologh, 1990; Morgan, 1992; Seidler, 1994).

THE RHETORIC OF EXPERIENCE

The candidate in a Canadian local election some years ago announced: "I am a graduate of the largest university in the world. The University of Hard Knocks." These statements provide a perfect illustration of the rhetoric of experience. Seidler's account of the ways in which modern masculinity comes to be identified with rationality, hence marginalising experience, provides some valuable and necessary insights into the conditions of modernity but does not tell us the whole story. In so far as experience enters into his masculinity story, it is in terms of a hardening process leading to a control of emotion and a holding of experience at arm's length. I would wish to argue that the rhetoric of experience continues to play an important part in the construction of modern masculinities; it is not simply a residue from some more traditional or prerational era. Men appropriate experience as well as reason although it is likely that these understandings or constructions of experience are different from those experiences associated with women and with femininity. Put another way, the distinction between reason and experience not only maps out differences between men and women, masculinity and femininity, but also maps out differences among men or styles of masculinity.

"Experience," then, creates hierarchies between men. There are a variety of features that we may identify with this gendered understanding of experience:

1. Experiences are seen as being "owned." The rhetoric of experience lays some kind of exclusive claim to this particular form of knowledge. I know because I was there or I had that experience; this is what makes the difference between us.
2. Experiences are quantitative and cumulative. It is not just a single experience that counts but rather a cumulative lifetime of experience. Hence, I do not simply have certain experiences denied to others but I have had more of a generalised and accumulated "experience."
3. Hence experience has a temporal dimension. It is associated with age or the membership of a particular cohort. When I was a National Service Man in the Royal Air Force, I was intrigued by the ways in which recruits would shout to one another, "get some in," meaning "I have had more time in the Service than you." Informal hierarchies were established around length of service, even amongst conscripts. Newcomers, with their careful attention to dress and saluting, were designated as "sproggs" (Morgan, 1987).
4. Experience is closely associated with physical or bodily experience, although it need not be actually based upon these. What is important is a contrast between direct and indirect experience, between the "real" world and between "book learning."
5. Experience, in these gendered constructions, is associated with the public/private distinction (Davidoff & Hall, 1987). The "real" world is whatever is designated as the public world, the world of public affairs where men gather and go about their business (e.g., employment, commerce, war, or politics).

REASON AND RHETORIC

The rhetorics of reason and of experience may be linked to different models of masculinity or different ways of doing masculinity. They do not necessarily differentiate between types of men; individuals may call upon either or both of these rhetorics as the occasion demands. As different constructions of masculinity, they are linked to other divisions between and within societies. Thus constructions of national identities, always gendered, may be woven around the contrasts between experience and reason. The construct of the bluff, no-nonsense, pragmatic Englishman may be contrasted to the more abstract thinking of the German or the excessive attachment to reason construed as being part of French culture.

Within societies, class may be a filter through which these contrasting ways of doing masculinity are presented. Generally speaking, industrial conflicts may be presented as representing a contrast between the logic of sentiment on the part of workers and the logic of rationality on the part of management. On one side, the mass meeting and angry speeches; on the other, men in suits, seated around desks or in boardrooms. This is not to say that members of ruling or dominant classes always or exclusively adopt the rhetoric of reason. They also lay claims to the rhetoric of experience, claiming that reason and intelligence are not enough and that some people, indeed, are "too clever by half."

The knowledges that men lay claim to are not simply based upon or expressed through the rhetorics of reason and rationality. They also have complex relationships with constructions of experience, experience that is valid, cumulative, and often public. Men lay claims to reason and reasonableness but these claims are commonly supported by and woven into claims based upon experience.

"Have You Had It Yet?"

Sexual knowledge, for both boys and girls, is one of the most important and most complex forms of gendered knowledge (Segal, 1990, 205–32; Walby, 1990, 109–27). Its complexities arise out of the cross-cutting currents of public and private, of knowledge and experience. It is significant not only in itself, but in the way in which it provides models for the acquisition and use of all kinds of other knowledges.

Insofar as I am drawing upon my own historically located biography at this point, I should stress that I am talking about growing up in the 1940s (I was born in 1937) and 1950s, my own experiences being refracted through a prism of a lower middle-class and Methodist family background. It was a time before the general availability of the pill, before the trial of Penguin Books for publishing *Lady Chatterley's Lover*, and before all that was associated with the "swinging sixties" and the "permissive society." The first time I heard anyone claim to have had sexual experience was during my period of National Service between 1955 and 1957. My own sexual experience (in the sense it was conventionally understood at the time) was deferred for some three or four years after the completion of National Service.

I have said that sexual understanding was a complex process arising out of the intersection of public and private, knowledge and experience. Public knowledge, in those pre-permissive days, was confined to the formal periods of "sex education" (although it was not designated as such) at school. These were the times when the normally mixed classes were divided into single-sex classes. There were two aspects to this pedagogy of sexual knowledge. "Hygiene," taught by the gym master, concentrated on the physical aspects and appeared to my youthful ears, to be mostly in Latin. Somewhat more lively were the classes in "Religious Knowledge." Here we were reassured that masturbation would not lead to venereal disease, that sex was a good thing in its place but should not be allowed to dominate our lives, and that we should recognise that girls were more than just "sex objects," although this particular term was not used at the time. We were advised to treat girls as intellectual equals and to enjoy their company. I remember being quite impressed by the advice at the time but cannot remember any discussion, either inside or outside of the classroom, of these lessons. This, then, constituted our formal pedagogy of sexual knowledge.

Private knowledge was gleaned from books, magazines, and dictionaries. In my case, access to these was fairly limited. I did not get more than a fleeting glance at the naturist publication *Health and Efficiency*, although I can remember lusting after a picture of a woman in a swimsuit on my first folder of developed snapshots. Dictionaries provided my first real experience of erotica, the occasional frision that could be encouraged by looking up, yet again, words such as "prostitute."

Between the public and the private was the semi-public or unofficial knowledge of the playground or the scout tent. This informal pedagogy was clearly most important since it not only imparted knowledge, or what was claimed to be knowledge, but also established informal hierarchies. There were those boys who claimed to have the "secret" knowledge and who had therefore the power to pass on or to withhold such knowledge. And there were those boys who were seen as innocent and who might, initially at least, be denied membership of the club. Narratives of the mechanics of sex, confined to penetrative heterosexual intercourse, were combined with appraisals of local girls, or girls (or teachers) at school, and sometimes assessments of their moral character. Again, discussion of homosexuality was, as far as I can remember, delayed until my National Service, although Marlowe's *Edward II* taught me much about homosexual desire.

Much of the talk about sex at that time seemed to be just that. Experience, on the other hand, was a more complex matter. There were the private experiences of wet dreams, erections, and wanking (although erections did have the unfortunate habit of becoming public). This was rarely, if ever, the subject of discussion or disclosure. I remember a classmate showing me a pin-up and semi-taunting me with questions like, "Don't you sometimes get the urge?" I tried to laugh off the question and move on to some less dangerous topic.

Indeed, most experience remained semi-private. While, during my National Service days, it was seen as a good thing to convey the idea that one was sexually experienced, that one had "had it," an individual was not required to go into details. Those who provided detailed accounts of last night's adventures were, I felt, regarded as slightly deviant. To say, in some general sense, that "I wouldn't kick her out of bed" could be the subject of discussion and group solidarity. To claim that one had actually had sex with an identified woman and to describe the process in some detail, was to threaten that diffuse solidarity.

The all-important question, "Have you had it, yet?," was significant in a variety of ways. At the most obvious, it was a mechanism of establishing informal hierarchies in terms of sexual experience while, at the same time, reaffirming the centrality of that experience. Further, it underlined the sense that experience was something that one possessed. And finally, there was no need to explain what "it" was.

In the case of sexual knowledge, therefore, experience and knowledge were interwoven. Since the words and the activities were so powerful, knowledge was itself a form of experience. And very often, experience had to be coded in such a way so that it masqueraded as knowledge. "There's nothing like it" could convey a sense of personal experience while reinforcing a general knowledge of the power of sexuality. More important were the ways in which knowledge and experience were deployed in the loose and informal groups that established hierarchies and created divisions between insiders and outsiders. To be a man was to be able to display oneself as knowledgeable and experienced in relation to women and to sexuality.

BULLYING

In Seidler's (1994) discussion, bullying becomes an almost prototypical example of masculine experience. As Sartre expressed it autobiographically:

At La Rochelle I discovered something that was going to mark the rest of my life: the most profound relationships between men are based on violence. (Quoted in Cohen-Solal, 1991, 41)

The boy experiences bullying at school. He feels pain and isolation but also learns to suppress these feelings, indeed to take pride in being able to "take it." Hence, in Seidler's account, these often intensely painful experiences are shaped into the making of masculinity through their denial.

There is a lot of truth in Seidler's account and it is one repeated in numerous other discussions, autobiographical or more general (see, for example, Mac an Ghaill, 1994). However, some of the complexities in the experience and knowledge around bullying need to be explored further.

First, the bullying experience is, like all experience, mediated through other less direct forms of knowledge. I cannot now remember which came first, my actual experience of being bullied or my reading of it in books such as *Tom Brown's Schooldays* or school stories in comics. Certainly I "knew" before I went to grammar school that bullies could be defeated, that bullies were basically cowards at heart but also that this was one of the expected hazards of school life for boys.

Second, there is a possible, if fluid, distinction between "normal" and "pathological" bullying. I experienced "normal" bullying on my first day at grammar school when all the first-formers, clearly identified by the newness of their uniforms and their general air of disorientation, were subjected to a hail of scorn from older boys. First-formers were called "weeds" and were frequently subjected to reminders of their weed status in the course of the first few weeks at school. This bullying was "normal" in that it appeared to be more or less a fact of life, that it was not subject to official sanctions, and that it was made partially bearable by the recognition that one would be on the other side next year. "Pathological" bullying (although frequent enough to have some "normal" features) was where some individual boy was identified as the object of more systematic mental and physical bullying. The target boy was one who was identified as having something different or some identifiable weakness. Such bullying was occasionally the subject of official sanctions or teachers' pronouncements.

Bullying involved patterns of inclusion and exclusion. Most of the accounts of bullying written by adults are from the point of view of the victim. Yet there is also the experience of being the bully, perhaps as an individual but more likely as a member of a group. The more "normal" the bullying, the more likely it was to contribute to group solidarity both on the part of the bullies and, often, the bullied. More patho-logical forms of bullying might also have had their group supports (especially where it operated on racial or some other divisions), but may also be denied this wider sense of participating in a generalised brotherhood.

Being able "to take it" was part of the bullying experience. At my school, as I suppose at most schools (all schools if the stories I read were anything to go by), it was not done to "tell tales," even when encouraged to do so by the teacher. You were supposed to take it, not to be seen to cry, and to develop strategies for dealing with it. While the heroic fights so lovingly described in the popular school stories rarely conformed to actual experience, there were ways of responding to at least some of the more routinised forms of bullying at school. One of mine was to develop an elaborate and imaginative set of insults and to shout them at the bigger boys in the playground. While this often ended in tears, my tears, it provided a measure of satisfaction of sorts.

It is worth noting that the boundaries of bullying have shifted. It has recently been the subject of scholarly inquiry and official interven-tion and defined as a problem that requires investigation and control (Besag, 1989; Tattum & Lane, 1989). As in the case of sexual harass-ment, what was once construed as normal and taken for granted, "just a bit of fun," has now been problematised. It is unlikely, however, that the importance of this particular set of experiences in the shaping of masculinities has been significantly reduced by scholarly analyses, although the long-term effects may be more important.

Bullying would seem to be the quintessential formative mascu-line experience, a key module in the "University of Hard Knocks." Yet men rarely confess to being bullied, less to having been a bully. How-ever, the lessons of group solidarity, of being able to take it, of not telling tales, carry over easily into male adult worlds of employment and public life in general. The rhetoric of public life routinely draws upon boyhood playground experiences of the importance of standing up to bullies whether these bullies be trades union leaders or military dictators such as Saddam Hussein. Men "know" that it is important to stand up to bullies and this knowledge comes in part from the secret but shared boyhood experiences of the playground.

HEROES AND THE HEROIC

Few autobiographical accounts of masculinity are without descrip-tions of childhood heroes, fictional or real, derived from comic books, television, the cinema, or the sports field. In keeping with this tradition, I could cite Dick Barton, the hero of a long-running radio series from 1946 to the early 1950s. The signature tune came to signify excitement even to those who had never listened to the daily quarter of an hour of adventure. A somewhat more sophisticated radio hero of the time was Paul Temple. I found myself particularly attracted to his affluent Home Counties life style and his companionate, if wholly unerotic, marriage to his wife, Steve, who shared in all his adventures. In a more serious vein, I can also remember being moved to tears by accounts of the last exploration of Captain Scott or impressed by the way in which the Methodist leader, John Wesley, dominated large and often initially hostile crowds.

I could also cite numerous other heroes from boys' publications such as the *Hotspur*, the *Wizard* and the *Champion*, Sexton Blake, Sherlock Holmes, Bulldog Drummond, and diffuse, if unnamed in memory, cowboy heroes. The American superheroes did not loom very largely in my imagination. Autobiographical reminiscences of such heroes usually imply that they had a direct influence on the boy who consumed such material, that they had a direct role in the construction of masculinities and masculine knowledge. I suspect, however, that the influence was a little more complex than that.

Consider Dick Barton. I never wished to miss an episode if I could help it, and his adventures were a common topic of discussion in the playground. But these discussions transformed and mediated the original experience. A process of ironicisation took place. We quickly became aware of the narrative conventions which became the object of comic parody. Rather than suspending disbelief, we revelled in our scepticism. If Dick Barton and similar heroes had any influence, it was mediated and transmuted through these narrative reframings and group relationships.

Many of my heroes were at the more cerebral end of a continuum. The physical rough and tumble of Dick Barton became a pretty poor second to the more obviously intellectual powers of a Sherlock Holmes. The idea of defeating one's enemies through reason and the application of science (together with the odd bit of disguise or other trickery) came to be more attractive than punch-ups or shoot-outs. There were clearly personal influences here: an asthmatic boy with little evidence of skill on the sports field could reassure himself that heroism did not necessarily depend upon the deployment of physical powers. I was beginning to learn that there was more than one way to be a man. I could secretly feel superior to those whose skills seemed to be more directly physical and this sense of superiority and identity could be reinforced through a small group of like-minded friends.

Heroes undoubtedly play an important role in the making of masculinities, but it is important not to oversimplify their contribution. It is probably less a matter of direct influence through imitation and more a matter of learning how heroism works and is constructed, of taking it to pieces and making use of those pieces that already fit in with an emerging construction of masculinity. Analyses of narratives of heroes can show how experience and rational knowledge combine, and how they are part of individual and collective experience and masculine identity formation.

CONCLUSION

I have made use of some of my childhood experiences, thoughts and feelings around such topics as sexuality, bullying, and heroism. In so doing, I am not seeking to claim that this happened to me therefore it must be so for all boys/men. Rather, I have argued that these accounts were part of my experience and that they can be included, along with numerous other such accounts, to illuminate the range of possible experiences in learning masculinities. More important perhaps is the recognition that these are not "raw" experiences. They are mediated and refracted through groups at school, through family or church influences, through class and ethnic identifications and, most importantly, through the numerous everyday experiences and reflections upon those experiences of adulthood. Thus, my reflections of the impact of heroism have been influenced by more recent encounters with feminism (e.g., Stanley, 1990; 1992), and the consequent critiques of masculinities, including my own.

I have also deployed many aspects of the rhetoric of reason. These include the citations of male authorities—Sartre, Weber, Seidler—and the deployment of a tone which connotes consideration and deliberation rather than simple assertion. I have attempted to show that both reason and experience are woven together in the construction of masculinities. The construction of a male heterosexual identity, for example, is achieved through the interplay between texts and talk, public and private experiences, processes of inclusion and exclusion in group encounters and in the troubled quiet of one's own bedroom. Even the physicality and misery associated with bullying may be mediated through other knowledges about bullying through which we learn to recognise, to understand and, perhaps, in some limited way, to control it.

If experience was really as straightforward as those who deploy the rhetoric of experience would often seem to suggest, then there would be little point in talking about a plurality of masculinities. The

"University of Hard Knocks" would produce a standard set of alumni. Yet what is learned from experience is that there is a variety of ways of using these experiences because they are never pure, raw, or unmediated. It is possible to claim that "boys will be boys," "bullying never did me any harm," "you need to rub a few corners off." But it is equally possible to claim that bullying is part of the taken-for-granted of boys' experiences which should no longer be taken-for-granted. Similarly, there is a range of possible heroes and a range of possible ways of making use of these heroic models.

In illustrating some of these themes I have drawn upon some well-established features of accounts of masculinity: the constructions of sexual difference and heterosexuality, violence and bullying, heroes and the heroic. These are part of the stock-in-trade of accounts and constructions of masculinity. They represent cultural resources out of which masculinities are constructed although some of these resources are also available to women.

What I have argued is that versions of reason and versions of experience combine in different ways to form masculine knowledge and are used by men within systems of patriarchal dominance. This does not suggest that experience or reason are irrelevant to the constructions of feminine knowledge but, rather, that in existing gender orders their significance may be different. As men, we do not simply learn from experience. Rather, we learn how to use experience in ways which may solidify or question masculinities. We do not simply learn how to reason but, rather, how to present ourselves as reasonable men.

REFERENCES

Besag, V. E. (1989). *Bullies and victims in schools*. Milton Keynes: Open University Press.

Bologh, R. W. (1990). *Love or greatness: Max Weber and masculine thinking—A feminist inquiry*. London: Unwin Hyman.

Cohen-Solal, A. (1991). *Sartre: A life*. London: Minerva.

Davidoff, L. & Hall, C. (1987). *Family fortunes*. London: Hutchinson.

Mac an Ghaill, M. (1994). *The making of men: Masculinities, sexualities and schooling*. Milton Keynes: Open University Press.

Morgan, D. (1987). *It will make a man of you: Notes on National Service, masculinity & autobiography*. Manchester: University of Manchester, Studies in Sexual Politics no. 17.

——— (1992). *Discovering men*. London: Routledge.

Segal, L. (1990). *Slow motion: Changing masculinities, changing men*. London: Virago.

Seidler, V. J. (1994). *Unreasonable men: Masculinity and social theory*. London: Routledge.

Stanley, L. (Ed.) (1990). *Feminist praxis: Research, theory and epistemology in feminist sociology*. London: Routledge.

——— (1992). *The auto/biographical I: The theory and practice of feminist auto/biography*. Manchester: Manchester University Press.

Tattum, D. P. & Lanc, D. A. (1989). *Bullying in school*. Stoke-on-Trent: Trentham Books.

Walby, S. (1990). *Theorizing patriarchy*. Oxford: Blackwell.

Weber, M. (1947). *The theory of social and economic organisation*. Glencoe, IL: The Free Press.

PART II

Popular Culture as Public Pedagogy

CHAPTER 5

HUNGER AS IDEOLOGY

Susan Bordo

THE WOMAN WHO DOESN'T EAT MUCH

We live in a time in which mass imagery has an unprecedented power to instruct. When I was a teenager in the 1960s, Twiggy's mascara-spiked stare and long, spindly legs represented our variant of the wide-eyed waif. We envied Twiggy's casual cool and elegantly elongated body. But few of us imagined that Twiggy represented a blueprint for the ordinary, adolescent girl to model herself after. She was a high-fashion mannequin, after all, and we all knew that they *had* to be skinny "to photograph well." Today, young women and men no longer experience much of a distinction between the commercially fabricated, artfully arranged images that surround them and the aspirations they hold for themselves. Women with eating disorders bring photos of ultra-thin model Kate Moss to their therapists as an example of the look they strive for, and the latest craze in cosmetic surgery is the "waif procedure," which vacuums out cheek-fat in order to achieve a hollowed-out look.

It would be a mistake, however, to imagine that what is being taught through mass images is only the desirability of a certain appearance of face and body. In layout after layout, Moss is arranged to look emotionally and mentally opaque, even vacant. She seems utterly without need, without expectation, without complaint. Without desire. Without hunger. Moss is an archetype of female recessiveness in an era of enormous gender-change and challenge. She assures us in interviews that she eats anytime and anything she wants. But even if this is true, it only adds to Moss's mystique for anorexics. For they know that the only way to eat whatever you like and look like Kate is either to remain in perpetual motion, or not to *want* to eat much of anything at all. And that, above all, is the state they aspire to—a state beyond appetite, beyond desire.

Some of the slickest advertisements appear to recognize the cultural potency of the imagery of the woman who is beyond hunger. In one television commercial, two little French girls are shown dressing up in the feathery finery of their mother's clothes. They are exquisite little girls, flawless and innocent, and the scene emphasizes both their youth and the natural sense of style often associated with French women. (The ad is done in French, with subtitles.) One of the girls, spying a picture of the other girl's mother, exclaims breathlessly, "Your mother, she is so slim, so beautiful! Does she eat?" The daughter, giggling, replies: "Silly, just not so much," and displays her mother's helper, a bottle of FibreThin. "Aren't you jealous?," the friend asks. Dimpling, shy yet self-possessed and deeply knowing, the daughter answers, "Not if I know her secrets."

Admittedly, women are continually bombarded with advertisements and commercials for weight-loss products and programs, but this commercial makes many of us particularly angry. On the most obvious level, the commercial affronts with its suggestion that young girls begin early in learning to control their weight, and with its romantic mystification of diet pills as part of the obscure, eternal arsenal of feminine arts to be passed from generation to generation. But far more unnerving is the psychological acuity of the ad's focus, not on the size and shape of bodies, but on a certain *subjectivity*, represented by the absent but central figure of the mother, the woman who eats, only "not so much." We never see her picture; we are left to imagine her ideal beauty and slenderness. But what she looks like is not important, in any case; what is important is the fact that she has achieved what we might call a "cool" (that is, casual) relation to food. She is not starving herself (an obsession, indicating the continuing power of food), but neither is she desperately and shamefully binging in some private corner. Eating has become, for her, no big deal. In its evocation of the lovely French mother who doesn't eat much, the commercial's metaphor of European "difference" reveals itself as a means of representing that enviable and truly foreign "other": the woman for whom food is merely ordinary, who can take it or leave it.

Another version, this time embodied by a sleek, fashionable African-American woman, playfully promotes Virginia Slims Menthol (figure 5.1). "Decisions are easy. When I get to a fork in the road, I eat." Here the speaker scorns obsessiveness, not only over professional or interpersonal decision-making, but over food as well. Implicitly contrasting herself to those who worry and fret, she presents herself as utterly "easy" in her relationship with food. Unlike the FibreThin mother, she eats anytime she wants. But *like* the FibreThin mother (and

FIGURE 5.1. Virginia Slims Menthol

this is the key similarity for my purposes), she has achieved a state
beyond craving. Undominated by unsatisfied, internal need, she eats
not only freely but without deep desire and without apparent consequence. It's "easy," she says. Presumably, without those forks in the
road she might forget about food entirely.

    The Virginia Slims woman is a fantasy figure, her cool attitude
toward food as remote from the lives of most contemporary African-
American women as from any others. For most women today—whatever their racial or ethnic identity, and increasingly across class and
sexual-orientation differences as well—free and easy relations with food

are at best a relic of the past.[1] Almost all of us who can afford to be eating well are dieting—and hungry—almost all of the time. It is thus Dexatrim, not Virginia Slims, that constructs the more realistic representation of women's subjective relations with food. In Dexatrim's commercial that shows a woman, her appetite-suppressant worn off, hurtling across the room, drawn like a living magnet to the breathing, menacing refrigerator, hunger is represented as an insistent, powerful force with a life of its own. This construction reflects the physiological reality of dieting, a state the body is unable to distinguish from starvation (Starvation stages, 1989, April 3). And it reflects its psychological reality as well; for dieters, who live in a state of constant denial, food is a perpetually beckoning presence, its power growing ever greater as the sanctions against gratification become more stringent. A slender body may be attainable through hard work, but a "cool" relation to food, the true "secret" of the beautiful "other" in the FibreThin commercial, is a tantalizing reminder of what lies beyond the reach of the inadequate and hungry self.

GENDER, HUNGER, AND DESIRE

Advertisers are aware, of course, of women's well-documented food disorders; they frequently incorporate the theme of food obsession into their pitch. The Sugar Free Jell-O campaign exemplifies a typical commercial strategy for exploiting women's eating problems while obscuring their dark realities. (The advertisers themselves would put this differently, of course.) In the "tip of my tongue" ad (figure 5.2), the obsessive mental state of the compulsive eater is depicted fairly accurately, guaranteeing recognition from people with that problem: "If I'm not eating dessert, I'm talking about it. If I'm not talking about it, I'm eating it. And I'm always thinking about it. . . . It's just always on my mind."

These thoughts, however, belong to a slender, confident, and—most important—decidedly not depressed individual, whose upbeat, open, and accepting attitude toward her constant hunger is far from that of most women who eat compulsively. "The inside of a binge," Geneen Roth writes, "is deep and dark. At the core . . . is deprivation, scarcity, a feeling that you can never get enough" (Roth, 1982, 15). In the Sugar Free Jell-O ad, by contrast, the mental state depicted is most like that of a growing teenage boy; to be continually hungry is represented as a normal, if somewhat humorous and occasionally annoying, state with no disastrous physical or emotional consequences.

FIGURE 5.2. Sugar Free Jell-O

Or consider the ad (shown in figure 5.3), depicting a male figure diving with abandon into the "tempered-to-full-flavor-consistency" joys of Häagan-Dazs deep chocolate. Emotional heights, intensity, love and thrills: it is women who habitually seek such experiences from food and who are most likely to be overwhelmed by their relationship to food, to find it dangerous and frightening (especially rich, fattening, soothing food like ice cream). The marketers of Häagen-Dazs know this; they are aware of the well-publicized prevalence of compulsive eating and binge behaviors among women. Indeed, this ad exploits, with artful precision, exactly the sorts of associations that are likely to

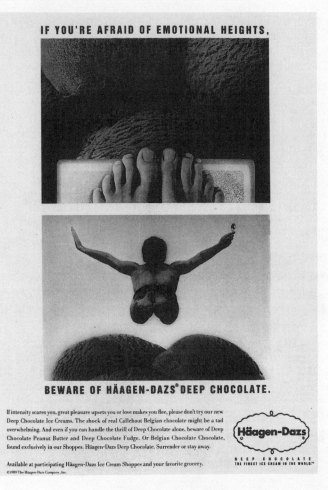

FIGURE 5.3. Häagen-Dazs

resonate with a person for whom eating is invested with deep emotional meaning. Why, then, a male diver? In part, the displacement is necessary to insure, as in the Jell-O ad, that the grim actualities of women's eating problems remain obscured; the point, after all, is to sell ice cream, not to remind people of how dangerous food actually *is* for women.

I would argue, however, that more than a purely profit-maximizing, ideologically neutral, Madison Avenue mentality is at work in these ads. They must also be considered as gender ideology—that is, as specifically (consciously or unconsciously) servicing the cultural reproduction of gender difference and gender inequality, quite independent of (although at times coinciding with) marketing concerns. As gender ideology, the ads I have been discussing are not distinctively contemporary but continue a well-worn representational tradition, arguably inaugurated in the Victorian era, in which the depiction of women eating, particularly in sensuous surrender to rich, exciting food, is taboo (Mitchie, 1987).

Men, of course, are *supposed* to have hearty, even voracious, appetites. It is a mark of the manly to eat spontaneously and expansively, and manliness is a frequent commercial code for amply portioned products: "Manwich," "Hungry Man Dinners," "Manhandlers." Even when men advertise diet products (as they more frequently do, now that physical perfection is increasingly being demanded of men as well as women), they brag about their appetites, as in the Tommy Lasorda commercials for Slim-Fast, which feature three burly football players (their masculinity beyond reproach) declaring that if Slim-Fast can satisfy *their* appetites, it can satisfy anyone's. But is it possible to imagine an advertisement depicting a young, attractive *woman* indulging as freely, as salaciously as the man in the Post cereal ad shown in figure 5.4? Such an image would violate deeply sedimented expectations, would be experienced by many as disgusting and transgressive.

When women are positively depicted as sensuously voracious about food (almost never in commercials, and only very rarely in movies and novels), their hunger for food is employed solely as a metaphor for their sexual appetite—as in the eating scenes in *Tom Jones* and *Flashdance*. Women are permitted to lust for food itself only when they are pregnant or when it is clear they have been near starvation—as, for example, in *McCabe and Mrs. Miller*, in the scene in which Mrs. Miller, played by Julie Christie, wolfs down half a dozen eggs and a bowl of beef stew before the amazed eyes of McCabe. Significantly, the scene serves to establish Mrs. Miller's "manliness"; a woman who eats like this is to be taken seriously, is not to be trifled with, the movie suggests.

The metaphorical situation is virtually inverted in the representation of male eaters. Although voracious eating may occasionally code male sexual appetite (as in *Tom Jones*), we frequently also find *sexual* appetite operating as a metaphor for eating pleasure. In commercials that feature male eaters, the men are shown in a state of wild, sensual transport over heavily frosted, rich, gooey deserts. Their total lack of control is portrayed as appropriate, even adorable; the language of the background jingle is unashamedly aroused, sexual and desiring:

FIGURE 5.4. Post cereal

"I'm thinking about you the whole day through [crooned to a Pillsbury cake]. I've got a passion for you."

"I'm a fool for your chocolate. I'm wild, crazy, out of control [assorted Betty Crocker cake mixes]."

In these commercials food is constructed as a sexual object of desire, and eating is legitimated as much more than a purely nutritive activity. Rather, food is *supposed* to supply sensual delight and succor— not as metaphorically standing for something else, but as an erotic expe-

rience in itself. Women are permitted such gratification from food only in measured doses. In another ad from the Diet Jell-O series, eating is metaphorically sexualized: "I'm a girl who just can't say no. I insist on dessert," admits the innocently dressed but flirtatiously posed model (figure 5.5). But at the same time that eating is mildly sexualized in this ad, it is also contained. She is permitted to "feel good about saying 'Yes'"—but ever so demurely, and to a harmless low-calorie product. Women may be encouraged (like the man on the Häagen-Dazs high-

FIGURE 5.5. Diet Jell-O

board) to "dive in"—not, however, into a dangerous pool of Häagen-Dazs Deep Chocolate, but for a "refreshing dip" into Weight Watcher's linguini (figure 5.6).

All of this may seem peculiarly contemporary, revolving as it does around the mass marketing of diet products. But in fact the same metaphorical universe, as well as the same practical prohibitions against female indulgence (for, of course, these ads are not only selling products, but teaching appropriate behavior) were characteristic of Victorian gender ideology. Victorians did not have *Cosmo* and television, of

FIGURE 5.6. Weight Watchers

course. But they did have conduct manuals, which warned elite women of the dangers of indulgent and overstimulating eating and advised how to consume in a feminine way (as little as possible and with the utmost precaution against unseemly show of desire). *Godey's Lady's Book* warned that it was vulgar for women to load their plates; young girls were admonished to "be frugal and plain in your tastes" (Brumberg, 1988, 179). And in the Victorian era, as today, the forbiddenness of rich food often resulted in private binge behavior, described in *The Bazaar Book of Decorum* (1870) as the "secret luncheon," at which "many of the most abstemious at the open dinner are the most voracious . . . swallowing cream tarts by the dozen, and caramels and chocolate drops by the pound's weight" (Mitchie, 1987, 193).

The emergence of such rigid and highly moralized restrictions on female appetite and eating are, arguably, part of what Bram Dijkstra has interpreted as a nineteenth-century "cultural ideological counteroffensive" against the "new woman" and her challenge to prevailing gender arrangements and their constraints on women (Dijkstra, 1986, 30–31). Mythological, artistic, polemical, and scientific discourses from many cultures and eras certainly suggest the symbolic potency of female hunger as a cultural metaphor for unleashed female power and desire, from the blood-craving Kali (who in one representation is shown eating her own entrails) to the *Malleus Malificarum* ("For the sake of fulfilling the mouth of the womb, [witches] consort even with the devil"), to Hall and Oates's contemporary rock lyrics: "Oh, oh, here she comes, watch out boys, she'll chew you up." In *Tom Jones* and *Flashdance*, the trope of female hunger as female sexuality is embodied in attractive female characters; more frequently, however, female hunger as sexuality is represented by Western culture in misogynist images permeated with terror and loathing rather than affection or admiration. In the figure of the man-eater the metaphor of the devouring woman reveals its deep psychological underpinnings. Eating is not really a metaphor for the sexual act; rather, the sexual act, when initiated and desired by a woman, is imagined as itself an act of eating, of incorporation and destruction of the object of desire. Thus, women's sexual appetites must be curtailed and controlled, because they threaten to deplete and consume the body and soul of the male. Such imagery, as Dijkstra has demonstrated, flourishes in the West in the art of the late nineteenth century. Arguably, the same cultural backlash (if not in the same form) operates today—for example, in the ascendancy of popular films that punish female sexuality and independence by rape and dismemberment (as in numerous slasher films), loss of family and children (*The Good Mother*), madness and death (*Fatal Attraction, Presumed Innocent*), and public humiliation and disgrace (*Dangerous Liaisons*).

Of course, Victorian prohibitions against women eating were not *only* about the ideology of gender. Or, perhaps better put, the ideology of gender contained other dimensions as well. In the reigning body symbolism of the day, a frail frame and lack of appetite signified not only feminine delicacy and spiritual transcendence of the desires of the flesh, but *social* transcendence of the laboring, striving "economic" body. Then, as today, to be aristocratically cool and unconcerned with the mere facts of material survival was highly fashionable. The hungering bourgeois wished to appear, like the aristocrat, above the material desires that in fact ruled his life. The closest he could come was to possess a wife whose ethereal body became a sort of fashion statement of *his* aristocratic tastes. If he could not be or marry an aristocrat, he could have a wife who looked like one, a wife whose nonrobust beauty and delicate appetite signified her lack of participation in the taxing "public sphere."[2]

MEN EAT AND WOMEN PREPARE

The metaphorical dualities at work here, whatever their class meanings, presuppose an idealized (and rarely actualized) gendered division of labor in which men strive, compete, and exert themselves in the public sphere while women are cocooned in the domestic arena (which is romanticized and mystified as a place of peace and leisure, and hence connotes transcendence of the laboring, bourgeois body). In the necessity to make such a division of labor appear natural, we find another powerful ideological underpinning (perhaps the most important in the context of industrialized society) for the cultural containment of female appetite: the notion that women are most gratified by feeding and nourishing *others*, not themselves. As a literal activity, of course, women fed others long before the "home" came to be identified as women's special place; Carolyn Bynum argues that there is reason to believe that food preparation was already a stereotypically female activity in the European Middle Ages (Bynum, 1987, 191). But it was in the industrial era, with its idealization of the domestic arena as a place of nurture and comfort for men and children, that feeding others acquired the extended emotional meaning it has today.

In "An Ode to Mothers" columnist Bud Poloquin defines "Moms" as "those folks who, upon seeing there are only four pieces of pie for five people, promptly announce they never did care for the stuff" (Poloquin, 1988, D1). Denial of self and the feeding of others are hopelessly enmeshed in this construction of the ideal mother, as they are in the nineteenth-century version of the ideal wife as "she who stands . . . famished before her husband, while he devours, stretched at ease, the produce of her exertions; waits his tardy permission without a word or a look of impatience, and feeds, with the humblest gratitude, and the shortest intermission of labor, on the scraps and offals which he disdains" (Dijkstra, 1986, 18). None of this self-sacrifice, however, is felt as such by the "paragon of womanhood" (as Charles Butler calls her), for it is here, in the care and feeding of others, that woman experiences the one form of desire that is appropriately hers: as Elias Canetti so succinctly puts it, "Her passion is to give food" (Canetti, 1962, 221).

In 1994, despite the increasing participation of women of all ages and classes in the "public" sphere, her "private" role of nurturer remains ideologically intact. Popular representations almost never depict a man *preparing* food as an everyday activity, routinely performed in the unpaid service of others. Occasionally, men *are* shown serving food—in the role of butler or waiter. They may be depicted roasting various items around a campfire, barbecuing meat, preparing a salad for a special company dinner, or making *instant* coffee (usually in a getaway-cabin or vacation boat). But all of these are nonroutine, and their exceptional nature is frequently underscored in the ad. In one commercial, a man fixes instant coffee to serve to his wife in bed on her birthday. "How tough can it be?," he asks. "She makes breakfast every morning." In another ad, a man is shown preparing pancakes for his son's breakfast (figure 5.7). "My pancakes deserve the rich maple flavor of Log Cabin Syrup," reads the bold type, suggesting ("my pancakes") male proprietorship and ease in the kitchen. The visual image of the father lovingly serving the son undoubtedly destabilizes cultural stereotypes (racial as well as gendered). But in the smaller print below the image we are told that this is a "special moment" with his son. Immediately, the destabilizing image reconfigures into a familiar one: like Dad's secret recipe for barbecue sauce, this father's pancakes make their appearance only on special occasions. Or perhaps it is the very fact that Dad is doing the cooking that *makes* this a significant, intimate occasion for sharing. (Imagine a woman instead of a man in the ad; would "special moment" not then seem odd?)

Continually, in representations that depict men preparing food, there will be a conspicuously absent wife or mother (for instance, in the hospital having a baby) who, it is implied, is *normally* responsible for the daily labor of food preparation and service. Even when men or boys are used to advertise convenience foods, the product has usually been

FIGURE 5.7. Log Cabin Syrup

left for them with expert instructions added by Mom. In the Jell-O Heritage ad (figure 5.8), this absent maternal figure (whether mother or grandmother is not clear) appears in the small insert to the upper right of the larger image, which depicts a young man away at college, well-supplied with Jell-O pudding snacks. Significantly (although somewhat absurdly), she is associated with the provision of a "strong foundation" by virtue of the fact that *she* prepares instant pudding from a mix rather than merely flipping the lid off an already prepared pudding snack. Men are almost *never* shown lavishing time on cooking. *Real* coffee is always prepared by women, as are all the cakes and casseroles that

FIGURE 5.8. Jell-O Heritage

require more than a moment to put together. When men *are* shown cooking an elaborate meal, it is always *with* one or two other yuppie men, converting the activity from an act of everyday service into a festive, "Big Chill" occasion.

FOOD AND LOVE

At the beginning of the 1992 U.S. Presidential campaign, Hillary Clinton, badgered by reporters' endless questions concerning her pursuit of a professional career, shot back defensively and sarcastically: "Well, I suppose I could have stayed home and baked cookies and had teas . . ." Media audiences never got to hear the end of her remark (or the questioning that preceeded it); the "cookies and teas" sound-byte became *the* gender-transgression of the campaign, replayed over and over, and presented by opponents as evidence of Hillary's rabid feminism and disdain for traditional maternal values. Rightly protesting this interpretation, Hillary Clinton tried to prove her true womanhood by producing her favorite recipe for oatmeal chocolate chip cookies. Barbara Bush, apparently feeling that a gauntlet had been thrown down, responded in kind with a richer, less fibre-conscious recipe of her own. Newspapers across the country asked readers to prepare each and vote on which First Lady had the better cookie.

That the cookie itself should have become the symbol and center of the national debate about Hillary Clinton's adequacy as wife and mother is not surprising. Food is equated with maternal and wifely love throughout our culture. In nearly all commercials that feature men eating—such as the cake commercials whose sexualized rhetoric was described earlier—there is a woman in the background (either visible or implied) who has *prepared* the food. Most significantly, *always*, the woman in the background speaks the language of love and care through the offering of food: "Nothin' says lovin' like something from the oven"; "Give me that great taste of love"; "Nothing says 'Cookie, I love you' like Nestle's Toll House Cookies Do." In these commercials, male eating is inextricably tied to female offerings of love. This is not represented, however, as female self-abnegation. Rather, it is suggested that women receive *their* gratification through nourishing others:

> *Her voice, heard off:* "He's like a little boy—normally serious, *then* he eats English muffins with butter . . . [shot of man's face transported with childlike delight] . . . and *I* get to enjoy watching him. A little butter brings a lot of joy."

My analysis, I want to emphasize, is not meant to disparage caring for the physical and emotional well-being of others, "maternal" work that has been scandalously socially undervalued even as it has been idealized and sanctified. Nor am I counterposing to the argument of these ads the construction that women are simply oppressed by such roles. This would be untrue to the personal experiences of many women including myself. I remember the pride and pleasure that radiated from my mother, who was anxious and unhappy in most other areas of her life, when her famous stuffed cabbage was devoured enthusiastically and in voluminous quantities by my father, my sisters, and me. As a little girl, I loved watching her roll each piece, enclosing just the right amount of filling, skillfully avoiding tearing the tender cabbage leaves as she folded them around the meat. I never felt so safe and secure as at those moments. She was visibly pleased when I asked her to teach me exactly how to make the dish and thrilled when I even went so far as to write the quantities and instructions down as she tried to formulate them into an official recipe (until then, it had been passed through demonstration from mother to daughter, and my mother considered that in writing it down, I was conferring a higher status on it). Those periods in my life when I have found myself too busy writing, teaching, and traveling to find the time and energy to prepare special meals for people that I love have been periods when a deep aspect of my self has felt deprived, depressed.

Nor would I want my critique to be interpreted as effacing the collective, historical experiences of those groups, forced into servitude for the families of others, who have been systematically deprived of the freedom *to* care for their own families. Bell hooks points out, for example, that black women's creation of "homeplace," of fragile and hard-won "spaces of care and nurturance" for the healing of deep wounds made by racism, sexism, and poverty, was less a matter of obedience to a tyrannical gender-norm than the construction of a "site of cultural resistance" (hooks, 1990, 42) With this in mind, it is clear that the Jell-O Heritage ad discussed earlier is more complex than my interpretation has thus far allowed. Part of an extensive General Foods series aimed at the African-American consumer and promoting America's historically black colleges, the ad's association of the maternal figure with "strong foundations" runs far deeper than a nostalgic evocation of Mom's traditional cooking. In this ad, the maternal figure is linked with a black "heritage," with the preservation and communication of culture.

However, at the same time that hooks urges that contemporary black culture should honor the black woman's history of service to her family and her community, she also cautions against the ideological construction of such service as woman's natural role. (Despite the pleasure I take in cooking, in relationships where it has been expected of me, I have resented it deeply.) It is this construction that is reinforced in the representations I have been examining, through their failure to depict males as "naturally" fulfilling that role, and—more perniciously—through their failure to depict females as appropriate *recipients* of such care. Only occasionally are little girls represented as being *fed*; more often, they (but never little boys) are shown learning how to feed others (figure 5.9). In this way, caring is representationally "reproduced" as a quintessentially and exclusively female activity. And here, it is significant and disquieting that the General Foods series does not include any ads that portray female students discovering their black heritage (or learning how to rely on convenience foods!) at college. Women appear only in the background, encouraging and supporting, "feeding" the development of others.

The ubiquitous configuration of woman-food-man, with food expressing the woman's love for the man and at the same time satisfying woman's desire to bestow love, establishes male hunger as thoroughly socially integrated into the network of heterosexual family and love relations. Men can eat *and* be loved; indeed, a central mode by which they receive love is through food from women. For women, by

FIGURE 5.9. General Foods

contrast (who are almost never shown being fed by others), eating—in the form of private, *self*-feeding—is represented as a *substitute* for human love. Weight Watchers transparently offers itself as such in its "Who says you can't live on love?" ad (figure 5.10). In these ads there is no partner, visible or implied, offering the food and thus operating as the true bestower of "love." In many ads—virtually a genre, in fact—the absence of the partner is explicitly thematized, a central aspect of the narrative of the ad. One commercial features a woman in bed, on the phone, refusing date after date in favor of an evening alone with her ice-cream bonbons: "Your Highness? Not tonight!" "The inauguration? Another year!" In another, a woman admits to spending a lot of time alone with her "latest obsession," a chocolate drink, because it gives her "the same feeling as being in love" and "satisfies her innermost cravings anytime [she] wants." She pleads with us, the viewers, not to tell Michael, her boyfriend.

These commercials hit a painful nerve for women. The bonbon commercial may seem merely silly, but the chocolate drink ad begins to evoke, darkly and disturbingly, the psychological and material reali-

FIGURE 5.10. Weight Watchers

ties of women's food problems. The talk of "obsession" and "innermost cravings," the furtiveness, the secrecy, the use of food to satisfy emotional needs, all suggest central elements of binge behavior. Frusen Glädjé supplies another piece and gives an important lie to the other, more upbeat commercials (figure 5.11): "He never called. So, Ben and I went out for a walk to pick up a pint of Frusen Glädjé. Ben's better looking anyway." Frusen Glädjé: "It feels so good." Here, as in the Häagan-Dazs ad discussed earlier, the sensuousness of the ice-cream experience is emphasized; unlike the Häagan-Dazs ad, however, Frusen-

FIGURE 5.11. Frusen Glädjé

Glädjé offers solace from emotional depths rather than the thrill of emotional heights. This is, indeed, the prevailing gender reality. For women, the emotional comfort of self-feeding is rarely turned to in a state of pleasure and independence, but in despair, emptiness, loneliness, and desperation. Food is, as one woman put it, "the only thing that will take care of *me*."

FOOD AS TRANSGRESSION

An extremely interesting fact about male bulimics: they rarely binge alone. They tend to binge at mealtime and in public places, whereas women almost always eat minimally at meals and gorge later, in private (Schneider & Agras, 1987, March). Even in our disorders (or perhaps especially in our disorders) we follow the gender rules. In the commercials I have been discussing, female eating is virtually always represented as private, secretive, illicit. The woman has stolen away from the world of husband, family, friends to a secret corner where she and the food can be alone. A "Do Not Disturb" sign hangs on the door to the room where the women sits munching on her "purple passion," New York Deli Potato Chips. A husband returns home to discover that in his absence, his wife, sitting on the floor, has eaten all the Frusen Glädjé; her voice is mildly defiant, although soft—"I ate all the Frusen Glädjé"—but her face is sheepish and her glance averted. Men sing openly of their wild cravings for Betty Crocker cakes; women's cravings are a dirty, shameful secret, to be indulged in only when no one is looking.

More often than not, however, women are not even permitted, even in private, indulgences so extravagant in scope as the full satisfaction of their hungers. Most commonly, women are used to advertise, *not* ice cream and potato chips (foods whose intake is very difficult to contain and control), but individually wrapped pieces of tiny, bite-size candies: Andes candies, Hershey's kisses, Mon Cheri bonbons. Instead of the mounds of cake and oozing frosting typical of commercials featuring male eaters, women are confined to a "tiny scoop" of flavor, a "tiny piece" of chocolate. As in the Weight-Watchers linguini advertisement ("Dive in"), the rhetoric of indulgence is invoked, only to be contained by the product itself: "Indulge a little," urges Andes Candies. "Satisfy your urge to splurge in five delicious bite-size ways." The littleness of the candy and the amount of taste that is packed within its tiny boundaries are frequently emphasized: "Each bite-size piece packs a wallop of milk chocolate crunch." Instead of the emphasis on undifferentiated feelings of sensuous delight that we see in commercials showing men, the pitch aimed at women stresses the exquisite pleasure to be had from a sensually focused and limited experience. The message to women is explicit: "Indulge a *little*." (And only out of sight; even these minuscule bonbons are eaten privately, in isolation, behind closed doors.) It is significant, too, that in all these commercials, the woman is found "indulging" only after a day spent serving others. In these commercials, it is permissible for women to feed the self (if such dainty nibbling merits this description) only after first feeding others: "For my angel, I sewed for days. Now I deserve a little praise. I thank me very much with Andes Candies."

These commercials, no less than the Victorian conduct manuals, offer a virtual blueprint for disordered relations to food and hunger.

The representation of unrestrained appetite as inappropriate for women, the depiction of female eating as a private, transgressive act, make restriction and denial of hunger central features of the construction of femininity, and set up the compensatory binge as a virtual inevitability. Such restrictions on appetite, moreover, are not merely about food intake. Rather, the social control of female hunger operates as a practical "discipline" (to use Foucault's term) that trains female bodies in the knowledge of their limits and possibilities. Denying oneself food becomes the central micro-practice in the education of feminine self-restraint and containment of impulse.

Victorian women were told that it was vulgar to load their plates; in 1990, women students of mine complain of the tortures of the cafeteria—the embarrassment of eating ice cream in front of the male students, the pressure to take just a salad, or, better yet, refuse food altogether. Later at night, when they are alone, they confront the deprived and empty feeling left in the wake of such a regimen. As in the commercials, the self-reward and solace is food. The problem, however, after a day of restraint, is the requirement for any further containment of the now ravenous self. Unlike the women in the Andes candy commercials, few women who have spent the day submerging their desires, either for the sake of their families or to project the appropriately attractive lack of appetite to a cafeteria full of adolescent boys, really feel rewarded by a bite-size piece of candy, no matter how much chocolate "wallop" it packs. In private, shamefully and furtively, we binge.

DESTABILIZING IMAGES?

When, in my classes, we discuss contemporary representations, I encourage my students to bring in examples that appear to violate traditional gender-dualities and the ideological messages contained in them. These ads almost always display a complicated and bewitching tangle of new possibilities and old patterns of representation. A television commercial for Hormel microwaveable Kid's Kitchen Meals, for example, opens with two young girls trying to fix a bicycle. A little boy, watching them, offers to help, claiming that "I can fix anything. My dad lets me fix his car. My mom lets me fix her dinner." When the girls are skeptical ("Yeah, well prove it!"), he fixes a Hormel's Kid's Kitchen Meal for them. Utterly impressed with his culinary skill and on the basis of this ready to trust his mechanical aptitude, they ask, "You know how to fix a bike?" "What? Yeah, I do!" he eagerly replies. Now, what pedagogy is contained in this ad? The little girls cannot fix their own bike, a highly traditional, "feminine" limitation. Yet they do not behave in helpless or coquettish ways in the commercial. Far from it. They speak in rough voices and challenging words to the boy, who is physically smaller (and, it appears, younger) than they; "Give me a break!" they scornfully mutter when he claims he can "fix anything." Despite their mechanical inability, they do not act deferential, and in a curious way this neutralizes the gendered meanings of the activities depicted. Not being able to fix a bike is something that could happen to anyone, they seem to believe.

Then, too, there is the unusual representation of the male cooking for and serving the females. True, it only required a touch of the microwave panel. But this is, after all, only a little boy. One message this commercial may be delivering is that males can engage in traditionally "feminine" activities without threat to their manhood. Cooking for a woman does not mean that she won't respect you in the morning. She will still recognize your authority to fix her bike (indeed, she may become further convinced of it precisely by your mastery of "her" domain). The expansion of possibilities for boys thus extracts from girls the price of continued ineptitude in certain areas (or at least the show of it) and dependence on males. Yet, in an era in which most working women find themselves with two full-time jobs—their second shift beginning at five o'clock, when they return from work to meet their husband's expectations of dinner, a clean and comfortable home, a sympathetic ear—the message that cooking and serving others is not "sissy," though it may be problematic and nonprogressive in many ways, is perhaps the single most *practically* beneficial (to women) message we can convey to little boys.

In its provision of ambiguous and destabilizing imagery, the influx of women into the professional arena has had a significant effect on the representation of gender. Seeking to appeal to a population that wishes to be regarded (at least while on the job) as equal in power and ability to the men with whom they work, advertisers have tried to establish gender symmetry in those representations that depict or evoke the lives of professional couples. Minute Rice thus has two versions of its "I wonder what 'Minute' is cookin' up for dinner tonight?" commercial. In one, father and children come home from work and school to find mother "cookin' up" an elaborate chicken stir-fry to serve over Minute Rice. In the other, a working woman returns to find her male partner "cookin' up" the dinner. The configuration is indeed destabilizing, if only because it makes us aware of how very rare it is to see. But, significantly, there are no children in this commercial, as there are in the more traditional version; the absence of children codes the fact that this is a yuppie couple, the group to which this version is designed to appeal.

And now Häagen-Dazs, the original yuppie ice cream, has designed an ad series for this market (figures 5.12 and 5.13). These ads perfectly illustrate the unstable location of contemporary gender advertisements: they attempt to satisfy representational conventions that still have a deep psychic grip on Western culture, while at the same time registering every new rhythm of the social heartbeat. "Enter the State of Häagen-Dazs"—a clear invocation of the public world rather than the

FIGURE 5.12. Häagen-Dazs

FIGURE 5.13. Häagen-Dazs

domestic domain. The man and woman are dressed virtually identically (making small allowances for gender-tailoring) in equally no-nonsense, dark business suits, styled for power. Their hair-styles are equivalent, brushed back from the face, clipped short but not punky. They
have similar expressions: slightly playful, caught in the act but certainly
not feeling guilty. They appear to be indulging in their ice-cream break
in the middle of a workday; this sets up both the fetching representational incongruity of the ad, and its realism. Ice cream has always been
represented as relaxation food, to be *indulged* in; it belongs to a different
universe than the work ethic, performance principle, or spirit of competition. To eat it in a business suit is like having "quickie" sex in the
office, irregular and naughty. Yet everyone knows that people *do* eat ice
cream on their breaks and during their lunch hours. The ad thus

appears both realistic and *representationally* odd; we realize that we are seeing images we have not seen before *except* in real life. And, of course, in real life, women *do* eat Häagen-Dazs, as much as, if not more than, men.

And yet, intruding into this world of gender equality and eating realism that is designed to appeal to the sensibilities of "progressive" young men and women is the inescapable disparity in how much and how the man and woman are eating. He: an entire pint of vanilla fudge, with sufficient abandon to topple the carton, and greedy enough to suck the spoon. She: a restrained Eve-bite (already taken; no licks or sucks in process here), out of a single brittle bar (aestheticized as "artfully" nutty, in contrast to his bold, unaccessorized "Vanilla Fudge"). Whether unconsciously reproduced or deliberately crafted to appeal to the psychic contradictions and ambivalence of its intended audience, the disparity comes from the recesses of our most sedimented, unquestioned notions about gender.

NOTES

A longer version of this paper originally appeared in Susan Bordo, *Unbearable weight: Feminism, Western culture, and the body,* (Berkeley: University of California Press, 1993). The present version has been edited to conform to space requirements of this volume and to highlight the theme of "pedagogies of everyday life."

1. True, if we survey cultural attitudes toward women's appetites and body size, we find great variety—a variety that is shaped by ethnic, national, historical, class, and other factors. My eighty-year-old father, the child of immigrants, asks at the end of every meal if I "got enough to eat"; he considers me "skinny" unless I am plump by my own standards. His attitude reflects not only memories of economic struggle and a heritage of Jewish-Russian preference for *zaftig* women, but the lingering, well into this century, of what was once a more general Anglo-Saxon cultural appreciation for the buxom woman. In the mid-nineteenth century, hotels and bars were adorned with Bouguereau-inspired paintings of voluptuous female nudes; Lillian Russell, the most photographed woman in America in 1890, was known and admired for her hearty appetite, ample body (over two hundred pounds at the height of her popularity), and "challenging, fleshly, arresting" beauty (Banner, 1984, 136). Even as such fleshy challenges became less widely appreciated in the twentieth century, men of Greek, Italian, Eastern-European, and African descent, influenced by their own distinctive cultural heritages, were still likely to find female voluptuousness appealing. And even in the late 1960s and early 1970s, as Twiggy and Jean Shrimpton began to set a new norm for ultra-slenderness, lesbian cul-

tures in the United States continued to be accepting—even celebrating—of fleshy, space-claiming female bodies.

Even more examples could be produced, of course, if we cast our glance more widely over the globe and back through history. Many cultures, clearly, have revered expansiveness in women's bodies and appetites. Some still do. But in the 1980s and 1990s, an increasingly universal equation of slenderness with beauty and success has rendered the competing claims of cultural diversity ever feebler. Men who were teenagers from the mid-seventies on, whatever their ethnic roots or economic class, are likely to view long, slim legs, a flat stomach, and a firm rear end as essentials of female beauty. Unmuscled heft is no longer as acceptable in lesbian communities. Even the robust, earthy actresses who used to star in Russian films have been replaced by slender, Westernized types.

2. Women were thus warned "gluttonous habits of life" would degrade their physical appearance and ruin their marriageability. "Gross eaters" could develop thick skin, broken blood vessels on the nose, cracked lips, and as unattractively "superanimal" facial expression (Brumberg, 1988, 179). Of course, the degree to which actual women were able to enact any part of these idealized and idolized constructions was highly variable (as it always is); but *all* women, of all classes and races, felt their effects as the normalizing measuring rods against which their own adequacy was judged (and, usually, found wanting).

REFERENCES

Banner, L. (1984). *American beauty*. Chicago: University of Chicago Press.

Berger, J. (1977). *Ways of seeing*. London: Penguin.

Brumberg, J. (1988). *Fasting girls*. Cambridge, MA: Harvard University Press.

Bynum, C. W. (1987). *Holy feast and holy fast: The religious significance of food to medieval women*. Berkeley: University of California Press.

Canetti, E. (1962). *Crowds and power*. New York: Viking.

Dijkstra, B. (1986). *Idols of perversity*. New York: Oxford University Press.

hooks, b. (1990). *Yearning*. Boston: South End Press.

Mitchie, H. (1987). *The flesh made word*. New York: Oxford University Press.

Poloquin, B. (1988, May 8). An ode to mothers. *Syracuse Herald American*, p. D1.

Roth, G. (1982). *Feeding the hungry heart*. New York: New American Library.

Schneider, J., & Agras, W. S. (1987, March). Bulimia in males: A matched comparison with females. *International Journal of Eating Disorders*, 6(2), 235–242.

Starvation stages in weight-loss patients similar to famine victims. (1989, April 3). *International Obesity Newsletter*.

Ward, H. O. (Mrs.) (1880). *The young lady's friend*. Philadelphia: Porter and Coates. (Quoted in Mitchie.)

CHAPTER 6

"GIRLS' MAGS" AND THE PEDAGOGICAL FORMATION OF THE GIRL*

Kerry Carrington
Anna Bennett

INTRODUCTION

While the body has an obvious biological practicality, its signification and association with a particular form of sexuality is nowhere near as fixed or certain. Sexuality is not defined by nature, although plenty probably think so. Rather it is a domain of meanings, a field of measurements and assessments, and most significantly a focus of much governmental intervention. Its formation is the pedagogical product of training in culturally and historically specific modes and manners of sexual conduct (Elias 1978; Mauss 1985). In other words, sexuality is an artifice—a product of much work of the self as well a site and product of considerable governmental interventions which provide it with access to certain capacities and attributes. While we are aware of recent

---

*Following the completion of this chapter for the book, a new book by Angela McRobbie (1994) was published. Within this text the author revisits her previous analysis of magazines like "Jackie." She suggests that feminist readings of girls' magazines, including her own, had concentrated too much on "the seamless text of oppressive meaning held together by ideology, rather than on the disruptions and inconsistencies and spaces for negotiation with the magazines" (McRobbie, 1994, 163). While it has to be acknowledged that magazines aimed at teenage girls have undergone significant changes in the 1990s, McRobbie concludes that these magazines are susceptible to a more open-ended reading than her previous research suggested. We concur and hope that our contribution, however small, has paved the way for a revitalisation of feminist analyses of cultural texts like, "Dolly," and "Cleo."

theoretical developments occurring in this larger intellectual terrain (see, for example, Meredyth, 1993), our focus is more limited. We shall restrict our analysis to an interrogation of the web of technicians and apparatuses of government that have encircled the girl within a dense and diverse network of governmentality, taking magazines aimed at the teenage market as one aspect of such a network.

Feminist scholars have tended to stress the sexually differentiated character of the social efforts that governmentalise children into forming masculine and feminine sexualities and subjectivities. Schools, families, government agencies, workplaces, and popular culture have variously been identified as sites which produce systematic sexual differences associated with masculinity and femininity (see Deem, 1978; Game & Pringle, 1983; Connell, 1987; Friedan, 1983; Oakley, 1972; Wolf, 1991). Adolescent femininity has been characterised in much of this feminist research as a stage in a woman's life crucial to the production of a hegemonic culture of femininity, trapped by the lure of romance and manipulated by the seductions of mass culture (see, for example, Lee, 1993 and McRobbie, 1991). Magazines such as *Seventeen, Cleo, Girlfriend, Dolly, Cosmopolitan, Woman's Own, Woman's Day,* and *Women's Weekly* tend to be represented in such analyses as the vile products of patriarchal culture (McRobbie, 1991; Radway, 1984; Winship, 1987). Through their consumption girls and women are said to be seduced into a culture of mass consumption and duped by the ideology of romance into a future of domesticity. The major aim of our chapter is to refute this overgeneralised reading of such highly variable cultural products. In particular, we refute the assumption which pervades much of this research that girls are the passive victims of a hegemonic culture of femininity and that culture is prepacked, sanitised, and sold to her through her consumption of "girls" magazines. Quite apart from the fact that there is no simple correspondence between these magazines and the pedagogical formation of adolescent femininity, the girl we argue is the product of a distinctively modern form of personage with attributes and characteristics which are historically specific and culturally diverse. The formation of such personal characteristics do not lend themselves to such levels of overgeneralisation and determination.

FEMINIST ANALYSES OF WOMEN'S MAGAZINES

Much of the feminist analysis of women's magazines aimed at age-segregated female markets within Australia, Britain, and the United States has been based on essentialist notions of gender. The basic argument to come out of this literature is that such magazines instruct the female sex how to fashion themselves into an object of the male gaze, as good wives, mothers, and daughters. A major difficulty with gender essentialism is that it projects onto men and women capacities and attributes which are culturally variable and historically specific (Fraser & Nicholson, 1990, 28). Another is that it totalises the "shared experiences" of "women as a group" into a unitary phenomenon. Our argument is that it is just not feasible to impose such a level of universality upon such diverse processes of pedagogical formation.

Gender essentialism follows a familiar line of feminist contention that patriarchal society necessarily and always disempowers women, constructing them in the image of men, as the other. Friedan (1965), for example, describes mass culture as one of the evils of the modern world lamenting the particular susceptibility of women to its powers. This popular feminist position on the media, and women's place within it, has until recently colonised the debate about women's magazines. There has been a tendency for feminist readings to dismiss the positive and productive aspects of such magazines in providing women with a series of devices, instructions, and techniques in transgressing and transforming their pedagogical formation as feminine subjects. Paradoxically, this tends to disempower rather than empower women, by constructing them almost entirely as hapless products of patriarchal culture!

Angela McRobbie's (1991) analysis of *Jackie* magazine establishes this particular path of feminist analysis. Her theoretical position asserts that women's magazines, particularly those aimed at the teenage market, mould girls into specific homogeneous female roles according to age. She argues that the magazines represent for girls agents of social control as the police do for boys (1991, 112). To McRobbie, *Jackie* is a system of messages, a signifying system, and a bearer of a patriarchal ideology which elicits consent from girls in their own leisure time to the ideologies of femininity, leisure, and consumption (p. 81). She identifies four codes which operate within such texts which together construct a totalising ideological system of meaning—the romantic code, the code of domesticity, the code of fashion, and the code of pop music (p. 94). According to McRobbie, girls occupy the passive role where "romantic individualism" dominates. She explains:

> Jackie sets up, defines and focuses exclusively on "the personal," locating it as the sphere of prime importance to the teenage girl. . . . Romance, problems, fashion, beauty and pop all mark out the limits of the girl's feminine sphere. Jackie represents

"romantic individualism" as the ethos par excellence of the teenage girl. The Jackie girl is alone in her quest for love; she refers back to her female peers for advice, comfort and reassurance only when she needs to do so or when she has nothing better to do. Female solidarity, or even just female friendship, has no real existence in the magazine. (1991, 131)

McRobbie's analysis of magazines like *Jackie* is, as she admits, one-sided. It is a textual reading of the ideology of the magazine—and not an analysis of how girls read *Jackie*—how much of the romantic individualism they take on board—or other ways in which these texts can be read (i.e., as playful texts or sex-instruction manuals). The major difficulty we have with this line of analysis is that the possibility is overlooked that girls may actually consume these texts in their cultural practices as objects of pleasure and play. The totalising notion of a "culture of femininity" upon which McRobbie's argument about these magazines rests, does not allow for what Hebdige (1978) calls bricolage, the reappropriation of cultural artefacts, such as *Dolly* magazines. It is prepacked, sanitised, sold, and consumed by the docile, unimaginative girl. Unlike the objects of style available to boys, the objects of style in the culture of femininity (i.e., magazines like *Jackie*, *Just Seventeen*, *Dolly*, and *Cleo*, fashion, music, and so on) are represented as determinant and unnegotiable features of patriarchal culture. Such an analysis of the culture of femininity leans toward a fatalism which constructs girls as the passive consumers of romantic individualism (see Carrington, 1993a; 1993b). This understanding of the role and effect of magazines aimed at the teenage female market fails to seriously consider the popularity of such textual mediums exclusively devoted to the teenage girl. What is ignored in such an analysis is that girls may actually consume these cultural products as sources of pleasure about *their sexuality* and as sources of knowledge a lot less prudish than that which is "officially" available to them (for example, sex-instruction manuals, biology classes, or parental advice).

A number of other pieces of research into women's magazines come to conclusions similar to McRobbie's. Windschuttle (1988, 254), in his chapter on "Glossy Sexuality," expresses a paternalistic concern about the "peculiarly vulnerable" state of female adolescence, where magazines seemingly "catch" them. He argues that far from creating sexual liberation, these magazines create an all-pervading anxiety and crisis of confidence which work to confine women to a restricted, oppressive social role (1988, 250). Ultimately, this dramatically argued position is both malevolent and patronising in that it constructs the genre of popular women's magazines as "the trash of low culture." Other writers such as Naomi Wolf and Janice Winship have followed suit, targeting the consumerism, promotion of heterosexuality, domesticity, and objectification of women's bodies as the essence and purpose of women's magazines. Janice Winship sees the positioning of women within these magazines as creating the "masculinisation of femininity," and a deepening dependence on both men and commodities. Very much like McRobbie, she argues that readers consume the ideology through the consumption of the product (Winship, 1987, 55–65) and that they "rarely aid women coming together independently of the magazine" (p. 80). Naomi Wolf (1991) runs a similar argument, stating that magazines targeted at women have consistently glamorised whatever the economy and their advertisers needed at that moment from women. She does, however, stress the importance that such magazines have played in the popularisation of women's liberation discourses and therefore recognises, though only fleetingly, some of their ambiguous effects.

Mica Nava points to the development of a more nuanced understanding of subjectivity flowing from the application of Foucault's work on media and textual analyses. These developments move away from the "notion of man and woman as duped and passive recipients of conspiratorial messages designed to inhibit their true consciousness" (Nava, 1987, 207). She argues that little attention has been paid to the way in which the relative status and power of women has paradoxically been enhanced by consumer society's providing women with new areas of authority and expertise. She says it is important to recognise this space as a source of power and pleasure for women and not to dismiss the mass consumption of products (such as women's magazines) as devices engaged in brainwashing, manipulation, and the creation of false needs (pp. 205–8).

It appears that some feminist writers are revising their past denunciations of these magazines. For example, in the introduction to her revised edition of the classic feminist text *Damned Whores and God's Police*, Ann Summers (1994, 25) provides a fairly positive endorsement of "girls' magazines."

> Only the magazines directed at younger women, *Cleo, Cosmopolitan, New Woman* and the teenage bible *Dolly*, offer anything like a realistic depiction of the actual lives of their readers and the issues and problems they have to contend with. These magazines do address subjects like sex, self-esteem, sexual harassment and the multitude of day-to-day hassles in any young woman's life, and in

this respect they are at least continuing to conform to the notion of women's service which was the editorial rationalization for what we used to criticize in the past.

What seems important to us then is a revisionist analysis of popular magazines aimed at the teenage female market, of the kind mooted in the passage above. In such an analysis it is important to interrogate these magazines in terms of the positive as well as the repressive effects they produce—as cultural products which multiply discourses, induce pleasure, generate power effects, and produce knowledge through which their readers can measure, realign or reinvent themselves as modern girls in ways which are highly variable (Foucault, 1978, 73).

SELLING THE DEVICES OF METAFEMININITY AND THE TECHNIQUES FOR THEIR DECONSTRUCTION

Our analysis is based on an examination of forty-eight recent editions (twelve of each) of four popular magazines—*Dolly, Girlfriend, Cleo,* and *Cosmopolitan*—aimed at the Australian and New Zealand teenage female markets. Some of the information about these magazines and their readership derived from phone conversations with their respective editors. Our revisionist analysis seeks to avoid reading these magazines in terms of a repressive or liberating dichotomy. The highly variable discursive nature of the discourses expressed within them, as opposed to the interpretation of them as little more than patriarchal vessels, will be a common theme. Moreover, an attempt is made here to problematise the various discourses produced in such magazines, paying particular attention to the ambiguity flowing throughout these texts.

One of the most striking aspects about these magazines is that they sell particularly well (Communications Update, 1993). *Cleo, Cosmopolitan,* and *Dolly* are the most popular, selling over 10 million copies among them in the Australian and New Zealand markets annually. All three are published by Australian Consolidated Press (ACP) and are owned by Kerry Packer. His company, ACP, owns a staggering 46.86 percent of the total circulation of magazines within Australia (p. 22). Other popular women's magazines owned by ACP include *Women's Weekly, Woman's Day,* and *Elle. Dolly* sells over 204,000 copies per average per issue (p. 21) and has a readership age of around 14 to 24. The magazine was established in November 1970, and seems most popular with the 13 to 18 age group. *Cleo* magazine sells over 322,000 per issue and targets an older age group between 18 and 34 (ibid.). *Cosmopolitan* sells 316,000 copies per issue (ibid.) and targets the 18 to 24 age group. These magazines are sold monthly and marketed throughout Australia and New Zealand.

Girlfriend is a relative newcomer to the Australian market. It was established in October 1988. The magazine is owned by Pacific publishers, a small company which tends to be overlooked in most of the statistical data available on the Australian media. The editors of *Girlfriend* claim that its readers are in the 13 to 25 age group. The largest concentration of readers, however, are more realistically between the ages of 11 to 16. Like the others, this magazine is also published in Sydney. The editors of *Girlfriend* we spoke to claim to sell 63,042 copies per issue. They based this figure on their access to the current audited circulation figures and told us they expect sales to rise 20 percent in the next six months. The relatively low circulation compared to competitors such as *Dolly*, it seems, would be related to two factors: the relative newness of the magazine and the reduced purchasing power of younger consumers.

On the basis of sales figures as large as those described above (and depicted in table 6.1) it has been estimated that just about every female beyond early childhood in Australia sees one of these magazines weekly (Windschuttle, 1993, 247). Australia presently has a population of 1,554,377 girls aged between 13 and 24 (see table 6.2). On the basis of our calculations, each one of these girls purchases an average of seven "girls" magazines per year. That's a lot of dupes, if feminist theorists like McRobbie and Winship are correct in their observations about their stupefying effects on adolescent girls.

Advertising fashion and beauty products constitute a large function of magazines aimed at the female market. This function has

TABLE 6.1
Sales Volume of Magazines Aimed at the
Australian and New Zealand Teenage Markets

Magazine	Sales per Issue	Sales per Year
Girlfriend	63,042	756,504
Dolly	204,000	2,448,000
Cosmopolitan	316,000	3,792,000
Cleo	322,000	3,864,000
TOTAL	905,042	10,860,504

Source: Communications Update, 85, February 1993—except for *Girlfriend*, whose circulation figures were kindly provided by the editors.

TABLE 6.2
Girls Aged 13–24, Australian Census, 1991

Age	Population
13	121,686
14	122,140
15	117,567
16	125,796
17	128,521
18	132,557
19	139,273
20	143,937
21	136,845
22	131,896
23	123,473
24	125,686
TOTAL	1,554,377

Source: Data retrieved from Supermap, Australian Census, 1991. We wish to thank Andrew Johnson, a postgraduate in the School of Humanities, University of Western Sydney, for retrieving this data from the CD ROM "Supermap" package.

attracted considerable criticism from feminists, who argue that women and girls fall prey to an all-pervading incitement to purchase such products. While we agree that advertising is used in these texts to promote the trappings of metafemininity, fashion, makeup, and other such accessories, we believe that this argument misses a number of crucial points and complex nuances.

First, there is no such homogeneity in advertising across the different magazines, in terms of audiences, products, or messages. *Cleo* and *Cosmopolitan* magazines are marketed to an older audience and therefore promote products aimed at such an audience. The markets are divided into a normative grid of what Tait calls "ages and stages." The demarcation of femininity into such a grid can then be understood as a disciplinary method which categorises girls according to the stage in the series they are moving through (Tait, 1993, 46). Advertisements for wedding gifts, domestic products, food and alcohol, more expensive consumer items such as French perfume, and cars regularly appear in them (see, for example, *Cosmopolitan*, April 1993). Older models are used in the promotion of such products. By contrast, *Girlfriend* and *Dolly* use younger models and concentrate on the promotion of cheaper products such as "Impulse" body sprays as substitutes for French perfume (see *Dolly*, January 1993). Obviously, domestic products are not advertised in their pages. The language, argot, and cultural pitch of the magazines also differ according to age specificity. *Girlfriend* and *Dolly* deploy schoolgirl slang as a means of constructing an intimate relationship between the reader and magazine. Whereas *Cleo* and *Cosmopolitan* tend to use more sophisticated language in promoting identification with its readership.

Second, and much more importantly, there is no simple homogeneity in either product promotion or in the messages they construct about girls' bodies. Not all the advertising in these magazines involves selling beauty products or fashion accessories aimed at fashioning girls in an image desired by men. In all four magazines we looked at, advertising covered a diverse range of products such as condoms (for example, *Girlfriend*, April 1993), tampons, erotic devices, music, literature, and public health announcements such as "the safe sex message." Pain relievers such as "naprogesic" were even promoted as alternatives to putting up with period pain (*Girlfriend*, January 1993). Clearly the advertising of such products to girls is not just a question of media manipulation. Most teenage girls do have a use for such products, almost monthly, so this is hardly a case of advertising creating unnecessary desires for superfluous products. In addition, some of these advertisements are critical in providing knowledge about the experience of femininity and menstruation of a *positive*, and not a negative nature. Tampon advertisements, for example (which are permanently located in *Dolly* on the front-page spread), routinely debunk traditional myths about use and insertion, using a question-answer format. For example, "Will I be a virgin after I use tampons? Absolutely (Provided you were before you used them)" (*Dolly*, November 1991). Another variation of the tampon advertisement uses a letter/response format to promote a positive response to menstruation and a confidence about its bodily experience. For example:

> *Reader:* I've never used tampons before but I think I'd like to try them now. The only thing stopping me is that I don't really know how to use them. I got my first quite early, so none of my friends know any more than I do. And before you tell me to discuss this with my mother, you should know I'd rather die than talk to mum about that sort of stuff.
>
> *Dear Early-Bird:* The first thing you should do is get to know your body a little better. There's a very helpful little pamphlet inside every pack of Libra Fleur. This will help you get to know where

and how to insert the tampon. The key to it is relaxation. If you're at all tense, insertion can be more difficult. It's a case of trial and error the first time, but you'll soon get the hang of it, I'm sure. And by the way, it might be tricky talking to mums at first, but they can be handy. . . . For more information and a free sample send your name and address to "Libra Personal Product Adviser . . . ." (*Dolly*, November 1991)

Third, it is too simplistic to assume any automatic commensurability between the product being promoted and the consumer. It is important to read these texts as more complex than just as vehicles for Wolf's so called "mass consumerism." Though we admit the magazines are owned almost entirely by the Packer and Murdock media monopolies, such concentration of ownership does not dictate a fixed, all-powerful unitary discourse of power or a single set of messages of the kind suggested by the critics of these magazines. As Mica Nava explains (1987, 209–10), there is no necessary relationship between consumption and production:

Cultural forms and meanings are not reducible to class and the economic. Consumerism is far more than just economic activity: it is also about dreams and consolation, communication and confrontation, image and identity. Like sexuality, it consists of a multiplicity of fragmented and contradictory discourses. . . . Consumerism is a discourse through which disciplinary power is both exercised and contested. While not negating its relation to capitalism, we must refuse to return it always to questions of production.

This is not to deny the transparent manipulation of beauty advertisements where the product promises perfection, or at least improvement in enhancing attractiveness to men. Indeed, the most worrying aspect of product promotion to us was the deployment of body fads fed by an international fashion culture and promoted by magazines as the desirable "body appearance." The contemporary preoccupation with the "waif" look is one such contemporary example. But this, it seems, has more to do with the structuring of our cultural preoccupation with fads rather than a deliberate attempt by magazines to impoverish girl's bodies. On the other hand, there was no shortage of beauty advertisements which promoted their products with the promise of pleasing men. Consider, for example, the following caption attached to an image of soft feminine hands caressing bulging hairy biceps.

He always felt my hands were too rough. But not any more. For longer, stronger nails and softer, smoother skin—Complete Care Hand and Nail Lotion or Hand and Nail Cream. With a money back guarantee. (*Cleo*, July 1993)

It *is* important to recognise, as many feminist researchers have before us, the role of these magazines in the constitution of what Craik has called a "sexual fix"—that is, in the construction of masculinity and femininity as polar opposites (Craik, 1984). The repetitive images of noseless cover girls and wafer-thin fashion models contrasted against seemingly endless images of boys with bulging pectorals and washboards stomachs provide plenty of empirical support for this argument (see, for example, *Just Seventeen*, April 1993). The packaging of ideals: supermodels, models, actors, pop stars, again extracted from various discourses, popularise and construct a desire to be like them. The pursuit of the desired look is encouraged in such articles as "How to Dress Like a Supermodel" (*Girlfriend*, December 1993), and by providing the "vital statistics" or measurements of personalities, beauty competitions, and make-overs[1] where the pursuit of fad looks are perpetuated. However, there are two important qualifications we wish to make about the constitution of the "sexual fix." First, it is important to recognise that there was a considerable difference in the images of femininity produced in the four magazines. *Girlfriend* stood out in particular for its promotion of stereotypical anglocentric images of femininity—that is, the pale-thin-blonde look. *Cleo, Cosmopolitan*, and to a lesser extent *Dolly*, made considerable efforts to represent a much wider range of "ethnic" and culturally diverse fashion models and cover girls in their representations of femininity. Secondly, just as the social practices of dress and adornment can create images of noseless girls and washboard boys, as Craik suggests, the deployment of such cultural practices can also operate as devices for disrupting the sexual fix. She explains: "Through fashion the 'sexual fix' is symbolically undermined by 'un-fixing' those categories of representation, body, 'women' and 'problem'" (Craik, 1984, 82).

It is thus equally important to recognise the role of these magazines in providing girls with the necessary skills and techniques for transgressing dichotomous representations of femininity and masculinity in popular culture. For example, make-overs while they may promote sexualised images of sorts, also promote girls experiencing their bodies as sites of aesthetic pleasure and experimentation. Make-up is not necessarily used to feminise the body in any unifying sense. The make-ups and make-overs provide girls with the techniques to undo and rework the sexual fix; to experiment with their sexual identity, to refuse the naturalness of a single feminine style and therefore to disrupt dichotomised images of femininity and masculinity. Take, for example, the promotion of multiple personae in the July edition of *Girlfriend*, where the same girl, Melissa, is made up in three different ways, as a "Glamour Girl," a "Natural Girl," and a "Sporty Girl." Of course, all promote a range of different beauty products, but the crucial point is that they also expose femininity as something constitutive, as made-up. A different example of what we mean here is the promotion of a range of androgynous beauty products, which actively attempt to break down binary opposites between masculinity and femininity. For example,

> Whether you're a guy or a girl, long hair needs extra attention and intensive conditioning. You and your boy share lots of stuff, so isn't it time you started swapping your styling secrets? . . . If you've ever stolen your boyfriend's shaving cream, or tried on his aftershave and like the effect, you'll know that sometimes it makes sense to raid his bathroom cabinet. But the reverse is true, too. Your guy can sometimes take a leaf from your book, especially when it comes to looking after his skin and hair. So sharing your beauty buys isn't just another way to demonstrate your togetherness—it also means you score some new beauty products, and he gets to brush up his look. (*Dolly*, August 1993)

Fourth, it is not at all clear that the objectification of bodies is a one-way street. While the historical construction of girls waiting "for their prince to come" is reminiscent of representations within the magazines (Walkerdine, 1984), it's not the only one. Take for example the full frontal nude "map of the modern male" depicted in the 1993 August edition of *Dolly*. The map summarises a list of essential male attributes. On the penis it states—"notice the way it just hangs there innocently, pretending not to have a mind of its own. Don't be fooled. It does." Male models are routinely represented in these magazines as objects to be "perved at." Their objectification in the pages of *Cleo*, for example, is regularly embodied in competitions like "The sexiest man alive" contest and narratives about "the man as heart-breaker," cheater, liar, the list goes on and on (*Cleo*, May 1991).

Fifth, like the editors of these magazines, we are not so sure that *only* girls read them. As boys do not have the same or even variations of this genre available to them, strangely it seems that some boys read them. Articles and especially advertisements aimed at teenage boys are increasingly apparent, for example, in advertisements promoting safe sex among young gay males (*Dolly*, July 1993). It could be that boys read these texts as an impersonal means of acquiring access to femininity and learning about adolescent female sexuality.

Sixth, though the magazines promote work upon the body in order to "catch" men, this work on the self is also promoted as an aesthetic activity—as a series of explorations of "the ages and stages" of girlhood. Dressing up is represented in such texts as pleasurable and fun. What's so wrong about this? While we don't deny that girls can receive advice of a highly sexualised nature from such magazines, it is important to see that their effects are limited, highly variable, and not totalising. When the magazine is put away, it cannot be assumed that an "ideology of femininity" overcomes the reader. In other words, reading magazines like *Dolly* is not necessarily such a serious exercise.

Lastly and *most* importantly, these magazines facilitate an important site and means for a positive transformation of sex into discourse for teenage girls. Dear Dolly, Dolly Doctor, Q & A Medical, and the reams of advice on relationships, familial, sexual, and platonic, in the pages of these texts constitute for the girls who consume them, an archive on the "truth about sex." We would not suggest that the "truths about sex" produced in these texts are even "truthful" or "revealing," but nor would we dismiss them as disabling or repressive in their effects. Sexuality is defined in such texts as a domain susceptible to pathology (Foucault, 1978, 68), and thus subject to a grid of judgments, measurements, and normalising interventions. Certainly, the images of femininity and sexuality promoted in such texts can act as a set of normalising devices for measuring failure, for example, through the completion of questionnaires like, "Am I Sexy?"; "Do I have charm?"; "What kind of girl am I"; and so on. The crucial point is that these magazines occupy an important part of a complex machinery for producing discourses in which sexuality as an aspect of person formation is problematised. It can hardly be denied that the advice about sexuality supplied by these magazines equips girls with a great deal of useful and positive knowledge about such matters, not easily acquired elsewhere. For instance, to whom does a thirteen-year-old girl ask how to masturbate, how to insert a tampon, what's petting, what's an orgasm, do I do it on the first, second, or third date, how do I know if I'm being used, how do I dump a guy, how do I tell my girlfriend I love her, when should I have my first pap smear, can condoms break, is the pill dangerous, where do I get an abortion, and so on? The traditional sources of such information include teachers, parents, and sex-educators often reluctant to answer such questions. Take, for instance, the frankness of the following advice about masturbation published in the August edition of *Girlfriend*.

> MASTURBATION. WHY DO GIRLS MASTURBATE. There are lots of myths about masturbation, but the truth is that it's a normal, harmless and healthy way of discovering how your body works and responds to sexual excitement. Most articles and books you read about sex tend to centre on how you and your partner can experience safe sexual pleasure together. But not everyone has a boyfriend and not everyone is ready to undertake sexual activities of this nature with a guy! This is why it's a good idea for you to explore what gives you pleasure enjoyment and sexual pleasure alone, before you even contemplate a sexual relationship. (*Girlfriend*, August 1993)

Consider also the following advice in response to a letter from a girl feeling anxious about her sexual attraction to a girlfriend.

> You've only known her for a few months so you don't really know what her reaction will be. It may scare her and she may reject you, which is the last thing you want. Just enjoy her company, have fun together and try not to dwell on deeper matters until you're sure how you really feel. If you believe your affection is deeper call the Gay and Lesbian Counselling Service on (02) 360 2211. (*Girlfriend*, July 1993)

Hardly a promotion for heterosexuality! How about the following advice to a thirteen-year-old girl under sexual pressure from a sixteen-year-old step-brother to massage his penis.

> Your stepbrother sounds like a creep who's using his power to abuse you and gain pleasure for himself. What he's doing is very wrong and it's also against the law. . . . If you don't think you can stand up to him by yourself, then you need to tell someone about it. Try telling your mum, or someone else in authority what he has been doing to you. You need to put an end to it now before he tries doing anything more serious. (*Girlfriend*, July 1993)

Sounds like the kind of advice about incest most feminists would want promoted to more than a million girls in Australia each year. We don't deny the pressure to consume, to always look good, and to conform to certain ideals, are promoted in such magazines, but it is important to recognise that they are matched by undercurrents of critique. Articles on "How Implants Ruined My Breasts" (*Dolly*, July 1993), "EAT" (*Just Seventeen*, April 1993), and "Be Confident" (*Girlfriend*, July 1993) are representative of this. The incitement for girls to use these magazines as techniques for acquiring confidence in themselves and knowledge about sex, their bodies, friendships, and sexual relationships cannot be easily dismissed as a stupefying form of "mass consumerism." Descriptions of pap smears (*Girlfriend*, July 1993), enticements to travel and join international youth exchange programs and to write scripts for novels and plays for example, encourage self-government, not repression.

Articles on the normality and pleasure of masturbation clearly free the girl, as an object of government, from some of the more repressive myths of traditional sexual behaviour. The magazines make it their business to educate girls about sex and their bodies, for instance: "Here at 'Girlfriend' we believe that sexual knowledge is vital for young women so they can make informed decisions about their relationships" (July 1993).

Cleo appears to be the most explicit in the depiction of sexuality. "Cleo's Directory" located in the back pages, advertises exotica for women, including vibrators (*Cleo*, July 1993). Articles such as "The Secrets of Easily Orgasmic Women" provide young women with useful information on their bodies and sex lives (*Cleo*, November 1991). Female sexuality is demystified and given a domain of importance. Bodies are deconstructed here. The problematisation of sex for the girl is related, as Ann Barr Snitow points out in reference to Harlequin novels, to the time and training involved in the pursuit of orgasmic sex: "it depicts the heroine struggling, against the hero's resistance (or ignorance), to get the right combination of elements together so that, for her, orgasmic sex can take place" (*Snitow*, 1984, 272). Rather than there being a repressive force for female sexual control, there is the production of a variety of discourses in such magazines of the complexity, ambiguity, and fragility of adolescent female sexuality. This explicitly represents the increasing emphasis, not on the sexualisation of women as objects, but on female sexuality and its remarkable capacities and variations.

There is one major qualification to our argument. We do acknowledge that these magazines construct themselves in positions of authority—as experts in that they claim to possess the "truth" of sex. The relationship between the reader and the text is a pedagogical one. The space between the reader and the text is also an intimate one. Dolly occupies the role of the friend, confidant, adviser and expert. Tait has suggested in reference to sex-education manuals, that "young people are defined as 'normal' by modelling their relationships, both to themselves and others, against a complex grid of available governmental manuals" (Tait 1993, 47). Guides about "Do's and Don'ts," "How To's" ("How to Kiss . . . Get Your Guy . . . Tell if You're Good in Bed"), and "Never Do's"—"10 Things You Should Never Do in Bed" (*Cleo*, May 1991), for example, set up a grid of norms about various conducts such as beauty, sex appeal, body shape, conduct, and personality from which girls can measure and evaluate themselves, of the kind Tait refers to in relation to sex-education manuals. Special editions or sections devoted to sex and relationships, such as *Dolly*'s June 1992 supplement "Relating and Dating," reflect the time and space which the magazines devote to providing the "truth" about such matters. "Info-lines" are promoted which provide answers to questions such as: "Is he the right guy for you?" (phone 005551460) and "The coolest things about being single" (phone 00555146265). There is a problematisation of sex in such texts which supports the Foucauldian thesis that the obsession with sexuality is unique to modernity.[2] "What Should I Do?," "Q & A Medical," and "Dolly Doctor" function as confessionary devices where "experts" help with readers' problems. It is apparent to us that these textual devices may serve a crucial and positive function in assisting girls to manage the complexities and anxieties of personal development that plague her pedagogical formation. These do-it-yourself surveys provide readers with a series of norms of performance (Am I Sexy?) and thus with a pedagogical source for relieving (or in certain instances fuelling) sexual and personal anxieties. They therefore constitute, among others, a technique through which the capacity for governmentalisation is installed in the lives of individual girls. These grids of knowledge provide advice about how to become a "better girl"—which as we have tried to demonstrate above can mean many things from doing work on self to catch a man, that is fashioning the self through the lens of the male gaze—but also reinventing the self by becoming more knowledgeable and confident about your body, about sexuality, about handling boys, girlfriends, and parents, and other such possibilities. But it would be a mistake to see the "better girl" as coerced or duped into submission (i.e., into developing such "feminine" capacities and attributes) through false consciousness or the ideology of romantic individualism. The "better girl" is the pedagogical product of a form of government which connects her desires to the objectives of the advertisers and the magazines.[3] Can more than a million girls be so stupid? There are no such equivalent magazines for boys as the feminist research so frequently points out. So who's missing out, and on what?

Just as feminists have argued that Madonna can be read as a transgressive text in the sense that her consumption as a cultural product transgresses the boundaries of femininity (Schwichtenberg, 1993, 140–42; Paglia, 1992, 5), so too can magazines like *Dolly* and *Cleo*. Just like Madonna, these cultural products expose femininity as an artefact—the product of a series of fashion devices and make-up techniques. Readers are provided with intricate instructions about how to transform their looks and image through such means as "make-ups and make-overs." The familiar feminist critique is that such instructions train girls how to present themselves from the point of view of the male gaze, what Winship refers to as the masculinisation of femininity and McRobbie calls "romantic individualism." Yet girls can use these devices to shape, reinvent, take on and off, or move the boundaries around femininity. As Johnson (1993, 131) suggests about the pedagogical role of such magazines in her analysis of the formation of the modern girl: "Indeed, if different images of femininity could be taken on and off, then so too, by implication, could femininity itself."

CONCLUDING NOTE

The theoretical purpose of our chapter has stressed that adolescent femininity is not a homogeneous product of patriarchal culture. Its pedagogical production is highly variable and tangential. Femininity, like other variants of what Tait (1993, 47) describes as "a youthful habitus" is an artefact of various forms of government, whose outcomes are always tangential, variable, and incomplete. The girl is not the fatalistic heir of hegemonic femininity and magazines aimed at the teenage female market are not necessarily the vehicles of romantic individualism, or the products of ideological representations of sexuality, femininity, and masculinity. These magazines comprise one such technology of government within which femininity is formed and reformed in everyday life. But, as we have tried to show, the consumption of such textual devices cannot be read off or reduced to the single solitary effect of one underlying discourse about the sexual repression of adolescent girls.

Metafemininity is exposed in the instructional discourses of such magazines as an artifice; as a construction or invention of a masculine gaze whose production is not found in nature, but in a masculinist discourse about sexuality which has fetishised women's bodies, carved them up into bits and pieces of flesh (tits, legs, and bums), adorned them with the devices of metafemininity (fashion, makeup, and accessories), and then served them up for consumption of the male gaze. When these various strategies come together magazines like *Dolly* and *Cleo* are transgressive texts which expose femininity as a prop, a put-on, a make-up and make-over. The consumers of these cultural products can then use them "in ways that challenge the stable notion of gender as the edifice of sexual difference" (Schwichtenberg 1993, 132), that is, to make the formerly unpresentable presentable (Lyotard 1986, 81).

NOTES

1. Make-overs are before and after shots of girls who after having sent pictures of themselves to *Dolly*, are chosen as models for "making-up."

2. Foucault's *The history of sexuality* (vol. 1) offers a different account of the formation of modern discourses about sex to the repressive hypothesis which sees the Victorian era as ushering in a silence over sex—confining it to the bedroom for the purposes of reproduction—closing off a history in which bodies "made a display of themselves." The repressive hypothesis constructs the modern era as enlightened—as the era of sexual liberation. Foucault argues that the history of sexuality far from undergoing restriction in Victorian times has on the contrary been subjected to a mechanism of increasing incitement; the techniques of power over sexuality have not obeyed a repressive principle, but rather one of dissemination and implantation of polymorphous sexualities; the will to knowledge about sex did not come to a halt during the repressive Victorian times, but persisted in constituting a science of sexuality (Foucault 1978, 9–13).

3. Here we wish to acknowledge the adaptation of original theoretical insights from Tyler 1993.

REFERENCES

Carrington, K. (1993a). Cultural studies, youth culture and delinquency. *Youth subcultures*. Hobart: Clearing House for Youth Studies.

—— (1993b). *Offending girls: Sex, youth and justice*. Sydney: Allen & Unwin.

Communications Update (1993). Issue number 85, February 1993.

Connell, R. W. (1987). *Gender and power*. Sydney: Allen & Unwin.

Craik, J. (1984). Fashion, clothes, sexuality. *Australian Journal of Cultural Studies*, 23, 259–268.

Deem, R. (1978). *Women and schooling*. London: Routledge & Kegan Paul.

Elias, N. (1978). *The history of manners, vol. 1: The civilising process* (Trans. E. Jephcott). New York: Pantheon Books.

Foucault, M. (1978). *The history of sexuality*. New York: Vintage Books.

Fraser, N. & Nicholson, L. J. (1990). Social criticism without philosophy: An encounter between feminism and postmodernism. In Nicholson, L. J. (Ed.), *Feminism/postmodernism*. New York: Routledge.

Friedan, B. (1983). *The feminine mystique*. Harmondsworth: Penguin.

Game, A. & Pringle, R. (1983). *Gender at work*. Sydney: Allen and Unwin.

Johnson, L. (1993). *The modern girl: Girlhood and growing up*. Sydney: Allen & Unwin.

Lees, S. (1993). *Sugar and spice: Sexuality and adolescent girls*. London: Penguin.

Lyotard, J. (1986). *The postmodern condition: A report on knowledge*. Manchester: Manchester University Press.

McRobbie, A. (1991). *Feminism and youth culture*. London: Macmillan.

—— (1994). *Postmodernism and popular culture*. London: Routledge.

Mauss, M. (1985). A category of the human mind: The notion of person; the notion of self (Trans. W. D. Halls). In M. Carrithers, S. Collins, & S. Lukes (Eds.), *The category of the person*. Cambridge: Cambridge University Press.

Meredyth, D. & Tyler, D. (Eds.) (1993). *Child and citizen: Genealogies of schooling and subjectivity*. Brisbane: Institute of Cultural Policy Studies, Griffith University.

Nava, M. (1987). Consumerism and its contradictions. *Cultural Studies*, 1(2), 204–210.

Oakley, A. (1972). *Sex, gender and society*. New York: Harper & Row.

Paglia, C. (1992). *Sex, art and American culture*. London: Penguin.

Radway, J. (1984). *Reading the romance: Women, patriarchy and popular literature*. Chapel Hill: University of North Carolina Press.

Schwichtenberg, C. (1993). Madonna's postmodern feminism. In C. Schwichtenberg (Ed.), *The Madonna connection*. Sydney: Allen & Unwin.

Snitow, A. B. (1984). Mass market romance: Pornography for women is different. *Desire: The politics of sexuality*. London: Virago.

Summers, A. (1994). *Damned whores and God's police*. Revised ed. Ringwood: Penguin.

Tait, G. (1993). Youth, personhood and "practices of the self": Some new directions for youth research. *The Australian and New Zealand Journal of Sociology*, 29(1), 40–54.

Tyler, D. (1993). Making better children. In D. Meredyth & D. Tyler (Eds.), *Child and citizen: Genealogies of schooling and subjectivity*. Brisbane: Institute of Cultural Policy Studies, Griffith University.

Walkerdine, V. (1984). Some day my prince will come. In A. McRobbie & M. Nava (Eds.), *Gender and generation*. London: Macmillan.

Windschuttle, K. (1988). *The media*. Ringwood: Penguin.

Winship, J. (1987). *Inside women's magazines*. London: Pandora.

Wolf, N. (1991). *The beauty myth*. New York: William Morrow.

CHAPTER 7

CHILDHOOD AND PARENTING IN CHILDREN'S POPULAR CULTURE AND CHILDCARE MAGAZINES

Carmen Luke

CHILDREN'S POPULAR CULTURE AS PUBLIC PEDAGOGY

From infancy, most children are immersed in the texts of popular culture. The texts and artifacts of popular culture frame children's understanding of the world and of themselves, of narrative, heroes and heroines, gender and race relations, cultural symbols, values, and social power. How children negotiate and experience the messages of popular cultural texts is crucial to any understanding of the relationship among cultural texts, artifacts, social subjects, and practices. However, my concern in this chapter is with the larger discourses—the rhetorical constructs—of childhood and parenthood in popular cultural representations.

Visual representations such as cinematic texts, stylized illustrations, cartoons, video, or photographs, are part of the landscape of meaning that social subjects encounter in everyday life. Television texts, the toy industry, and popular culture more generally teach powerful lessons about the social world which are variously reinforced by the discourses and pedagogies of home and school (Luke, 1990a,b,c; 1993). Together these discourses provide cultural meaning systems of concepts such as 'childhood', 'family', 'femininity', 'masculinity', 'race', and so forth.

I use the term discourse here following Foucault (1972) to define how theoretical and "commonsense" knowledges are produced historically and in specific sociocultural contexts. Self-other understandings, according to Foucault, are always contingent upon subjects' various positions within a range of discourses available at particular historical moments and in specific cultural locations. So, for instance, how one understands one's location within a class structure, racial, gender, or national identity is made possible through the symbolic meaning systems available to social agents. Cultural meaning systems are inscribed on social relations and innumerable texts, textual sites and practices (e.g., television, schools, play) which, in turn, give meaning to a range of gendered social and cultural identities and styles (Bourdieu, 1984). These, in turn, are made concrete through the social relations of lived experience in which variations of 'community', 'family', 'childhood', or 'gender' are enacted. Since contemporary Western culture is organized around a cult of the image (Ewen, 1988), then any analysis of mass cultural discourses must go beyond attention to the linguistic text and consider as well the representation of meaning encoded in images, objects and spaces (cf. Luke, 1994; 1996, in press). This is what I attempt here.

Foucault suggests that "discourse transmits and produces power": it is a product of and produces power relations (1981, 101). Western discourses of childhood and motherhood derive their power and "truth value" from a longstanding scientific history in disciplinary sociology, psychology, and social psychology. Variations of these discourses circulate through daytime talk shows, parenting self-help books and childcare magazines, mothercraft courses, in parent-child relationships, in daycare centres, schooling, and so on. These sites, texts, and social relations are the public forum in which specialized, disciplinary knowledges are transformed into public pedagogies and commonsense knowledges of everyday life.

As feminist scholarship has repeatedly shown, historically the author-authorities of theories of childhood, motherhood, and femininity have been men. From Aristotle to the social contract theorists to Freud, the relegation of women and symbolic femininity to nature and the private sphere, to identities of lack, inferiority, affect, and unreason, is testimony to the discursive production of femininity as both the product of historical power relations and the continuing (re)production of unequal real and symbolic power that structures gender relations from birth. Constructs of femininity and masculinity in the discourse of children's toys or parenting magazines attest to the remarkable historical consistency of such differential gender valuation. And, the power of discourse—in this case, that of childhood and motherhood—is sustained by its proliferation in popular cultural forms such as television, cinema, toys, videogames, lifestyle magazines and—paramount in late capitalist economies—by its ability to be transformed into consumer goods.

WALL-TO-WALL POWER RANGERS, TURTLES, AND BARBIES

The possibility for discourse to be transformed into merchandise is a fundamental requirement within contemporary capitalist logic. Learning the games of childhood play, learning gender, or parenting is enabled through mass cultural, media, and commodity forms. Today's niche marketing of childhood, demands detailed product knowledge of mothers, whose nurturing role is closely tied to responsible consumption of an increasingly wide range of age-appropriate instructional toys, infant gear, medicines, and nursery technologies (e.g., vaporisers, SIDS heart rate monitors, closed-circuit cameras). The discourse of mothering is a public and commodified discourse played out in the images of television talkshows and sitcoms, in magazines, advertising, and on the shelves of toy and department stores. These public sites and texts encode constructs of childhood and parenthood, and act as powerful public pedagogies in the production of social identities of the 'child', 'family', 'gender', or 'race'.

If we consider the scope of children's popular culture—not the adult romanticized version of what children's culture is or ought to be—it becomes evident that children spend a lot of their waking hours with television and the video games, comic books, and toy spin-offs from television or movies (Luke, 1990b). Television has the highest market-saturation rate of home information technologies, but other media texts also cross-reference to the artifacts of children's popular culture, which create an intertextual universe, a network of desire, that few children exist outside of. It is in this intertextual network of commodity and visual symbolic sign systems in which childhood is experienced (Luke, 1996, in press). Children's television programs today function primarily as thirty-minute commercials, and successful new toy launches increasingly rely on movie and TV program promotions. The hugely successful Smurfs, Ninja Turtles, Transformers, My Little Pony, She-Ra, He-Man, or Care Bears toylines were entirely dependent on television programs and movies as advance organizers of children's material desire (Kline, 1993). Children grow up in this intertextual universe which ties TV programs to movies, toys, T-shirts, pyjamas and shoes, games and action figures, bedlinens and towels, pencil cases and lunchboxes, and even wallpaper. What Ien Ang (1985) called "wall to wall *Dallas*" is as applicable to the child's world of wall-to-wall Simpsons, Ninja Turtles, *Jurassic Park*, or Power Rangers.

For children, the jump from narrative to commodities—from Tranformer cartoons to Tranformer toys; from Muppet cartoons to McDonald's promotion of Muppet Babies; or from Spielberg movies to spin-off television cartoons, fast-food-outlet contests, or the movie-linked action figures and video games—seems relatively natural. It is naturalized because it *is* the background cultural tapestry in which childhood is lived, and in which (social or biological) parents experience childhood and parenthood with their children.

Buying into the system means both buying into particular ideological narratives of social structure, gender roles, and power relations, and into a social construction of reality which is real, material, and constitutes the lived experience of childhood and adults (Kinder, 1991). Parents *do* take their children to Pizza Hut or McDonald's and purchase the latest figurines; parents *do* buy the advertised cereal or peanut butter children insist on to avoid embarrassing conflicts in supermarket aisles; parents *do* buy the Turtle or Power Ranger towel or bedsheet set, the latest kiddie Reeboks, Nikes, Nintendo games, and *Jurassic Park* T-shirts.

These everyday consumer and social practices exemplify the cultural postmodernism of Baudrillard's (1981;1988) world of simulacra— a world of images and signs which refer only to other images and signs, none of which have a concrete referent in "The Real." The family trips to Disneyland, movieworld themeparks, or the consumer practices requisite for entering contests to meet media characters, are a case in point. They constitute actual social practices and yet are based on media(ted) referents which "bear no relation to any reality whatever: it is its own pure simulacrum" (Baudrillard, 1988, 170). According to Baudrillard (p. 72),

> the Disneyland imaginary is neither true nor false: it is a deterrence machine set up in order to rejuvenate in reverse the fiction of the real. Disneyland is there to conceal the fact that it is the "real" country, all of "real" America, which *is* Disneyland. . . . It is no longer a question of a false representation of reality (ideology), but of concealing the fact that the real is no longer real, and thus of saving the reality principle.

The hyperreal imaginary of social practices constitutes much of contemporary experience for children and adults—in the West, and increasingly on a global scale. Postindustrial capitalism has given rise to postmodern global economies of culture: anyone anywhere can buy into innumerable cultural styles. Hill-tribe kids in Thailand wear Chicago Bulls hats, Slovenian kids wear O.J. and Nike T-shirts (Homer Simpson T-shirts are still sighted in New Guinea), and women in the American Midwest sport "ethnic dress." In remote Australian Aboriginal or

Guatemalan highland communities, people gather around the glow of the screen watching old reruns, *Beverly Hills 90210*, Academy Awards, or Miss Universe, brought to you by Coke, Pepsi, Nike or Toyota. I take Baudrillard's point that contemporary cultural experience is not a false representation of reality but that it *is* reality, a reality principle different in kind from Enlightenment guarantees of reified truths about the real. But if we consider that everyday social, economic, political, and cultural practices have long functioned in relation to the hyperreal imaginary of religious metaphysics, then perhaps in principle there is nothing particularly different—ontologically—about the postmodern turn. Form (i.e., media) and content (i.e., secularized) have changed to be sure. Yet the political economy of the sign, its "fundamental non-existence," its imaginary relation to an alleged Truth or Real encoded in forms of symbolic, iconographic, or totemic spiritual belief systems, has always configured the moral and political consciousness of people in Western and non-Western cultures. I now turn to look at constructs of gender in childhood cultural industries.

CHILDHOOD AND TOYWORLDS: GENDERED ORGANIZATION OF SPACE

The adult leisure market boomed in the 1980s and had a direct impact on the commercialisation of children's leisure (Butsch, 1990; Engelhardt, 1986; Kline, 1993). Advances in computer technology, refinements of niche marketing strategies, and the expansion of megamalls emerging as new micro-cities and revisioned "community" centres with safe play-zones and child-oriented events, all had direct spin-offs to the child market. Niche marketing to a "concept" and "identity" oriented generation of parents, meant the development and marketing of "quality" toys, children's designer clothing and shoes, alongside the hugely successful mass marketing of cross-linked toy, media, fast-food, and soft-drink product tie-ins. During the 1980s, retail toy chains expanded nationally and internationally, and the children's market entered an historically unprecedented retail profit boom (Kline, 1993; McNeal, 1987; Seiter, 1992).

A recent study by Seiter (1992) reveals some interesting insights about the gendered discourse underlying the organisation of space, color, and merchandise at Toys 'R' Us. As part of the postmodern globalisation and normalisation of experience, Toys 'R' Us, like McDonald's and other fast-food chains, has strict franchising requirements so that consumer experience is the same no matter where one shops or eats. In all stores, customers encounter high-tech toys and computer games first (marketed to boys and fathers) before moving on to licensed action figures and dolls. Moving from the high-tech "first encounter," boys' toys are available in the next sections, and towards the rear of the store are the girls' toys. What this means is that girls have to pass through the boys' section to get to the girls' ware, whereas boys can avoid the girls' merchandise altogether. All merchandise sectors are color-coded from signs to racks and packaging. The boys' section is coded in metallic, primary colors, whereas the girls' section consists of a riot of pinks and purples.

The girls' section is surrounded by arts and crafts goods, by preschooler instructional toys and gear, and the infant goods section. This arrangement suggests a natural connection between real baby bottles, infant gear, cribs, strollers, baby buggies, and "pretend play" baby toys. In one aisle merchandise for "real" babies is available paralleled in the next aisle by those same commodities at reduced size (and price). One sector for mothers, the adjacent sector for their girls. This gendered structural layout reproduces the domestication of femininity and functions as a silent pedagogy of gender differentiation—what Foucault calls social discipline and normalization through the organization of space.

The boys' sections, by contrast, are adjacent to sporting and outdoor and the computer and high-tech merchandise. The connection between "real" masculine interests such as sports, camping, or technology and "pretend" play is similarly assured. Yet there appears to be less of a disjunction between male adult leisure commodities and boys' toys since there are no reduced-size play replications of tents, bicycles, inflatable rafts, computer games, and so forth. In other words, unlike the girls' world of miniature household appliances and childcare paraphernalia, boys enter the world of male leisure interests earlier and more directly than girls.

Boys' toys are generally more expensive than girls' toys, and girls' toys keep them confined in more limited space compared to the spatial range enabled by boys' toys. Hot shots radical recoiler, radio-controlled vehicles, or cybertronic blaster guns keep boys on the move, whereas playing house requires less space, movement, and is far less action-oriented. One of the all-time best-selling toys "Supersoaker"—a watergun shaped like a handgun—en-genders different kinds of social and bodily behaviors than its equivalent for girls. "Flirt Squirts" waterguns for girls are shaped like compacts, lipsticks, and nailpolish bottles, all in fashion colors. Handgun action is oriented towards others, in pursuit of others, and structures social relations in conflict, opposition, and violence, whereas compacts and lipsticks are turned on the self in a discourse of self-adornment, not combat with others.

The gendered discourse in the toy industry's construction of childhood is not a subtext but a very explicit pedagogy of gendered identity. Marketers of childhood have produced an intensified dynamic between the cultural symbolic of television narratives and commodity "materiality" (Williams, 1980). Television programs and ads model the social narratives, the imaginary worlds of pretend and play, and the cultural goods of toyworlds enable and make concrete those play repertoires, and the shaping of identities and social relations. Corporate visions of 'childhood', 'gender', 'parenthood', or 'family' saturate the symbolic, spatial, material, and social environment to such an extent that, increasingly, we fail to take much note of them. How lessons on femininity and masculinity are constructed in the world of toys and toystores, or childcare magazines, are a case in point. I now turn to examine childcare magazines as one other discursive site in which particular visions of childhood and parenthood are inscribed.

CHILDHOOD AND PARENTING IN CHILDCARE MAGAZINES

In liberal theory and modern or postmodern capitalism the child is situated in the social and economic unit of the idealized nuclear family and as the primary focus of labor for women. Childhood and motherhood are inseparable sociocultural and economic practices and discourses—theoretical and "commonsense." Put simply, mothering implies children, and children are reared primarily by women whether in nuclear, single-parent, extended family, daycare, or primary school contexts.

Women's magazines all feature editorials and advertisements which not only celebrate bourgeois notions of motherhood and the pampered child within a heterosexual and nuclear-family formation, but are implicitly based on theoretical narratives of moral, cognitive, social, and behavioral development (cf. Phoenix, Woollett, & Lloyd, 1991). Such implicit public pedagogies are intertextually linked to, for instance, Fisher-Price toy ads which "responsibly" mark their toys with age-appropriate labels, environment-friendly stickers, or guidelines on the kinds of psychomotor skills a particular toy claims to develop. And it is up to the informed consumer, most commonly mothers, to make the appropriate product choices. This section takes up these issues through a focus on constructs of childhood and motherhood in parenting magazines.

Most first-time mothers buy or are given pregnancy, childbirth, and baby-care books which they consult religiously (cf. Urwin, 1985). These texts, according to Urwin, help women learn about normative constructs of mothering, and about children's cognitive, behavioral, and physical development. Such texts are consulted by women both as a check on, and in anticipation of, expected development. Given the paucity of information many women receive from their doctors and clinics, and their reluctance to consult their doctors with questions they might find trivial (Todd, 1989; Waitzkin,1991), women rely heavily on information exchanged with other mothers, books, television, and magazines. Unlike books, magazines are relatively cheap, the articles are usually short, written in nonmedical jargon and therefore easy to read, and the glossy illustrations provide appealing imageries of happy and good-looking mothers, babies, and toddlers.

Magazines offer visions of childhood and motherhood which both model and reinforce normative ideas of feminine desire located in idealized motherhood and childhood: of cute babies and stylishly dressed toddlers, of powerful emotional moments of bonding, tranquillity, and symbiotic identification which these texts and images consistently claim as intrinsic to the "most important time in a mother's and baby's life." Such visions of feminine destiny are socialized into girls early beginning with the toys parents buy to initiate girls into feminine discourses of nurture and domesticity. Toys come and go, but the "bread and butter" staples of girls' toys remain remarkably constant: from little ironing boards, miniature kitchens, stoves and toasters, to dolls, mini strollers, baby buggies, snugglipacks, and cribs. My analysis below suggests that parenting and childcare magazines both reinforce traditional gender values and experiences most women learned as girls, and prepare new mothers to reproduce those experiences with their own children.

Parenting/Mothering Texts

I collected magazines on parenting and mothering over a six-month period in 1992. The total textual corpus consisted of twenty-three magazines of which six were analysed in detail for this study.[1] I had not purchased or read magazines about babies for some twenty years. My initial reading of these magazines for this study was radically different from how I think I first read those magazines as a young mother. Once I started reading issues of *Parents*, I became fascinated with the discourse and quickly started gathering other magazines: American *Mothering*, *Parent's Digest* and *Parents*, and British *Practical*

Parenting.[2] On a first glance through the magazines, three things became immediately apparent. First, without reading any of the (mostly redundant) articles, I was struck by the complete absence of women and children of color in Australian and British magazines. Secondly, I was also surprised at the overwhelming amount of advertising in American magazines compared with British and Australian ones. The construction of infancy and early childhood in the baby gadgets and world of instructional toys has produced ever finer distinctions within childhood by the increased segmentation of mothering activities, developmental stages, and mother and baby needs that the infant commodity discourse claims to cater to.

Finally, as I had anticipated, the concept of parenting by which most magazines identify their readership has very little to do with male parenting or fatherhood. All magazines address a woman who is implicitly assumed to be in a heterosexual relationship with a relatively comfortable male wage to support many of the commodity-based fantasies of motherhood. Men for the most part are excluded from the visual and textual discourse of these magazines. Their presence is token, stereotyped, disengaged from domestic and child care, and most often positioned in relation to articles on divorce, marriage problems, insurance or car ads, as celebrity endorsements or medical "experts." In the discussion below, I will take up representations of race first, followed by an analysis of children's gender representation before considering the gendered dimension assumed under the concept 'parenting'.

CONSTRUCTS OF RACE

In six monthly issues of Australian *Parents*, not one photo of mothers, fathers or children of color was published in either feature articles or advertisements. Over a six-month period, only one item under the regular column "The Growing Years: 6–10 Years" addressed race/ethnicity. Titled, "Higher Marks for Asian Children," the short 200-word column explained how "cultural motivation for academic achievement" helps Asian children achieve (August/September 1992, 72). The September 1992 issue of Australian *Mother & Baby* featured children of color in an article on a Kenyan baby adopted by the magazine through Foster Parents Plan ("Our Boy Moses"). Five photos accompanied the article all featuring Kenyan children, aid, and adoption workers, and one photo of Moses and his mother. The text focuses primarily on the benefits and costs of child sponsorship, and profiles Moses and his mother. Identifying Moses as "our boy" co-opts him as commodity purchased with

Western aid dollars, and "Moses" erases his cultural identity and names him as one of ours: a Westernized, christian, "spiritual" kin.

While the efforts of Foster Parents agencies is unquestionably laudable, this vision of children and mothers of color is one that is reproduced across televisual and other magazine texts in innumerable Third World aid appeals. Western aid appeals for colonized peoples elsewhere reinforce the stereotypes of Third World destitution and does little to foreground persons of color in positive contexts in the very culture in which this magazine is located. American *Mothering*, *Parents*, and *Parent's Digest*, however, tell a slightly different pictorial and textual story.

Out of thirty ads with photos in the Winter 1992 issue of *Mothering*, only one featured an African-American mother and infant, the rest were Anglo-American. Out of sixty-seven nonadvertising photos, only eight featured mothers and children of color. *Parent's Digest* (Winter 1992) also scores poorly in its representation of children of color. A total of 163 children appeared in photo illustrations of which 29 (18%) were of identifiably racial and ethnic origin. Of 119 photo illustrations of various combinations of adults and children, only three featured adults of color, one of whom is Magic Johnson talking to a group of school-aged children. Clearly, *Parent's Digest* has little to offer in the way of multi-racial and multicultural visions of childhood or parenting. The context in which children of color are featured in this issue portrays them primarily on their own, as product users, and as audience for male celebrities involved in "charity" work (e.g., Paul Newman, Magic Johnson).

The October 1992 issue of American *Parents* is a 267-page issue featuring a total of 182 photo representations of babies, toddlers, and children of which only 29 (15.9%) are identifiably children of color: mostly African-American, followed by Asian, and Latina/Hispanic. Of those 29 representations, 12 featured girls, 15 featured boys, and two featured gender neutral shots, mostly of babies. Only three composite photos showed children of color with what the reader is to assume are adults in parenting roles. One portrays an African-American woman with her three sons as part of an article on what parents think about schools. Another features an African-American mother and her daughter mixing what looks like cookie mix in a bowl as part of an article on getting preschoolers ready for school. A third photo features an African-American mother with two children as part of a vaccination ad. The caption reads: "I never realized my kids might need a second measles vaccination." The fourth photo features an African-American mother, father, and young boy in a stressful situation to reflect the article's focus on children's jealousy.

Most of the children of color in this issue were featured with other children or alone. Three out of four child-parent portrayals featured women only with their children. The one photo which included a paternal figure featured a relatively negative family portrayal: a young boy clings to his mother and rebukes his father with a hostile look. The ideological underpinning of this visual representation implicitly supports the worst of negative stereotypes about the African-American family. Since this is the only image of an African-American father-son relationship in a 266-page issue, the hostile and negative imagery of the photo (further supported by the "problems" addressed in the article) represents a negative and stereotyped construct of African-American male relationships and family.

Three other photos signifying "family contexts" show only women with children which can be interpreted to represent and reinforce the current dominant image of African-American households as female-headed. On my reading, the vaccination ad provides an implicit racist and sexist commentary by positioning the woman as uninformed, naive, and potentially negligent. While it is not uncommon for pharmaceutical advertising to construct women in stereotypical roles, as irresponsible, unreliable, and not the best judges of their health, illness, or symptoms, the use of an African-American woman in this ad enables both race and feminine gender to intersect at the nodal point of ignorance and potential maternal negligence: "I never realized my kids might need a second measles vaccination!"

The photo of a mother and daughter whipping up batter with a mixmaster is a classic portrayal of feminine gender socialisation. Of interest, however, is that such an image should feature as part of an article on "school readiness." The article points out that the "Three Rs" should be replaced with the "Four Cs": communication, curiosity, creativity, and cooperation. The "Four Cs" seem commonsense enough. However, the "Four Cs" do not conceptually or pedagogically translate into the kinds of stereotypical mother-daughter tasks portrayed in the photo or its association with "school readiness." The gendered subtext of this particular article is discussed in further detail in the next section.

CONSTRUCTS OF GENDER

Each issue of Australian *Parents* is approximately 100 pages in length and includes an average of twenty-five feature articles, nine regular columns, and forty advertisements of which approximately twenty per issue include photos. One issue (August/September 1992) carried 21 photo ads which featured five boys, two girls, and the remaining 14 showed infants in gender neutral outfits. Articles in *Parents* consistently reproduce gendered play patterns. One article, "I Can Do It Myself," draws on the wisdom of developmental psychologists and advises mothers how to help children emulate tasks that parents and caregivers do routinely around the house: from buttering bread, to mopping up, making phone calls, and carrying dishes. The gendered division of play/labor in this layout is unmistakable: girls are shown arranging flowers, putting on makeup, doing dishes, and putting on boots. Boys are shown in only two photos: one mopping the floor, the other on the phone.

Parent's Digest (Winter 1992) features 163 images of children of which 61 are identifiably female, 64 are male, and the remainder are in sexually neutral representations (table 7.1). Of 61 female portrayals, 38 showed girls in relation to products and actively engaged in activities; the remainder were portrayed doing nothing in particular. Of those 38 images, the largest percentage (29%) associated girls with food, eating, fashion and hair (N=13). Boys were portrayed in 30 activities and in relation to products, and were most frequently associated with eating (N=7) and reading (N=6).

Although girls appeared more frequently and were shown in a greater variety of activities than boys, girls and boys in this text are positioned in traditional gendered play and activities. Proportional to total male representations, boys in this text are more frequently shown outside, associated with reading, writing, sports, and computers. Girls are shown more frequently indoors and concerned with fashion, hair, and jewellery.

CONSTRUCTS OF PARENTING

In the sense that parenting is most commonly understood to mean maternal and paternal involvement in childrearing, parenting in the magazines surveyed here is not about parenting at all. Magazines like *Parents* or *Parenting* may claim to address mothers and fathers, and to tackle childrearing issues of joint concern, but parenting remains firmly associated with women and mothering.

Of all the magazines surveyed, only *Mother & Baby* (November 1992) and American *Mothering* (Winter 1992) included an article on homosexual parenthood. Titled "Being Gay," the article in *Mothering* constructed homosexuality as a "normal variation" and emphasized

TABLE 7.1
Representations of Gendered Activities in *Parent's Digest* (1992)

Girls	Boys
Engaged with food/eating, fashion, hair (N=13)	Reading/holding books (N=7)
Playing musical instruments (N=5)	Eating (N=6)
Reading/holding books (N=4)	Writing (N=2)
Smiling for detergent (N=2)	Playing in a creek (N=2)
Painting/drawing (N=2)	Rollerblading (N=2)
Blowing dandelions (N=2)	Boating (N=2)
Skipping rope (N=2)	Playing on a swing (N=1)
Sitting at a computer following instructions from a boy (N=2)	Playing tug-of-war (N=1)
Playing with Playskool busy balls and beads (N=2)	Giving instructions at a computer (N=1)
Sitting on a Playskool locomotive (N=1)	Playing with a Playskool computer (N=1)
Riding a bike (N=1)	Playing chess (N=1)
Playing teacher (N=1)	Sitting in a wheelchair (N=1)
Playing with mother's jewelry (N=1)	Playing softball (N=1)
	Playing with Playskool busy gears (N=1)
	Sitting on a Playskool locomotive (N=1)

that sexual orientation has little to do with desires and commitment to fatherhood or motherhood. The article provides strategies for lesbian mothers and gay fathers to cope with homophobia and the negative messages children bring home from school, peers, and playground. The accompanying photo illustrations feature two men in embrace on the title page, a photo of two women and one child on the following page, and a photo of a man holding an infant on another page.

Australian *Mother & Baby*, by contrast, constructed gay parenting as an exclusively lesbian relationship. Two women were featured in "Two Mums & a Baby." Two photos accompany the text showing two women and an infant smiling happily at the camera. The text, much like that in *Mothering*'s "Being Gay," outlines the negative sociocultural responses communities often level against gay family formations, and presents arguments in favor of families headed by two women. In my estimation, the photo illustrations and text portray a positive image of lesbian parenting. However, the failure to address male homosexual parenting implicitly reaffirms parenting as mothering, as fundamentally connected to women.

Parent's Digest presents a less inclusive pictorial record of men. The 161-page Winter 1992 issue features a total of 119 photo illustrations of adults and children in various combinations. I excluded photos of the editorial staff and their children. Of the 119 shots featuring adults, only 18 featured men. Six were of celebrities, three portrayed men demonstrating lifesaving strategies for choking victims, one male featured in an insurance ad, and another accompanied an article advising readers "to put marriage first." One photo shows a male playing a board game with a boy and girl accompanying an article on divorce, and partial masculinity is featured in one ad for Johnson's which shows a male hand and forearm holding an infant.

The remaining five photos show a man and young boy on a tire swing for Oshkosh; a small photo of a family on bicycles accompanies a "bike safety" article; one black and white photo shows a mother helping youngsters into a school bus while the father waits in the background. In an article titled "Raising Daughters, Raising Sons," two photos feature dads and their boys. One is of a white male and his preschooler son cutting up some food on the kitchen table. On my reading, this is the only image that depicts active male parenting in a nontraditional context. The other photo accompanying this article is the only representation of African-American fatherhood in this issue: it features a father and son embracing with a big grin for the camera.

Of eighteen male images in this issue, then, only one can be interpreted to count as active and nonstereotyped male involvement in childcare. Only three other images feature a male in a parenting context: the father-son play scene for Oshkosh, the family bike ride, and the anonymous male arms holding a nude Johnson's baby. While a father riding bikes with the family and playing with his son on a tire-swing are predictable stereotyped representations, the Johnson's ad featuring male hands holding a newborn infant breaks with traditional imageries of fatherhood. However, by showing only hands and forearms as iconic shorthand for a male, the disembodied relationship between father and infant precludes both symbolic and actual (i.e., visual) confirmation of any emotional or physical ties between father and infant. The male is shown without head or body, and there is no bonding look between adult and infant—a visual connection which pervades almost all shots of mothers and infants in all the magazines surveyed.

American *Parents* featured a total of 133 adults in individual and group shots with children and other adults. Out of a total of 133 adults, 29 were men, and 104 were women. Only six out of twenty-nine images showed men engaged with children, and only five of those could be construed as active engagement in parenting activities. One features a variation of the father-son ad series for Oshkosh; another features an African-American father with a woman and young boy in an article on jealousy (discussed earlier); the third image shows a father's face close to an infant in what could be read as a "bonding moment" for Baby Fresh wipes; the fourth shows father and son reading a book together; lastly, one image portrays a family of four washing the family car as part of an article on "Ten Simple Ways to Add Years to the Life of Your Car."

The remaining male images feature men as Santa Claus, experts (doctors, professors), and in connection with ads for cars, car seats, insurance, gourmet kitchenware, and toys. Others show men accompanying articles on the death of a child, fitness programs, jealousy in marriage, raising children after divorce. Men also appear in celebrity endorsements such as Bill Cosby for Kodak, Carl Lewis for Panasonic, and Paul Newman for "Newman's Own." As in other magazines, men frequently appear in humorous "comic corners": literally as a joke.

Men in *Parents*, as in other magazines surveyed here, do not function as paternal signifiers in active male parenting roles. Men primarily function as expert signifiers, as celebrity endorsements, and as counterpoint to women in the context of "social problems" such as jealousy, divorce, separation, and other marriage and relationship issues. Men's peripheral role in parenting across all the magazines surveyed suggests that infant and childcare remains women's work and destiny.

Girls' and boys' numerical representation is about equal in these magazines, but they remain positioned in retrograde traditional roles. Men, gay and lesbian parents, and parents and children of culturally different backgrounds, are largely absent, or else cast in stereotypical and often culturally offensive representations. The way sexuality and race/ethnicity are commonly represented in media texts and commodity forms tends towards reified and simplistic identities which occlude differences among groups. In childcare magazines, not only are adults and children of color marginalized visually and textually, but for the most part they are appropriated into a bourgeois middle-class discourse which homogenizes cultural differences and constructs their token inclusions within the discourse, fantasies and desires of ruling class culture.

CONCLUSION: CONTRADICTORY IMAGES
OF PARENTHOOD AND CHILDHOOD

I have here shown how the marketplace of childhood promotes highly gender-differentiated constructs of the child in the media and toy industries, and in parenting magazines. Whether in the toystore, on television, or in magazines—childhood and parenthood are made intelligible through a vast array of niche-marketed cultural goods, embedded in sexist and racist discourses. But cultural texts and markets are never simple either/or choices for "reader"-consumers, and there is a danger of viewing such texts as monoglossically or unproblematically pro- or anti-woman, pro- or anti-gay or particular cultures—as tends to happen in media, public and often academic debate over so-called "political correctness." I wish to conclude by highlighting the contradictory and often ambiguous status of such texts.

Within "mass access" public discourses of television, cinema, and lifestyle magazines, the social and economic restructuring of the Western family are being re-presented, albeit within ideologically disciplining limits. Starting in the mid-1980s, "new age fathers" began to appear on television, in clothing and scent ads: the man of the moment was shown with laptop computer in one hand, a briefcase in the other, and a baby tucked in a "natural fibre" designer baby-backpack. American Calvin Klein ads were in the forefront of celebrating the new sexy male whose appeal and virility was constructed not only in relation to a sexy partner, a sculpted body, and good taste in clothes, but in relation to a new sexualized object—an infant or young child. The child in such ads functions as a culturally and ideologically significant prop in redefinitions of upscale 1990s female-male relationships, the politics of choice, sexual and social identity.

In the 1980s, the marketing of "new" visions of family and lifestyle choices emerged in television family sit-coms which brought us the postfeminist family (cf. Probyn, 1990), and in mainstream cinema which celebrated fatherhood (*Raising Arizona, Three Men and a Baby, Look Who's Talking*), and valorized motherhood over devastating career choices (*Fatal Attraction, Baby Boom*). Whereas television narratives and lifestyle magazine ads glamorize parenthood as a designer add-on to affluent, white, two-career couples and, indeed, can be read to signify the politics of choice, that vision disappears altogether in parenting and childcare magazines. In these discourses a far more traditional regime of femininity, motherhood, and domesticity is at work. Here, career, new age male partners, or sexuality are excluded from visions of feminine identity which are reconstructed solely around the pleasures of maternity and nurturing an other. Care of the self is displaced by care and nurture of a child which depends crucially on an implicit but assumed heterosexual marriage within a nuclear family.

Raising infants in this discourse is a lonely and isolated task. Daycare, friends, neighbors, and partners are absent from the pictographic and textual landscape. Women are on their own, most commonly shown inside the house, and engaged only in activities centred on a child. Her socially isolated relationship with an infant or toddler suggests that she is solely responsible for the early formation of a child's values and behaviors. She has sole moral responsibility for the upbringing of a new generation, and is thus positioned as the only candidate to blame for children's subsequent dysfunctional development.

The magazines' specialized sections map the stages not only of child development but normative expectations of a mother's psychological orientation and social responsibility in relation to those stages. These stages are invariably tied to the consumer products which claim to facilitate and enhance those stages. Advertising text exhorts women to become informed consumers in the best interests of their children's welfare. The importance of being well informed and one step ahead of her child's development in order to make the appropriate product choice (whether of snugglipacks, nappies, cereals, or medicines) is a recurring message for women. The lessons for women encourage them to study up on child development, to learn about product ranges, and to exercise informed consumer judgment in making correct product choices that match children's stage/age-related needs. The construction of childhood, childcare, and motherhood as niche markets, and situating parentchild social bonds and familial relationships as crucially dependant on that market—product choices that guarantee "those special moments"—subtly provides women with the illusion of choice (cf. Knijn, 1994). The daily demands of childcare may not leave women much choice other than to respond to the child's immediate needs. Yet at the same time, the choice offered on the marketplace of childhood enables her to reclaim some measure of self-directed, albeit illusory, choice and agency.

The child in this discourse is an object of feminine desire, and yet it is a desiring and consuming subject in its own right. The child's maturing social and cognitive needs are intelligible primarily through the product ranges available to enhance and develop those needs: from Fisher-Price pedagogy to the tiny tots identity business of fashion offered by "Esprit," "Benetton," Reeboks' "Weeboks," or the latest McDonald's "McKids" designer wear (cf. Willis, 1991).

How-to and self-help books and magazines can teach us lessons in manners, cooking, health and fitness, childcare, building construction, financial planning, car maintenance, or skills for career success. All of us have, at some time or another, taught ourselves from these books or magazines. Like television, books and magazines address us individually, but we nonetheless read and view collectively as mass readership or viewing audience. In staffrooms across the nation, people talk about last night's television programs or the weekend sports event. Kids enact media heroes or favorite programs in schoolyard play and interweave those texts in their written work. Women buy and share childcare magazines with other women, and they are also the primary purchasers of children's commodities. In short, popular cultural texts are indeed constitutive of "real" experience, and they do provide a mass cultural ideological framework which people variously dismiss, engage in, or buy into. Because public culture is woven into every crevice of everyday experience and cuts across traditional boundaries of class, ethnicity, age, and, certainly, nation and geography, the public texts of popular culture are probably a more powerful pedagogy than the generally decontextualized knowledge and skills taught in formal institutions of learning, disconnected as they are from what is referred to as "the real world."

Parenting magazines present only one version of motherhood. Yet specialized parenting magazines such as those analysed here provide a conservative and traditional vision of femininity, motherhood, and family. It is a vision which largely excludes women and children of color, single mothers, poor mothers, fathers, and nonheterosexual family formations. In contrast to "postfeminist" visions of family and parenthood in other mass media and cultural texts, the discourse of parenting magazines remains decidedly prefeminist.

How parents are to understand childhood and structure their children's experiences is today increasingly determined by the production of childhood as a market. And while many parents refuse or can't afford to buy into the system, the global expansion of commercialized childhood culture and massive profit returns, suggest that the majority of parents, indeed, *are* buying. What parents buy into, however, is a commodified cultural narrative that is highly gender segregated, almost exclusively white, middle-class, and heterosexual. Toys and toystores, movies and television, parenting books and magazines, or videogames and corporate mall playgrounds, weave a mass cultural construct of affluent Western childhood and parenthood, "winking" seductively at parents and kids. Many women in at some point in their life trajectories will assume the positioning and practices of mothering: how the texts and artifacts of mainstream culture construct motherhood and childhood stands as a powerful normalising discipline with and against alternative and feminist constructs.

NOTES

An earlier version of this chapter was originally published in the *Australian and New Zealand Journal of Sociology* (La Trobe University Press), 30(3) (1995).

1. One issue per magazine was selected for analysis on the basis of what I judged to be the most representative issue in a six-month period. Initially, my interest was in Australian *Mother & Baby* (AU $4.20) and *Parents* (AU $3.95), both published by the same company. The circulation staff of *Parents* advised that it has the highest exposure of all Australian childcare magazines with a monthly readership of 178,000, which includes household subscriptions, over the counter and hospital/clinic sales, shared and/or exchanged magazines. *Mother and Baby* is a relatively expensive magazine and has a readership of 166,000. I also sought circulation figures from British *Practical Parenting*, (£1.20) and American *Mothering* (US $5.95), *Parents* (US $2.25), and *Parent's Digest* (US $2.95), but received a reply only from *Mothering*, which claims a circulation of 66,342 excluding shared or exchanged magazines.

2. I considered overseas magazines relevant for analysis because they are available on Australian news-stands and, clearly, women are buying them in volume.

REFERENCES

Ang, I. (1985). *Watching Dallas: Soap opera and the melodramatic imagination*. London: Methuen.

Baudrillard, J. (1981). *For a critique of the political economy of the sign* (C. Levin, Trans.). St. Louis: Telos Press.

—— (1988). Simulacra and simulations. In M. Poster (Ed.), *Jean Baudrillard: Selected writings* (pp. 166–184). Originally published in *Semiotext(e)* (1983), 1–13, 23–49.

Bourdieu, P. (1984). *Distinction: A social critique of the judgement of taste*. New York: Routledge & Kegan Paul.

Butsch, R. (Ed.) (1990). *For fun and profit*. Philadelphia: Temple University Press.

Engelhardt, T. (1986). Children's television: The shortcake strategy. in T. Gitlin (Ed.), *Watching television* (pp. 68–110). New York: Pantheon.

Ewen, S. (1988). *All consuming images*. New York: Basic Books.

Foucault, M. (1972). *The archaeology of knowledge* (A. Sheridan, Trans.). New York: Harper.

186   POPULAR CULTURE AS PUBLIC PEDAGOGY

———— (1981). *Power/knowledge: Selected interviews & other writings 1972–1977* (C. Gordon, Ed.). New York: Pantheon Books.

Kaplan, E. A. (1992). *Motherhood and representation: The mother in popular culture and melodrama.* New York: Routledge.

Kinder, M. (1991). *Playing with power in movies, television and video games: From Muppet Babies to Teenage Mutant Ninja Turtles.* Berkeley, CA: University of California Press.

Kline, S. (1993). *Out of the garden: Toys and children's culture in the age of TV marketing.* Toronto: Garamond Press.

Knijn, T. (1994). Social dilemmas in images of motherhood in the Netherlands. *The European Journal of Women's Studies,* 1(2), 183–206.

Luke, C. (1990a). *Constructing the child viewer.* New York: Praeger.

———— (1990b). *TV and your child.* Sydney: HarperCollins.

———— (1990c). On reading the child: A feminist poststructuralist perspective. *Australian Journal of Reading,* 14(2), 109–116.

———— (1993). Television curriculum and popular literacy: Feminine identity politics and family discourse. In B. Green (Ed.), *The Insistence of the letter: Literacy studies and curriculum theorizing* (pp. 175–194). London, Falmer Press.

———— (1994). Feminist pedagogy and critical media literacy. *Journal of Communication Inquiry,* 18(2), 27–44.

———— (1996, in press). Media and cultural studies. In P. Freebody, A. Muspratt, & A. Luke (Eds.), *Constructing critical literaries,* Norwood, NJ: Hampton Press.

McNeal, J. (1987). *Children as consumers.* Lexington, MA: Lexington Books.

Phoenix, A., Woollett, A., & Lloyd, E. (Eds.) (1991). *Motherhood: Meanings, practices and ideologies.* London: Sage.

Probyn, E. (1990). TV does the home. *Screen,* 31(2), 147–159.

Seiter, E. (1991). Toys are us: Marketing to children and parents. *Cultural Studies,* 6, 232–247.

Todd, A. (1989). *Intimate adversaries: Cultural conflict between doctors and women patients.* Philadelphia: University of Pennsylvania Press.

Urwin, C. (1985). Constructing motherhood: The persuasion of normal development. In C. Steedman, C. Urwin, & V. Walkerdine (Eds.), *Language, gender and childhood.* London: Routledge & Kegan Paul.

Waitzkin, H. (1991). *The politics of medical encounters*. New Haven, CT: Yale University Press.

Williams, R. (1980/1962). *Problems in materialism and culture*. London: New Left Books.

Willis, S. (1991). *A primer for daily life*. Routledge: New York.

CHAPTER 8

PLAY FOR PROFIT

Susan Willis

Amusement is the assimilation of all sorts of imaginative and spontaneous forms of play to the commodity form; hence it is play's negation. I am fascinated by play because I see it as a practice that promotes the creative imagination, challenges social order, and facilitates communal social relations—all the things that capitalist consumer culture aims to eradicate. Conversely, I am appalled by the insistant availability of amusements, that turn fun into something you buy and parenting into a negotiated relationship between avid child consumers and put-upon parental nay-sayers.

In working with a definition that opposes play to amusement, I challenge the common practice in cultural studies today which tends to read resistance into practically anything and everything that people do to make meanings and define themselves in consumerist society. I maintain that the great majority of everyday leisure-time activities are so assimilated to consumerism and the commodity form that they leave little room for imaginative meaning making, let alone oppositional or utopian practices. I also realize that there is no form of play available to us that either pre-dates capitalism or escapes its ideologies and social formations. Most play involves a commodity—a toy of some sort, a media concept, or media-generated identity. So, I'm not suggesting play as an idealized category, but an imaginative social practice so remarkable that when you witness it you realize you are seeing something that cannot obtain in the culture of amusement. Indeed, one particular form of play, children's role-playing games, so clearly distinguishes itself from amusement activities as to provide a means for critically assessing capitalist culture as a whole. Role-playing games often enact contradiction. Such is the case when children use play to imagine expanded gender possibilities such as a female spaceship pilot or basketball star who is at the same time a nurturing agent. Enactments of gender such as these offer imaginary resolution to the contradictory inequalities between men and women that children perceive in the larger society. Similarly, when children play at working, they set aside economic and social constraints that typify adult labor. Performing the activites of carpenters, fire fighters, secretaries, and check-out clerks, they situate work in an imaginary system aimed at the production of fun rather than wages and profits. In *Minima Moralia*, Theodor Adorno remarked the utopian possibilities of play when he observed how a child playing with a toy truck and its cargo transformed the alienation of purposeful behavior that characterizes labor into a performative negation of production and a means for experiencing pleasure (Adorno, 1989, 228).

I realize, too, that a great many sociologists of play will not agree with my definition of children's role-playing games as a form of play that challenges received social identities. The predominant tendency in ethnographic studies of play is to see children's role-playing games as enforcing social stereotypes. Vivian Paley, a teacher who studies and writes about her pupils' play, sees "kindergarten [as] a triumph of sexual self-stereotyping" (Paley, 1984, ix). According to Paley, three-year-olds display a fluid relationship to gender in their play. Boys and girls in preschool, play together and exchange or mix costume accoutrements and gender roles. "Policemen sweep the floor and dress the baby, and mothers put men's vests over negligees while making vague appointments on the telephone" (Paley, 1984, x). According to Paley, these hybrid gender identities tend towards polarization in four-year-olds and finally produce in kindergarten a dramatic opposition between boys who play at being weapon-toting superheroes and girls who represent themselves in "good little families" (Paley, 1984, 3).

In Paley's accounts, the girls are typically in the classroom doll corner working out the dynamic between "Mother, Sister, Baby, and Maid" (Paley, 1984, 1) when they are invaded by a boy gang of robbers, "'Do you got any gold?' 'No,' Charlotte says, stirring an empty pot" (Paley, 1984, 1). I don't refute the scenario (I've witnessed many similar instances of play) nor would I dispute the gender stereotyping that informs much of children's play. But I would question whether observations drawn from a kindergarten classroom ought to be taken as indicative of all play. What seems most problematic in this particular ethnography is the existence of gender-specific play areas such as a "doll corner," and Paley's role as a teacher that requires her to maintain the "appearance of control" (Paley, 1984, x). My own observations of play lack the daily regularity of a kindergarten teacher, but because I observe children outside of school as well as in the classroom, in playgrounds, in community parks and schoolyards, and in private homes, I can expand on Paley's findings. First of all, I would say that gender hybridization or the mixing of genders in play doesn't cease at age five. I recently observed three children (two boys and one girl) ranging in age from six to ten who were playing at caring for two stuffed animals (a teddy bear and a buffalo). This version of "playing house" was initiated by the youngest child, the girl; but it was clear by their conversation that the imaginary contours of their "house" did not conform to a traditionally defined female domestic setting. The boys played at teaching the bear and buffalo how to use a computer, and the computer blew up, injuring the buffalo. "Give Buffy his medicine," ordered the girl. This was achieved by poking a crayon into a salt shaker and pouring the imaginary brew down the buffalo's throat. The rest of the game involved lots of nurturing with pillows and blankets for the buffalo, lots of disputes over the care required and who would administer it, and occasional outbursts of roughhousing when the buffalo would revive to become a weapon for bopping one or the other child over the head. Outside the classroom, boys play at nurturing long past kindergarten and girls can act assertive, rebellious, and disruptive, or even take on the role of superhero.

Rather than confirming polarized gender stereotypes, I would say that children's play has the power to liberate the imagination and transform traditional social identities. This is because the players are constantly testing, challenging, and redefining their relationships to each other and to society at large. I have witnessed countless role-playing games where children stretched, bent, or broke their social realities. They play at being the opposite sex, the "other's" race, or another's age. And they do so not as individuals, but as participants in the ever-changing context of the game's system of social relations. I know of no practice available to adults—not even the study and articulation of critical theory—that offers an analogous pleasurable means for estranging all the existing, normalized social forms and behaviors so as to scrutinize them and enact their transformation.

Even when children evoke gender stereotypes, their play may be an ironic enactment of a critical distance from the stereotype. Not long ago I observed two young girls playing "Halloween." It was a blazing hot day in the middle of summer. Although the girls were dressed in shorts and T-shirts, they enacted imaginary princess costumes and spent a lot of time admiring and adjusting invisible long skirts and complicated bodices. They were pulling a wagon from imaginary house to house which transmuted from a carriage intended to transport one or the other princess to a booty barge for the imaginary Halloween loot.

On the basis of visual evidence, they looked like two girls pulling a wagon, gesturing, and talking. Their conversation sketched out an elaborate fantasy that shifted the season from summer to fall and produced a game that fluctuated between two girls pretending to be "trick-or-treating" in princess costumes and two girls pretending to be "real" princesses who encountered demons, witches, and monsters in the course of journeying from one castle to the next.

This role-playing game dramatizes the strength of creative imagination. It also reveals that identity need not be conceptualized as a "type" but may instead be a fluid category that emerges out of social practice and relationships. Moreover, in this game the female stereotype of princess is both uncritically accepted by the two young girls and at the same time the object of critical scrutiny. The pleasure of optimal femininity embodied in being a princess and wearing long, elegant dresses is balanced against the equal pleasure of turning princesshood into a Halloween farce. The game is an imaginative performance where two real girls play at being unreal girls, testing in their game the likelihood of playing the way they do in the dresses they imagine. Imaginative role-playing games such as this are so complicated that everything I write seems to confine its fluidity and transformative power to reductive conceptual categories. I know of only one study that comes close to demonstrating how play creates allegorical reverberations in the construction of both real and fantasy meanings. This is an essay by Ana Mayanovic-Shane published in *Play and Culture*, a journal devoted to analyses of play whose main body of offerings tends more towards sociology than theory. Mayanovic-Shane contends that in play children construct a "fictive plane" (Mayanovic-Shane, 1989, 227) which remains in communication with the children's reality and enables them to deconstruct meanings in both fiction and reality. This, she suggests, is laden with more complicated meanings than the adult activity of making metaphors, but it's one whose implications can always be avoided by labelling the entire activity as "pretend."

Opposed to imaginative play is an amusement culture that presses play into a pedagogy of prescribed purposeful activites. The spontaneous, sometimes quirky activites and gender definitions that characterize creative play have no place in amusement, which is instead dominated by a controlled environment and menued choices. I find the notion of a menu an appallingly explicit reference to a society that equates doing with consuming and democracy with expanded consumer choice. Ours is a society that instructs categorical thought. If it's not in the computerized menu and its possible combination of ingredients, then it can't be imagined. Nintendo heroes race through elaborate mazes, beset by foes and unexpected shifts in the terrain—all of it pre-programmed and packaged in software. Children's commercial culture boasts an extravagant array of media images; but the virtual reality, mixed media graphics, and interactive formats bespeak a culture where the utopian imagination is pushed to the margins of daily life and haunts its elsewheres. You're not likely to get disruptive social models such as Gameboy heroes who befriend their opponents or win by turning rivalry and combat into play or festival, nor are you likely to find a balloon at the end of a fishing line or anything that smacks of surrealism.

Conformity to normative thought was not born with amusement culture, but is endemic to the process of socialization and is particularly enforced in public education. I recall that one of my children was told she was "wrong" for having drawn a fish at the end of a kite string. Maybe the kindergarten teacher hadn't read George MacDonald's classic *The Golden Key* and so knew nothing about "air fish." As frustrating as public education can be, there is, nevertheless, a huge difference between the way normative thought is enforced in school and the computerized logic of Nintendo. The classroom is a socially constructed and negotiated space which interactive video is not. As I parent, I get upset when my children come home from school with stories of having been criticized for their imagination or rebuked for behaviors that contest restrictive gender definitions (such as the time my eight-year-old son was admonished for holding hands with his best friend: a boy). But schooling is as much a pedagogy of enforced disciplinary norms as it is the laboratory for their resistance.

The only recognizable drawback to amusement culture, besides the need to secure spending money and transportation, is menu tedium: a hundred eventualities and all of them predictably rational. "This game's no fun." "What I really want is 'Tetris' or 'Carmen Sandiego,' maybe 'Final Fantasy'." The rational universe of consumer culture expands by replication, filling up internally with more of the same. Imagination finds no outlet but to generate the trivial details that distinguish one game from the next. Our culture may be dominant but it lacks the flights of fantasy that characterize García Marquez's magical realism. Colombia's Nobel laureate has often spoken out against Western logic and its assimilation to the mass commodity market. In a videotaped interview aired on the Bravo channel, he commented, "The moment you have Cartesianism, a rigour of thought that doesn't allow the imagination to fly, there's bound to be lots of things people miss. If a French person really saw a girl fly up into the sky in body and soul, he'd never dare tell anyone for fear of appearing crazy. There's no place for it in his realism" (García Marquez, 1989). Marquez's response to Western imperial logic is to strategize appropriations of the mass forms. He went so far as to propose radical teledramas or soap operas. If Marquez can conceptualize a critical soap opera, might he or someone like him invent the equivalent of magical realism in a Nintendo format? I think not. The abstracted hyperspace of interactive video is the cancellation of magical realism's more human landscape.

Nowhere is the antithesis between play and amusement more evident than at Disney World. At this, the world's most highly developed private property "state" devoted to amusement, play is all but eliminated by the absolute domination of program over spontaneity. Every ride runs to computerized schedule. There is no possibility of an awful thrill, like being stuck at the top of an old-fashioned ferris wheel. Disney is not carnival. Order prevails particularly in the queues for the rides which zigzag dutifully on a prescribed path created out of stanchions and ropes; moreover, the visitor's assimilation into the queue does not catapult him or her into another universe, as it might if Jorge Luis Borges had fabricated the program. The Disney labyrinth is a banal extension of the ride's point of embarkation, which extends into the ride as a hyper-themed continuation of the queue. The longest queue in the world is the "Backstage Movie Tour" at Disney's MGM Studios which has done away with the distinction between the ride and its queue by condemning the visitor to a two-and-a-half-hour-long pedagogical journey that preaches the process of movie production. Guests are mercilessly herded through sound stages and conveyed across endless back lots where one is treated to the banality of conventional ranch-style houses used in television commercials and a couple of wrecked cars from movie chase scenes. Happily, there are a few discreet exit doors, bail-out points for parents with bored children.

To date, three five-day-long research trips to the Magic Kingdom have netted me only one observed instance of play. This occurred when a group of youngsters tried on the sombreros at an open-air display booth and began their version of the Mexican Hat Dance. Their playful cavorting was clearly disruptive of the programmed flow of traffic. Visitors had trouble getting around and through them and into the designated attractions. In doing something that Mickey, Donald, and Goofy might have done in one of the early cartoons, these kids were breaking unwritten codes of conduct that are built into Disney World's designed environment.

What's curious about what's not at Disney is that there is no way of knowing what's missing until an aberrant event occurs and provokes the remembrance of the social forms and behaviors that have been left out. This was the case with the episode of spontaneous play. Until I saw real play, I didn't realize that it was missing. The incident stood out against a humdrum background of uniform amusement: hundreds of kids being pushed from attraction to attraction in their strollers, hundreds more waiting dutifully in the queues or marching about in family groups—all of them abstaining from the loud, jostling, teasing, and rivalrous behaviors that would otherwise characterize many of their activities.

Closing time promotes particularly dutiful and passive behavior amongst Disney guests. Rather than racing to snag one last ride or lag behind in an attempt to prolong the Magic Kingdom experience, tens of thousands of visitors feed themselves into the prescribed exit channels like the *Dawn of the Dead* zombies that George Romero portrayed in their final sleepwalking visit to a shopping mall. Everyone laboriously exits, funneling themselves towards the Magic Kingdoms' portal, thence into snaking queues for the monorail, which will convey them to more snaking queues to Disney trams, which will convey the lucky ones to hotels and the unlucky ones to parking lots with their inevitable vehicle queues.

Conformity with the park's program upholds the Disney value system. Purposeful consumption—while it costs the consumer a great deal—affirms the value of the consumer. "Don't forget, we drove twenty hours to get here." This is how one father admonished his young son who was squirming about on the floor of EPCOT's Independence Hall, waiting for the amusement to begin. The child's wanton and impatient waste of time was seen as a waste of the family's investment in its amusement. Everyone but the kids dancing the Mexican Hat Dance seemed to have accepted the park's unwritten motto: "If you pay, you shouldn't play." To get your money's worth, you have to do everything and do it in the prescribed manner. Free play is gratuitous and therefore a waste of the family's leisure time expenditure. If a family is to realize the full value of its leisure time consumptions, then every member must function as a proper consumer.

The success of Disney World as an amusement park has largely to do with the way its use of programming meshes with the economics of consumption as a value system. In a world wholly predicated on consumption, the dominant order need not proscribe those activities that run counter to consumption, such as free play and squirming, because the consuming public largely polices itself against gratuituous acts which would interefere with the production of consumption as a value. Conformity with the practice of consumption is so widespread at Disney that occasional manifestations of boredom or spontaneity do not influence the compulsively correct behavior of others. Independence Hall did not give way to a seething mass of squirming youngsters even though all had to sit through a twenty-minute wait. Nor did other children on the margins of the hat dance fling themselves into the fun.

I have been characterizing the absence of real play at Disney World in terms of its assimilation to amusement as a commodity form. I want now to consider the effects of privatization on the culture as a whole. The Reagan/Bush era saw a massive boost to private sector economics and the subsequent deepening of privatization in social and cultural forms. Following the election of President Clinton and the hope that a Democratic administration might revive a public sector bled dry for more than a decade, I realized how strongly my own work has been shaped by a struggle against the social and cultural manifestations of privatization. It remains to be seen if change at the level of politics can produce significant effects in society; or, more pessimistically, if the development of global capitalism transcends national politics, making the distinction between conservative and more liberal administrations epiphenomenal to deeply structured social relations that are locked into the global dominance of the corporations. In either case, the coming years will be a challenge for propenents of public life.

What's clear is that culture in the United States is fundamentally privatized in the various forms it delivers up for consumption. What I mean by a privatized culture has to do with the everyday ways that an economy dominated by the private sector translates itself into our trivial practices and intimate lives. The most striking and crippling manifestation of privatization is the way the culture is geared for individual consumption and enforces the separation of individuals from possible communal relationships. I recall that the advent of small, affordable computers (as opposed to those hulking consoles that inhabited an entire room of a university "computer center") was heralded by predictions of democratized public use. People imagined that computers would be made available in post offices, public libraries and schools, town halls, and community centers—all the underfunded sites that today define our embattled public sector. One year later the utopian vision had been superceeded by a mass advertising campaign that debuted on Super Bowl Sunday, where the personal computer was promoted for individual in-home use. Today many middle-class homes include one or more personal computers with an additional laptop for each of the household's traveling professionals. I see nothing democratizing in a technology so readily put to private use, wherein the individual user is necessarily separated from his or her immediate, practical relations with others and where the technology is available on a class-exclusive basis which then serves to enhance a class bias in the job market and society at large.

The proliferation of a private consumer culture is best exemplified by the popularity of interactive video, particularly Nintendo and the portable Gameboy. In her book, *Playing With Power*, Marsha Kinder praises Nintendo, seeing it as a means for enhancing cognitive skills in children and facilitating children's play relationships. She observes that many Nintendo games allow two players, some as many as four; and that children involved in joint play talk among themselves, often providing each other with helpful strategies (Kinder, 1991, 115). I find this an improverished form of interaction. Indeed, interactive video is a nice name for a technology that defines the individual's primary relationship to the program by way of the screen and joy stick, and only secondarily links the player to others who are by definition incidental. The machine mediates everything that would otherwise be socially defined from the actual physical relationship between the players, to their conversation, and thoughts about each other.

Most often children play as individuals with a friend hovering over the primary player's shoulder, witnessing and commenting on the play emanating from the screen. In such play scenarios, children need not interact except to dispute playing time and to argue over whose turn it is to play. Some children's primary attachment to Nintendo is so fundmental that they can't manage an invitation to play or sleep over at the house of a friend who does not have Nintendo. Such children are apt to bring their Nintendos with them like technological teddy bears which offer the security of continuing habitual practice in unfamiliar surroundings. The host child's home, family, and quirky behaviors need not be dealt with as long as Nintendo centers the child's reality.

Commercialized private play is both a program and a spatial system. Jody Berland has argued that the sort of spatial relationships that obtain in capitalist culture emerge out of a dialectic between productive technologies and audiences. According to Berland, audiences are as much the producers of space as are the parameters of technology. She points to the transformations in entertainment beginning with fairs, which were superceeded by music halls, which in turn gave way to the cinema. If fairs were disorderly sites of consumption, the music halls represented an initial move to reconcile "order and indulgence" (Berland, 1992, 42). As Berland describes it, "seats were gradually fixed to face the stage, and the architecture was renovated to permit clearer stratification between the pits and the boxes" (Berland, 1992, 42); regulations were imposed that separated pubs from theaters and more regulations that contributed to the professionalization of the performers.

Once they became syndicated, music halls "spread outwards to sub-urbs and provincial towns whose own entertainments had gone into decline as a consequence of these innovations. Then, of course, with this structure in place, cinema was introduced; it both appropriated and displaced the earlier structures in order to extend the logic of their production" (Berland, 1992, 42). Berland's point is that in the process of consuming a particular entertainment, audiences function as productive agents of technological innovation.

I want to apply this reasoning to Disney World, which Scott Bukatmin has astutely interpreted as a cinematic space. According to Bukatmin, the entire park is laid out and visualized as if through the lens of a camera (Bukatmin, 1991, 61). Visitors to the park are in fact constituted as an audience and positioned as they would be in a cinema taking in the vistas and taking rides that track them through scenes from a movie. Recognizing that the visitor participates as a viewer does a lot to explain the amused absorption of most folks at Disney World and their relative lack of spontaneity.

It's interesting to note that the dialectic between productive tech-nologies and audience has already given rise to a new spatial configu-ration, wherein the cinematographic space of Disney World has been superseded by the video game format of "Discovery Zone." A franchized chain of private indoor playgrounds, "Discovery Zone" does Disney World one better by assimilating the child (who is already skilled as a viewer/reader of film and filmic space) into the action/reac-tion programmed space of Nintendo.

Endemic to the suburbs where it crops up in strip malls among sprawling development tracts and lots of bumper-to-bumper traffic, "Discovery Zone" features a built environment consisting of brightly colored plastic tubing, sliding boards, foam-covered mountains, and vats filled with plastic balls. Besides a lounge for adults, each "discovery zone" includes a snack bar and a carnival-like game area, whose addi-tional fees for drinks, munchies, and game tokens is apt to boost the ini-tial entry price of $4.99 per child to an overall expenditure of $15.00 or more.

"Discovery Zone" makes play an occasion for reaping profits. It represents what may well be capitalism's first attempt to fully colonize play by turning it into commercialized amusement. Unlike the not-for-profit indoor play areas that I have visited such as YMCA gymnasi-ums where mats and other equipment are randomly made available for children's play, "Discovery Zone"'s layout is always the same and replicated in each of its 180 installations coast to coast. This means that frequent trips to "Discovery Zone"—and families are encouraged to buy the year pass—will induct the child into a programmed play space whose structure is always the same. While it might be argued that public parks and playgrounds include a similarly rigid play environment defined by the arrangemnt of swing sets, see-saws, and slides, program and structure are balanced against the undefined spaces between play apparatus where all sorts of spontaneous interaction takes place, making the public playground a negotiated site for play. By comparison, there are absolutely no undetermined spaces at "Discovery Zone"— nowhere for a kid to simply hang out or invent a game with friends. Instead, every inch is programmed, as is every second, for optimal and constant movement. At "Discovery Zone" the child is incorporated into a Nintendo-like game format. Kids race through the tubing, scale the mountains, slide into the ball vats, and give the overall impression of highly charged energy bleeps on a computer screen. Outside of "Have you tried this"; "Let's do that again"; and "Hey, follow me," conversation is minimal. Invented by a gymnastics instructor appalled by the low cardiovascular endurance and agility skills of American youths, "Discovery Zone" promotes itself as a means for building children's strength and self-esteem. It does so at the price of cancelling the social relations that typify real play and turning the kids into hyperactive, adrenalized rats in a maze. "Let's play volcano." This young girl's invitation to engage in a role-playing game was instantly cut short by a cascade of boys who tumbled into the ball vat where the game of volcano might have taken place, catching the girl up in their headlong rush to keep moving.

Margaret Morse sees a continuity between freeways, malls, and television which she characterizes as constituted by "distraction," whose lived effect is "a partial loss of touch with the here and now" (Morse, 1990, 193). We use our remote controls to surf through television menu selections, shopping from channel to channel. We take the freeway, disengaged from the world by the windshield and the abstraction of the roadway, to arrive at a mall where we shop some more. We all recognize the plight of *Dawn of the Dead*'s zombies as an experience that approximates our own. Daily life becomes what Morse calls an "elsewhere" (Morse, 1990, 145), a "nonspace" (Morse, 1990, 195) which is not "mysterious or strange" (Morse, 1990, 196) as such a place might be imagined by Borges or García Marquez, but is instead a muffled banality. "Discovery Zone" adds the playground to the circuit of "distraction." The pace in this nonspace may be more rapid than in a mall, but the plastic barrier against reality is just as secure. Although Morse makes no claims for gender bias in her description of "distraction," I sense that the inequalities of parenting put more women than men in the daily life loop of "distraction." The pedagogical effect of "distraction" at "Discovery Zone" is to teach children to conceptualize themselves apart from the social world, which might not be the way we want it to be, but it is at least a real terrain of struggle. If "distraction" inhibits the urge to political activity and if it is disproportionately lived by women, then it is a factor in the subordination of women and children.

"Discovery Zone" is capitalist culture in miniature, where many of the features that characterize capitalism as a system of production and an ideology are laid out for the child to rehearse and informally learn to accept as natural. First of all, play, like everything else that's worth doing, is something you buy. And, like everything else in a private economy, the ability to pay creates a social distinction between those who can afford to pay for goods and services and those who cannot. Privatization drives a wedge between the classes and casts everything associated with the public sector as inferior. What's interesting about "Discovery Zone," indeed with most amusements, is the relatively low price of admission, which gives the appearance of a society defined by democratic consumerism. The fallacy is that were daily life to be wholly dominated by the private sector, it would be as costly as a lifetime stay at Disney World. Seemingly low entry fees also function to deter the question of why profits are made off services that ought to be free.

Besides learning that play is something you buy, the "Discovery Zone" child also "discovers" that time is money. Upon purchasing admission, the child is given a sticker to wear throughout his or her stay. The sticker indicates the hour and minute when each child's two hours of paid play comes to an end. Play is allotted and rationalized. It is made to conform to the temporal constraints that typify alienated labor time. Play is, thus, the abstract inverse equivalent of work. Rather than work's antithesis, it is the child's means for learning how to mesh self and pleasure to a time clock. What's more, when told that their time is up, kids don't rebel, hide out, or attempt to find ways to prolong their play. Like dutiful soldiers, they leave the field, often with their parents policing the temporal constraints—"Five more minutes"; "Don't waste your time, we have to leave soon." Kids and parents internalize the rationalization of play, making it inconceivable that anyone would fail to conform.

The alternative to consumerist play lies in the struggle to revive the public sector, whose most embattled institution in the United States is public education. Massive cutbacks in funding during the Reagan and Bush administrations have decimated public schools, making them ripe for corporate investment and ready for salvation by such private concerns as Burger King, which now runs ten high schools in the West and Midwest. Debates around public education have received media attention as well as coverage by investigative journals such as *The Nation*. Much less—if anything—has been said or written about our country's system of local, regional, and national parks and playgrounds. More devastatingly underfunded than public education, many playgrounds have been taken over by social outcasts and drug dealers, making them hazardous sites for play. Moreover, most playgrounds—even those in comfortable neighborhoods—are deemed unsafe in the context of the overall ideological denigration of everything having to do with the public and the compensatory value our society places on the private commercial sector. Parks and playgrounds are presumed unsafe while malls and amusement parks are thought to be secure. Such thinking makes it reasonable for Boy Scouts to "camp out" on a battleship (as reported to me by a father who chaperoned the event) and for nineteen Poughkeepsie Girl Scout troops to "camp out" in a shopping mall (as reported in *The New York Times*). The prevailing tendency in popular culture criticism would interpret such incidents as imaginative appropriations of the military and the commercial for the sake of popular entertainment. It's not clear to me that appropriation is possible in an environment that engulfs the campers in the gender-specific benefits of the military for boys and the pleasures of shopping for girls. While I don't want to suggest that nature is the only proper site for campouts, I do want to pose the question of the absent public alternative. Why do we not have a multitude of varied public sites for peoples' use?

The parks and playgrounds that we do have are the legacy of the Play Movement, a turn-of-the-century organization of philanthropists who urged the creation of sandlots first in Boston, Chicago, and New York; and later strove to open public school play grounds nationwide for community use. Appalled by crowded and unhealthy urban conditions, members of the Play Movement advocated vigorous directed activity—what we would call games and sports as opposed to free play—as a means for ameliorating the life of the working class. Significantly, the Play Movement saw play as an endeavor whose social implications far outweighed its physical benefits. Play was meant to steer kids away from the evil temptations of the street: pool halls, taverns, and general loitering.

Not long ago, the Play Movement became the object of critical reassessment by leftist theorists of education, who condemned it as an organization whose only concern was to establish control over the largely immigrant and potentially unruly urban working class. The enactment of child labor laws had turned a great number of children and adolescents out of the factories. New methods were needed to occupy their time and hold them in readiness for reentry into the workforce. This line of argument sees the Play Movement as the social extension of industrial capitalism. Directed activity under the leadership of playground supervisors was a means for indoctrinating children in the precepts essential for an efficient and docile workforce including a respect for leadership and expertise; and for the acceptance of specialized skills, team spirit, and social hierarchy. As Paul Violas puts it, the Play Movement was simply a vehicle for "training the urban working class" (Violas, 1978).

While the reformist movements of the Progressive Era certainly did have the desire for social control on their agendas, something is overlooked in the leftist critique of the Play Movement. This is the significance of the public sector generally; and specifically the fact that public education and public play don't have the same meanings for us today that they had for the philanthropists in 1910. As I see it, the public sector is a zone of contention, the site where communally defined interests meet the dominant social forces, which are often embedded in the governing agencies and committees that oversee our public institutions. While there are few clear victories for communal interests, there is, nevertheless, always a possibility for change. Such is definitely not the case when popular interests contend with the private sector, which is supported by a legal system that overwhelmingly values private property over communal use. So, if public playgrounds were initially created as informal laboratories for instilling the values and practices deemed essential for a happy, healthy working class, they do not serve such a function today. Indeed, as I have argued, this is currently the function of play for profit at commercial playgrounds whose technologically programmed definition of play fits the needs of managerial capitalism. Moreover, even in the heyday of Progressive politics, the Play Movement had its transcendent utopian impulses (also overlooked by contemporary critics on the left). Carried away by the social implication of play, Henry Curtis, a long-time secretary of the Play Movement, suggested a number of possibilities for radically transforming the urban environment (Curtis, 1917). He recommended that certain streets be blocked off, thus turning the conduits for trade into parks for play. He also suggested that tenement courtyards might be freed up for play if residents would develop a single communal laundry rather than rely on the individualist method of washing clothes with its proliferation of clothes lines. Curtis went so far as to imagine rooftop playgrounds connected by bridges to other rooftops, a truly utopian conceptualization of a public mall.

Such utopian flights of fancy are sadly lacking in our current beleaguered and retrenched attitudes toward the public. The commercial sector is felt to be the repository of all that's worth imagining. Disney World and Nintendo—if it's not on the menu it can't be had. The decimation of the public sector has been produced as much by the waning of communal conceptualizations of social life as by the withdrawal of funds. If we are to invent alternatives to privatized commerical culture, we must draw upon the daily life experiences and desires that give a sense of what the communal might be were it to be fully realized socially. Childhood social relations supply more possibilities for tapping into communal experience than do the routinized practices available to most adults. Yet childhood is the most ardently sought after market today.

Contrary to many who write on pedagogy, I don't see reformist tactics as offering viable strategies for opposing capitalist culture. While I've argued the need to support public education (as opposed to elitist private schools and insular in-home instruction), I don't see the public sector as we know it (not even a reinvigorated one) as a solution in itself nor an actual alternative to capitalism. The public sector is important because it embraces communal social relations and can give a sense of what a more communitarian society might be like. The problem with reformist strategies, no matter how well intentioned, is that they, like the Play Movement, are necessarily embedded in and shackled to the social and economic forces that they enforce even while representing opposition to them. Utopia can't be institutionalized. While we might wish to imagine reformist pedagogical strategies organized around the imaginative gender bending and transformational possibilities inherent in children's creative play, such strategies would be doomed to reinscribe disciplinary norms once congealed in a prescribed pedagogical practice. I offer creative play, especially imaginative role-playing games, as a deconstructive lever meant to set the accepted "normalcy" of children's commercial culture and the broader leisure time industry at a critical distance. Play is a pedagogy for reversing capitalist social formations. It can't be instructed; but its example can be used to empower alternative vision.

References

Adorno, T. (1989). *Minima Moralia*. London: Verso.

Berland, J. (1992). Angels dancing: Cultural technologies and the production of space. In L. Grossberg, C. Nelson, & P. Treichler (Eds.), *Cultural Studies*. New York: Routledge.

Bukatmin, S. (1991). There's always tomorrowland: Disney and the hypercinematic experience. *Cotber*, 57 (Summer 1991).

Curtis, H. (1917). *The Play Movement and its significance*. New York: Macmillan.

Kinder, M. (1991). *Playing with power*. Berkeley: University of California Press.

García Marquez, G. (1989). Tales beyond solitude. London: British Film Institute.

Mayanovic-Shane, A. (1989). You are a pig: For real or just pretend? Different orientations in play and metaphor. *Play and Culture*, 1989, vol. 6, 2.

Morse, M. (1990). An ontology of everyday distraction: The freeway, the mall, and television. In P. Mellencamp (Ed.), *Logics of Television*. Bloomington: Indiana University Press.

Paley, V. (1984). *Boys and girls*. Chicago: University of Chicago Press.

Violas, P. (1978). *The training of the urban working class*. Chicago: Rand McNally.

CHAPTER 9

WOMEN IN THE HOLOCENE: ETHNICITY, FANTASY, AND THE FILM *THE JOY LUCK CLUB*

Rey Chow

THE SCAR

In the early scenes of *The Joy Luck Club* (directed by Wayne Wang, 1993), we notice a detail that does not at first seem significant. Auntie An-mei's neck looks somewhat unusual, and she seems always to wear clothes that hide it. Only much later for An-mei's story is among the last to be told—do we find out that what we did not see very well earlier is a scar.[1] When An-mei was a little girl back in China, she was in the house of her grandparents one day, when a heart-rending scene of cursing and rejection took place. Her mother, who had been newly widowed, was being accused of having had sexual relations with another man. As a daughter she had thus brought shame to her family by her lack of the chastity befitting a widow. In spite of her mother's pleading, An-mei's grandparents did not want her back. In a moment of heated gesticulation, the adults caused a boiling pot of soup to spill on the young An-mei, scorching her neck with what was to remain a scar—a scar that, as she would tell us, was the only thing with which she had to remember her mother for a long time to come. Eventually, An-mei would see her mother again and discover the truth of her mother's so-called "lack of chastity." Her mother had been raped by a rich man, Wu Tsing, and had become pregnant. Since no one believed she had been raped, she had no choice but ask to be taken into his house as his fourth concubine. When she delivered her child, a baby boy, he was immediately taken to be raised as the son of the second wife. Living in a house full of suspicion, distrust, rivalry, and bad will, An-mei's mother had no sense of her own worth. Even though her untimely death from some pastries stuffed with opium was rumored to be an accident, An-mei knew it was suicide. At her mother's funeral, An-mei bravely demanded the repentance of all those who had caused her mother to die. Her mother killed her own weak spirit, she says, so that she could give An-mei a stronger one, and from that day on, An-mei learned how to shout.

In spite of its smallness, the scar is, in a number of ways, a crucial key to the narrative action of *The Joy Luck Club*. Structurally, it is a narrative hinge: it provides a means for An-mei's story to unfold and takes us back to a past that is otherwise unavailable to us. But it is not simply a narrative hinge in the abstract. As a mark, a closed-up wound left permanently on a female body, this scar is what links different generations of women together. If the daughter is scarred for life, it is because her mother was scarred for life: the daughter's body stands as a permanent witness, a testifying piece of evidence for the rejection, humiliation, and suffering of the mother. This piece of evidence, created by what happened to the mother but inscribed corporeally on the daughter, is the sign of an unforgettable relationship, in which the lonely and self-sacrificing mother is given companionship and comradeship.

Toward the end of my chapter I will come back to this scarring as the site of an ambiguous, ambivalent idealism in the age of "multiculturalism." Before doing that, I would like to discuss some of the problems inherent in the general reception of *The Joy Luck Club*.

"HOW AUTHENTIC AM I?": THE "ETHNIC FILM" READING

It would not be an exaggeration to say that the success of the film *The Joy Luck Club*, much like the success of the novel by Amy Tan, has largely been the result of a trendy enthusiasm for celebrating what are in the North American context called "minority cultures." In keeping with the major pedagogical tenets of cultural pluralism, which aim at (re)educating us about the existence of cultures "other" than the predominant WASP cultures of the West, an increasing number of representations of what are considered "minor" identities and ethnicities are found in our mainstream media.[2] Regardless of the contents of their works, "minority" authors are primarily identified as targets of "ethnic" information: we cannot mention Amy Tan or Maxine Hong Kingston without being reminded that their stories are about the "Asian-American" or "Chinese-American" experiences, the same way we cannot mention Toni Morrison, Alice Walker, or Spike Lee without being reminded that their works pertain to the "African-American" heritage. In highlighting the process in which these "ethnic" authors are received, my point is not to question the Asian-American or African-American writers' rights to investigate their peoples' histories; rather, it is to challenge a fundamental difference between the treatment of such writers and that of mainstream cultures. My question is not exactly why "ethnic" writers are considered "ethnic," but what politics is in play when we hear about the "Asian-American," "Latin American," "African-American" experiences without at the same time hearing about the ethnic origins and ethnic sensitivities of, say, Madonna, Arnold Schwarzenegger, Mickey Mouse, Bart Simpson, or H. Ross Perot?[3] What would happen if indeed we were to view these figures of mainstream cultural representation the same way we view the "Asian-American" or "African-American"?

With these questions in mind, it seems to me that there are two issues at stake in the reception of *The Joy Luck Club* as an "ethnic film." First, representations such as *The Joy Luck Club* are socially prescribed in a certain category, namely, as a representation of "people of color" and of "ethnicity"—while many of their contemporaries (such as Sally Potter's *Orlando*, Martin Scorcese's *The Age of Innocence*, Jane Campion's *The Piano*, or James Ivory's *The Remains of the Day*) are not. Second, to this categorical distinction of "ethnic film" is moreover attached a pedagogical function, namely, that these "others" are trying to rediscover their "origins," which are "Chinese," "Japanese," "African," "Latino," and so forth, and which are essentially different from the normative and well-understood baseline represented by the white man and the white woman. In terms of the conventions of representation, the West and its "others" are thus implicitly divided in the following manner: the West is the place for language games, aesthetic fantasies, and fragmented subjectivities; the West's others, instead, offer us "lessons" about history, reality, and wholesome collective consciousnesses. This division has much to tell us about the ways "ethnicity" functions to produce, organize, and cohere subjectivities in the "multicultural" age.

If we juxtapose against the multiculturalist narratives of "ethnicity" the work of Michel Foucault, we see that ethnicity is fast acquiring the kind of significance and signifying value that Foucault attributes to sexuality in the period since the seventeenth century.[4] One of the most well-known of Foucault's arguments is that sexuality is not natural but constructed, and that in the multiple processes of discursive constructions, sexuality has, however, always been produced as the hidden, truthful secret that intimate something people take turns to discover and confess about themselves. The discursive, narrative char-

acter of the productions of sexuality means that even though our institutions, our media, and our cultural environment are saturated with
sex and sexuality, we continue to believe that it is something which
has been repressed and which must somehow be liberated. Foucault
calls this "the repressive hypothesis," by which he refers to the restrictive economy that is incorporated into the politics of language and
speech, and that accompanies the social redistributions of sex. Foucault
is clear on the didactic and indeed religious implications of the repressive hypothesis:

> the essential thing is . . . the existence in our era of a discourse in
> which sex, the revelation of truth, the overturning of global laws,
> the proclamation of a new day to come, and the promise of a cer-
> tain felicity are linked together. Today it is sex that serves as a
> support for the ancient form so familiar and important in the
> West—of preaching.
>
> The statement of oppression and the form of the sermon
> refer back to one another; they are mutually reinforcing. To say
> that sex is not repressed . . . not only runs counter to a well-
> accepted argument, it goes against the whole economy and all the
> discursive "interests" that underlie this argument. (*History of Sex-
> uality*, 1, pp. 8–9)

In other words, the great progress of sexuality-as-signification in Western modernity has been going hand in hand with two tenacious collective beliefs—first in repression, then in emancipation. For Foucault, the
question is thus not why we are repressed, but how we came to believe
we are: how do we, he asks, construct scenarios in which sexuality must
be "liberated"? One response is that the proliferation of discourses concerned with sex would not be possible without the concurrent proliferation of fields of power:

> more important was the multiplication of discourses concerning
> sex in the field of exercise of power itself: an institutional incite-
> ment to speak about it, and to do so more and more; a determina-
> tion on the part of the agencies of power to hear it spoken about,
> and to cause *it* to speak through explicit articulation and endlessly
> accumulated detail. (*History of Sexuality*, 1, p. 18; emphasis in the
> original)

The discursive ferment and mechanisms that surround "ethnicity"
in our time share many similar features with the "repressive hypothe-

sis" that Foucault attributes to the discourse of sexuality. Chief of all is the belief in "ethnicity" as a kind of repressed truth that awaits liberation. In order to facilitate this liberation, it is not enough that we identify the hidden motifs and inscriptions of ethnicity in all cultural representations; it is believed that we also need to engage in processes of confession, biography, autobiography, storytelling, and so forth, that actively resuscitate, retrieve, and redeem that "ethnic" part of us which has not been allowed to come to light.

Moreover, while ethnicity can no doubt hold a subversive, progressive value for individuals faced with institutions that are traditionally blind and deaf to the inequities and iniquities created by ethnic difference, the institutions themselves are already busily incorporating within them various kinds of "ethnic consciousness." If, as Foucault tells us, schools, hospitals, bureaucracies, military camps, and other public establishments register "sex" even when they put on a sexually "neutral" front, then increasingly and transindividually, the same establishments are creating the information networks for the inscription, institutionalization, and active utilization of ethnicity as a form of practice that is steadily subjected to methodical systematic calculation. For instance, while giving "minority" candidates a better chance of being selected, "equal opportunity" and "affirmative action" employment policies also provide institutions the means of monitoring what are supposedly "private" and "personal" elements such as family history, "racial" heritage, sexual preference, and so forth. As E. San Juan writes, in the United States

> "Ethnicity" is the official rubric to designate the phenomenological plurality of peoples ranked in a hierarchy for the differential allocation and distribution of resources. This hierarchy in turn is guaranteed by the taken-for-granted doctrines of liberal democracy premised on individual competition, the right to acquire property and sell labor power, and so on.[5]

Whenever institutions mobilize themselves this way, we are in the realm, as Foucault's arguments show, not of personal liberation but rather of disciplinary subject formation. Would it be far-fetched to say that precisely those apparatuses that have been instituted for us to gain access to our "ethnicities" are at the same time accomplishing the goal of an ever-refined, ever-perfected, and ever-expanding system of visuality and visibility, of observation and surveillance, that is not unlike Bentham's Panopticon, the model of the ideal prison which Foucault uses to summarize the modern production of knowledge—a production that is inseparable from discipline and punishment, from the ubiquitous "economy" of sociopolitical control?[6] It is in the light of a generalized panopticism that William Spanos, for instance, discusses the pluralistic regimentation of humanistic inquiry in the modern Western university as the paradigm case of what Foucault means by the production of knowledge:

> However invisible and unthought by administrators, faculty, students, and historians, the polyvalent panoptic diagram thematized on the ontological level by Heidegger and on the sociopolitical level by Foucault traverses the heterogeneous structure of the modern "pluralist" university. It saturates the domain of higher education from the physical organization of institutional and classroom space to the "spiritual" space of inquiry and knowledge transmission: the "author function," research, journals, learned societies, conferences, hiring, professional advancement, and both pedagogical theory and practice. The university as we know it has its historically specific origins in the Enlightenment and reflects and contributes to "the gradual extension" and "spread" of the mechanisms of discipline "throughout the whole social body."[7]

Panopticism is ultimately the extreme form of an efficient socializing gaze which oversees and conditions us even in our most "private" beliefs and "solitary" activities. The power of the Panopticon owes not so much to its existence as a tangible architectural structure monitoring our behavior from the outside, as to its capacity to be internalized by us as an ever-vigilant Other demanding from us our secrets, our histories, our collaboration. Implicit in the conception of the Panopticon was, as Foucault writes, the ideal of

> an architecture that is no longer built simply to be seen (as with the ostentation of palaces), or to observe the external space (cf. the geometry of fortresses), but to permit an internal, articulated and detailed control—to render visible those who are inside it; in more general terms, an architecture that would operate to transform individuals: to act on those it shelters, to provide a hold on their conduct, to carry the effects of power right to them, to make it possible to know them, to alter them. (*Discipline and Punish*, p. 172)

This power is evident as we think of the frequency with which, in the "multicultural" age, we answer the call and demand to narrate our "ethnic" pasts and lineages. The invisible interrogation behind the multiculturalist "ethnicity" apparatuses is: "How authentic are you?"—to which everyone voluntarily responds with self-conscious reflections, descriptions, and appellations. Once we respond, however, we are helping to complete the circuit set off by the panopticist interrogation process. The more detailed and earnest our research into our ethnic histories as such, the more successful the panopticist interrogation is in accomplishing its task.

It is not an accident, therefore, that this panopticist interrogation is usually most effective—that is, that it exhibits its disciplinary "gaze" most luringly—when it is "investigating" those "others" who are supposedly far from what is held to be the cultural "norm." As in the cases of the clinic, the prison, the madhouse, and other such institutions for social outcasts, the systemic production of knowledge here is most efficient not only through the internalization of discipline by individuals—what Louis Althusser calls the "interpellation" of the subject[8]—but also through the active creation of what we might call the *National Geographic* of the soul—the observation platforms and laboratories in which the "perverse" others—the "inmates"—can be displayed in their "nonconforming" and "abnormal" behavior, in their strangely coded practices and rituals. Such observation platforms and laboratories would include the confessional, autobiographical narratives told voluntarily by these "others" in their interaction with the panopticist gaze, which solicits from them not only their life stories but a sustained belief in the necessity of their confessions as arising from genuine "experience." In Joan Scott's terms, such "experience" is now given the value of a kind of foundationalism whose truth lies beyond the discursivity that is, in fact, its basis.[9] In an age when the sexual revolution is drawing to a close in part because of epidemics such as AIDS, the arena of panopticist interrogation that was previously monopolized by sexuality now gives way to experiences of "ethnicity," which in turn generate spectacular results.

This, then, is certainly one manner in which we can view *The Joy Luck Club*. If cinema, together with other types of technologized visuality, is one of the most effective apparatuses of subject-formation in our age, then *The Joy Luck Club* can certainly be described as playing up to the panopticist multiculturalist gaze in a number of ways. The film centers on life experiences that are revealed to us through autobiographical narratives. Each in her turn, the four mothers—Lindo, Ying Ying, Anmei, and Suyuan—reveal to us the historical layers of their subjectivities, each with a tale of the horrors and sufferings they had to go through as young women in another time and another land. Lindo lost her own mother and family when she entered the Wang family as a child bride, but she was eventually able, with courage and intelligence, to extricate herself from the sad fate that awaited her as an "infertile" daughter-in-law. Ying Ying fell in love with a playboy, who abandoned her for other women soon after they were married. In her resentment and anger, she drowned her own baby while bathing him. An-mei witnessed her mother's rejection by her own family and the humiliation she suffered in the Wu family. Suyuan, who had twins, had to abandon them during wartime, when she herself was so ill that she thought she was going to die. She never found out that the babies lived. (Suyuan's story came to us from her widower-husband.)

Even though the mothers' stories are not the only events that take place in the film, we feel that they are where the emotional densities of the film are most invested. These stories, (re)narrated with lush, sensuous colors, with characters and settings that stand in memorably bold contours, deliver into the contemporary English-speaking world of the daughters some kind of truth from a faraway past. At the same time, if the effect of these stories is one of liberation, it is also one of exoticism. Not only are the images of the past always given in aesthetically distinct frames that mark them off from the present, but even the mothers' idiosyncratic voices—their intonations, their exclamations, their stubbornness, their accents which are supposedly a mixture of English words and Chinese syntax—add to this aura of an otherness that is unknowable except through their acts of autobiographical narration. If these memories exist only in the mothers' minds, the film becomes in effect an opening, a disclosure of these minds, a rendering-in-visibility of the hidden dramatic forces that make up their magical, archaeological appeal.

In terms of the panopticist interrogation, *The Joy Luck Club* could thus be seen as an instance of the many current contributions toward the new discursive obsession called "ethnicity." Relying on some of the most used conventions of cinema—voice-over narration, sentimental music, melodramatic events, sensuous cinematography—the film generates a potentially endless process in which the past is "emancipated" for the present and the future. While we are given four sets of stories, the film could theoretically have included many more, with the same kind of emancipatory structure and utopian ending, whereby the dead and absent mother becomes precisely the point of narrative closure, of family reunion across continents, across vastly different cultural settings, and across time lost. As in Foucault's argument about sexuality, the repressive hypothesis—which in the present context amounts to the belief that the origins of Asian-American cultural experiences have been forgotten, neglected, or silenced—goes hand in hand with the proliferation of dialogues, narratives, images, details, in such a way as to turn filmic representation itself into precisely the kind of "observation platform" in the terms described above. Ethnicity is here the "secret"— the truth of subjectivity—that must be released into the open in order for human social identity to be properly established. But as it is consciously dramatized, ethnicity also becomes a transparent sight/site, enabling the emergence of a clear, legible subject and the rich but essentially family-oriented communication within the identified "ethnic" group. Thus the young Chinese-American woman June, whose narrative voice organizes the entire filmscript, finally takes the place of her mother (Suyuan) and returns to the homeland, China, to meet her half-sisters and complete a journey that began decades ago.

If my reading were to stop at this point, then it could be summarized as a reading that basically understands the film as an instance of loyal service to the dominant American ideology of multiculturalism. A Foucauldian reading such as the one I have been following, with its tendencies to point to the institutional streamlining of subjectivities though the repressive hypothesis, would dovetail very well with a reading by way of Althusser's theory of ideology and Edward Said's *Orientalism*.[10] The criticism of an institutionally normalized subject who is effectively interpellated by society's practices of discipline and coercion in the name of "ethnicity" would, in this instance, accompany a criticism of *The Joy Luck Club* as a work of Orientalism that simply panders to the tastes for "ethnic diversity" among white readers and audiences alike.[11] In such a reading, all the signifiers of ethnicity, of "Chineseness," including the sceneries, costumes, mannerisms, verbalisms, acts of violence, and so forth, would have to be written off as a mythification, a degradation and distortion that has little to do with the "real" China and "real" Chinese people.[12]

Even though we cannot understand *The Joy Luck Club* without the insights of Foucault, Althusser, and Said—for those insights reveal in an indispensable manner the kinds of subjection and subjugation our technologies of representation entail, in ways that no individual human being can escape—it is my belief that a responsible reading of the film, precisely if it is sensitive and responsive to the issues of contemporary cultural politics, cannot stop at this point. While Foucault, Althusser, and Said would move our reading toward mechanisms of institutional control, networks of subjective manipulation, and other devices of the exercise of panopticist power, their insights must also be reciprocated by a form of reading that would (re)discover in the various systems of surveillance traces of resistance that survive in what Michel de Certeau calls a "proliferating illegitimacy."[13] We need, in other words, to supplement the overtly Foucauldian, anti-Orientalist reading with one that attends to some of the peculiarities of the film itself.

LEGENDS OF FANTASY: THE ILLEGITIMATE READING

To do this supplementary reading, we need to begin where the other type of reading tends to end—namely, the place of the stereotypes, the myths, the melodramatic details. We will go back to the scar on Auntie An-mei's neck.

In many ways the scar is a banal element. As I already mentioned, it is a means to indicate the bond between mother and daughter; it is a narrative hinge that allows us to return to the scene of crime and explore the history of An-mei's mother and grandmother. In terms of narrative conventions, the scar is a stereotypical device for a return to the "origin." But precisely what does it tell us about"origins"?

Upon close reading, the scar reveals itself to be the place of a profound ambivalence. If it does serve the conventionalized turns of narrative, it also exists as a unique kind of mark—a physical *defect* at the juncture between the female body and the larger "lineage" of so-called "Chineseness" or "ethnicity." The significance of this defect is twofold: it displaces the patriarchal obsession with "origins" onto a bonding among women; it highlights women's place in patriarchy as itself always already a dis-place-ment. On the scarred female body, the patriarchal idea and ideal of a continuous ethnic lineage are violently disrupted. The "origin" to which the scar leads back is not a plenitude but a war zone; it is not about the joys of ethnicity but about sex, fertility, marriage, widowhood, rape, concubinage, and other forms of oppression—all with the female body as its battleground. If ethnicity, like sexuality, is ultimately about the management of human reproduction, then what the bond/scar between mother and daughter demonstrates instead is *sexuality and ethnicity as enslavement*, as something that they have to resist together rather than help perpetuate. The scar signifies not so much the continuity of ethnic "origin" as its seriality—rather than being a definite beginning, the origin "exists" only insofar as it is a series, a relation, a mark-made-on-the-other. Behind each mother is thus always another mother. Mothers are, in other words, not a replacement of "fathers" but their displacement; not simply another self-sufficient "origin" but always already a mark-on-the-other, a signifier for another signifier, a metaphor. Most of all "mothers" are legends: as much as being popular "stories," they offer, in themselves, *ways of reading*.

It is hence important that we wrest the "mothers" of this film from the anthropomorphic or humanistic realism in which they are bound to be lodged in most interpretations. Rather, I suggest reading these mothers as, first and foremost, metaphors and stereotypes. As much as their stories, the mothers themselves, including the very physical details about them, are part and parcel of a skillful use of metaphors and stereotypes in the cinematic production of a new kind of fantasy. We think here not only of An-mei's scar, but also of Suyuan's bad teeth and bleeding hands (as she pushes the wheelbarrow with her babies in it during wartime), the expressive looks of all the mothers' eyes, the articulate tensions of their facial muscles, their tears, their smiles, and their strong and determined voices. . . . All in all such physical details constitute the mothers as encrypted texts, gestural archives, and memory palaces.

But what is the point of showing that mothers are metaphors, stereotypes, larger-than-life figures? First, it is to break away from a connotatively negative reading of melodrama. The usual assumption about melodrama, even for many who take serious interest in it, is that it is about the polarization of good and evil, of black and white, and so forth—in other words, melodrama has always been assumed to be the opposite of subtle and nuanced representation.[14] My argument is rather that melodrama, especially as it appears in film, offers a privileged view of the basically machinic or technologized nature of what we call sentimental emotions. As filmic devices such as the close-up and the slow-motion make visible previously unseen/undetected dimensions of human life, revealing therein what Walter Benjamin calls the "optical unconscious,"[15] so the figure of the mother, insofar as it is presented in affectively enlarged and amplified—that is, melodramatized—terms, reveals the gendered "unconscious" that is our "maternal linkage."[16] Enlargement and amplification: these are, concurrent with affect, terms of machinic magnification—of visual and aural intensification. We may thus say that, with the intensified focus on the mother, human emotions are magnified *technologically* the way pictures are "blown up." The resulting aesthetic effect is not one of identity with but one of a distant fascination for this awesome "animal" and "being" which strikes us as spectacle and drama, and in front of which we lose control of our bodies—we cry.

Second, by making a deliberate theoretical move away from the realistic "ethnic film" reading, my point is to situate *The Joy Luck Club* within our postmodern explorations of human origins *in general*. At this juncture, it would be useless to compare and contrast *The Joy Luck Club* with films such as *The Wedding Banquet* or *Farewell My Concubine*, since these films are also received in the same classification of "ethnic film." Instead, I think we need to juxtapose *The Joy Luck Club* with a film such as—of all wild leaps of the imagination—*Jurassic Park* (directed by Stephen Spielberg, 1993). My purpose in making this conjunction is to problematize the politics behind the prevalent categorical difference of the "ethnic other," a politics which organizes and hierarchizes what are in fact contemporary representations.

What do *The Joy Luck Club* and *Jurassic Park* have in common? In order to put my argument across, let me be very schematic. First, both films are about ancestry; both are about a certain fascination with a type of being that precedes younger groups of people and to which/whom the younger generations owe their present condition. Second, both films set up fictive scenarios in which the fascination with this ancestral other—mothers in the one case and dinosaurs in the other—leads to the unfolding of historical life details. The crucial point is that our access to these ancestral others is inevitably *coded*. In *The Joy Luck Club*, the ancestral land—China—is reconstructed through narrative codes, through memories that unfold in the characters' new environment—America—and that are in turn made into film. In *Jurassic Park*, the extinct environment of the dinosaurs is reconstructed through "scientific" codes, which include DNA cloning and the innovative technology that goes into the making of Jurassic Park; this artificially "reproduced" dreamland with its gigantic animals is in turn simulated through computerized effects on the movie screen.

Third, in both films the relation between the ancestors and the descendants is not at all an easy one. Amid fascination are feelings of horror, danger, and repulsion, as well as a definite sense of the pastness of the world of these others. The fictional exploration of these otherworldly beings goes hand in hand with a knowledge of the chronologically and experientially alien nature of their existence. This alien Ness is conveyed through exotic details—in *The Joy Luck Club*, through the elements that compose the phantasmagoric visual present we see in flashbacks; in *Jurassic Park*, through the elements that compose the phantasmagoric spatial present, the make-believe setting of *Jurassic Park*. Fourth, in spite of the knowledge of their alienness, part of the fascination with these others lies in the feeling that the younger generations and the ancestral beings are deeply related, and that these others represent, whether in historical, ethnic, or biological terms, our predecessors, our previous life forms. In *The Joy Luck Club*, the mothers' narratives are merged into the daughters'; in *Jurassic Park*, returning from the fantasy land to the world of modern cities in a helicopter, the characters see below them against the surf a line of ungainly dinosaur-like pelicans.

A possible objection to my juxtaposition of the two films would perhaps stem from my apparent dismissal of the sacredness of the human stories. Am I not committing the enormity of virtually equating "ethnics" and ethnic (m)others with animals? I will respond to this type of question by saying, first of all, that the notion that humans, who are animals, are superior to "animals"—since such would be the assumption behind this type of question—is not one to which I subscribe. A detailed response to the question would necessitate a problematizing of the age-old philosophical, epistemological, and ethical constructions of such a notion of superiority, and it would take us far beyond the parameters of this chapter. But the question of whether humans are superior to animals, important though it is, is not really the main issue here.

The main issue is that the multiculturalist conceptions of "ethnicities," following the steady progress toward the disciplining and fragmentation of knowledge since the Enlightenment, are ultimately part of an ongoing systemic splintering of the whole notion of "humanity" into manageable units of information. In the age of cyberspace, hypertext, and virtual reality, "humanity" can no longer be conceived without numbers, statistics, computerized processes of digitization, documentation, and permutation. If the status of "humanity" is that of "the real," the real itself is, in this age of simulations, "produced from miniaturized units, from matrices, memory banks and command models."[17] And yet, if high-tech fragmentation of "humanity" as such is the *general* condition of life in a rationalistic, speed- and efficiency-driven world, the ideological burden of "humanity" lingers with weight when it comes to "ethnicity." Precisely when the surfacing of "ethnic others" and the production of "ethnicity" as knowledge should further break up the notion of "humanity" as it was traditionally conceived in white, European, masculinist terms, such a notion of "humanity"—of humans as "higher" animals, as "subjects" with "consciousnesses," as "voices" of truth awaiting emancipation—reemerges in "ethnic" forms.

In what amounts to the same argument from a different perspective: even while "humanity" is irreversibly exploded and imploded with scientific advances such as genetic engineering, in-vitro fertilization, test-tube babies, surrogate mothers, and so forth—advances of experimentation with biological (re)production which are inextricably part of the *mise-en-scène* of science fiction fantasies such as *Jurassic Park*—the same old myth of "humanity," complete with blood ties, kinship bonds, and tribal identity, is fabricated through the "others" in the name not of fantasy but of reality, history, and ethnicity. The politics of the division between "science fiction" and "ethnic film," insofar as it tends to disallow precisely the kind of allegorical juxtaposition of the two films I am suggesting, is very much a reconfirmation of the racist ideology which sees the world in terms of "West" and "East," "us" and "them," and which has been, since the heyday of European imperialism, the main epistemological support of an academic discipline such as anthropology.

Even though it is likely to be considered illegitimate, then, the juxtaposition of *The Joy Luck Club* and *Jurassic Park* enables us to see precisely the process of the "delegitimation" of knowledge that François Lyotard describes as characteristic of the postmodern condition. Lyotard holds that the crisis of knowledge—which he defines in terms of the disappearance of what he calls metanarratives—occurs in both the speculative/philosophical and the political spheres. In the speculative/philosophical sphere, the crisis is caused by "an internal erosion of the legitimacy principle of knowledge" and can be summarized as "a process of delegitimation fueled by the demand for legitimation itself." The failure of speculative knowledge to sustain, from within its principled parameters, its claim to truth leads ultimately to the perspectivizing of "truth" itself. In the political sphere, meanwhile, there is an increasing discontinuity between truth and justice: while the emancipation apparatus derived from the Enlightenment "grounds the legitimation of science and truth in the autonomy of interlocutors involved in ethical, social, and political praxis," there is "nothing to prove that if a statement describing a real situation is true, it follows that a prescriptive statement based upon it (the effect of which will necessarily be a modification of that reality) will be just."[18]

In our present context, the two films correspond to the two interrelated aspects of this postmodern "delegitimation." On the one hand is the science fiction fantasy with its infinitely multiplying *perspectival* inquiries—multimedia, simulated, hyperreal—into the truthful origins of biological life forms such as birds. Such inquiries call into question the traditional boundaries between the various fields of knowledge, in particular the boundary between science and myth. On the other hand is the so-called "ethnic work of art" with its implicit *political* imperative of vindicating the neglected fate/history of an entire culture and people, an imperative whose claim to truth is, however, always mediated by narratives, institutions, and apparatuses of representation. These narratives, institutions, and apparatuses of representation give the "ethnic work" the value of equivalence with other similar works but little proof of justice: all such works are now seen to have equal claims to "truth" through their equally autonomous, but always local, "subjectivities." While I do not necessarily agree with Lyotard's conclusion that the world has therefore become a matter of "language games" since the grand narratives have lost their credibility, I think his explanation of the delegitimation of knowledge helps clarify the mutually implicated epistemological/discursive functions of the science fiction fantasy and the "ethnic film," and the way they participate *concurrently* in the critical condition he calls the postmodern.

I have therefore borrowed the title of my paper from Max Frisch's novella *Man in the Holocene*,[19] to gesture toward the much larger implications of fantasy with which *The Joy Luck Club* should, I think, be seen.

The Joy Luck Club, for all its apparent historical elements, is ultimately a legend—and a legend of fantasy at that. The fantasmatic mother-daughter relationships could be seen not so much as corresponding faithfully to Chinese American "history" as a dramatization of its metaphoricity, its textuality and seriality, and its "reality" as a kind of continual storytelling.[20] However, precisely because it uses "local" signifiers which are nonwhite, the film will continue to be read as "ethnic" and always be recuperated into a Western notion of otherness, of us-versus-them. Between the film's material signification and its inevitable recuperation, there is no exteriority, no outside position. This in-between-ness—between fantasy and recuperation—is the very space in which the politics of representation will always be played out in the age of cultural pluralism.

Pedagogically, then, *The Joy Luck Club* can be seen as the kind of mainstream film that is valuable precisely because it is ambiguous. When we see the film not in terms of the realistic register of "ethnicity" in which it is inevitably cast by the forces of multiculturalism, but instead as a kind of idealism production through cinema, then it would be possible to locate it within a libidinal economy that will always imagine its "origins" in another time and another place. We would see that it is a contemporary of other Hollywood monuments such as *Jurassic Park*, with which it shares a present of the imaginary, of fantasy. For these reasons I will call the female characters of *The Joy Luck Club* women in the Holocene—as a way to emphasize that they are full members of a geological present that must be understood not as a separatist subculture but rather as our contemporary culture, with its continual, even if very old, attempts to (re)imagine, (re)make, and (re)invent itself.

To return to the detail with which I began: the film is, ultimately, a kind of scar. It is a mark of the historical discrimination against peoples of color, a sign of the damage they have borne alongside their continual survival. The recuperation of this scar as an entertaining embellishment—as a new, exotic way to tell stories in postmodern America—will always be the function of the dominant technologies of power with their capacity for panopticist searches and invasions. But the scar is, as well, the mark of a representational ambivalence and inexhaustibility—in this case, the ambivalence and inexhaustibility of the so-called "ethnic film," which participates in our cultural politics not simply as the other, the alien, but also as us, as part of our ongoing fantasy production. The film, in other words, is a scar blown up to the size of a motion picture, in which we see the veins, the tissues, the traces, and the movements of scar formation. It is a legend in which and with which we read—how the scar attempts to heal and how, despite the scarification, the skin has taken on new life.

NOTES

1. In the novel, An-mei's story appears in the second chapter, which is entitled "Scar." See A. Tan, *The Joy Luck Club* (New York: Vintage, 1989). In this chapter, I am primarily following the order of events as they appear in the film.

2. For an example of how multiculturalism has become a mainstream media issue, see the special issue of *Time*, Fall 1993: "The new face of America."

3. Examples of this fundamental perceptual difference abound in our everyday contexts. Let me cite two briefly.

At a conference on feminism and film theory held in Spain, a white American feminist told the audience that she wished there were black feminists present to tell them about the experiences of "women of color." I was ready to overlook her oblivion to my presence as a "woman of color," but the larger assumption behind her stated wish was alarming—namely, that "white" experiences like her own were somehow in a different category, that "white" was not "colored" and not "ethnic."

The second example is the mirror opposite of the first one. In Minneapolis, Minnesota, a black woman, Sharon Sayles Belton, recently became mayor. Minneapolis police chief Tony Bouza is reported to have said about her: "She doesn't think in terms of race. Sharon is the least black person I know." See S. Perry, "Our Ronnie: Notes on Sharon Sayles Belton and Her Unlikely Soulmate," *City Pages*, Minneapolis, 17 November 1993, p. 8. As Perry comments succinctly: "It practically goes without saying that to elect a black woman mayor flatters all our egalitarian primping and posturing; her half of the bargain is that she never, never calls us on our betrayals. . . . For her the cost of admission to the halls of power (whether it was paid consciously or not) has been to embody a fantasy of black life as seen through the eyes of middle-class white people: starting from humble origins, rising through luck and determination and the goodwill of white mentors, and finally *becoming like us*" (emphasis in the original).

4. M. Foucault, The history of sexuality. vol. 1, trans. R. Hurley (New York: Vintage, 1989). Hereafter page references are indicated in the text.

5. E. San Juan, Jr., *Racial formations/critical transformations: Articulations of power in ethnic and racial studies in the United States* (London: Humanities Press, 1992), 15. This book contains incisive criticisms of the ways "ethnicity" has been enlisted to serve the interests of mainstream cultural pluralism; see especially chapter 2, "The cult of ethnicity and the fetish of pluralism."

6. See M. Foucault, *Discipline and punish: The birth of the prison*, trans. A. Sheridan (New York: Vintage, 1979). Hereafter page references are indicated in the text.

7. W. V. Spanos, *The end of education: Toward posthumanism* (Minneapolis: University of Minnesota Press, 1993), 43. Spanos' argument (in chapter 2, "Humanistic inquiry and the politics of the gaze") is that Bentham's Panopticon as theorized by Foucault was an instance of the post-Enlightenment culmination of a disciplinary supervisory schema that actually began much earlier in the West—among writers of the humanist Renaissance and philosophers of classical antiquity: "Bentham's Panopticon brings to fulfillment the coercive potential latent in metaphysical 'oversight' *and*, by way of this excess, makes explicit the disciplinary genealogy of the idea and practice of the modern synoptic humanist university that the metaphysical tradition authorized and elaborated. A careless reader of Foucault might object that Bentham's model applies essentially to a historically specific and appropriate architectural instance within modern Western society: the reformatory prison. But such an interpretation is what Foucault's genealogical scholarship insistently denies" (Spanos, p. 40; emphasis in the original).

8. See L. Althusser, "Ideology and ideological state apparatuses (notes towards an investigation)," *Lenin and philosophy and other essays*, trans. B. Brewster (London: New Left Books, 1971), 127–186.

9. See J. Scott, "The evidence of experience," *Critical Inquiry*, Summer 1991. A shorter version of this essay is reprinted as "Experience," in J. Butler & J. Scott (Eds.), *Feminists theorize the political* (New York: Routledge, 1992), 22–40.

10. See Althusser, "Ideology and ideology state apparatuses"; E. Said, *Orientalism* (New York: Vintage, 1978).

11. For a recent discussion of Orientalist representations of Chinese people in America, see J. S. Moy, *Marginal sights: Staging the Chinese in America* (Iowa City: University of Iowa Press, 1993). However, if *The Joy Luck Club* were indeed to be read in the light of Orientalism, the kind of binary logic on which Moy's arguments depend—Western artists and viewers on the one hand, Chinese spectacles on the other—would break down since the writers and director in this case are themselves Chinese-American.

12. This is a problem of cross-cultural reading that demands a detailed discussion. Since I have dealt with it at length elsewhere, I will not repeat myself and will ask interested readers to see my book *Primitive passions: Visuality, sex-*

uality, ethnography, and contemporary Chinese cinema (Columbia University Press, 1995), in particular the chapter entitled "The force of surfaces."

13. See M. de Certeau, "Walking in the city," *The practice of everyday life,* trans. S. Rendall (Berkeley: University of California Press, 1984); excerpted in S. During (Ed.), *The Cultural Studies Reader* (London: Routledge, 1993), 151–160.

14. See, for instance, P. Brooks, *The melodramatic imagination: Balzac, Henry James, melodrama, and the mode of excess* (New York: Columbia University Press, 1985).

15. W. Benjamin first used the term "optical unconscious" in the essay "A small history of photography" (1931), *One-Way Street*, trans. E. Jephcott & K. Shorter (London: New Left Books, 1979), 240–257; he again refers to "unconscious optics" in "The work of art in the age of mechanical reproduction," *Illuminations*, trans. H. Zohn (New York: Schocken, 1969), 217–251.

16. Cf. note 15 above: Space constraints mean that I can merely point to the vast implications of the linkages between the "optical unconscious," filmic melodrama, and excessive emotions associated with cultural stereotypes. For a related argument about excessive emotions and technologized visuality, see my "Postmodern automatons," in J. Butler & J. Scott (Eds.), *Feminists theorize the political* (New York: Routledge, 1992), 101–117.

17. J. Baudrillard, *Simulations*, trans. P. Foss, P. Patton, and P. Beitchman (New York: Semiotext(e), 1983), 3.

18. F. Lyotard, *The postmodern condition: A report on knowledge*, trans. G. Bennington & B. Massumi (Minneapolis: University of Minnesota Press, 1984); see especially pp. 31–41.

19. M. Frisch, *Man in the Holocene*, 1979; translation by M. Frisch and G. Skelton (New York: Harcourt Brace Jovanovich, 1980). The novella describes an old man who is losing his reason and who is aware of it. He approaches his doom by projecting his gradual insanity onto his natural surroundings. In the process he becomes obsessed with paleontology: as his mind disintegrates, he reintegrates into the history of the earth, into the Holocene, the geological period when human beings are caught in the act of evolving from their Neolithic stage. The paradox is, of course, that the Holocene is not only the geologically recent past but also the geological present; it is the period of our world as well. Frisch's imaginative juxtaposition of vastly different time frames (the life of a human being and the duration of a geological period) foregrounds their incommensurability and disorientates the reader on the whole question of "origins."

20. For an interesting discussion along these lines, see M. Fischer, "Ethnicity and the postmodern arts of memory," in J. Clifford & G. Marcus (Eds.), *Writing culture: The poetics and politics of ethnography* (Berkeley: University of California Press, 1986), 194–233.

PART III

Pedagogies of
Academic and Legal Discourse

CHAPTER 10

THE PEDAGOGY OF SHAME

Sandra Lee Bartky

I

With few exceptions, women are subjected to a powerful disciplinary pedagogy which teaches us that we are Other and which prepares us for the "lesser life" that many of us are destined to live. Simone de Beauvoir has told us that women are not born but made: I take this to mean that our subjectivities are formed within an interlocking grid of social ensembles—school, family, church, workplace, media—that teach us our destiny, which is to serve and to please. Each of these institutions has its characteristic kind of teaching, each its peculiar pedagogy. The media, for example, teach us to internalize the gaze of what I have called elsewhere a "hostile witness" to our bodily being: hence we become obsessed with an "inferiorized" body—a body that is too fat or too thin, whose nose is too wide or too narrow and whose skin certainly lacks the perfection of alabaster. In the daily bombardment with images of perfect female beauty, we are made anxious and ashamed of our "imperfections," of the myriad ways in which we fail to measure up.[1]

While each of the social institutions I have mentioned has its characteristic pedagogy of shame, shame, of course, is by no means only or always what they teach us. Consider however that a shame-ridden subject lacks a sense of entitlement, she settles for less than she deserves; she is more easily dominated. To the extent that we so often accept the lesser lives that are offered us, and insofar as we internalize intimations of inferiority, we must assume that the inculcation of shame and guilt in women is a pervasive feature of social life. While all social ensembles are "pedagogical" in an extended sense, in what follows, I shall examine in some detail the teaching to girls and women in a particular site of social life—the classroom—that is a site of pedagogy in a narrower and more conventional sense. But before I proceed, I shall offer some general remarks on the nature of shame itself.

It is likely, I think, that some patterns of mood or feeling tend to characterize women more than men. Here are some candidates: shame; guilt; the peculiar dialectic of shame and pride in embodiment consequent upon a narcissistic assumption of the body as spectacle; the blissful loss of self in the sense of merger with another; the pervasive apprehension consequent upon physical vulnerability, especially the fear of rape or assault. Since I have no doubt that men and women have the same fundamental emotional capacities, to say that some pattern of feeling in women, say shame, is gender-related is not to claim that it is gender-specific, that is, that men are never ashamed; it is only to claim that women are more prone to experience the emotion in question and that the feeling itself has a different meaning in relation to our total psychic situation and general social location than a similar emotion has when experienced by men. Some of the commoner forms of shame in men, for example, may be intelligible only in light of the presupposition of male power, while in women, shame may well be a mark and token of powerlessness. We recognize in everyday speech the proneness of certain classes of persons to particular patterns of feeling: it is often said of ghetto Afro-Americans, for example, that they have feelings of hopelessness and that they are depressed and despairing. This is not to say that rich white people never despair or feel depressed, only that members of the "underclass" are more given to feelings of hopelessness than more privileged people and that the despair they feel is peculiarly disclosive of the realities of their lives.

In the following sections, I shall examine a particular manifestation of women's shame, not the alteration of pride and shame called forth by the imperatives of feminine body display, nor the shame of women who feel that they are fat, old, or ugly. The shame I want to pursue now is less specific; its boundaries are blurred; it is less available to consciousness and more likely to be denied. This shame is manifest in a pervasive sense of personal inadequacy that, like the shame of embodiment, is profoundly disempowering; both reveal the "generalized condition of dishonor" which is woman's lot in sexist society.[2] I shall maintain that women typically are more shame-prone than men, that shame is not so much a particular feeling or emotion (although it involves specific feelings and emotions) as a pervasive affective attunement to the social environment, that women's shame is more than merely an effect of subordination but, within the larger universe of patriarchal social relations, a corporeal disclosure of self in situation.

II

Shame can be characterized in a preliminary way as a species of psychic distress occasioned by a self or a state of the self apprehended as inferior, defective, or in some way diminished.[3] For the Sartre of *Being and Nothingness*, shame requires an audience: shame is "in its primary structure shame *before somebody*": it is "shame *of oneself* before the Other."[4] "Nobody," he says, "can be vulgar all alone!" To be ashamed is to be in the position of "passing judgement on myself as on an object, for it is as an object that I appear to the Other."[5] Only insofar as I apprehend myself as the Other's object, that is, through the medium of another consciousness, can I grasp my own object character. Hence, shame before the Other is primordial: I must feel shame before some actual Other before I learn to raise an internalized Other in imagination. Furthermore, "shame is by nature recognition": unless I recognize that I *am* as I am seen by the Other, the Other's judgment cannot cast me down.[6]

Sartre's discussion of shame is highly abbreviated: preoccupied with the role of the Other as audience, he has little to say about the mechanisms that can forge an identification of self and Other in an experience of shame, much less a gendered identification. Once an actual Other has revealed my object-character to me, I can become an object for myself; I can come to see myself as I might be seen by another, caught in the shameful act. Hence, I *can* succeed in being vulgar all alone: in such a situation, the Other before whom I am ashamed is only—myself. "[A] man may feel himself disgraced," says Arnold Isenberg, "by something that is unworthy in his own eyes and apart from any judgement but his own."[7]

Here is a fuller characterization of the structure of shame: shame is the distressed apprehension of the self as inadequate or diminished. It requires, if not an actual audience before whom my deficiencies are paraded, then an internalized audience with the capacity to judge me, hence internalized standards of judgment. Further, shame requires the recognition that I *am*, in some important sense, what I am seen to be.

Like Sartre, John Deigh underscores the intersubjective structure of shame. We should "conceive shame, not as a reaction to a loss, but as a reaction to a threat, specifically the threat of demeaning treatment one would invite in giving the appearance of someone of lesser worth."[8] But this seems excessively narrow. Surely, shame is sometimes a reaction to real loss, to loss of face, this occasioned by the disclosure to oneself or to others or defects in the self that may come suddenly and horribly to light. At any rate, Deigh's definition bears clearly upon additional aspects of the shame experience: the cringing withdrawal from others; the cringing within, this felt sometimes as a physical sensation of being pulled inward and downward; the necessity for hiding and concealment. All are typical responses to threat. The painful disclosure of one's shortcomings, actual or feared, may lead to "a shattering of trust in oneself, even in one's own body and skill and identity" and, since whatever is found shameful in oneself may reflect the character of one's normal social network, "in the trusted boundaries or framework of the society and the world one has known."[9] Hence, "Shame, an experience of violation of trust in oneself and in the world, may go deeper than guilt for a specific act."[10]

Deigh takes issue with John Rawls' account of shame in *A Theory of Justice*.[11] For Rawls, shame is an emotion felt upon the loss of self-esteem. Self-esteem, in his view, is rooted in the belief that one's aims and ideals are worthy and that one has the personal capacities—the abilities, talents and qualitites of character—one needs to pursue such ideals. Shame is called forth by the recognition either that one lacks these capacities or that one's aims themselves are unworthy. But Deigh disagrees: he invites us to imagine situations in which the loss of self-esteem occasioned by the realization that one has failed to realize an important goal is productive of sorrow, perhaps, but not necessarily of shame; moreover, he notes that we may feel ashamed of something about ourselves (e.g., an outlandish name or our table manners) which may be quite unconnected to what Rawls regards as the ordinary sources of self-esteem. Deigh notes that shame is often occasioned by the recognition that we have violated norms appropriate to our station in society: in such a case "the subject neither realizes that his aims and ideals are shoddy nor discovers a defect in himself that makes him ill-suited to pursue them."[12] Rawls' mistake was to have associated identity too closely with achievement: he makes no distinction between "who one is and how one conducts one's life."[13] This omission reflects the privilege of "persons who are relatively free of constraints on their choise of life pursuits owing to class, race, ethnic origins" and, I would add, to gender.[14] In my view, Deigh's way of characterizing shame marks an advance over Rawls, recognizing as it does the extent to which the worth of persons is determined not only by their achievements as measured against their ideals, but by something which may have little to do with their achievements, namely, their "status in the context of some social hierarchy."[15] One disclaimer, however: I find that the subjunctive mood in which Deigh's definition is formulated fails to distinguish sufficiently between shame as a response to demeaning treatment one fears one would invite in appearing to be a person of lesser worth and the shame of someone subjected routinely to such treatment.

Shame, then, involves the distressed apprehension of oneself as a lesser creature. Guilt, by contrast, refers not to the subject's nature but to her actions: typically, it is called forth by the active violation of principles which a person values and by which she feels herself bound. Deigh puts it well: "Shame is felt over shortcomings, guilt over wrongdoings."[16] Shame is called forth by the apprehension of some serious flaw in the self, guilt by the consciousness that one has committed a transgression. The widely held notion that shame is a response to external and guilt to internal sanctions is incorrect: shame and guilt are alike in that each involves a condemnation of the self by itself for some failure to measure up; it is the measures that differ. While useful conceptual distinctions can be drawn between shame and guilt, the boundaries between them tend to blur in actual experience. Psychological studies have shown that most people are hard put to state the difference between shame and guilt, nor can they easily classify their experiences under one heading or the other.[17] This is hardly surprising, since each must call forth the other with great frequency. The violation of a cherished moral principle is likely to be taken by anyone without satanic ambitions as the sign of some shameful weakness in the personality.

III

Textbooks in the psychology of women tend to confirm the everyday observation that women are in general less assertive than men, have lower self-esteem, less overall confidence and poorer self-concepts.[18] The terms on this list refer to traits and dispositions such as assertiveness and to beliefs: to have a poor self-concept, presumably, is to have one set of beliefs about oneself, while to have a good self-concept is to have another. Missing here is any sense of the affective taste, the emotional coloration of these traits and beliefs. Certainly, everyone understands how painful it is to have low self-esteem or too little confidence. Let us pursue this: what, precisely, is the character of this pain?

Several years ago, I taught an upper-level extension course in a suburban high school. The students were mostly high school teachers, required by their school district to earn periodic graduate credit as a condition of continuing employment. None of the students was very young: most were in their forties and fifties. Women outnumbered men by about two to one. The women, who tended on the average to be somewhat academically better students than the men, displayed far less confidence in their ability to master the material. I found this surprising, since the female teachers, pedagogical authorities in their own classrooms, did the same work as the male teachers, had comparable seniority, similar educational credentials and, I assume, pay equity. The school in which both men and women taught had an excellent reputation. There is nothing unique about the classroom I am about to describe: I have observed in other classrooms what I observed there. I select this particular class as an example because male and female students were mature and well-matched professionally and because their relationships seemed to be free of sexual tensions and courtship games that sometimes complicate the relationships of younger men and women.

Though women were in the majority, they were noticeably quieter in class discussion than the men. The men engaged freely in classroom exchanges and seemed quite confident—in view of the quality of some of their remarks, overconfident. Women who did enter discussion spoke what linguists call "women's language": their speech was marked by hesitations and false starts; they tended to introduce their comments with self-denigrating expressions ("You may think that this is a stupid question, but . . ."); they often used a questioning intonation which in effect turned a simple declarative sentence into a request for help or for affirmation from without; they used "tag" questions which had the same effect ("Camus' theme in *The Myth of Sisyphus* is the absurdity of human existence, isn't it?") and excessive qualifiers ("Isn't it true that sometimes, maybe . . .").[19] This style of speaking, whatever its substance, communicates to listeners the speaker's lack of confidence in what she is saying and this, in turn, damages her credibility.

In addition to their style of speech, I was struck by the way many female students behaved as they handed me their papers. They would offer heartfelt apologies and copious expressions of regret for the poor quality of their work—work which turned out, most of the time, to be quite good. While apologizing, a student would often press the edges of her manuscript together so as to make it literally smaller, holding the paper uncertainly somewhere in the air as if unsure whether she wanted to relinquish it at all. Typically, she would deliver the apology with head bowed, chest hollowed, and shoulders hunched slightly forward. The male students would stride over to the desk and put down their papers without comment.

Now every female student did not behave in this way all of the time. Nor is this all that the women communicated. To the casual observer, the atmosphere in the classroom was both relaxed and stimulating: both men and women took an evident interest in the material and managed a lively exchange of ideas. But, like an organ-point that sounded faintly but persistently all term, something else was detectable too: it became clear to me that many women students were ashamed of their written work and ashamed to express their ideas in a straightforward and open manner. Indeed, it would not be unusual for a student just to say "I'm really ashamed of this paper" while handing it to me. I have no doubt that these utterances were accurate reports of feeling. At the same time, I suspect that they were rituals of self-shaming undertaken in order to bear more easily a shaming they anticipated from me: an ordeal is often easier to endure if we can choose its time and place. These apologies served also to underscore the students' desire to do well in the course, hence, to get into my good books and, by arousing pity in me for such evident emotional distress, to soften my judgment of their work. Behind a facade of friendliness and informality, two very different dramas of relationship to the teacher were being enacted: the men regarded me as a rival or as an upstart who needed to prove herself, the women, as potentially a very punitive figure who needed to be placated and manipulated.

Given the extent to which psychotherapeutic discourse has permeated ordinary speech, it might seem more natural to say that my female students displayed not shame, but "feelings of inadequacy." In point of fact, it is difficult to distinguish the two. To confess to "feelings of inadequacy" is to do more than merely acknowledge one's limitations: it is to admit to having done some suffering in the contemplation of these limitations. I would not say, for example, that I had "feelings of inadequacy" in regard to auto mechanics. What I feel in regard to my ignorance of auto mechanics is indifference, not anguish. If, however, I say that I feel inadequate in regard to something, I imply that according to my own lights, I ought not to be inadequate in regard to this thing and that my real or putative inadequacy pains me. But what is this pain but a species of psychic distress occasioned by a sense of the self as lacking or diminished—just the definition of shame offered earlier? "When you lack what you do not want, there is no shame."[20]

It seems to be that the demeanor of my female students in that suburban classroom bore the characteristic marks of shame, of a shame felt directly or anticipated: in their silence, the necessity for hiding and concealment; in the tentative character of their speech and in their regular apologetics, the sense of self as defective or diminished. The fear of demeaning treatment could be seen in the cringing before an other from whom such treatment was anticipated; shame could be read even in the physical constriction of their bodies.

Now if the primordial structure of shame is such that one is ashamed of oneself before the Other, who is the Other before whom my female students were ashamed? Since I have a kindly and permissive style and make a point of never subjecting my students to ridicule, let us assume for the sake of argument that I am not this Other. The identity of this Other, whoever it turns out to be, will be hugely overdetermined, for women in a sexist society are subjected to demeaning treatment by a variety of Others: they bring to the classroom a complex experience of subordination and an elaborate repertoire of stereotyped gestures appropriate to their station. One wonders too whether there is any relationship between women's shame—both the shame that is directly linked to embodiment and the shame that is not and the persistence of religious traditions that have historically associated female sexuality with pollution and contagion. But whatever the character of this overdetermination, it remains the case that female subjectivity is not constructed entirely elsewhere and then brought ready-made to the classroom: the classroom is also a site of its constitution. What I shall suggest in the next section is that the Other so feared by my female students is, to a surprising degree, especially in light of the overdetermination of shame to which I have just referred—a composite portrait of other and earlier classroom teachers who had, in fact, subjected them but not their male counterparts to consistent shaming behavior. It should be kept in mind in what follows that the classroom is perhaps the most egalitarian public space that any woman in our society will ever inhabit.

IV

The Project on the Status and Education of Women of the Association of American Colleges has produced an extraordinary report which details the many ways in which the classroom climate at all educational levels may produce a diminished sense of self in girls and women. While every instructor is by no means guilty of the kinds of demeaning treatment described in this report, such treatment is widespread and pervasive. The report itself is well-documented, its claims supported by a variety of empirical studies.[21]

Females, it turns out, are less likely to be called upon directly than males; indeed, women and girls are often ignored, even when they express a willingness to speak. Teachers in grade school talk to boys wherever they are in the room, to girls only when they are nearby. Teachers tend to remember the names of male students better and to call upon them by name more often. Women are not given the same length of time to think a problem through and come up with an answer.

Nor are men and women asked the same kinds of questions: women are often asked factual questions ("When did Camus publish *The Stranger*?"), while men are asked questions that require some critical or analytical ability ("What do you see as the major thematic differences between *The Stranger* and *The Plague*?"). Some instructors may make "helpful" comments to women that imply, nevertheless, women's lesser competence ("I know that women have trouble with technical concepts, but I'll try to help you out"). Instructors tend to coach men more than women, nodding and gesturing more often in response to men's comments and pushing and probing for a fuller response: this suggests that the points men make in discussion are important and that they can stretch themselves intellectually if they try. Women may well receive less praise than men for work of the same quality, for studies have shown repeatedly that work when ascribed to a man is rated higher than the same work ascribed to a women, whether the work in question is a scholarly paper, a short story, or a painting. There is evidence that men's success generally is viewed as deserved, women's as due to luck or to the easiness of the task.[22]

Women are interrupted more than men both by their teachers and by their fellow students. Teachers are likelier to use a tone of voice that indicates interest when talking to men but to adopt a patronizing or dismissive tone when talking to women. Teachers have been observed to make more eye contact with men than with women; they assume a posture of attentiveness when men speak but look away or look at the clock when women speak.

Ignorant of the fact that styles of communication are gender-related, instructors may assume that women's use of "women's language" means that women have nothing to say. On the other hand, women may be viewed negatively when they display stereotypically masculine traits such as ambition, assertiveness or a pleasure in disputation. The female student may receive direct sexual overtures in the classroom, but even if this does not happen, she is far likelier than her male counterpart to receive comments about her appearance: this may suggest to her that she is primarily a decorative being who is less serious and hence less competent than the men in her class.

Instructors may use sexist humor or demeaning sexual allusions to "spice up" a dull subject. They may disparage women or groups of women generally. Or they may use sexist language, referring to human beings in generic masculine terms or calling male students "men" but female students "girls" or "gals." The linguistic disparagement of women may be echoed in a course content from which the history, literature, accomplishments or perspectives of women have been omitted.

Here, as elsewhere, women of color are in double jeopardy, for the demeaning treatment that is visited upon women, whatever their race, is similar in many ways to the demeaning treatment that is suffered by students of color, whatever their gender. Instructors may interpret student's behavior in the light of racial stereotypes, taking, for example, the silence of a black woman as "sullenness'" of an Hispanic woman as "passivity." Black women, in particular, report that their instructors expect them to be either academically incompetent or else academically brilliant "exceptions." A black woman may be singled out, in ways that underscore her sense of not belonging, by being asked for the "black woman's point of view" on some issue rather than her own view.

College teachers have been better mentors to men than to women; they are likelier to choose men for teaching and research assistantships and to contact men when professional opportunities arise. In laboratory courses, instructors have been observed to position themselves closer to men than to women, giving men more detailed instructions on how to do an assignment. They are likelier to do the assignment for women or just allow them to fail. In such courses, men are often allowed to crowd out women at demonstrations. Classroom teachers are unlikely to recognize, hence to try to alter the dynamics of mixed-sex group discussion which are not different in the classroom than they are elsewhere:

> Despite the popular notion that in everyday situations women talk more than men, studies show that in formal groups containing men and women: men talk more than women; men talk for longer periods and take more turns at speaking; men exert more control over the topic of conversation; men interrupt women more frequently than women interrupt men and men's interruptions of women more often introduce trivial or inappropriately personal comments that bring the woman's discussion to an end or change its focus.[23]

These behaviors, considered *in toto*, cannot fail to diminish women, to communicate to them the insignificance and lack of seriousness of their classroom personae. When one considers the length of this catalogue of microbehaviors and senses what must be its cumulative effect, one is tempted to regard the shaming behavior visited upon women in the modern classroom as the moral equivalent of the dunce-cap of old.

The classroom, as we noted earlier, is only one of many locations wherein female sense of self is constituted. Behaviors akin to the ones just listed are enacted in many other domains of life, in, for example, family, church, and workplace. If, as I claimed earlier, women are more shame-prone than men, the cause is not far to seek: women, more often than men, are made to feel shame in the major sites of social life. Moreover, it is in the act of being shamed and in the feeling ashamed that there is disclosed to women who they are and how they are faring within the domains they inhabit, though, as we shall see, this disclosure is ambiguous and oblique.

V

A number of contemporary philosophers have maintained that "over a wide range of emotions, beliefs are constitutive of the experience in question."[24] The so-called "emotions of self-assessment," such as pride, shame, and guilt, seem to lend themselves well to analysis in terms of belief. DeSousa, for example, holds that shame appears "to be founded entirely on belief," a view, as we saw earlier, that Rawls seems to share.[25] Now what are the relevant beliefs in which shame is said to consist? Gabrielle Taylor offers an account of the common structure of belief in emotions of self-assessment: "in experiencing any one of these emotions, the person concerned believes of herself that she has deviated from some norm and that in doing so, she has altered her standing in the world."[26] Presumably, then, shame would consist in three beliefs: first, the general belief that deviation from *this* norm marks someone as a person of lesser worth; second, the belief that *I* have deviated from this norm; third, the belief that in so doing I have altered my standing in the world.

If this analysis is correct, one would expect students who behave as if they feel *generally* ashamed of their performance to believe in their general failure to measure up to the ordinary standards of academic performance. Now I do not think that my students held any such general beliefs about themselves at all; indeed, I suspect that if confronted with such a claim, they would angrily deny it. Could they not point to evidence of past academic accomplishment? Seemingly ashamed, they do not believe they have anything in general to be ashamed of; it is merely *this* paper, so hastily written she's ashamed to give you, *that* remark she fears you'll find stupid. My students felt inadequate without really believing themselves to be inadequate in the salient respects: they sensed something inferior about themselves without believing themselves to be generally inferior at all.

What transpires in the classroom, it should be noted, goes on behind everyone's back. The shaming behavior is typically quite subtle, so much so that those responsible for it are largely unaware of what they are doing. Students believe that the classroom is a meritocracy, teachers that they treat all students fairly, irrespective of race, class, or gender. Both are wrong. The biases that invade consciousness are so pervasive and so little available to consciousness that they can sabotage good intentions—or even good politics. Hence, the earlier assumption that I myself had done nothing to provoke shame in my female students is very likely wrong as well. Without an alternative interpretive framework wherein their meanings might be differently understood, the comment on a student's appearance is merely a compliment, the sexist joke, mere harmless fun. Because the sexist messages of the classroom are transmitted in a disguised fashion or else both sent and received below the level of explicit awareness, what gets communicated to women does not take the form of propositional meaning and what they take away from the situation is not so much a belief as a *feeling* of inferiority or a *sense* of inadequacy. Female self-awareness in the situation I describe is importantly constituted by a certain contradiction between appearance and reality: on the one hand, the presumption of equality on the part of all actors in this drama, on the other hand, its actual though covert and unacknowledged absence. An ambiguous situation, affirming women in some ways and diminishing them in others, holding itself out as fair while oftentimes violating its own standards of fairness, tends to produce in women a confused and divided consciousness: believing themselves to be fully the competitive equals of men, many women yet feel somehow diminished and inadequate, this in the absense of any actual evidence of failure.

In sum, then, the "feelings" and "sensings" that go to make up the women's shame I describe, do not reach a state of clarity we can dignify as belief. For all that, they are profoundly disclosive of women's "Being-in-the-world," far more so than many fully formed beliefs women hold about themselves and about their situation, beliefs, for example, that, like men, they enjoy "equality of opportunity" or that the school or workplace is meritocratic in character. What gets grasped in the having of such feelings is nothing less than women's subordinate status in a hierarchy of gender, their situation not in ideology but in the social formation as it is actually constituted. Not only does the revelatory character of shame not occur at the level of belief, but the corrosive character of shame and of similar sensings, their undermining effect and the peculiar helplessness women exhibit when in their power, lies in part in the very failure of these feelings to attain the status of belief. Once elevated to the relative lucidity of propositional belief, the suspicion that one's papers are poor, one's remarks stupid, indeed, that one's entire academic performance is substandard, would quickly vanish, overwhelmed by a mass of contrary evidence. With the collapse of these suspicions-cum-beliefs, the shame of which they are said to be constitutive, having no longer any foundation would likely disappear.

VI

In conventional moral philosophy, shame is a penance that restores the miscreant to the proper moral equilibrium; this is taken to be the normal and ordinary use of shame in ethical life. Unpleasant though they may be, philosophers regard emotions such as shame and guilt a price we pay for the very capacity to be moral, for only persons with an emotional investment in the doing of good deeds could feel distressed by their misdeeds. But for the shame-ridden and shame-prone, there is no moral equilibrium to which to return: "feeling inadequate" may color a person's entire emotional life. Under conditions of oppression, the oppressed must struggle not only against more visible disadvantages but against guilt and shame as well. It was not for nothing that the movement for black empowerment called not only for black civil rights and economic advancement, but for "black pride." Nor should we forget that this was the movement that needed to invent the slogan "Black is beautiful." What figures in much moral philosophy as a disruption in an otherwise undisturbed life is, for whole categories of persons, a pervasive affective attunement, a mode of disclosure wherein their inferiority is disclosed to inferiorized subjects, though, paradoxically, as I have been arguing, what is *disclosed* fails, in the typical case, to be *understood*.[27] Better people are not made in this way, only people who are weaker, more timid, less confident, less demanding and, hence, more easily dominated. The experience of shame may tend to lend legitimacy to the structure of authority that occasions it, for the majesty of judgment is affirmed in its very capacity to injure. The heightened self-consciousness that comes with emotions of self-assessment may become, in the shame of the oppressed, a stagnant self-obsession. Or shame may generate a rage whose expression is unconstructive, even self-destructive. The need for secrecy and concealment that figures so largely in the shame-experience isolates the oppressed from one another and in this way works against the emergence of a sense of solidarity. In all these ways, shame is profoundly disempowering.

What is to be done? What practice is suggested by this theory? The growth of feminist consciousness has made it possible for many students to detect overt sexism in the classroom. A long story could be told about the efforts, both successful and unsuccessful, to change the behavior of the more benighted classroom teachers. But sexism that is overt, to those who can recognize it for what it is, is less corrosive to the souls of students than the covert sexism that is detailed in "The Classroom Climate"—the sexist practice that "goes on behind everyone's back." What is to be done about *that*?

We can, first of all, give copies of reports such as "Classroom Climate" to all our colleagues and students. We can make a point of keeping up with the relevant research. Those of us who are qualified to do such research can contribute to this research ourselves. We can have our classes videotaped. We can, in public forums, discuss ways in which subtle disparagement can diminish the student—male or female, white or nonwhite—who is "Other." We can encourage our schools, whatever their level, to sponsor such sessions and to invite both students and faculty to attend. Women students complain to me often about the sexism of some of their instructors; rarely can I persuade them to do anything whatever to stop it. Occasionally, I have written politely worded letters to these instructors in an attempt to articulate what so discomfits some of their students. But students are more timid than they need to be; they ought to be empowered to fight on their own behalf. They need somehow to be assured—by policies that have yet to be invented—that their complaints about a teacher's classroom practice need not lead inexorably to lower grades or withdrawal of patronage. But there are dangers here. "Troublesome" students *are* often punished. Teachers stick together and the confidentiality of students' complaints cannot always be guaranteed. Teachers need protection, too, from the occasional malice or paranoia of students. Many people will be made uncomfortable by this increased vigilance; I myself worry that heightened consciousness might turn our schools into gulags where everyone fears the informer. But doing nothing at all is equally unacceptable. While individual grievances cannot be ignored, I myself would prefer a meta-pedagogical practice that encouraged general discussion of covert sexism in an atmosphere of civility, discussion in which noone is scapegoated and from which all might learn. In spite of the possibility of risks and discomfitures to everyone, ourselves included—we must never forget what we are about—a pedagogy that "sets out to 'reserve feminine silence,' to 'voice' and to value girls' and women's writing, reading and knowledges."[28] We have come far in the last two decades, yet we must not allow ourselves to forget that most of the pedagogy now in place maintains, both overtly and covertly, a powerful patriarchal grasp on what our society holds out to its youth as "truth."[29]

NOTES

1. See S. L. Bartky, *Femininity and domination* (New York: Routledge, 1990), chapters 3 and 5.

2. H. A. Bulhan, *Frantz Fanon and the psychology of oppression* (New York: Plenum, 1985), 12. Bulhan uses this phrase to characterize slaves and oppressed persons of color. Citing the work of psychologists Orlando Patterson and Chester Pierce, Bulhan characterizes a "generalized condition of dishonor" as a status in which one's person lacks integrity, worth, and autonomy and in which one is subject to violations of space, time, energy, mobility, bonding, and identity.

3. S. Miller, *The shame experience* (Hillsdale, NJ: The Analytic Press, 1985), 32.

4. J.-P. Sartre, *Being and nothingness* (New York: Philosophical Library, 1956), 221–222.

5. Ibid., 222.

6. Ibid.

7. A. Isenberg, "Natural pride and natural shame," in A. Rorty, (Ed.), *Explaining Emotions* (Berkeley: University of California Press, 1980), 366.

8. J. Deigh, "Shame and self-esteem: A critique," *Ethics*, 93 (January 1983), 242.

9. H. M. Lynd, *Shame and the search for identity* (New York: Harcourt Brace and Co., 1958), 46.

10. Ibid., 47.

11. J. Rawls, *A theory of justice* (Cambridge, MA: Harvard University Press, 1971), 440–446.

12. Deigh, "Shame and self-esteem," 235.

13. Ibid.

14. Ibid.

15. Ibid., 241.

16. Ibid., 225.

17. Miller, *The shame experience*, 3.

18. Some relevant studies are discussed in M. W. Matlin, *The psychology of women* (New York: Holt, Rinehard and Winston, 1987), 129–132.

19. For discussions of "women's language," see R. Lakoff, *Language and women's place* (New York: Harper & Row, 1975); B. Thorne & N. Henley (Eds.), *Language and sex: Difference and dominance*. (Rowley, MA: Newbury House Publishers, 1975); N. Henley, *Body politics: Power, sex and non-verbal communication* (Englewood Cliffs, NJ: Prentice-Hall, 1977).

20. Isenberg, "Natural pride," 370.

21. R. M. Hall, with the assistance of B. R. Sandler, "The classroom climate: A chilly one for women?" Prepared by the Project on the Status and Education of Women of the Association of American Colleges, 1818 R St., NW, Washington, DC 20009. The claims I make in this section about differences in treatment of male and female students are drawn almost entirely from empirical studies cited in the body of the report or in the Notes and Selected List of Resources. See esp. pp. 17–21.

22. An excellent review and evaluation of this research can be found in S. Riger and P. Galligan, "Women in management: An eploration of competing paradigms," *American Psychologist*, 35(10) (October 1980), 902–910. See also P. R. Clance, *The imposture phenomenon* (New York: Bantam, 1985), also P. R. Clance and S. Jones, "The imposture phenomenon in high-achieving women: Dynamics and therapeutic interventions," *Psychotherapy: Theory, research and practice*, 15 (1978), 241–247.

23. "Classroom climate," 8.

24. G. Taylor, *Pride, shame and guilt: Emotions of self-assessment* (Oxford: Oxford University Press, 1985), 2.

25. R. R. DeSousa, *The rationality of emotion* (Cambridge, MA: MIT Press, 1987), 137.

26. Taylor, *Pride, shame and guilt*, 1.

27. "Phenomenally, we would wholly fail to recogize both *what* mood discloses and *how* it discloses, if that which is disclosed were to be compared with what Dasein is acquainted with, knows and believes 'at the same time' when it has such a mood." Martin Heidegger, *Being and time*, trans. MacQuarrie and Robinson (New York: Harper & Row, 1962), 173. See also section 29, pp. 172–179.

28. C. Luke & A. Luke, "Pedagogy," in J. M. Simson (Ed.), *The encyclopedia of language and linguistics* (London: Pergamon Press, 1993), 566.

29. This essay draws heavily from my longer and differently focused chapter 6, "Shame and gender," in Bartky, *Femininity and domination*. I wish to thank Carmen Luke for her patience and encouragement, as well as for her incisive editorial and theoretical help in the preparation of this manuscript.

CHAPTER 11

RECONSIDERING THE NOTIONS OF VOICE AND EXPERIENCE IN CRITICAL PEDAGOGY

Anneliese Kramer-Dahl

While deconstruction has been widely used to disrupt the textual staging of knowledge in disciplines such as literary, social, and cultural theory, its powerful resources have only recently come to be applied to pedagogy and its theoretical metanarratives. A small body of deconstructive readings, performed foremost by women in literacy education, has emerged, asking profoundly unsettling questions which challenge what we claim to be doing in the name of education. Their focus has been largely on the texts of what has been termed 'critical' or 'liberatory' pedagogy, a pedagogy which theorizes and attempts to practice literacy education as a form of social and political empowerment of those silenced in conventional institutions of schooling. Founded on Brazilian educator Freire's notion of teaching for critical consciousness (conscientization), the project of critical pedagogy—elaborated by educational theorists Giroux, McLaren, Simon, Shor, and others—aims at opening institutional spaces for marginalized students to give voice to their experience and to develop a critical analysis of oppressive social systems in order to transform them in accordance with their interests.

That it is women who question the claims of empowerment of these largely male texts is not surprising, given that literacy training is overwhelmingly the work of women, who, as mere executioners of theories and curricula constructed for them by men, had their positionings and identities defined for themselves for too long by those in control. In this emerging tradition of deconstructive readings by feminist pedagogues, Ellsworth (1992) examines the key discourses of critical pedagogy in light of her own experience as a teacher of a university anti-racism course. Gore (1992), in her Foucauldian analysis of power and pedagogy, demonstrates that these discourses of empowerment function as much as "regimes of truth," with their normalizing and oppressive tendencies, as the discourses whose "will to power" they so clearly expose. Similarly, Luke (1992) points to the First World masculinist subject that these discourses consistently construct, and Lather (1991) examines how their attempts to empower actually maintain and reinforce relations of dominance. In short, these authors agree that even if the goal of our work, as is that of critical approaches to literacy, is the emancipation of heretofore marginalized groups, we need to be aware that it is bound to be, as educational systems generally are, in Foucault's terms, a way of "disciplining the body, normalizing behavior, administering the life of populations" (Rajchman, 1985, 82). Nevertheless, they also agree that by taking up the challenges deconstruction offers to the discourses of empowerment, their practice is what Spanos (1987, 12) calls "a forwarding, a postmodern critical" one, intended not to destroy the work done in the name of empowerment, but to test and continually revise it.

When applying the resources of deconstruction to the discourse of critical pedagogy and confronting it with the particularities of my own attempts to put into practice its agenda for empowerment, I run a considerable risk; after all, up until recently women have not been considered a source of knowledge legitimate enough to engage in reflection upon their own experience. Ellsworth's attempt to do so, when she problematized key assumptions of critical pedagogy in light of her experience of teaching an anti-racism course, was dismissed by established theorists as a "careerist" move, an act of rebellion of the "daughter" out to discredit her fathers via the assumedly inadequate "proof" of her account of her "failed" practice (Giroux and McLaren's readings as quoted by Lather, 1991, 45–47). Yet, at the same time, it is because of the existence of particularistic, life-written presentations like hers that my attempt to reflect upon my own experience in the following becomes much less an act of courage. Furthermore, given the conflicting readings her account elicited, I have learned that a less agonistic way of telling allows for a more productive way of disagreeing among pedagogues who claim to be part of the same struggle.

The particular local teaching site I have been most heavily involved in is that of the introductory university composition class, particularly the course for basic or remedial writers. It is in its context that I can deconstruct the assumptions and prescriptions of critical literacy pedagogy best since they guided my practice in many ways. I will begin my project by looking at the kinds of curricular practices this course was trying to go beyond, and its own assumptions and goals, and the roots these have in larger ideological structures. This will be crucial when it comes to understanding the correctives I am proposing later—correctives which are not to be taken as yet another model of critical pedagogy, or, worse yet, a set of prescriptions for practice. Instead, they are intended as provocation to reconsider what is really at issue when we claim to be empowering students and helping them discover their "voices."

CONTEXTUALIZING TRADITIONAL AND ALTERNATIVE BASIC WRITING PEDAGOGIES

Both the basic writing course in its then dominant form and the alternative version I constructed can only be understood as complex responses to an array of historical and social circumstances. In what follows I will briefly review some of these, which range from university-wide to smaller departmental factors, especially hierarchies which informed the then current place of writing courses, and, more specifically, basic writing courses, within the university. As for my own alternative teaching agenda, it also emerged, as we shall see, in reaction to the tensions and controversies surrounding the university's efforts at the time to promote "educational equity." At the same time, it was also the result of my increased interest in poststructural critical theory and Freire-inspired pedagogies, which put in question a number of assumptions upon which the dominant approaches to basic writing classes were founded.

When I joined the writing faculty of the English department of a major Californian state university in the late 1980s, I was caught in the midst of a new "crisis of standards." At least that was what educational commissions and university administrations, who are fond of speaking a discourse of crisis, claimed we were facing. As usual, it was seen as being brought about by yet another change in the social characteristics of the student population. At the time the new "illiterates" who "darkened the doors" (Collins, 1993) of the University of California campuses were largely Asian-American students, already making up more than 40 percent of the undergraduate student body and on the increase. Moreover, yet another wave of drastic cuts in the permanent faculty was underway. As a writing teacher, I was also caught in hierarchies and dichotomies that had increasingly solidified in English departments over the decades. In their historical studies of writing instruction in the United States, both Rose (1985) and Ohmann (1988) have shown that the writing course, especially that targeted at incoming undergraduates, has held a strange position in the curriculum of English studies. To be sure, with the decline in students majoring in their subject, English departments need to hold on to this course, since it services the university at large, is often generously funded and thus ensures that English studies does not have to share the unhappy fate of so many other humanities departments, which are constantly on the verge of elimination. Yet English faculty consider teaching undergraduate writing intellectually demeaning and at most volunteer to help in its administration. After all, they have been trained and hired as literary critics, their job being to teach the close reading of literature to those select few who have the leisure to indulge in its consumption. Writing, on the other hand, is work, training for all in skills to survive in university and in the workforce. It is no coincidence, then, that its teaching is left largely to temporary and part-time hires, most of them women. Holding so-called "non-career" jobs, they are not entitled to time off for research and can be given more and larger classes than permanent staff. Also, not only are they robbed of the status that permanent faculty have, but as "casual labor" (Collins, 1993, 170), they are left with very little autonomy as far as the curriculum of their courses is concerned.

At the time I started teaching, divisions and struggles did not just exist within the university at large, pitting departments against the university administration, tenured against temporary faculty, and men against women. Even within the writing curriculum itself, "nontraditional," often ESL students, who typically score low on the entrance test, were separated from traditional ones by being placed in remedial or basic writing classes. In the regular writing classes, under the then increasing influence of social-constructivist approaches to composition, the emphasis was largely on familiarizing students with the discourse conventions of various academic disciplines—with the exception of the occasional more traditional teacher who, spurred on by the contemporary calls of neoconservatives like Bloom, Hirsch, and the then Secretary of Education to uphold the canon, made his students engage with what Bloom (1987, 62) calls "the greatest texts" of Western civilization, or at least of American culture. Basic writing courses, in contrast, were defined by "an absence and a process" (Collins, 1993, 169).

Since they lacked academic discourse skills, it was argued, students placed in basic writing classes should first be encouraged to write narratives of personal experience and then slowly move outward to essays in which they had to take a public position. The reasons given for this were convincing, or so at least they seemed to be to me at the time. Exposing them to models of "good prose" or to typical genres of disciplinary writing, as was happening in the regular classes, would easily encourage the students' mindless imitation of forms and, given their lack of preparation, would magnify the relative advantage of those with prior exposure to such types of texts over those in basic writing classes even more. If there was to be any "text in the class" at all, it was the texts the students themselves wrote in response to experience-eliciting assignments. In line with the emphasis on personal growth, basic writing course curricula advocated the use of the process model of writing, arguing that with its emphasis on "free" and "authentic" expression, it would help inexperienced writers gain confidence and overcome their fear of using their own opinions, notwithstanding the fact that teachers had the right to judge to what extent the students' expressions were free and authentic.

It was then emerging writing research influenced by poststructuralist theories of languages, such as that of Bartholomae (1985) and Bizzell (1982), and its particular focus on the situation of basic writers that led a number of us teachers to reconsider the existing course curriculum. Not only were general notions like the integrity of experience, "originality," "individual authorship," and the "naturalness" of the act of writing put in question, but more specific curricular practices were interrogated as well. To what extent does a textless, expressivist-oriented curriculum address the problems of underprepared, nonmainstream students, especially those problems they face when called upon to read and write in other classes? Effective writing in any academic course involves the construction of one's own text out of and in critical response to prior texts—texts and response-strategies which basic writers, typically from less privileged home and educational backgrounds, where language practices are most unlike those of the academy, have not been exposed to.

More and more we realized that a curriculum exclusively focused on the students' personal experience was a problematic way of responding to the challenge of their underpreparedness. Rather than fostering the students' questioning and synthesizing of the ideas of others, it did nothing but make them reproduce their own commonsense (McCormick, 1989; Christie, 1989). Thus the division as it had been set up between regular and basic writing courses—one which restricted the teaching of writing that is highly valued in academia to students already privileged and which continued, in high-school fashion, to mine the personal everyday experience of those already marginalized— clearly was a means of ensuring the successful perpetuation of the very race- and class-bound differences in performance, and hence inequalities, that the students had entered the university with. To quote Collins

(1993, 169), ironically "the students most defined as structurally 'lacking,' as needing special, remedial courses, were given the most 'polite' curriculum, one in which the discursive demands of the institution were soft-pedaled and their experience was given pride of place." By maintaining this polite, benevolent curriculum, we had, however unintendedly, become complicit in the further marginalization and stigmatization of our basic writing students.

One way of challenging the use of writing instruction as a gatekeeper of inequalities had been suggested by Bartholomae and Petrosky (1986) in their guidelines for a basic writing course. They argued for direct, explicit instruction in the conventions of academic discourse, thus hoping to narrow the gap that had existed between students in basic writing courses and those enrolled in regular ones. This way, according to Bartholomae (1985, 156), students would be taught "how to speak in the voice and through the codes of those of us with power and wisdom." As he and Petrosky saw it, documents of personal experience were no longer ends in themselves, mere breakthroughs in students' confidence as writers, but were to become the objects of directed scholarly investigation. In guided assignments, the students would be asked to rework these prior texts of theirs, taking them as "case studies," in the context of standard academic accounts of these kinds of experiences. Activities like these would, to quote Bartholomae and Petrosky (1986, 38), "enable these marginal students to participate in an academic project" and "to demonstrate to them, and to the university that such participation is possible." And perhaps even more importantly, it would lead to a critical recasting of their attitudes towards written texts, especially those of experts, which they tend to see as "speaking with an oracular authority" (Bartholomae and Petrosky, 1986, 38), and which at best they have learned to write *with* and not *against*.

However, in their effort to initiate their students into the discursive activities of the university, Bartholomae and Petrosky's curriculum left behind, or at least left undeveloped, an important concern of a literacy intended to empower, which is to get them to play an active role in the challenging and transformation of these activities. Also, reading Aronowitz and Giroux's (1985) radical critique of education in America, I began to see that, however laudable the emphasis on the social construction of knowledge and on literacy as socialization is, pedagogies like these amount to necessary but limited interventions. For, despite their keen awareness of the power-and-knowledge asymmetries and resulting conflicts in the context of the classroom, they often fail to acknowledge similar ideological factors at work in academic discourse communities, for the characterization of which key concepts such as power, conflict, and difference are equally crucial. In their optimistic belief that to teach students ways of academic writing and knowledge creation will help them overcome their problem of academic marginalization, writing specialists like Bartholomae and Petrosky tend to ignore the fact that discourse communities are usually more concerned with excluding new members and new knowledges than with admitting them. Or at least, they feel that it is pedagogically more effective to conceal any sign of conflict or dissonance within such discourse communities from their student newcomers. A discursive practice is after all much easier to approximate by novice writers when it is presented as fixed and unified. From a perspective of critical pedagogy, on the other hand, teaching any discursive practice, whether academic or nonacademic, without a careful cultural analysis and critique will reinforce the culture's dominant ideological structures and thus render Freirean conscientization difficult if not impossible. More specifically, our students, so Giroux (1983, 219) argues, many of whom are submerged to a "culture of silence" and accept their social positions as natural, need to learn how writing works in the world, a world where "social practices situated in issues of class, gender and race shape everyday experience."

This latter point was brought home to me most urgently at that time through recent political developments on campus and in the community around it. In the winter of 1986, anti-racist groups of academics and students had just faced a major setback. Despite their month-long community wide demonstrations in favor of bilingual state policies, the people of the state of California had voted in large majorities to support the "official English" memorandum on their ballots. Worse still, the powerful lobbying groups advocating "English only" laws, who had succeeded in swaying the public's vote, also had been fanning their resentment over policies in general which "cater" to immigrants and other minorities. In the weeks that followed the election, on campus Asian and Chicano student speakers took the stage demanding that community programs be launched to maximize awareness of racial issues, and that historically silenced cultures and their knowledges be represented equally in American education through the institution of courses in, for example, Asian-American and Chicano studies.

It was these minority student demonstrators and their demands that helped me finally shape my alternative curriculum, one which was to emphasize difference, diversified voices, and the possibility of education leading to cultural self-recognition rather than a blind acceptance of "the way things are." In the articulation of its rationale and aims, I was encouraged by the attempts at revision which were being undertaken at other universities, most notably that by Herrington and Curtis at the University of Massachusetts. Sensitive to the problems of a personal-growth type and a social-constructivist writing curriculum, an alternative basic writing course had to be reinvisaged as one which helped students write "experience" neither as isolated individuals, emphasizing the unhistorical and personal, nor as members-to-be of discourse communities, emphasizing the apolitical and universal of knowledge-construction. Instead, experience, and the knowledge that is subsequently constructed, had to be seen as contingent upon race, gender, language, and history (e.g., Ellsworth, 1992; Mohanty, 1990) and hence as complex and frequently politically volatile. Effective writing instruction, thus reconceptualized, had to provide marginalized students with "the tools that enable [them] to appropriate those dimensions of their experiences and history that have been suppressed" (Giroux, 1983, 231), thus no longer simply consenting to a construction of the social world which has for so long acted against their interests. The appropriation of this diversity of experiences and histories is especially crucial for students in basic writing courses, as, according to Herrington and Curtis (1990, 490–491),

> Our writers are on the so-called "margin" both academically and socially: academically, as students in Basic Writing, and socially, as citizens of color in a predominantly White, Anglo-European, English-speaking institution traditionally unreceptive to their cultural and linguistic heritages. . . . By bringing their varied cultures and life experiences from the margin into the center of the course—a relatively easy task—we can help them cross that academic boundary or, perhaps more accurately, we can begin to erode this false boundary and the institutionally constructed impediment to education it represents.

The way to achieve this movement to the center was by "finding ways of working with students that enable the full expression of multiple 'voices' engaged in dialogic encounter" (Simon, 1987, 380), encouraging them to speak in self-affirming ways about their experiences and differences and to investigate how these have been shaped by their own social positions and those of others. Accordingly, "no privileged place" was to be accorded "to Western culture" (Aronowitz and Giroux, 1991, 13) and its texts. Instead, the course was to be focused on subaltern texts, ones which represented the students' own diverse histories, dreams, and experiences and thus to enable them to recognize marginal voices, including their own, as voices of authority.

PROBLEMATIC ASSUMPTIONS OF MY EMPOWERING CLASSROOM

It is this kind of classroom I was trying to create for my students. I selected minority-authored texts, such as Richard Rodriguez' *Hunger of Memory*, Maxine Hong Kingston's *The Woman Warrior*, David Hwang's play *Family Devotions*, and Frank Chin's short stories, texts which reflect students' own diversified experiences as Chicanos and Asian-Americans. Through these textual models I hoped to encourage my students to articulate their own experiences in dialogue with these texts and with each other, and then take the necessary further step to provide them with a language of critique that would enable them to critically interrogate the discourses that give meaning to these experiences. What I did not realize then was that, however obvious my rationale behind these goals may have been, much less so were the ideological assumptions behind it, many of which were highly problematic. For one thing, as mentioned earlier, I had assumed, along with Herrington and Curtis, that bringing the students' varied cultures and experiences from the margin to the center was a "relatively easy" task, when in actuality it turned out to be an extremely complicated process. My lapse into this traditional view of the learner as a kind of blank slate is apparently characteristic of most critical approaches to literacy. Freirean approaches quite commonly assume that students are basically "innocent," more or less free of conflict, not people whose subjectivities have been formed in ways that they are likely to have "internalized" what are considered normative behaviors. To illustrate, Barkley Brown (1989, 921) describes her own pedagogical practices when teaching African-American women's history:

> How do our students overcome years of notions of what is normative? While trying to think about these issues in my teaching, I have come to understand that this is not merely an intellectual process. It is not merely a question of whether or not we have learned to analyze in particular kinds of ways, or whether people are able to intellectualize about a variety of experiences. It is also about coming to believe in the possibility of a variety of experiences, a variety of ways of understanding the world, a variety of frameworks of operation, without imposing consciously or unconsciously the notion of the norm.

Even if I had anticipated this difficult pedagogical process of reassessing center and margin, there were other crucial issues that required equal consideration. For instance, in light of Foucault's description of the panopticon and other expressions of disciplinary power, how can we assume that a pedagogical practice which asks students to make public information about their experiences and cultures in the presence of others, could ever grant them a safe, egalitarian place in which to speak? Indeed, as Bernstein's work on invisible pedagogy emphasizes, a more "open" classroom "encourages more [of the student] to be made public" and so more of the student will be "available for direct and indirect surveillance and control" (1977, 135). Furthermore, arguing for such a practice skirts the issue of who, in the classroom, has the authority to judge what kind of experience counts as relevant and what kind of reading of it is "correct."

This fiction of empowering pedagogy's democratic classroom will be even more difficult to maintain if we bear in mind the impending prospect of interrogation, carried out in the often alienating language of critique, which is likely to threaten students' values, desires and their willingness to openly voice their understandings and experiences of the world (for an extensive discussion, see Orner, 1992). In my own classroom I could observe that especially among the more recently immigrated Asian-American students, the "empowering knowledge" they were offered posed a threat to the stasis of their lives at home and their ability to adjust to their new host culture. The foregrounding of questions of social and political inequality in the university and in the larger community did not always carry the same weight for them as they did for their American-born counterparts. In fact, some of them found it disturbing constantly to have to consider such issues. As one of my students, a recently arrived Chinese-American from Malaysia, wrote in her journal, "I realize that as a Chinese I am not being treated equally, but it's a lot better than my situation was in Malaysia. In this class we seem to keep on dwelling on what's bad about this country. I don't understand why!" Others, especially two Chicano students who worked a night job at a local executive all-white golf-course in order to finance their university education, found that extending the critical stance on racism which they had displayed in class discussions to conditions at work, as I had encouraged them to do, made it almost unbearable to go to work any longer. Lewis (1990, 484), writing about her own experience in teaching women's studies, puts it like this:

> We cannot expect that students will readily appropriate a political stance that is truly counter-hegemonic, unless we also acknowledge the ways in which our feminist practice/politics creates rather than ameliorates feelings of threat: the threat of abandon-

ment, the threat of having to struggle with unequal power relations, the threat of psychological/social/sexual, as well as economic and political marginality.

Furthermore, in our call for critical interrogation other questions
arise: how is such a critical interrogation possible if only marginal voices
and texts are authorized in the classroom? As Freebody, Luke, and
Gilbert (1991) have argued, without a reading of these voices and texts
against the more dominant, canonical ones, how can the various reading
positions and practices each calls upon be made apparent to students?
Also, familiarity with the dominant tradition of representing the marginal
is necessary in order to understand the constraints on any attempt of
marginal writers themselves, including our students, to represent their
experiences. And, even if we consider these factors, what about the analytical method, the "language of critique," which we as critical pedagogy's transformative teachers are supposed to give to our students in
order to reveal the ideological distortions in their texts? Is this method of
analysis really neutral or is it one "designed to reveal and to command
assent" (Buckingham, 1986, 43) to these revelations? If that is so, then,
ironically, albeit in the name of empowerment, the radical teacher may
well give them yet another controlling scheme of interpretation, which
imposes the "correct" answers on the students, thus making them once
again the objects of what Freire himself rejected as "banking education"—
only this time the passive recipients of the teacher's ideological enlightenment (Lather, 1991, 137). Considering all these issues carefully, it
becomes apparent that critical pedagogy and its teachers often overesti-
mate their transformative powers. For they are too eager to assume that
granting marginalized students and texts of marginalized authors equal,
if not exclusive, space from which to speak in classrooms and encouraging critical classroom dialogue, will somehow enable the alteration of a
social world whose controlling institutions continue to derive much of
their strength from the quiet effectiveness with which they ensure systematic patterns of advantage and exclusion.

     While these concerns merit much more attention than I can give in
this context, all of them hinge critically on the notions of "experience"
and "voice," which I will examine more carefully in the following section. When left untheorized, as they were in my class, these notions are
highly problematic. Undoubtedly, the authorization of their marginal
experiences can be a crucial form of empowerment for students, but
more often than not this authorization takes place purely at an attitudi-
nal, interpersonal level, thus making the liberatory classroom an
accomplice of a false metaphysics of presence. Experience is under-

stood as a transparent window on reality, not, as poststructuralist work on language and subjectivity insists, the product of our insertion into particular practices and discourses that have been made available to us in our specific times and places. To enable students to understand experience in such discursive, nonessentialist terms is difficult, and even more so if one's classroom effectively separates, as mine did, minority students and texts from the dominant Anglo-American ones.

The emphasis on the centrality of minority experiences of both students and texts read and written about, led to exclusions, as it quickly silenced those whose experience was seen to be that of the dominant groups; that is, the occasional Anglo-American and European ESL student who was placed in this class, and the more canonical texts which students in other writing classes had on their reading lists. As for the students, my pedagogy created a classroom situation where, to borrow Fuss' (1989) term, they "one downed" each other on the oppression scale. The minority students viewed themselves as the ones with superior "insider-knowledge" of more "authentically" experienced oppressions, relegating the white students to marginal observer-status, with no legitimate contributions of their own to offer (see also Luke, 1994). Although there was the occasional moment of ambivalent satisfaction about the tables-being-turned in our class, with the students' marginality all of a sudden reconstructed as the more privileged and dominant discourse, there also was the recognition that this moving to the center was located in a different and separate space from the centrality white students usually occupied. Still more importantly, as Mohanty (1990, 195) has characterized the effect of this oppositional arrangement in the liberatory classroom:

> Potentially this implicitly binary construction [minority students versus white students] undermines the understanding of the co-implication that students must take seriously in order to understand "difference" as historical and relational. Co-implication refers to the idea that all of us . . . share certain histories as well as certain responsibilities: ideologies of race define both white and black peoples, just as gender ideologies define both women and men. Thus, while "experience" is an enabling focus in the classroom, unless it is explicitly understood as historical, contingent, and the result of interpretation, it can coagulate into frozen, binary, psychologistic positions.

The hierarchical identity politics in my classroom came to separate not merely minority from white students, but even differentiated some individuals amongst the minority ones. Especially among those students who were the sole representatives of certain race or ethnicity groups in the class, the most unique, usually most visible part of their identity came, in synecdochal fashion, to stand for the whole (Fuss, 1989, 116). For example, the Japanese-American student was typically reduced to his or her "Japanese-Americanness." Or the specific "differences" (of personality, history, language) of one Ethiopian-American predictably came to represent the difference of the African-American collective, thus reinforcing the understanding of experience in individualistic, essentialist terms.

This tendency to homogenize minority experience could have been problematized if we had examined more closely how minority cultural identities were constructed in our texts, especially if we had juxtaposed contemporary Asian-American writing to conventional white-authored texts. Reading Maxine Hong Kingston or David Hwang, for example, against and from within the discourses of, say, Willa Cather's short stories which feature Chinese-American characters, would show how these recent writers construct minority experience as shifting, contingent, unstable, whereas Cather positions it in binary opposition to the dominant.

My decision to "ban" texts by white authors because of their "bias" against or their silencing of minority experiences, proved problematic for a number of other reasons as well. My students, though initially enjoying the relevance of the material and the ease with which it allowed them to interact with it, on the whole did not respond positively to this exclusion. In the beginning I thought that their negative reactions were exclusively prompted by the fact that as "natural Hirschians" (Bacon, 1993) they were looking for initiation into the dominant public culture. Yet upon prompting them further I discovered that a number of them felt that having been victims of Otherness for so long, often in high school classes led by white teachers who foregrounded and almost fetishized the race issue (e.g., "in my senior high school year they made us do projects on the boatpeople and their acculturation problems here, just because I am Vietnamese-American"), they were eager to assume "common ground," stressing their experience as one of "difference within identity." A few of the American-born Chinese students went as far as to vehemently object to what they considered a patronizing selection of readings which dwelt on Asian cultural origins they, unlike their foreign-born classmates, wanted to separate themselves from in order to be considered truly American. To put their reactions into high-theoretical terms, this basic writing class for them was just another "pocket of difference and otherness" that had been created by the dominant to prolong their marginality (Radhakrishnan, 1987).

Upon reflection now, I find it revealing that even among literary critics and writing specialists it is usually the ones from the dominant culture, speaking in the interest of those marginalized, who tend to call for mandatory diversity in the name of empowerment, while the marginalized ones themselves warn of such developments. Sanchez (1987), for instance, cautions that to affirm uncritically all the efforts of universities in their programs and courses to take issues of difference and diversity on board, is to run the risk of idealizing what is often motivated by an effort to carry on "business as usual" in the face of overwhelming challenges posed by changing demographics in their student populations. More specifically with respect to the issue of representation of experience in curricular texts, Elizabeth Fox-Genovese (1986), an African-American literary critic, argues forcefully that sacrificing the "classics of the Euro-American tradition" in favor of minority-authored texts is more frequently than not some "misguided liberal attempt" to make matters more relevant for students:

> Very likely, our students feel colonized in relation to that elite western culture that has constituted the backbone of our humanistic education. Female and minority students in particular are, as it were, being asked to look at someone else's picture and acknowledge it as their own mirror image. To throw out the canon does not solve their problem any more than expurgating all traces of western technology solves the problems of colonial peoples. From one perspective, throwing out the received histories and cultures only makes things worse. For, if you do not include a heavy dose of the history of elite males, how do you explain why women and members of minorities are not running the world? One of the more difficult tasks facing those who have been excluded from the corridors of political and intellectual power is to accept the history of their oppression or exclusion and to transform it into a base for future action. (Fox-Genovese, 1986, 136–137)

Furthermore, it is most readily in juxtaposition with texts from the dominant formation that students can recognize that and how minority texts write experience differently. In fact, it is when comparing such texts in the ways they are produced and received that students can come to accept a redefinition of experience in the sense of the continuous worldly construction of subjectivity. In other words, they can see that minorities write and read experience differently because they live out their lives as socially categorized Chicanos or Chinese-Americans or whatever, and because their texts circulate and are read differently from those signed by Anglo-American writers.

Just as "experience" is a crucial political term when it comes to formulating a critical pedagogy, so is the notion of "voice." And as Orner (1992) has convincingly shown, the calls of transformative teachers for students to "find their own voices" (Freire and Giroux, 1989, viii) are grounded in the same essentialist epistemological assumptions. Freireans assume that by speaking in their "authentic voices," those who have been silenced by traditional pedagogical practices and the dominant culture, can make themselves audible and become "authors of their own world" (Simon, 1987, 380). Of course, the reasons given for soliciting these authentic voices are radically different from those offered by progressivist literacy pedagogues since the social and political commitments of a liberatory teaching agenda are allegedly much stronger. But what both have in common is that the metaphor itself, assumed to be a self-evident way of describing ethical and intellectual development, is left unexamined. Yet, given poststructural theorizing on subjectivity, can the process which critical pedagogy attempts to initiate any longer be seen as one of the students "finding" a voice that is already there, independent and pre-existent? Or isn't it more apt to view it as a process of "fashioning a voice" from the discursive environments into which students have been inserted (see Finke, 1993)?

Admittedly, unlike progressivist discourse, the discourse of critical pedagogy acknowledges the possibility of each student being able to locate a variety of authentic voices in her/himself, but this corrective move through pluralization "loses sight of the contradictory and partial nature of all voices" (Ellsworth, 1992, 104). Ellsworth explains this further:

> [Critical pedagogy] does not confront the ways in which any individual student's voice is already a "teeth-gritting" and often contradictory intersection of voices constituted by gender, race, class, ability, ethnicity, sexual orientation or ideology. Nor does it engage with the fact that the particularities of historical context, personal biography, and subjectivities split between the conscious and unconscious will necessarily render each expression of student voice partial and predicated on the absence and marginalization of alternative voices. (Ellsworth, 1992, 103)

The situation in my basic writing class was very similar to the one Ellsworth describes: their complex and contradictory positioning made it very difficult for some of my students to "fully express their multiple voices" (Simon, 1987, 380), especially not, as mentioned earlier, in the sort of trusting and committed "dialogic encounters" which critical pedagogues envision in the liberatory classroom. Several of my Korean-American women students were reluctant to join their voices with those of their male Korean-American classmates since it involved subordinating the gender oppression they felt so strongly in their minority subculture. Even though this keen awareness of gender oppression united them with their Chicano women classmates, the latter rarely spoke up with them, as it threatened to silence the racial oppression they felt as Hispanic-Americans in relation to Asian-American "model minorities." Then again, my two international students from Central America found it difficult to join their American-born Hispanic classmates because such privileging of ethnic concerns meant marginalizing their oppressions as people living under U.S. imperialism.

Most problematic, perhaps, is an element of dishonesty when liberatory teachers claim to give equal space to the students' diverse voices and cultures. Is the affirmation of these voices automatic, or is our commitment to diversity and tolerance predicated on the acceptance of certain values and ideals? Or, to put it more specifically, as Kalantzis and Cope (1993, 53–57) do, how easily can critical pedagogy "give voice to cultures which revere textual authority or which elevate teachers as the source of educational knowledge? If every culture or point of view is as good as the next, how does it handle cultures with hallowed traditions of sexism and racism?" Obviously, when confronted with such questions we realize that we privilege certain kinds of voices over others and that, in fact, "we want our students to fashion a particular kind of voice that corresponds to our own desires" (Finke, 1993, 17) as liberatory teachers. Critical educators ask us to invite our students' yet undisciplined journal writing or initial personal responses to texts as an idea-generating device, but insist, in a paternalistic gesture, that subsequently these initial confessions and narratives must be worked over and their "critical interrogation" be encouraged (Giroux and Simon, 1989, 231).

It is only then that, according to critical pedagogy, empowerment can take place. Equipped with a 'language of critique,' which we transformative teachers are supposed to have provided, our students are then ostensibly ready to have "the false attractions and myths" (Giroux, 1983, 213) exploded and their initial "mystified" narratives replaced by "politically correct" ones. Once these tools of critical analysis have been given to our students, as Giroux (1988, 165) would have it, "the authoritative discourse of imposition and recitation" will be replaced with a

voice "capable of speaking in one's own terms, a voice capable of listening, retelling and challenging the very grounds of knowledge and
power." But what if we give this scenario another, more skeptical reading, this time drawing from deconstruction which seeks to foreground
how our interventionist moves as teachers are always invested with
our own social, political, and personal interests, despite our desire to
make our students critical agents? This kind of reading would acknowledge the material reality surrounding the production of such empowered voices in the classroom. It would be aware of the possibility that
what is offered in the name of empowerment could easily itself turn
into another "authoritative discourse of imposition and recitation." That
is, being constituted under our gaze, the students' responses which we
as teachers elicit and authorize as voices "capable of speaking in [their]
own terms" (Giroux 1988, 165), are often nothing more than our students' successful attempts, however unconscious, to learn the "group
think" in the classroom and to anticipate the "ideologically correct"
disclosures the teacher wants to hear.

AN ALTERNATIVE POSTCRITICAL WRITING PEDAGOGY

In the preceding narrative of my own search for an alternative
practice, I have tried to demonstrate that the current curricular problems we face in our basic writing classes are the result of deeply
entrenched political problems and antagonisms. I have also tried to
show that these problems and antagonisms cannot be adequately
resolved by a counter-practice which, in the name of empowerment,
invisibly redefines what writing, basic writers, and their transformative teachers should do. The problem is that it continues to assume, to
paraphrase Donald (1989, 28), that if we only teach students how to
respond to and write about texts properly (whichever type of writing,
whichever texts, whichever "properly"), then "somehow [we] will produce a particular subjectivity" which will "in turn lead to [our] desired
social ends." Of course, the kind of subjectivity we favor in our classrooms may vary—the culturally literate citizen, the authentically voiced
individual, the effectively socialized member of an academic discourse
community, or, as in my case, the empowered minority voice—and, so
with it will the desired social ends, ranging from integration or personal growth and independence over upward mobility all the way to
liberation and transformation.

As an alternative agenda, critical literacy pedagogy is most comfortable with practices of ideology critique, with a binary logic which

focuses on unmasking the distortions of some Other—be it traditional-ist, progressivist, or apolitical social constructivist writing agendas. At the same time critical pedagogy refuses to admit its own "regime of truth" (Gore, 1992, 63), insisting that its transformative teachers have somehow managed to escape the very power politics which it can so astutely pinpoint in dominant pedagogies. But in order to effectively counter dominant discourse and practices, our pedagogy must, to quote Wilden (1980, vii), "be of a higher logical type than that with which it is in conflict." That is, it must go beyond substituting one type of dis-course about writing for another. To echo Baker and Luke's (1991) account of a reconceptualized pedagogy for reading, it must bring writ-ing discourses and practices themselves to the fore as the object of a writing pedagogy.

Such a metagesture involves denaturalizing the ways in which basic writing classrooms and their pedagogical practices work together as cultural technologies in the production of preferred discourses about writing and preferred writing positions for students. More specifically, in my basic writing course my responsibility would be to make my stu-dents aware of the ways in which both the texts we read and the oral and written discussions about these texts we conduct in our classroom, are framed. This may well be best achieved by confronting them with contesting texts and contesting ways of writing about texts, as it allows the denaturalization of reading and writing positions and portrayals of experiences and voices. Only then can the students realize that (1) what is admitted as minority writing into the enlarged canon, and thus into our classroom, is inevitably some discursively based invention of a minority cultural identity, one authorized by a dominant, Anglo-Amer-ican culture, and (2) what counts as effective writing about these texts in our classroom likewise is not a natural product but one authorized by us teachers, the pedagogies we advocate and the daily interactions around written texts we invite and legitimate.

REFERENCES

Aronowitz, S. & Giroux. H. (1985). *Education under siege*. South Hadley, MA: Bergin and Garvey.

———— (1991). *Postmodern education: Politics, culture and social criticism*. Min-neapolis, MN: University of Minnesota Press.

Bacon, J. (1993). Impasse or tension? Pedagogy and the canon controversy. *Col-lege English*, 55(5), 501–514.

Baker, C. & Luke, A. (1991). Discourses and practices: A postscript. In C. Baker & A. Luke (Eds.), *Towards a critical sociology of reading pedagogy* (pp. 257–268). Amsterdam: Benjamins.

Barkley Brown, E. (1989). African-American women's quilting: A framework for conceptualizing and teaching African-American women's history. *Signs*, 14(4), 921–929.

Bartholomae, D. (1985). Inventing the university. In M. Rose (Ed.), *When a writer can't write* (pp. 134–165). New York: Guilford.

Bartholomae, D. & Petrosky, A. (1986). *Facts, artifacts and counterfacts.* Upper Montclair, NJ: Boynton Cook.

Bernstein, B. (1977). *Class, codes and control,* vol. 3. Boston: Routledge and Kegan Paul.

Bizzell, P. (1982). College composition: Initiation into the academic discourse community. *Curriculum Inquiry*, 12(2), 192–207.

Bloom, A. (1987). *The closing of the American mind.* New York: Simon & Schuster.

Buckingham, D. (1986). Against demystification: A response to *Teaching the media. Screen*, 27, 80–95.

Christie, F. (1989). Language development in education. In R. Hasan & J. R. Martin (Eds.), *Language development: Learning language, learning culture* (pp. 152-198). Norwood, NJ: Ablex.

Collins, J. (1993). "The troubled text": History and language in American university basic writing programs. In P. Freebody & A. Welch (Eds.), *Knowledge, culture and power* (pp. 162–186). London: Falmer Press.

Donald, J. (1989). Beyond our ken: English, Englishness, and the national curriculum. In P. Brooker & P. Humm (Eds.), *Dialogue and difference: English into the nineties* (pp. 13–30). London: Routledge.

Ellsworth, E. (1992). Why doesn't this feel empowering? Working through the repressive myths of critical pedagogy. In C. Luke & J. Gore (Eds.), *Feminisms and critical pedagogy* (pp. 90–119). New York: Routledge.

Finke, L. (1993). Knowledge as bait: Feminism,voice and the pedagogical unconscious. *College English*, 55(1), 7–28.

Fox-Genovese, E. (1986). The claims of a common culture: Gender. race, class and the canon. *Salmagundi*, 72(2), 131–143.

Freebody, P., Luke, A., & Gilbert, P. (1991). Reading positions and practices in the classroom. *Curriculum Inquiry*, 21(4), 435–457.

Freire, P. & Giroux, H. (1989). Pedagogy, popular culture and public life: An introduction. In H. Giroux & R. Simon (Eds.), *Popular culture, schooling and everyday life* (pp. vii–xii). New York: Bergin and Garvey.

Fuss, D. (1989). *Essentially speaking.* New York: Routledge.

Giroux, H. (1983). *Theory and resistance in education: A pedagogy for the opposition.* South Hadley, MA: Bergin and Garvey.

―――― (1988). *Schooling and the struggle for public life: Critical pedagogy in the modern age.* Minneapolis, MN: University of Minnesota Press.

Giroux, H. & Simon, R. (1989). Schooling, popular culture and a pedagogy of possibility. In H. Giroux and R. Simon (Eds.), *Popular culture, schooling and everyday life* (pp. 219–235). New York: Bergin and Garvey.

Gore, J. (1992). What we can do for you! What can 'we' do for 'you'? Struggling over empowerment in critical and feminist pedagogy. In C. Luke and J. Gore (Eds.), *Feminisms and critical pedagogy* (pp. 54–73). New York: Routledge.

Herrington, A. & Curtis, M. (1990). Basic writing: Moving the voices on the margin to the center. *Harvard Educational Review,* 60(4), 489–496.

Kalantzis, M. & Cope. B. (1993). Histories of pedagogy, cultures of schooling. In B. Cope & M. Kalantzis (Eds.), *The powers of literacy: A genre approach to teaching writing* (pp. 38–62). London: Falmer Press.

Lather, P. (1991). *Getting smart: Feminist research and pedagogy with/in the postmodern.* New York: Routledge.

―――― (1992). Post-critical pedagogies: A feminist reading. In C. Luke & J. Gore (Eds.), *Feminisms and critical pedagogy* (pp. 120–138). New York: Routledge.

Lewis, M. (1990). Interrupting patriarchy: Politics, resistance and transformation in the feminist classroom. *Harvard Educational Review,* 60(4), 467–488.

Luke, C. (1992). Feminist politics in radical pedagogy. In C. Luke & J. Gore (Eds.), *Feminisms and critical pedagogy* (pp. 25–53). New York: Routledge.

―――― (1994). Women in the academy. The politics of speech and silence. *British Journal of Sociology of Education,* 15(3), 211–230.

McCormick, K. (1989). The cultural imperatives underlying cognitive acts. *Reading-to-Write Report* 9. Berkeley, CA.: Center for the Study of Writing.

McLaren, P. (1988). Schooling the postmodern body: Critical pedagogy and the politics of enfleshment. *Journal of Education,* 170(1), 53–83.

Mohanty, C. T. (1990). On race and voice: Challenges for liberal education in the 1990s. *Cultural Critique,* 14 (Winter), 179–206.

Ohmann, R. (1988). *The politics of letters*. Middlesbury, CT: Wesleyan University Press.

Orner, M. (1992). Interrupting the calls for student voice in 'liberatory' education. In C. Luke & J. Gore (Eds.), *Feminisms and critical pedagogy* (pp. 74–89). New York: Routledge.

Radhakrishnan, R. (1987). Culture as common ground: Ethnicity and beyond. *Melus*, 14(1), 5–20.

Rajchman, J. (1985). *Michel Foucault: The freedom of philosophy*. New York: Columbia University Press.

Rose, M. (1985). The language of exclusion: Writing instruction at the university. *College English*, 47(3), 341–359.

Sanchez, R. (1987). Ethnicity, ideology and academia. *The Americas Review*, 15(1), 80–88.

Simon, R. (1987). Empowerment as a pedagogy of possibility. *Language Arts*, 64(4), 370–382.

Spanos, W. (1987). *Repetitions: The postmodern occasion in literature and culture*. Baton Rouge, LA: Louisiana State University Press.

Wilden, A. (1980). *System and structure*. London: Tavistock.

CHAPTER 12

LEGAL PEDAGOGY AS AUTHORIZED SILENCE(S)

Zillah Eisenstein

Pedagogy is about teaching and, therefore, learning. Here, I will focus on how law(s) operates as a state-authorized pedagogy.[1] Legal pedagogy is both straightforward *and* complex. It is structured by silences and subtle equations.

Law teaches us what is acceptable and what is suspect; what is right and what is wrong; what is permissible and what is not. This oppositional epistemological framework underlines the simplicity of law and its powerfulness. It simultaneously constructs the man/woman divide through the silent privileging of white male standards. This exclusionary stance presumes the absence of white women and people of color.

We (?) are brought up to obey the law(s). Laws are supposed to be fair. They are supposed to be reasonable. They are supposed to be just. They are most often meant not to be questioned or challenged.

As such, law is a pedagogy of silencing and quieting. It is a pedagogy of state authority. It is meant to protect and sustain.

But law as a discourse—as a "power" language, as "the" authorized discourse of society—also subverts itself. Liberal democratic law promises equality. When equality is uncovered as exclusionary, it legitimates a self-critique. Then, law is a pedagogy of privilege and sex/race discrimination *and* it is also promissory of a more radical practice. Let me now address a specific argument: that law as a pedagogy establishes racialized gender privilege *and* it also contains its own subversion.

NEUTRALITY, OBJECTIVITY, AND THE "NATURE" OF LAW

Law, as the text or the word, is supposed to be disinterested. And the lawmaker is supposed to adjudicate impartially, to balance interests in a neutral and fair-minded way. Law authorizes what is meant by right and wrong, truth and falsity, and fact and value from this stance. It presents power as rational and just and even neutral. Catharine MacKinnon has termed this presentation "the point-of-viewlessness" of law: "Objectivist epistemology is the law of law. It ensures that the law will most reinforce existing distributions of power when it most closely adheres to its own highest ideal of fairness."[2]

Ronald Dworkin,[3] from a different vantage point, recognizes the power of law to determine right and wrong. He argues that the "idea" that there is always a right and wrong way of doing something is "real" within law because people believe it to be so.

An objectivist standpoint sets up a series of oppositions: true/false, right/wrong, and so on. My point is not that there are not times when things are true or false or right or wrong, but rather that these oppositions can be clearly distinguished less often than legal positivists assume and that the distinctions are not based on an objective truth. The objectivist standpoint makes clear-cut demarcations rather than continua the basis of its epistemology. Law recognizes duality rather than diversity. Instead of being able to recognize complexity *within* the relationships between true and false, right and wrong, law constructs dichotomous oppositions that deny the complexity. In the courtroom, subtleties do not count: winning and losing do.

Although the masquerade of neutrality often disguises and misrepresents power, it also does something else. The discourse of law, which establishes the idea that law is neutral and fair, simultaneously fosters the expectation that law *should* be neutral, even if it is not. And this "idea" does not remain an idea; it has become part of legal discourse. This is what legal equality for the sexes means: law should be neutral in terms of sex. There are serious problems with this conception, given the already racialized and engendered discourse(s) of law(s), but the idea that law should be sex neutral can be used to decenter the white phallus along with its objectivist, dualistic standpoint.[4]

The supposed objectivity of law is often established in and through the "law(s) of nature." Natural law is presumed to be necessitated by nature itself. Natural rights, which are derivative from natural (white) "man," stand as abstract givens in this view. The privileging of nature authorizes natural law, natural rights, natural "man." It is the power of the meaning of "natural"—its supposedly a priori status—that gives law its authority *within* society. Nature is both disorderly and tempestuous and harmonious and rational. In the first instance, law makes sense of the disorder of nature and tames "her." In the second instance, nature is extended to society through law. In both instances, natural law is the law of reason; law is therefore reason itself. Rationality and the laws of nature are encoded as part of the objectivist standpoint.

Law as a politics is made invisible by the inevitability of nature. Hierarchy is presented as the differences *in* nature, and natural law is in part the reasonable way to interpret these differences. In other words, "natural law [is] what reason discovers, and natural law was discovered by reason."[5] Reason establishes its own universality. Reason is not partial like passion is; reason is impartial, fair-minded, and just.

THE ENGENDERED FORM OF PHALLOCRATIC LAW(S)

Liberal democratic law helps to structure patriarchy in the way it differentiates woman from man; law embodies the relations of racialized patriarchy through the differentiation, by sex, of racialized gender. Woman is part of nature; white men, like law, must sometimes tame and control her. The *reason* of men suppresses the passion of woman.[6]

Problems of legal practice have roots deep within the engendered "nature" of law. "Law privileges objectivity, individualism, and rights over their binary opposites, subjectivity, collectivity, and responsibility, and this privilege is identified with the more general male privilege over females."[7] Law does not exist alongside the privilege but inside it. It establishes a gendered series of hierarchical differences.

The language of law silences woman and this is doubly true for women of color. Luce Irigaray argues that the presence of woman seems impossible to imagine within law as it is presently formed. "That would not fail to challenge the discourse that lays down the law today, that legislates on everything, including sexual difference, to such an extent that the existence of another sex, of an other, that would be woman, still seems, in its terms, unimaginable." She believes that the only way to create space for women is to develop a new language, one which no longer assumes that men are "everything"—"that [the masculine] could no longer, all by itself, define, circumvent, circumscribe, the properties of anything and everything."[8] We need a starting place other than Jefferson's "All men are created equal," because it leaves us with a vision that equality can be articulated through a homogeneous standard: white men.

This is not *just* a problem of language, because language is always more than it seems/means. This is a problem of how language operates as discourse, as symbolization of a racialized and gendered notion of nature, of human(ity). "As male is the implicit reference for human, maleness will be the measure of equality."[9] Men are the norm, so women *are* different (from men). But for women to be treated as equal, they must be treated *as* men, *like* men, because equality is premised on men. If one is treated as different *from* men, one is not treated as equal. "Women are permitted to compete with men under the same rules and within the same institutions, but those institutions were designed in accordance with normative male values, priorities and characteristics."[10] Requirements and standards are designed with men in mind.[11]

Gendered law (which is also simultaneously coded by race) is constructed through the differentiation of woman *from* man, and this differentiation takes several forms. Some laws explicitly treat women as different from men—for example, in the denial of the rights to tend bar, administer an estate, or engage in combat. Before 1971 these kinds of prohibition were not seen as problematic in United States constitutional law. They were rather seen as necessitated by the "real" differences of women (from men). Today there is much less closure on this issue, as is reflected in the very idea of sex discrimination. After all, sex discrimination as a legal concept makes the treatment of someone in terms of sex (difference) or classification by sex problematic.

We need to recognize that much of the gendered nature of law masquerades subtly, whereas racial privilege often has not. The differentiation by sex is not explicit, but implied through a silencing of difference in a supposedly neutral language, such as the notions of "veteran" or "worker" or "individual." There are also laws in which the term "men" supposedly applies to women as well, but the male standard is expressed explicitly in these cases.[12]

The engendered nature of law privileges man as the referent by making woman "the" different "other," and thereby it homogenizes the differences among women. Woman's "difference" is assumed to be a part of the preferred order of things. Given this view, which treats the sex (biological nature) and gender (cultural mediation) of woman as one and the same, "classification by sex" is not viewed as problematic. As Justice Joseph Bradley stated in his concurring opinion in *Bradwell v. State*:

> On the contrary, the civil law, as well as nature herself, has always recognized a wide difference in the respective spheres and destinies of man and woman. Man is, or should be, woman's protector and defender. . . . The constitution of the family organization . . . indicates the domestic sphere as that which properly belongs to the domain and functions of womanhood.[13]

Although few would argue today, as Bradley did in 1873, that *the* "difference" of sex requires separate spheres for men and women, differentiation by sex still underlies law.

So far, this discussion has treated engendered law as a unity; the phallus is centered in and by law. I now want to show how this unity of patriarchal privilege establishes a coherence of hierarchical relations in law, while presenting an often incoherent, dispersed, and contradictory view of the phallus. Law is both unified and contradictory: the symbolization of the white phallus underlines multiple and sometimes incoherent interpretations of racialized gender.

There is little clarity or consistency of legal thought about the meaning of *the* "difference" of sex—the difference of woman *from* man—and with it sex discrimination. Biology, according to MacKinnon, "is used to define both the grounds on which different treatment may be recognized as discriminatory and the grounds on which different treatment may be recognized as a consequence of 'real' sex differences: hence, reasonably based and not discriminatory."[14] In other words, if what is considered a "real" sex difference exists, one cannot argue categorically that differential treatment of "classification by sex" is discriminatory; instead, the specific treatment must be seen as warranted by *the* "difference." The problem here is the meaning of "real" in the phrase "real sex difference." What does "real" mean if we view reality as continua rather than as a construct in the dualism of truth/falsity? What if there are multiple differences of sex that are complexly related to differences of gender rather than *a* "difference" of sex established in nature that differentiates all women from all men? The problem is that the meaning of "real" cannot be established from *inside* the engendered meanings of "classification by sex" within law.

The engendered nature of law limits the possibility of recognizing sex discrimination. According to the Fourteenth Amendment, individuals deserve equal (similar) protection if they are similarly situated.[15] Women, however, are often not similarly situated to men. The pregnant female is not similarly situated to the nonpregnant male. MacKinnon writes that "similarly situated" should mean "that people who are the same should be treated the same"—that persons in relevantly similar circumstances should be treated relevantly similarly.[16] But what is relevant similarity? And who is the standard?

Equal protection doctrine masks its male referent in the guise of neutrality. "Current equal protection doctrine fails to look beyond the appearance of neutrality and refuses to recognize that actions based on sexually unique physical characteristics such as pregnancy are sex based."[17] Under the equal protection clause, all persons are entitled to equal protection, unless some legitimate state purpose justifies differentiation by sex. Then treatment according to sex is legal as long as the classification of sex is not unreasonable or arbitrary. So women can be treated as women—that is, as different from men—if they are not similarly situated (to men) and if the reasoning is not arbitrary. The white phallus is privileged here—through men and/or the state.

The "legitimate state purpose" and "compelling reasons" qualifications to equal protection doctrine allow the state to interpret the "laws of nature" (*qua* biology) as it sees fit. Whether and to what purpose the state invokes the "name" of nature is utterly arbitrary. It does so when citing the immutable differences in nature and when recognizing the likeness of women and men. While doing both, the state condenses and unifies varying and competing discourses about racialized gender. Law has changed to permit the treatment of women and men as the same while preserving a notion of the "natural difference" of woman from man. Even though law has shifted to accommodate a notion of similarity between the sexes, it operates as if there is one objective reality, which establishes "real" sex difference. Interestingly enough, although nature and its derivative—"real" sex difference—are treated as givens in phallocratic discourse, law shifts and continues to renegotiate their meaning. Let us turn to this issue of the meanings(s) of sex "difference" in law(s), the dispersed and contradictory versions of the phallus.

Sex "Difference" and Classification by Sex

Supreme Court cases document the shifting and contradictory views of woman's difference from man and establishes these views as legal pedagogy. I have chosen Supreme Court cases because of their particularly symbolic resonance as the highest law of the land. Let us see how the law treats "classifications by sex" under the guise of equal protection doctrine.

In common law there was no problem of sex difference. Women had no independent status; hence, no difference. The husband and wife were one, and that one was the husband. This view was clearly articulated by William Blackstone: "By marriage, the husband and wife are one person in law: that is, the very being or legal existence of the woman is suspended during the marriage, or at least is incorporated and consolidated into that of the husband; under whose wing, protection, and *cover*, she performs everything."[18] By the middle of the nineteenth century, this view was replaced by the separate spheres doctrine as defined in *Bradwell v. State* (1873). Both these views deny women's autonomous status to contract as an independent being. In 1873 Myra Bradwell applied for a license to practice law and was denied because "as a married woman [she] would be bound neither by her express contracts nor by those implied contracts which it is the policy of the law to create between attorney and client." Further, "God designed the sexes to occupy different spheres of action, and that it belonged to men to make, apply and execute the laws, was regarded as an almost axiomatic truth."[19]

The sexes were viewed as "different," occupying different spheres, and this viewing was seen as almost an axiomatic truth. Variations on this theme dominated most court decisions until 1971. Women were excluded from activities that appeared to conflict with their roles as wives and mothers, such as tending bar unless one was the wife or daughter of the owner, or serving as a juror. Justice Frankfurter in *Goesart v. Cleary* (1948) stated: "The fact that women may now have achieved the virtues that men have long claimed as their prerogatives and now indulge in vices that men have long practiced, does not preclude the state from drawing a sharp line between the sexes, certainly in such matters as the regulation of the liquor traffic."[20] He also argued that "nature made men and women different. . . . The law must accommodate itself to the immutable difference of Nature."[21] The Court made no distinction between sex and gender. They are treated as one and the same.

Nature defines woman *by* her sex difference. And nature is taken as fact. This view lays the basis for the decision in *Muller v. Oregon* (1908), in which the Court upheld the constitutionality of an Oregon statute restricting to ten the daily working hours of women in laundries, factories, or mechanical establishments because of the limitations of their bodily strength.

> The two sexes differ in structure of body, in the functions to be performed by each. . . . *This difference justifies a difference in legislation* and upholds that which is designed to compensate for some of the burdens which rest upon her.[22]

The Court found woman disadvantaged by her physical makeup and her maternal function. The limitation of working hours for women, when there is no such limitation for men, would only be a violation of a woman's right to equal treatment if women were similarly situated to men, and given the Court's interpretation that they are not.

The differentiation of woman from man in its various articulations in law is acceptable as long as such treatment is justified by a legitimate state purpose and is not arbitrary. If, however, categorization by sex were viewed as suspect within the law, such classifications would have to be justified by "compelling" reasons. Although sex has yet to become a suspect category, like race, the standards for establishing "legitimate government objectives" that justify classifications by sex have become more rigorous. In *Reed v. Reed* (1971), the Court decided unanimously to overrule an Idaho statute that gave men preference over women in appointments as administrators of deceased persons' estates.[23] After the *Reed* decision, the Court insisted that the government would have to offer substantial justification for treating men and women differently, otherwise the practice would be in violation of the Equal Protection Clause of the Fourteenth Amendment. "By providing dissimilar treatment for men and women who are thus similarly situated, the challenged section violates the Equal Protection Clause."[24]

From the engendered standpoint of the law, men and women will seldom be similarly situated; indeed, standards are articulated from the male point of view, which defines combat as man's territory in the first place. This male viewing assumes a series of starting points that really aren't starting points at all, but rather points within a racialized and engendered discourse.

The engendered discourse of law is *already* a series of racialized gender classifications based on what are considered "real" differences between the sexes. One cannot recognize discrimination if one believes that the different treatment of the sexes is required by the "real" differences of woman from man as established in nature, or biology. When differentiation of the sexes according to their engendered meaning(s) is said to be constitutional, the politics of sex inequality masquerades in law as legal.

Although Justice Stewart argued in the *Michael M. v. Superior Court* (1981)[25] that there are "narrow" circumstances when men and women are *not* similarly situated and seems to have assumed that these instances are defined by *the* biological "difference" of women from men in terms of their childbearing capacity (pregnancy), the gendered bias of law is not limited to these instances, nor is pregnancy, as a basis for classification by sex/gender, used with any consistency. Sometimes it is used to define women as a class, but sometimes, such as when women are being treated "like" men, it is ignored as an issue. Justices Rehnquist and Stewart argued in the *Michael M.* case that the key question was "whether women and men are 'different in fact' in the context of the law at issue."[26] They determined that sex-based laws and disproportionately burdensome neutral rules are not harmful because they reflect "natural" differences between men and women; "the 'real' differences

between the sexes have necessary—not undesirable—social consequences" (SESD, p. 918).

Ann Freedman calls this the "real differences" standard; if differences are found to be "real," based in "fact," then differential treatment
is acceptable. She notes that the initial notion of "different in fact" comes
from the case *Tigner v. Texas* (1940).[27] Justice Frankfurter used this reference while upholding the exclusion of women from tending bar in
Goesart v. Cleary (SESD, p. 929). The interpretation of "different in fact"
is supposed to apply to the distinctive reproductive and sexual characteristics that define the membership of a sex. The standard's meaning,
however, is much more varied. The Court seldom agrees about how to
interpret this "fact" of "real difference."

Justices Brennan and Marshall have often been joined by Justice
White, and more recently Justice O'Connor, in arguing that alleged differences of nature do not in themselves justify sex classifications. "All
rules based on sex, whether or not the underlying differences between
women and men can be characterized as biological, must be tested
against the same standard of social justification: Is the sex-based classification 'substantially related' to an 'important' governmental goal?"
(SESD, p. 949). Justice O'Connor similarly held the position in *Missis-
sippi University for Women v. Hogan* (1982) that classifications based on
sex "must be applied free of fixed notions concerning the roles and abilities of males and females" and that the statutory objective itself must
not reflect stereotypic and anachronistic notions about woman's role.[28]
Although there is disagreement within the Court regarding the justificatory status of sex-based classification, the justificatory status of governmental goals in and of themselves stands outside the critique. The
(patriarchal) state is privileged within law; its needs can justify sex discrimination and make it constitutional.

"SIMILARLY SITUATED" AND (NOT) PREGNANT

Pregnancy defines women as not similarly situated to men and
therefore different from men. On this basis, differential treatment is
acceptable—it is not a problem. In much the same way, most classifications based on pregnancy have not been viewed as sexually discriminatory; rather, they have been treated as neutral. Several cases deal
with the issue of pregnancy in this light: *Geduldig v. Aiello* (1974), *General
Electric Co. v. Gilbert* (1976), and *Nashville Gas Co. v. Satty* (1977).[29]

In *Geduldig v. Aiello*, a California district court held that the exclusion of four pregnant women from a disability insurance system vio-

lated the equal protection clause. The Supreme Court reversed this decision, claiming that the insurance company did not discriminate "against any definable group or class in terms of the aggregate risk protection derived by that group or class from the program" (417, p. 496). They found that not gender, but rather a physical condition (pregnancy), was at issue in this exclusion. "While it is true that only women can become pregnant, it does not follow that every legislative classification concerning pregnancy is a sex-based classification" (417, p. 496n20). Pregnancy is *not* a category of sex, because *non*pregnant persons are both men and women. "The program divides potential recipients into two groups—pregnant women and nonpregnant persons. While the first group is exclusively female, the second includes members of both sexes" (417, p. 497).

The standard of evaluation here is the phallus. In other words, the male, as nonpregnant, is made the subject. The engendered nature of the law privileges nonpregnant persons. It is this category—which includes *all* men and *some* women—that is used to deny the sex-class status of pregnancy—which applies to no men, but a majority of women. The interpretation of pregnancy is what is at issue here. It can be used both to differentiate women from men by institutionalizing *the* "difference" of the female body and to assume that men and women are the same if not pregnant: either way, the phallus rules.

This kind of thinking—which claims the male standard as a neutral standpoint—reappeared in *Personnel Administrator of Massachusetts et al. v. Feeney* (1979). In this case, granting preference to veterans when hiring was challenged as discriminatory against women and in violation of equal protection doctrine. The Court found the statutory classification to be neutral—that is, not gender based. Significant number of *non*veterans are men—and all *non*veterans (men and women) are at a similar disadvantage.[30] The Court's classification scheme once again advantages the male standard. The privileged category is men through the category *non*veteran. Because veterans are men and because nonveterans are also men, women are not discriminated against as a class as nonveteran.

The Court argued that "the distinction between veterans and nonveterans . . . is not a pretext for gender discrimination." Although the Court also acknowledged that few women benefit from veteran preference, it said, "The non-veteran class is not substantially all female. . . . Too many men are affected by [the statute of preference] to permit the inference that the statue is but a pretext for preferring men over women" (442, p. 275). The distinction is between veterans and nonveterans, not between men and women. This is how an engendered discourse defines neutral law: it erases the presence of sex class at the same time it constructs it. Woman is made absent by the presence of the male standard, in this case through the category of the nonveteran, which is supposedly sex neutral. Men and women—as in *non*veteran—are similarly situated and treated as alike. This line of argument is used to erase the sexually discriminatory aspects of the classification "veteran."

This kind of thinking has made it very difficult to recognize sex discrimination as problematic, especially when the issue is pregnancy. Here due process has proved to be a more progressive approach than equal protection. In *Cleveland Board of Education et al. v. La Fleur* (1974), pregnant public school teachers challenged the constitutionality of mandatory maternity leave rules and won on the basis of due process. The Court decided that terminating women's employment during pregnancy for the school's convenience was insufficient reason to infringe on women's basic constitutional liberty. The regulations "imply irrebuttable presumptions that unduly penalize a female teacher for deciding to bear a child."[31] More specifically, the Court argued that "freedom of personal choice in matters of marriage and family life is one of the liberties protected by the due process clause" (414, p. 639). The choice of how long to work during pregnancy is an individual matter that must be protected. Justice Rehnquist dissented from this opinion, arguing that law-making requires presumptions that may appear arbitrary.

Equal protection doctrine silently assumes a stance of sexual homogeneity through its criterion of "similarly situated." It is not always clear on what basis women are *not* seen as similarly situated, but most often the basis is their capacity to bear children and their obligation to rear them. The other side of this coin—how pregnancy and veteran status are most often seen as neutral rather than as sex-specific categories—further highlights the engendered basis of law. It makes clear that the standards, in terms of either how they are defined or how they are applied, are explicated through a phallocratic discourse that either marginalizes woman (as in *non*veteran status) or makes her absent (as in pregnant person). The engendered discourse of law treats women as "different," as in less than men, or treats them as equal, as in the same as men. The problem is that women are neither simply one or the other in terms of their sex of gender.

One sees woman's complicated status of "same/different" in the 1991 case *International Unions et al. v. Johnson Controls*.[32] In 1982 Johnson Controls instituted a "fetal protection policy" that barred all women, except those with medically documented infertility, from jobs involving potential lead exposure. The Court held that the policy was discriminating on its face because gender was not a bona fide occupational qualification. Fetal protection policies were found in this instance to be a form of sex discrimination: fertile men were allowed to choose whether to risk their reproductive health so women should also be able to choose. This of course is a mixed victory. The decision does *not* take the "difference" of pregnancy into account in order to treat women the same as men.

CONTRADICTORY (LEGAL) PEDAGOGIES

Because the law treats women differently from men, and as more different from men than they are, it exposes its own gendered partiality. The positioning of sex-neutral law is contradictory. To treat women as the same as men challenges the phallocratic structure of law from inside but also upholds the core of meaning that makes law's normative standard the "rational man."

The impact of changes in law that presumably create a greater equality between the sexes reflects this contradictory position. Further, many changes in law(s) presume the "sameness" standard, while society continues to treat men and women differently. This is very much the case for women in divorce and custody proceedings. On the one hand, no-fault divorce, equitable distribution of property, and the accompanying shifts in legal discourse that these developments encompass provide significant room for improving women's situation. On the other hand, there is a problem with treating men and women as the same in divorce when the social expectations that have defined their life in marriage have not done so. This is most true in the case of the homemaker. Law as pedagogy about equality reflects the way equality is thought about in society and instigates new ways to think about equality, even though it does not completely change the way we think or the way society operates. But legal discourse, as well as society, can also remain static, anachronistic, and resistant to change. This is why it is so difficult to assess exactly the impact of the shifts in the discourse of engendered law(s) and what they "really" mean.

This is particularly true in issues of child custody, where the disjuncture between legal discourse and social practice can be troubling. Historically, the mother was viewed preferentially as the custodial parent. Recently, though, the "tender years" doctrine, which assumes that young children need to live with their mother, has been replaced with the sex-neutral phrase "best interests of the child" and "joint custody." By 1985, more than thirty states had adopted some form of joint custody law, to allow—and possibly encourage—fathers' involvement in post-divorce parenting. This is an instance, however, in which law has shifted more than the practices of men. On the whole, women remain the childrearers, both in marriage and after divorce.

One realm in which changed custody law seems to have had an impact, and not necessarily to women's advantage, is contested custody. Whereas women remain the custodians of children in uncontested custody cases, men very often win custody in contested cases with the help of the "best interests of the child" as the revised legal standard. The preference for mothers in these cases is replaced by sex-neutral determinations. Although the "best interests of the child" standard appears "to be sex neutral, it is increasingly being undermined by the development of criteria that discriminate against women."[33] The courts are minimizing the value of past day-to-day care and instead are emphasizing the parent's economic resources and lifestyle. Thus, women "are faced not with sex-neutral custody standards applied appropriately to whoever does the primary caretaking, but rather with standards that ignore or devalue primary parenting and are sex discriminatory.[34]

Joint custody opened doors for fathers who wanted custody.[35] Nevertheless, the number of fathers asking for custody is small. Of those who do seek custody, a disproportionate number receive it. The New York Task Force found that "there is substantial evidence that when fathers do litigate custody, they win at least as often as mothers do."[36]

A further problem with the "best interests of the child" standard is that if and when custody is contested, the mother, particularly if she is a wage earner, is very often viewed by a judge as not like a woman, a good parent, because a mother who works in the labor force doesn't have time to be a good mother. A father who works—as men are expected to do—is seen as able to be a good father and still hold a job.

This kind of thinking does not characterize all judges. As frequently as not, judges are still swayed by the "tender years" doctrine, but there are problems either way. Although maternal preference may seem like a way to protect women's interests within the family structure as it presently exists, "the stereotype of a mother on which it is based has negative consequences for the custody-seeking woman who does not conform to an image which is both sexist and out of touch with reality."[37] This is more and more the case, because a majority of women with children work in the labor force.

Whatever the problems with joint custody as a doctrine having disproportionate and unfair impact on women, it represents a shift in the gendered discourse of law. It recognizes both mothers and fathers as parents and thus stands ahead of much-needed change in the actual societal relations of parenting. We are still, however, left with the question: How can we take the differential effects of gender-neutral law into account without reestablishing engendered law as acceptable?

RADICALIZING LEGAL PEDAGOGY

We need to adopt a radical pluralist pedagogy for envisaging how difference constitutes the meaning of equality. Such pedagogy assumes that differences and plurality constitute society, but understands that hierarchy and unequal relations of power presently structure those differences. Radical pluralism differs from liberal pluralism. Liberal pluralism assumes, through the process of abstraction and generalization, that equality *already* exists; further, the silent male referent masks the hierarchy and inequality.

A radical pluralist and feminist theory of equality must recognize the specificity of the female body and the variety of ways this is expressed: individually (as in differences of health, age, body strength, and size) and in terms of a woman's race and economic class. The unique aspect of the female body—its capacity for childbearing—makes women a sex class, even though differences exist among them. The engendered meaning of the mother's body plays a large part in this designation. Neither the female body nor the pregnant body is uniform in kind or meaning. A middle-class, black, pregnant woman's body is not one and the same as a working-class, white, pregnant woman's body. The pregnant body of a woman in her mid-thirties is not identical to the pregnant body of a woman in her early twenties. A welfare woman's pregnant body may not be the same an an upper-middle-class woman's pregnant body, or a diabetic's pregnant body, or an insemi-nated lesbian's pregnant body, or a surrogate mother's pregnant body.

It is the engendered meaning of the woman's body that homogenizes her "difference" from men and constructs her similarity to other women. Because the engendered viewpoint treats sex and gender as one, gender establishes similarity among women. The unity of women as a sex class is located in the intersection between sex and gender: a place in between that defines heterogeneous females as a homogeneous class. The pregnant body is plural in and of itself, whereas the "idea" of the mother's body is one: diversity and unity, differences and sameness exist simultaneously.

Biology—as the body—is always mediated through its discourses. The meaning of the pregnant body is therefore established in and through the ideas and practices that define an individual's body. Instead of recognizing the heterogeneous expressions of racialized pregnancy and motherhood along individual, economic class, sexual preference, and racial lines, phallocratic discourse abstracts the mother's body as middle class, heterosexual, and white, because acknowledging the plurality of differences among women would undercut the sameness/"difference" opposition.

Phallocratic power—which is plural, dispersed, and sometimes incoherent, as well as hierarchical and unequal in its dispersion—sets the limits of sex and race equality. The multiple existing political discourses regarding sex and gender and race, along with "difference" and sameness, constitute and reflect these relations of power. They position our viewing of power in between ideas and practice, in between truth and falsity of racialized gender. Given this, one's pedagogy must be located within "in-between" spaces.

NOTES

1. For a much fuller discussion of the engendered nature of the law, please see Z. Eisenstein, *The female body and the law* (Berkeley: University of California Press, 1989), especially chapter 2.

2. C. MacKinnon, "Feminism, Marxism, method, and the state: Toward feminist jurisprudence," *Signs*, 8 (Summer 1983), 645.

3. R. Dworkin, *Taking rights seriously* (Cambridge, MA: Harvard University Press, 1977), 290. And see his *A matter of principle* (Cambridge, MA: Harvard University Press, 1985), *Law's empire* (Cambridge, MA: Harvard University Press, 1986), and *The philosophy of law* (New York: Oxford University Press, 1977).

4. For a detailed accounting of the racialized aspects of gender, see Z. Eisenstein, *The color of gender: Reimaging democracy* (Berkeley: University of California Press, 1994).

5. *Encyclopedia of Philosophy*, s.v. "natural law."

6. The dualism of man as rational and woman as passionate should not be overgeneralized; this distinction takes many different historical forms, and in some periods defines woman as passionless, although not necessarily rational. These distinctions are also encoded racially.

7. D. Cole, "Strategies of difference: Litigating for women's rights in a man's world," *Law and Inequality: Journal of Theory and Practice*, 2 (February 1984), 45.

8. L. Irigaray, *This sex which is not one*, trans. C. Porter and C. Burke (Ithaca, NY: Cornell University Press, 1985), 85, 80.

9. MacKinnon, *Feminism, Marxism, method, and the state*, 644.

10. L. Krieger and P. Cooney. "The Miller-Wohl controversy: Equal treatment, positive action, and the meaning of women's equality," *Golden Gate University Law Review*, 13 (1983), 545.

11. See M. Wittig, "The Mark of Gender," *Feminist Issues*, 5 (Fall 1985), 3–12.

12. See R. Stilwell, "Sexism in the statues: Identifying and solving the problem of ambiguous gender bias in legal writing," *Buffalo Law Review*, 32 (Spring 1983), 559–587.

13. 83 U.S. (16 Wall) 130, 141 (1873).

14. MacKinnon, *Sexual harassment of working women* (New Haven, CT: Yale University Press, 1979), 110.

15. Section 1 of the Fourteenth Amendment reads: "All persons born or naturalized in the United States, and subject to the jurisdiction thereof, are citizens of the U.S. and of the state wherein they reside. No state shall make or enforce any law which shall abridge the privileges or immunities of citizens of the U.S., nor shall any state deprive any person of life, liberty, or property without due process of law; nor deny to any person within its jurisdiction the equal protection of the laws."

16. MacKinnon, *Sexual harassment of working women*, 107.

17. P. Segal, "Sexual equality, the Equal Protection Clause, and the ERA," *Buffalo Law Review*, 33 (Winter 1984), 129. And see D. A. Campbell, "Equal protection and gender based discrimination," *Villanova Law Review*, 27 (November 1981), 182–197; R. B. Conlin, "Equal protection vs. Equal Rights Amendment— Where Are We Now?" *Drake Law Review*, 24 (Winter 1975), 259–335; and E. Maltz, "Sex discrimination on the Supreme Court: A comment on sex equality, sex difference, and the Supreme Court," *Duke Law Journal*, (February 1985), 177–194.

18. William Blackstone, quoted in Wendy Williams, "The equality crisis: Some reflections on culture, courts, and feminism," *Women's Rights Law Reporter*, 7 (Spring 1982), 176. Also see Blackstone, *Commentaries on laws of England* [1765], vol. 1 (Chicago: University of Chicago Press, 1979).

19. 83 U.S. (16 Wall) 130, 131, 132 (1873).

20. 335 U.S. 464, 466 (1948).

21. Felix Frankfurter, quoted in William Chafe, *The American woman: Her changing social, economic, and political roles, 1920–1970* (Oxford: Oxford University Press, 1972), 125–126. Also see D. Kirp, M. Yudof, and M. Strong Franks, *Gender Justice* (Chicago: University of Chicago Press, 1986), 40.

22. 208 U.S. 412, 422-23 (1908).

23. See R. B. Ginsburg, "Sexual equality under the Fourteenth and Equal Rights Amendments," *Washington University Law Quarterly*, 1 (Winter 1979), 164. Also see her "From no rights, to half rights, to confusing rights," *Human Rights*, 7 (May 1978), 12–47; "Gender and the Constitution," *University of Cincinnati Law Review*, 44 (1975), 1–42; and "Some thoughts on the 1980's debate over special versus equal treatment for women," *Law and Inequality*, 4 (1986), 143–152.

24. 404 U.S. 71, 77 (1971).

25. 450 U.S. 464 (1981).

26. 540 U.S. 464, 450, 469. Also see A. Freedman, "Sex equality, sex differences, and the Supreme Court," *Yale Law Journal*, 92 (May 1983), 913–968, for a discussion of the "real difference" argument. All further references to this work, abbreviated as SESD will be included in the text.

27. 310 U.S. 141, 147 (1940).

28, 458 U.S. 716, 724–25 (1982).

29. See 417 U.S. 484 (1974)—all further references to this work, abbreviated as 417, will be included in the text; 429 U.S. 125 (1976); and 434 U.S. 136 (1977).

30. 442 U.S. 256, 257 (1979); all further reference to this work, abbreviated as 442, will be included in the text.

31. 414 U.S. 632, 648 (1974); all further reference to this work, abbreviated as 414, will be included in the text.

32. 111 S.Ct. 1196 (1991)

33. C. Lefcourt, *Women and the law* (New York: Boardman, 1984), chapter 6, p. 3.

34. Ibid.

35. See N. Polikoff, "Gender and child-custody determinations: Exploding the myths," in I. Diamond (Ed.), *Families, politics, and public policy: A feminist dialogue on women and the state* (New York: Longman, 1983), 183–202.

36. *Report of the New York Task Force on "Women in the Courts,"* March 1986, p. 161.

37. Ibid., 166.

CHAPTER 13

EVERYDAY LIFE IN THE ACADEMY: POSTMODERNIST FEMINISMS, GENERIC SEDUCTIONS, REWRITING AND BEING HEARD

Terry Threadgold

Donna Haraway has argued that "an adequate socialist-feminist politics should address women in the privileged occupational categories, and particularly in the production of science and technology that constructs scientific-technical discourses, processes and objects" (1991, 169). She asks some interesting questions about the roles that new groups doing science in different ways might be able to play, and about the kinds of connections they might be able to make with progressive social and political movements, and with scientific and technical workers. At the same time she is insistent that there can be no restructuring of the social relations of technology and science without theory and practice aimed at understanding the "myths and meanings structuring our imaginations."

That understanding, and the possibility of "doing things in different ways," then, depends on the kind of critical social literacies which may be developed as a result of the rewriting of patriarchal theories and of new ways of making and teaching knowledges. Change in the social relations of science, as in the social relations of the law, politics, the media, pedagogy, and a whole range of other areas is in part dependent on how we go about teaching reading and writing, and what sorts of things we teach that texts are, as well as how we theorise and go about the teaching. Changing any of these things, or indeed leaving them alone, is crucially related to the questions raised by the making of literate bodies (the embodiment of pedagogy that begins with the earliest contacts with the reading and writing practices of the community), the disciplining of subjects (their training within specific disciplinary fields), and questions raised by feminist theories of the relations between body and consciousness and theories like Bourdieu's of the embodied *habitus* (Threadgold, 1993). It is also related to the question of genre, the roles and functions of institutionally or discipline specific genres, their intersections with the making of the discourses, narratives, and myths that constitute the social world, the culture, and embodied subjectivities, and their discipline-based propensity to appropriate and homogenise difference.

To be disciplined, in any of the major disciplines in the sciences or the humanities/social sciences, is to learn to embody, to perform, and to enact on a daily basis, in the workplace, as everyday pedagogy, not only the academic genres that constitute the theories and practices of the discipline, but also the genres of social relations and embodied subjectivity that construct the discipline as "a body" of knowledge, and that determine its intersections and social relations with other disciplines, and other institutions, other "bodies" of knowledge. To succeed in the discipline means to be able to perform its genres, and to speak and write and embody its favorite discourses, myths, and narratives. When those are patriarchal to the core, the female disciplined subject may be seduced into occupying the positions offered by the discourses and genres of various versions of the male "other," or she may find her labours of rewriting, of not being seduced, the subject of critique or appropriation. It is particularly the latter problem I want to address in this chapter.

This poses two questions, and they are relevant not only to the position of white, middle-class, privileged women and the question of academic genres, but indeed to all of patriarchy's others, and at whatever level in the hierarchy of pedagogies that constitute schooling. How, once the discourses and genres of the other have been embodied, do you set about erasing the voices of the master, and learning to speak your own (women's/black/aged and so on) bodies, while still remaining credible within the academy? Is it possible to construct a different kind of *habitus* from the outset, or to reconstruct a made *habitus* and thus to remake the academy from within. Perhaps even more important, given recent critiques and appropriations of feminist work, are there any real connections between feminist pedagogies and the politics of praxis: are postmodernist and feminist pedagogies and theories just part of the "linguistic turn" (Norris. 1993; Rorty, 1991) of recent theory or can they have real social effects?

These are not new questions, but I would like to return to their relations with science. It is now both a feminist and a poststructuralist/postmodernist catchcry, in some places, that one does not analyse texts, one rewrites them, one does not have an objective metalanguage, one does not use a theory, one performs one's critique. I want to suggest that there are also seductions involved in allowing oneself to be positioned totally by the discourses and genres of rewriting and refusal of metalanguages, the seductions of an anti-science metaphysics. If we have accepted that science and theory are stories told from some body's position, and that they can be rewritten, then I think we must also accept that stories (rewritings) are theories, and that they always involve a metalinguistic critique of the stories they rewrite. To accept this means to rewrite the notion of metalanguage or theory in ways that may make it useful again for an explicit feminist critique, and it forces a rethinking of the politics and poetics of "rewriting." That politics and poetics is, after all, largely derived from the work of male theorists and it often comes perilously close to what Foucault has called "commentary" within disciplinary structures.

To "rewrite" in any case always involves an agency which recent theory has been eager to deny. Many feminists have been quick to ask whether it can be coincidence that the death of the subject is announced just as many of us are learning to voice our subjectivity. Yet others have been very concerned to find ways of sexing the subject of knowledge without replicating patriarchy (Probyn, 1993, 136):

> This task is to put oneself into the cultural landscape in order to throw it into relief and to allow new vectors and relationships to be seen, to be created. As 'man' fades away, the face of this discursive and effective landscape changes radically. Seen from the position of an alternative conception of the self, the self as an enunciative and theoretical strategy, this new landscape contains the possibility of ways of living within the social, of new sexual and gender ethics, of constructing theoretical accounts, and of experiencing oneself in relation to others in the historical present of oneself. . . . In less heroic terms, Foucault's care of the self allows me to consider a way of speaking and of theorising that proceeds from 'me' without reifying me as the subject of my speaking.

It is then these complex issues of feminisms, pedagogies, seductions, appropriations, agency and the relations between pedagogy, theory, subjectivity, and social change that I want to address in this chapter. Certain kinds of feminisms are often equated these days rather loosely with poststructuralism, deconstruction, or postmodernism, and the latter, together or in unison, are often constructed (often by men but also by women, namely McKinnon, 1987, 59) as apolitical and dangerous. I want to talk about these issues in relation to a very specific site of pedagogic and social activity, recent work in critical legal studies and in the semiotics of the law. There is a very real sense in which these issues and their consequences are about everyday life in the academy and its consequences in other places. This will be my focus here.

POSTMODERNISM, DECONSTRUCTION, FEMINISMS, AND THE LAW

I want to state at the outset that although I will talk about the confusions and incommensurabilites involved in various understandings of the terms postmodernism and deconstruction, I will not offer definitions as such. In the final section of this chapter I will discuss in detail some examples of what I consider to be postmodernist feminist and theoretical practice in the Australian context now. Those examples of praxis will articulate such definition as I am prepared to offer. There are reasons for this.

In the current context of critical legal studies, deconstruction and postmodernism are the two critical terms which are most often encountered. They are the two phenomena credited with a major rewriting of the theoretical practices and underpinnings of the law in recent times. Semiotics has also had its effects and feminisms sit somewhat uneasily either within or beside these practices in the current literature and debates. Feminist jurisprudence has at least been recognised and increasingly has effects in and through the teaching in law schools, but the role of the feminist within the legal academy and within the practice of the law outside the academy is still far from easy (Thornton, 1994; O'Shane, 1993). I want to talk then about the uses, political or otherwise, of deconstruction and postmodernism in relation to the law. Doing that immediately involves also talking about undecidability and indeterminacy, phenomena to which, in certain discourses, postmodernism and deconstruction (and thus by implication feminisms) are frequently reduced. Connected with these terms are a whole network of equally slippery concepts—the differend (Lyotard, 1988), femininity/masculinity, intertextuality, rewriting, the other and alterity, plurality and politics—to name only a few. All of these terms and concepts are used in radically incommensurable ways in different contexts. Let me begin with a considerable reduction of this complexity and a comparison of contexts:

1. Law is decidable (not indeterminate), is not political (for which read subjective), and can therefore "incorporate" deconstruction (for which read a care for the other) (Rosenfeld, 1992, in the context of U.S. uses of deconstruction).
2. Law is undecidable already (that is, it has always involved rewriting and intertextuality and has thus always been indeterminate, from indeed the time of Moses). It is therefore demonstrated to be already both postmodern and deconstructive (of itself). It is therefore also politically correct in relation to recent theory (Jacobson, 1992, again in the context of U.S. uses of deconstruction; see also Threadgold, 1994, for a counter to this position).
3. Undecidability and indeterminacy are associated with postmodernism (for which here read both the condition of late capitalism, the theoretical refusal of all forms of enlightenment critique and the "poststructuralist" belief in the discursive construction of reality) and they constitute a culpable neglect of the political (the belief in the possibility of truth, and the refusal of a Baudrillardian or Fish type belief that "truth" is always relative). Deconstruction (cf. Derrida, de Man) has nothing to do with the postmodern (cf. Lyotard, Baudrillard) although it has been co-opted by it. It "sustains the impulse of enlightenment critique" even as it subjects that tradition to a radical reassessment. Deconstruction is also associated with "close reading" the use of theory "to avoid reading stupidly, accepting language at face value," and with a stress on conserving (in Derrida's recent writing) the engagement of philosophy with ethical, political, and epistemological issues which cannot be reduced to textual "freeplay." (Norris, 1989, 11–13; 1992, in the context of U.K. work in theory and critical legal studies).

It is important to note that these three positions are all those of men and that many feminist positions available on these issues, which we will come to, are very different. There is much to agree with in Norris' position although his nostalgia for both the enlightenment and close-reading is incompatible in many ways with feminist deconstruction and postmodernism. What the uncertainties and incommensurabilities in these three examples demonstrate in some small measure are the conflictual and political textual processes through which meanings are produced and contested and the social relations of power constructed in the everyday life of the academy.

I want to argue that positions 1 and 2 above involve an uncritical appropriation of deconstruction/postmodernism within critical legal studies in the U.S. context which is very like what feminists have called the appropriation of the feminine by deconstruction and postmodernism themselves (Spivak, 1983). What actually occurs is a becoming-feminine (where feminine equals irrational, heteroglossia, plurality, rewriting, the relativity of truth) of the masculine (law) which protects it from the charge of being patriarchal (a charge that is explicit of course in feminist jurisprudence and deconstruction but implicit in these masculine uses of deconstruction). This feminisation then does not involve any need for the law to change. It is already postmodern and internally deconstructive and therefore can proceed with business as usual.

As Joan Scott, speaking of the discipline of history, has argued, this is "not a conspiratorial politics, nor is it narrowly self-interested; rather it protects an established corporate tradition" (1988, 9). Nevertheless, the form that knowledge has taken within the law—the remarkable absence of women in legal narratives of contract and equity, the narratives that sustain the law as institution, the relegation of women to a private sphere (the Englishman's home is his castle) where law does not operate—indicates a specific politics that sets agendas and enforces priorities, naturalises some categories and disqualifies others. It is in this way that the law functions as a cultural institution endorsing particular constructions of gender, race, age, and ethnicity and it continues to do this in the American context through the uses to which it puts deconstruction and postmodernism. This American appropriation is a restorative, recuperative, or normative phenomenon which mimics law's systemic appropriation of the private into the public, the local, the individual, and the specific into the universal, the unruly into the normative. The issues that this raises have to do with institutions and systems, and specifically with theories of how they operate in relation to subjectivity, embodiment and social change or stasis, a set of questions which are already disputed terrain among neo-pragmatists like Fish (1992), legal theorists like Ronald Dworkin (1982), Foucauldians, and feminist theorists. They are crucial questions, of course, for the issues of feminist agency and voice with which I began.

Let me begin then by looking a little more closely at the uses of postmodernism and deconstruction in the two chapters from the book *Deconstruction and the Possibility of Justice* (1992) from which I extracted positions 1 and 2 previously. *Deconstruction and the Possibility of Justice* has a place in the chain of readings/rewritings (in Dworkin's (1982) sense) that constitute the field of recent and emerging Australian work in Law and Literature and Critical Legal Studies. At the same time, it is a book that is marked by an extraordinary difference to the Australian work. Perhaps in this case *differance* (in Derrida's sense) would be the better term since there is within the chapters of the book a constant deferral of the business of deconstruction in favor of the assertion of the possibility of justice in abstract theoretical terms. The theme of the difference of deconstruction in the United States context is one that is constantly reiterated in the book, a book which begins with an essay by Derrida. That Derrida may have some anxieties about this difference/*differance* is indicated early in his chapter 'Force of Law: the "mystical foundation of authority"' when he makes some explicitly critical comments on the context of his encounter with critical legal studies in the U.S. and concludes: "Respect for contextual, acedemico-institutional, discursive specificities, mistrust for analogies and hasty transpositions, for confused homogenizations, seem to me the first imperatives the way things stand today" (p. 9).

Part 11 of the book is entitled "Deconstruction and Legal Interpretation" and begins with a chapter by Arthur J. Jacobson, "The Idolatry of Rules: Writing Law According to Moses, with Reference to Other Jurisprudences." In this extraordinarily masculinist context, Moses and his encounters with writing and rewriting are indeed read and rewritten as a postmodernist metaphor for the workings of contemporary dynamic jurisprudences which, in the face of positivism and naturalism, and like Moses, refuse to treat rules as idols and continually struggle to remake them. The premise of this chapter is that "to erase is to rescue writing from idolatry" (p. 106). The story of the three rewritings of the law in Moses' case becomes an allegory (an allegory of reading in de Man's terms) of the liberal humanist notion of the constant evolution of the common law in the direction of positive social change.

Nowhere is there any mention of class, race, or gender as implicated in these processes. The simple similarity between "rewritings"—as postmodernist evasions of fixity and rigid meanings—and "rewriting"— as involved in normal legal procedures of interpretation—is adduced as constituting law's own potential internal deconstruction of its own processes. That is, the proof of indeterminacy is adduced as evidence of deconstruction, without any of the careful strictures on the reading of indeterminacy suggested by Derrida in this book and elsewhere.

What is at stake here is the very political question raised in Drucilla Cornell's (1992) chapter in the same book, whether just any "rewriting" constitutes deconstruction—and whether in fact some forms of rewriting are actually forms of "restoration." It could be argued that the system within which Moses writes and rewrites the law (even if he does it three times), and the dynamic jurisprudences of which Jacobson speaks, are precisely the kinds of closed referential systems that constitute gender hierarchies and, rather than *constituting deconstruction*, actually *require deconstruction*. Indeed, in much feminist and critical legal studies work that is precisely what has been argued of late. There is a radical confusion here between the nature of the social conditions post-modernism has made it possible to see (that is, the law as institution) and the political or other consequences of rigorous deconstruction. Samuel Weber in his chapter in the book (p. 234) comments explicitly on this confusion when he talks of the "familiar and uncanny" nature of deconstruction in the context of a social system whose very "constitution" depends on the reading and rereading/rewriting of a written text (the Constitution, p. 238).

This use of deconstruction to maintain business as usual is particularly pertinent to the reading of the chapter in this book which demonstrates the full extent of the "restoration" made possible by a self-justificatory system like legal argument when confronted with "the crisis in legal interpretation" produced by nonrestorative uses of deconstruction. Michel Rosenfeld's chapter, "Deconstruction and Legal Interpretation: Conflict, Indeterminacy and the Temptations of the New Legal Formalism," is an extraordinary exercise in what Stanley Fish has called the law's tendency to incorporate its others. First, it is structured around the binary opposition between law and politics and is determined to maintain the proposition that "legal practice is irreducible to the practice of politics" (p. 156), and second it is convinced and sets out to prove that the American legal and constitutional system is already a deconstructive practice. To this end, it first rewrites deconstruction as liberal humanist democratic practice, reversing the deconstructive enterprise (whereby "texts" are usually subject to deconstruction) by declaring that whether deconstruction actually provides a solution to the crisis in legal interpretation "depends on whether its ontological and ethical presuppositions are compatible with law and legal interpretation" (p. 166). In other words, law and legal interpretation remain uncontested while deconstruction may be "incorporated" (the term is Rosenfeld's) provided that it is compatible with them.

At this point, in an exemplary pair of paragraphs (p. 167), "legal systems prevalent in Western democracies" are proved to be already instances of deconstruction now defined as "a care for the other," and we find that "so long as a legal system operates in the context of group pluralism, and through the application of general laws that are universally applicable, therefore, law meets the two conditions that entitle it legitimately to embrace deconstruction." Moreover the American legal system in particular encompasses a conception of law particularly well suited "to incorporate deconstruction" (p. 168).

What follows this ambiguity of agency and this semantic muddle (or hermeneutic circle) over who is deconstructing, embracing or incorporating whom is a strange conclusion that the "incorporation" of deconstruction in these terms will inform the practice of legal interpretation so as "to repel the threat of absorption into mere politics." What is never clear is how a "law having embraced deconstruction" would be in any sense different from an undeconstructed law. What we are left with is a law which will "channel disparate self interests to a common ground" (p. 197) with absolutely no substantive indications of how, no recognition of the gender hierarchy (to use Cornell's term) in which legal processes are implicated, and no recognition of the appropriation of the discourses of deconstruction by liberal humanist legal discourses which we have described in this chapter.

Far from demonstrating how a law which has embraced deconstruction might effect social change or solve the crisis in legal interpretation, this chapter shows precisely wherein that crisis lies by demonstrating (1) the "resistance to theory" (Paul de Man, 1986) that is built in to the processes of legal interpretation themselves, and (2) their systematically coercive powers of restoration and appropriation in the face of external attacks or challenges. In this case a close reading of Rosenfeld's text "uncovers . . . contradictions that go completely against" this particular reader's "received, canonical understanding" of deconstruction (to misquote Norris 1989, 152, speaking of deconstructions of legal texts). The system reasserts itself and deconstruction, embraced and incorporated into the body of the law, is effectively feminised, seduced, and disempowered. One is reminded here of Geoffrey Bennington's comment: "we have to try to understand that deconstruction is neither something done at a given date by an active and wilful or even heroic subject to a more or less resistant or complicit object, nor quite something that that object is shown to do to itself anyway whether we like it or not" (1994, 178).

It is clear that in the American context the work of Dworkin and Fish intersects in interesting ways with the curious uses of deconstruction reported above. Dworkin's (1982) account of legal interpretation as a system like that of imagined literary collaboration in the production of a novel—what Fish (1992) later popularised as "working on the chain gang"—each move constrained by the one before, and thus protecting the whole enterprise from sudden subjective swings, is actually not dissimilar to Fish's position on systems, despite the latter's critique of Dworkin (1992). Fish, working with notions of the interpretive community that have connections with Foucault's work on discipline and commentary, also argues that subjective or radical moves are impossible within the interpretive community or the system. This is why he argues that theory can change nothing, it is always a product of the system it tries to change and is therefore doomed to failure. This anti-theory agenda is different to Dworkin's insistence on the already socially evolving and therefore positive aspects of law as system, but both theories seem designed to protect the law and the academy, as community, and as collaborative practice, from the dangers of subjectivity or of radical political involvement. They also both explicitly deny the possibility of agency or of radical change. In both versions systems evolve, either producing democratic change inevitably or changing in ways impervious to agency. In both cases the complacent appropriation of recent literary theory is again enlisted to protect the corporation. As Norris has pointed out, this is "the kind of all-purpose pragmatist argument that can be used to discredit oppositional thinking in law, criticism, or any other field where professional interests are at play" (1989, 15).

It was then my reading of these American contexts that first prompted me to try to sort out what on earth we think that postmodernism and deconstruction and systems—evolving, open or closed, transformative or static—might be. One finds some remarkable differences in the stories that people tell. The following quotation is from Peter Goodrich, writing of the semiotics of the common law:

> The notion of time out of mind describes legal method most exactly; it is time unbound to any life or object, free of any specific temporality, a time of repetition and so a thoughtless time. It is what Legendre terms *the 'delirium of the institution'* which unravels itself within the discrete confines of the legal form, as a prisoner not of life but of normative governance (1976). The law is a prison of the deep historical structures which time treats badly. . . . *The institution hallucinates standard forms of procedure and norms of usual behaviour on the strength of half-remembered arguments,* through the dazed recollection of unreported cases or largely forgotten conversations. . . .
>
> These were the tools of the common law, these were their memories, a *communis opinio,* a collective memory, as law. Law is a presence which implies the totality of its history, but this implication is not logical or historical: rather, it is traditional and mythic. *The hallucinating mind is in strict terms a mind that wanders, that 'lucinates', that goes astray.* That is the source of common law, of unwritten law, the meandering of the legal mind, a temporal and geographic nomadism that snakes its path across the justificatory texts, the judgements, the year books and the law reports. *Here we can understand how the text is also the unwritten structure of*

everyday life, a reality which time treats badly and transmits very slowly over long periods. (Goodrich & Hachamovitch, 1991, 174; the emphasis is my own)

Goodrich's account of the legal system is of a hallucinatory system, a system based on myth and narrative, a system which is also the unwritten structure of everyday life, in which change may occur, but randomly, a system which is unconscious of its own workings and has no agenda for change. In some ways it is rather like Norris' reading of postmodernism, but it bears little relationship to the accounts of Fish, Dworkin, Jacobson, and Rosenfeld discussed above. It calls to mind Haraway's argument (1991) that to change the social realities and everyday worlds we live, we need to understand the myths and narratives that structure them.

These accounts however all in various ways also recall (and are to some extent influenced by) Foucault's (1971) account of commentary and its paradoxical relations to discipline, a proliferation of text which simultaneously produces citation (more of the same) and difference (the "new" which is the means of perpetuating the discipline but must always remain "in the true" of the discipline):

The infinite rippling of commentary is agitated from within by the dream of masked repetition: in the distance there is perhaps nothing other than what was there at the point of departure: simple recitation. Commentary averts the chance element of discourse by giving it its due: it gives us the opportunity of saying something other than the text itself, but on condition that it is the text itself which is uttered and, in some ways, finalised. (p.10)

But the principles involved in the formation of disciplines are equally opposed to that of commentary. In a discipline, unlike in commentary, what is supposed at the point of departure is not some meaning which must be rediscovered, nor an identity to be reiterated; it is that which is required for the construction of new statements. For a discipline to exist there must be the possibility of formulating—and of doing so ad infinitum—fresh propositions. . . . Within its own limits, every discipline recognises true and false propositions, but it repulses a whole tetralogy of learning. . . . In short, a proposition must fulfil some onerous and complex conditions before it can be admitted within a discipline; before it can be pronounced true or false it must be, as Monsieur Canguilhem might say, 'in the true'. . . . Disciplines constitute a system of control in the production of discourse, fixing its limits through the action of an identity taking the form of a permanent reactivation of the rules. (pp. 16–17)

While it is possible to read in this the makings of Fish's position or of Goodrich's, Foucault actually did not leave the matter there. The situation he describes above was one that he sought to change and he had a very specific agenda for doing this. Arguing that the four notions—signification, originality, unity, and creation—had dominated the traditional history of ideas for centuries, he suggested replacing them with the following—event, series, regularity, and the possible conditions of existence. This would, he said, enable us "to question our will to truth, to restore to discourse its character as an event, to abolish the sovereignty of the signifier" (p. 229). What he proposed of course was a "rewriting" of the disciplines. However deterministic his anti-humanist and anti-Enlightenment critique may have seemed, and however problematic his later work on "self-fashioning" and "technologies of the self" is as an account of agency to some critics (Norris, 1993), it was always clear that his was an oppositional position, dedicated to establishing the conditions of possibility for that permanent critique which Norris is so keen to associate (I think contra Foucault) with a rewritten Enlightenment ethos (1993, 99).

For poststructuralist feminisms Foucault's work has offered very different readings—the possibilities of stories of resistance not determinism, and of new, transformed selves. Chris Weedon's (1987) account is typical:

Although the subject in poststructuralism is socially constructed in discursive practices, she none the less exists as a thinking, feeling subject and social agent, capable of resistance and innovations produced out of the clash between contradictory subject positions and practices. She is also a subject able to reflect upon the discursive relations which constitute her and the society in which she lives, and able to choose from the options available. (p. 125)

Feminist readings, which find empowering the notion that reality and their own subjectivities are discursively constructed and can therefore be reconstructed, seem much closer to the spirit of Foucault's agenda for critique than the various male readings I have quoted above. Like Derrida, they also do not see deconstruction or postmodernism as having to do with indeterminacy or relativism. Derrida insists that he has never spoken of "indeterminacy":

> I do not believe I have ever spoken of "indeterminacy" whether in regard to meaning or anything else. Undecidability is something else again. . . . I want to recall that undecidability is always a *determinate* oscillation between possibilities (for example of meaning but also of acts) . . . there would be no indecision or *double bind* were it not between *determined* (semantic, ethical, political) poles, which are upon occasion terribly necessary and always irreplaceably singular. Which is to say that from the point of view of semantics, but also of ethics and politics, "deconstruction" should never lead to relativism or any sort of indeterminism. (1988, 148)

Nor do all feminist readings of Derrida have the problem with his use of the term 'text' that bothers Norris (1992, 19), writing of the postmodernist "takeover" of Derrida's "there is nothing outside the text") and MacKinnon (1989, 129). Derrida, as Cornell has argued (1993, 133: "Derrida shows us that social reality (including the very definition of power) and 'empirical' experience cannot be separated from the meanings they are given"), insists that his notion of 'text', contra Norris' anxieties about the "linguistic turn" in postmodernism and the textualism of Lyotard and Baudrillard (1992, 16), never meant that there was "nothing outside the text" in quite that way:

> I wanted to recall that the concept of text I propose is limited neither to the graphic, nor to the book, nor even to discourse, and even less to the semantic, representational, symbolic, ideal or ideological sphere. What I call "text" implies all the structures called "real," "economic," "historical," socio-institutional, in short: all possible referents. Another way of recalling once again that "there is nothing outside the text." That does not mean that all referents are suspended, denied, or enclosed in a book, as people have claimed, or have been naive enough to have accused me of believing. (1988, 148)

And then against these very positive feminist uses of Foucault and Derrida, to transform the system, to stop it evolving in that inevitable way, to deny Fish's argument "that any form of life or language game can shut itself into a totality that would identify the subject completely with any system of shared norms and deny the possibility of transformative change" (Cornell, 1993, 4). Spivak (1983) reminds us of the ever present restorative and recuperative powers of the system. Her discourse on the double displacement of woman in deconstruction itself is a paradigm case of the way the discourse of the other can be incorporated in and by the most radical of narratives. Spivak's account has many implications for the texts on aboriginality, homosexuality, and woman/rape/murder with which I will conclude this chapter, for the U.S. "incorporation" of deconstruction discussed above and for feminist attempts to rewrite themselves, the academy, or the social world:

> It is my suggestion however that the woman who is the "model" for deconstructive discourse remains a woman generalized and defined in terms of the faked orgasm and other varieties of denial. (1983, 170–171)

> Derrida's view of the textual operation—of reading, writing, philosophizing—makes it finally clear that however denaturalized and non-empirical these images (of hymen, orgasm etc.) might be, it is the phallus that learns the trick of coming close to faking the orgasm here, rather than the hymen coming into its own as the indefinitely displaced effect of the text. Thus the hymen is doubly displaced. Its "presence" is appropriately deconstructed, and its curious property appropriated to deliver the signature of the philosopher. . . . [D]issemination remains on the ascendant. The hymen remains reactive. It is "dissemination which affirms the already divided generation of meaning." Textual operation is back to position one and fireworks on the lawn with a now "feminized" phallus: "dissemination in the fold (*repli*—also withdrawal) of hymen." (1983, 175–176)

In 1993 Spivak rereads her polemic against Derrida in this passage and suggests ways of using deconstruction (affirmative deconstruction) for feminism:

> This is one paradoxical way of saying "yes" to the text, but it entails understanding from within, as it were, so that the moments that lend themselves to the so-called misappropriation are understood in the text's own terms. It is then that one can begin to develop a politics of reading, which will open up a text towards an as yet unknown horizon so that it can be of use without excuse. Let us now call this: negotiating with the structures of violence. It is in that spirit of negotiation that I propose to give assent to Derrida's text about woman as a name for the nontruth of truth, upon the broader terrain of negotiation with other established structures, daily practised but often disavowed, like the Law, institutional education, and, ultimately, capitalism. (1993, 129–130).

This multiplicity of contradictory positions (which without due care may indeed end up back at position one and fireworks on the lawn), this "negotiating with the structures of violence" is of course the stuff of which the myths and meanings and actions of everyday life in the academy are made. So is "affirmative deconstruction" (Spivak 1993, 130). There are many ways of doing this and I want now to turn to some women's stories of how, in part to redress the balance after so many men's stories of the impossibility of postmodernist feminist politics and social change.

Drucilla Cornell's (1992) chapter "The Philosophy of the Limit: Systems Theory and Feminist Legal Reform," in the book from which I quoted previously, insists that Derrida's deconstructive readings of Lacan and Levinas make it very clear that unless we challenge Lacan's and Levinas' reduction of woman to an imaginary fantasy, "to the *phenomenologically* asymmetrical other," equal citizenship is impossible and the violation of women in patriarchal societies will continue (p. 88). She is concerned here with what Joan Scott has called "restoration"— with understanding the reasons why "the conditions of women's inequality are continually restored" (p. 68). She rewrites Luhmann's systems theory to include "gender hierarchy," showing how gender functions as a closed semantic system, structured around a binary opposition. She is then able to show, using Lacan, Luhmann, and Derrida, how gender and law function as different subsystems within the social system and how, together, they continually restore women's inequality. Deconstruction, as a political force, is enlisted as a way of changing that system and stopping the process of restoration. It is what makes it possible to deconstruct the gender hierarchy which law supports, to challenge the status of dichotomies, to expose the internal instabilities in the system, and to study systematically the conflictual processes that produce meanings.

In *Transformations* (1993, 3) Cornell also argues, contra Fish, that no system is actually impervious to change, and that that change can be accomplished through "habit-change" or education. "Peirce offers us a convincing account of how we as lawyers, law professors, and judges come to be open to the invitation to create new worlds" (1993, 23). For her the lesson of deconstruction is like that of poststructuralism for Weedon:

The lesson is that no reality can perfectly totalize itself, because reality, including the reality of male domination, is constituted in and through language in which institutionalised meaning can never be fully protected from slippage and reinterpretation. (1993, 132)

These limits to institutionalised meanings are what makes it possible to conceive of feminine sexual difference and agency in ways that are not possible within their stabilised definitions within gender hierarchy (1993, 133). What makes this feminist account of systems theory different is the theorising of sexual difference, of sexuality and the body, an understanding of semiotics and Lacan's theory of the unconscious, and a different theory of "agency" or "freedom." As Judith Butler has explained:

> What we might call 'agency' or 'freedom' or 'possibility', is produced by gaps opened by the regulatory norms in the process of their self-repetition. (Quoted in Cornell 1993, 4)

It is this which allows a theory of agency to remain compatible with theories of poststructuralist subjectivity in ways which writers like Norris and Rorty seem unable to imagine. Cornell is worth quoting at length here. Speaking of psychoanalysis and the need to deal with racism, she says:

> Geertz reminds us that we cannot even begin to understand suffering if we don't grasp the limits of our imagination as it has become ensnared in the latest conventions. I have suggested that this very effort to free the imagination involves a journey into the depths so that we can see how this process of ensnaring took place. We return to the past through the very process of envisioning "what is" differently. To try to imagine a society without racism demands that we come to terms with the significance "race" has come to be given in our reality. We remember the future as we involve ourselves in this very process of reimaging the past so that the present world seems to give way under our feet in the wake of new meanings we did not dream of before. Psychoanalysis then can play a crucial role in Geertz's "science of imagining difference," a paradoxical phrase which not only captures our responsibility to respect the other, but allows us to understand that our political obligations can not be separated from our dreams and fantasies. (1993, 194)

C. S. Peirce then offers her a "postmodern" pragmatism with which to challenge neopragmatist thinkers like Rorty and Fish (1993, 3, 23ff.). Here I want to turn briefly to the work of Teresa de Lauretis (1984), who also works with Peirce's notion of habit-change, rewriting Eco's theory of semiotics (1976) to include embodied subjectivity. Peirce, as

Cornell (1993, 25) points out, was among the first to explore the truth of indeterminacy. It is Peirce whom Derrida (1967/76) and Eco (1976) appropriate to develop their concepts of "undecidability" and "infinite semiosis" respectively. Like Derrida and Eco, Peirce believed that "indeterminacy" could only ever be explored within a context where the interpretations of signs were established, that is, we use meaning as the basis for our questioning of meaning. Peirce explained indeterminacy through the concept of the interpretant. Every sign refers to some referent, but that referent is immediately the interpretant for another sign and so on. "If the chain of meaning comes to a halt, however temporarily, it is by anchoring itself to somebody, some body, an individual subject. As we use or receive signs we produce interpretants" (de Lauretis, 1984, 178). The conclusion of every single process of semiosis then is a modification of consciousness, a habit-change (de Lauretis, 1984, 178).

De Lauretis traces the process by which Eco excises that body from his theory of semiotics: "I am only suggesting that from the point of view of the theory of signification, *we should perform a sort of surgical operation*. . . . [T]he analysis of content becomes a cultural operation which works only on physically testable cultural products" (Eco, 1985, 198). For Eco, human action "must be excised of its psychological, psychic and subjective component" (de Lauretis, 1984, 176), and testable cultural products, in the materialist tradition within which Eco is working, are the those processes of production which produce "actual texts."

For de Lauretis there are many other kinds of social practice (family relations, workplace activities, classrooms, for example) which are interpretants that result in habit-change or "changes of consciousness" (1984, 178). Thus where Eco reads Peirce to argue that each act of semiosis produces "human action," and is prepared to read only the results of the actions as cultural products, de Lauretis argues that no process of semiosis can have any effect on the world except by passing through bodies (1984, 178–179). The nature of that body, of the subject who lives the body, is then directly relevant to understanding the processes by which meanings are made. This subject is always divided from itself because of its relationship to the chain of interpretants, provisionally joined to social and ideological formations, temporarily *there* as the chain of semiosis comes to a halt and each interpretant results in a habit-change, but never fixed by the system, always capable of further change. This embodied process of course deconstructs the opposition between subjective and social modes of signification that Eco works so hard to maintain (de Lauretis 1984, 181).

This feminist work, although it calls itself postmodernist (in the sense of a refusal or critique of modernist theories of systems) and

accepts indeterminacy as a condition to work with and through, is neither apolitical, nor unconcerned with ethics nor deprived of agency as
some people's versions of the postmodern are supposed to be (Norris,
1993). It is useful here to introduce Judith Butler's carefully articulated
arguments about the claims of 'poststructuralist' (a term she chooses in
preference to 'postmodernist') feminisms. She has accused "the scep-
tics" who lump together a diverse range of critical perspectives "under
the sign of the postmodern" of engaging in a "self-congratulatory ruse
of power" which in itself entirely misses the point of poststructuralism.
That point is the recognition that even the terms of criticism and the
subject position of the critic are implicated in the power structures
they seek to negotiate. To recognise that is *"not* the advent of a nihilis-
tic relativism incapable of furnishing norms, but rather the very precondition of politically engaged critique" (Butler 1992, 5–7; Howe
1984, 173).

Nor do these feminist theorists suffer from the kind of nostalgia
for an older Marxism or Enlightenment values that is constantly in evidence in Norris' and other neo-Marxist work (Norris, 1993; Eagleton,
1985; Jameson, 1983, 1984). Feminists like de Lauretis, Cornell, Butler,
Scott, and others do not forget categories like ideology, false-con-
sciousness, class, and so on. They do re-member subjectivity and the
body and that means that they must rewrite these older categories, but
having rewritten them they cannot go back. Their feminist poststructuralism, deconstruction, postmodernism, is remade by those rewritings and moves on. If history and politics and agency are rewritten,
lived differently, that does not mean you can no longer pursue political
ends or that action is impossible (Scott, 1988). I am reminded here of
Anna Yeatman's point in 1990 that the neglect of gender by the custodians of Marxist class analysis extends to an "extraordinarily incuri-
ous" attitude towards what she then called "the gender segmentation of
the intelligentsia" (p. 64).

If the above discussion of arguments about systems, theories, and
the possibilities of change is any indication that segmentation is alive
and well in 1995 as a part of the everyday lived and sexual/textual
realities of the academy, then it centres around an acceptance and
refusal of change expressed as an acceptance or refusal of what is
loosely called "postmodernism." Nowhere is this difference more hotly
argued than in the current context of debates about legal reform which
have been instigated and motivated by postmodernist, deconstructive,
and feminist agendas. I want to quote here from one more feminist
writer because it will bring me back to the law and the examples of
praxis with which I want to conclude.

Diane Elam, in a recent book on *Deconstruction and Feminism*, referring to Derrida on undecidability and indeterminacy has the following to say:

> The affirmative potential of feminist politics is that such a politics takes the undecidability of the multiple determinations of women, the clash of virgin, whore, mother etc., as the aporetic space within which a freedom arises. (1994, 84)

Turning to Barbara Johnson on abortion she adds:

> To win the debate on abortion would be to allow the undecidable in so far as abortion would be neither a decision which could be made in advance or made once and for all for all women. . . . By acknowledging the undecidable, deconstruction and feminism allow us to imagine other political spaces—spaces of political otherness. An ethical or just politics must recognise that this handling (of difference) cannot itself become the object of a contract, cannot be given a determinate meaning.
>
> A just politics must seek to handle these differences, to respect them, without implying that what is other can be made identical by means of that handling. This is the lesson of Lyotard's *Differend*. (1994, 84–85)

It is notable that for Elam, as for other feminists, the *differend* is a liberating concept which bears little relation to its offensiveness to theorists like Norris (1993, 18–19). She concludes with a discussion of Derrida on duty:

> Thus the understanding of politics as undecidable is not about refusing to make decision: it is about refusing to ground them in universal laws. We might even go so far as to say that the politics of the undecidable is an insistence that we have to make a decision, each time, in each case—that we cannot avoid making a decision by just applying a pre-existing law. (1994, 87)

With these things in mind then, I want to turn to look at how systems work and at some practical textual examples, examples of textual and theoretical practice, which may help to clarify what postmodernism, political feminisms, poststructuralism, and deconstruction *are*, how they conform themselves, and what actual political effects they may have, in some very specific local Australian sites now. All of my examples have to do with rewriting the law, the topic you will remember with which I began.

Praxis, Politics, and Social Change: Changing the Subject

Linda Hutcheon, speaking of the inevitably political consequences of postmodernism as it works to "de-doxify" the political import of cultural representations, has also made explicit the reasons why the terms I have been using in this chapter are so hard to define except as a network of intersecting practices: "In other words, it is difficult to sep-arate the 'de-doxifying' impulse of postmodern art and culture from the deconstructing impulse of what we have labelled poststructuralist theory" (1989, 4). My first example then is about the politics of post-modern representation, about what Althusser (1969, 231–232) called ideology as both a system of representation and an inevitable part of daily life, and about fictions which self-reflexively and self-consciously confront both documentary historical actuality and traditional formalist impulses and question the supposed transparency of representation. The concept of art as politics has emerged from the impact of Marxist, feminist, gay, black, poststructuralist, and postcolonial theory on the traditional foundations of the literary and visual arts (expressive, mimetic, and formalist). The result has been a change in the way some representations work, not as mimetic and subjective, but to explore the ways in which narratives, images, and languages structure the way we see ourselves and the way we have constructed ourselves and our social realities in the present and the past.

My example then is about the de-naturalising of the natural and the representation of the textual politics of recuperation in Mudrooroo Narogin's novel *Doin Wildcat* (1988). The novel is one of a trilogy in which the same narrative, the story of a young aboriginal man and his early encounters with the law and with various facets of white society, is constantly retold, rewritten, and reconstructed, from different and often conflicting perspectives, by that aboriginal grown old, recently released from goal after serving twenty-three years for the accidental murder of a white policeman. Identities are fluid, constantly changing, as they reappear in different versions of the narrative. The story, in this novel, is about the way a white filmmaker "steals the aboriginal's script," the film script (of the novel we are reading), by rewriting it in ways that again appropriate aboriginality for a white world. The speaking subject in this novel, black, educated through the experi-ence of the violence of the law, is doubly divided from himself, doubly displaced, ventriloquist, able to mimic the discourses of the master, a monolingual master who cannot hear or read *his* stories and lan-guages, and who constantly recuperates them, makes them safe by reappropriating them into his white narratives and worlds.

This double displacement is in fact a place from which to confront not only white histories of aboriginality but white formalisms, white genres, and forms of the novel (Narogin, 1990), and from which to negotiate the power of white linguistic capital. The novel is written in what the sociolinguist would call "nonstandard" English, aboriginal English, but the nonstandard speaker in this novel is multilingual, able to "read" and deconstruct the monolingual blindness of the guardians of standard English, its genres of power (Luke, 1993), and their violently recuperative tendencies. What the novel deconstructs as it represents are the powerful hierarchies of race, class, and gender inherent in all textual processes. Nowhere is this politics of deconstruction and re-presentation (rewriting) more poignant than in the re-presentations of the narrativity of legal process in the novel.

At fifteen the by now already "institutionalised" (p. 87) hero of the novel is let loose on a society he has few means to deal with. The narrative he tells is of both agency and lack of it: victim of a white world which cannot hear his story, he learns to fend for himself; streetwise, he steals to clothe himself with an identity; he makes himself a self in the milkbar world where he is arrested. Arrested he confides the details of this narrative to his probation officer ("Ee wanted me to talk about meself, an I obliged im," p. 89) who, asked to give evidence in court "does the dirty on me" (p. 88). It is worth comparing the details of the two narratives which confront the reader in the novel, two incommensurable constructions of differently lived and understood realities:

> I get outa Swanview, or rather am pushed out when I reach fifteen. Naturally by then I can't fend for meself, and so they get the Catholic Welfare to elp me. They get me a job an a place to stay in an ouse that specialises in puttin up coloured people. There's a couple more stayin along with me, but after the ome an bein outa that ome, I think there must be somethin more to the outside. I get outa that place, find meself another one across the tracks on the wild side of town, an then the job gets rid of me, an I've to use me wits to survive. Its pretty easy but I ate bein on me own. Then one night I wander into the Royal Milk Bar, an feel a bit at ome. (p. 87)

The probation officer's story, as courtroom evidence, constructed in the novel by the speaker of the narrative above, is a classic example of the way the discourse of the other is regularly reclaimed for normative public discourse by institutional practices like the law. The probation officer is that kind of expert reader who has learned to distrust the evidence of the eye-witness (Smith 1990, 120) and is practised precisely in normalising (and thus misreading) unruly and "nonstandard" discourses:

> Robinson: Unfortunately *there is little that can be said for this boy.* The Child Welfare Department has had nothing but trouble from him since his release from Swanview Boy's Home. At the age of nine he was sent there for breaking and entering a number of stores in the town in which he was then living with his mother. *The family to put it mildly were a bunch of drifters.* Reports show that he was not unintelligent, and he was quite good at school. . . . I found him a job and accommodation but he left these almost immediately. . . . *He is of aboriginal descent, on his mother's side, and I believe that this goes a long way towards explaining his behaviour.* (p. 89).

The significance of the *differend* here, of the narrative incompatibility of these two accounts, of the deafness of the public version to the private and individual and here very specifically black and juvenile one, is made yet clearer in the narrator's account of the cross-examination, a genre not known at the best of times for its propensity to listen to what it does not already know (Matoesian, 1993, 103):

> Magistrate: *You say in your statement that you do not believe in God?*
> Juvenile: 'Yeah that's right'. (A nudge from Robinson makes me remember the sir).
> 'Yes, that's right, sir!'
> Magistrate: *And so you have no time for such things as the bible and oaths made before God, and this court?*
> Juvenile: 'No I don't . . . Sir!'
> Magistrate (with a smile): And so, we may presume that you'll swear to tell the truth on your honour?
> Juvenile: *What is ee gettin at?* I shrug, but another nudge from Robinson makes me realise that ee wants an answer. Well, what else to say, but 'Yes, Sir!'
> Magistrate: Well, we'll have to take that on good faith won't we?
> Juvenile: Is words scare me, frighten me to ell an back. *They out to get me, an suddenly I don't want to be got. I blurt out just like the frightened kid I am inside:* "Sir, couldn't find no job. No matter what ee says, couldn't find no job. Ad no money either. Ad to pay me rent, ad to eat, ad nuthin to live on, or for!'

Magistrate: Mr. Robinson was there for you to appeal to. Did you?

Juvenile: *'Im! Ee wouldn't elp me if I was dyin.'*

Magistrate: And these articles of clothing that are on the table. I suppose you were going to sell them for food and shelter?

Juvenile: 'Me own gear was dirty and outa fashion. Me mates expect me to dress sharp.'

Magistrate: Oh . . . Now remember you have given me your word of, of honour to tell the truth. This is very important. *Do you feel any remorse for the crimes you have committed?*

Juvenile: *'Dunno what that is. I was ungry, the rent was due, and I needed some dough.'*

Magistrate: I think we have heard more then enough. Mr. Robinson will you come here please. (p. 89; the emphasis is my own)

Mudrooroo's juxtaposition of these different realities in this novel is specifically and self-consciously postmodern and deconstructive. His own position as educated aboriginal in a white world makes him as author a powerful deconstructive mimic and rewriter. He knows, and can use, the theories for political ends: his stories are in every sense theoretical, as well as theorised, even as they deconstruct the norms of canonical white literature and its languages (genres) of power.

His novels are now becoming part of that small group of canonical texts set as part of the final year English literature curriculum in many Australian states. This itself is an interesting postmodern phenomenon (Stephens, 1992) but the political implications of the reading and teaching of a fictional text like this one in Australian schools cannot be underestimated. The powers for the recuperation of Mudrooroo's deconstruction of institutionalised literary and linguistic power are of course enormous in that context, and in some ways its inclusion in the curriculum might be seen as a mode of reappropriation, but the text itself is remarkably resistant to the recuperative powers of public discourse on a number of levels simultaneously (linguistic, literary, narrative, and generic). It is through the careful interweaving of conflicting narratives that Mudrooroo is able to "voice" and "make heard" what the narratives themselves cannot hear, cannot read, cannot speak. The teaching of the novel then as postmodernist re-presentation and critique of re-presentation has the potential to result in the kind of habit-change, a change of habitus, that Cornell and de Lauretis have theorised.

The significance of his achievement is evident the minute that Mudrooroo's messages (for they are multiple) are projected into other places where conflicting narratives and meanings and the deafness of the guardians of public stories have similar but still more violent effects. In 1990 a little boy called Daniel Valerio was killed in Victoria, a victim of child abuse. Social worker Chris Goddard has written of the many narratives of violence and child abuse that circulated in the last weeks of Daniel's life, stories told to police, health and community services, doctors and nurses and teachers, none of which were heard by the experts presumed to know about such things. The deafness of the probation officer and the magistrate in Mudrooroo's novel take on a new poignancy in the context of Goddard's sad comment on the inquest into Daniel Valerio's death:

> There are no children present in Coroner's Court number one, just heart-rending photos and gloomy x-rays of a little boy long dead. Adults decide what is significant and what events and words mean at this inquest, just as adults decided what was significant and what events and words meant in the last painful days and weeks of Daniel's life. (*The Age*, Tuesday, 22 November 1993, 13)

What Goddard recognises in his writing about this case is the contingency and narrativity that postmodernism has made us see and that modernist stories of reality made invisible (even if they were always there). Acknowledging that contingency and narrativity is a crucial part of changing the way the law operates to perpetrate violence on those it purports to protect.

I quoted Peter Goodrich earlier in this chapter as someone working in critical legal studies who had reached something of an impasse in discovering precisely that contingency of which I have just been speaking. For him the common law had become a fabric of myth and narrative, a delusory and hallucinatory institution. He has since taken up a position which is closer to those of many of the feminists I have quoted, using Kant to develop a new ethics to enable a new agency in the face of what postmodernist critique has shown the modernist versions of law to be:

> Critical legal theory cannot return to (legal) reason or to the subject as the measure or account of law. But similarly it can no longer accept with modern jurisprudence the complacent view that ethics is not a proper concern for law or lawyers. . . . As against the moralism of maxims and codes, as against the complacency of established institutional ethics or more properly institutional

ethos, the critical concern with the ethical is a return to the political and an embrace of responsibility: for the other, for the stranger, the outsider, the alien or underprivileged who needs the law, who needs, in the oldest sense of the term, to have a hearing, to be heard. It is the responsibility of all law to heed the appearance of she who comes before the law (Cornell, 1991, 1992). (Douzinas et al., 1994, 22)

The postmodern judge is implicated, he stands in proximity to the litigant who comes before the law and hears his speech or request. Justice returns to ethics when it recognises the embedded voice of the litigant, when it gives the other in her concrete materiality a locus standi or place of enunciation. The law is necessarily committed to the forms of universality and abstract equality, but a just decision must also respect the requests of the contingent, incarnate and concrete other, it must pass through the ethics of alterity in order to respond to its own embeddedness in justice. (Douzinas et al., 24)

It is to the question of the postmodern judge that I now want to turn and again I do this with the intention of arguing for the positive value of postmodernism and for its part in changing habits.

The case to which I will refer here was an appeal in the Supreme Court of New South Wales, Equity Division, against a decision that the homosexual partner of a deceased man was not eligible, under the Family Provisions Act, N.S.W., to share in his deceased partner's estate. (*McKenzie v. Baddeley*. Priestley JA Meagher JA Hope A-JA: Judgment, 3rd. December, 1991). The majority and dissenting judgments involve just those negotiations over meaning, power, sexual, and class difference which Goodrich once described as the hallucinations of the common law, but the majority judgment delivered by Priestley JA is indicative and productive of habit-change. Priestley's intervention here is significant precisely because it represents an attempt to stop the system evolving in its normal hallucinatory way and to transform it, albeit in a local and perhaps transitory site. Priestley is an interesting judge, patron of the academic Law and Literature Society of Australia, and one who has listened in recent years to many poststructuralist feminist and deconstructive interventions in that postmodern context. There is evidence in his recent judgments that he is beginning to position himself self-consciously in other's stories, to hear other voices, and to let other voices be heard as they come before the law.

The consequences of this change of habitus are evident in the way he rewrites the genre of the judgment itself. This is nowhere more apparent than in the contrast between his judgment in this case, upholding the appeal, and that of the dissenting judge, Meagher JA, and the earlier judgment of Master Windeyer which the dissenting opinion supports. Priestley begins his judgement with the typical judicial narrative of "the story so far" but it is already worth comparing his story with Maegher's. Priestley acknowledges the homosexual relationship between the two men, and specifies as relative to this case the fact that "there was an emotional attachment between them." Meagher begins: "First, to my mind the fact that the relationship was homosexual is of no legal relevance. . . . The case should admit of the same answer as if either of the pair were a woman. . . . The fact that he crept into his lover's bed in the house when it suited him does not establish dependency." The first (Priestley's) retelling of the narrative acknowledges difference in its own terms as legitimate grounds for the appeal, the second reappropriates that difference into a heterosexual narrative and one of illicit, and therefore guilty, love, and thus denies the grounds for the appeal.

The case revolves around the question of dependency. It is argued that the amount of money the appellant earned by growing vegetables on his deceased partner's land constituted a financial dependency which legitimates his claim on his partner's estate. The matter is constructed as "trivial" in both the original and the dissenting judgment. Priestley quotes the Master as having said: "So far as the vegetable growing is concerned . . . there is nothing to show that the plaintiff needed or required the small amount of income raised from vegetables for his material needs." Maegher again recuperates this story of difference into one more familiar to him, another story of heterosexual relations, again feminising the issue of homosexuality: "For example, if my housekeeper uses some of her employment hours in knitting garments which she occasionally sells at the church bazaar, nobody would allege that the knitting activities made her dependent on me, even partly." Priestley is at pains to deconstruct this version of events, even if it involves deconstructing courtroom practice or the opinion of the Master. The matter of evidence is crucial to his arguments, particularly the wilful or patriarchal neglect of evidence when it does not fit a lived judicial reality or a public or commonsense story. He thus demonstrates the interconnections between evidence, narrative, and habit (lived and embodied subjectivity).

Listing the names of a considerable number of witnesses who had given affidavit evidence that the growing of vegetables was a "business," he comments that none of these witnesses was cross-examined, and then expresses his own very different view of the affidavit evidence the Master had so easily discounted:

> In commercial terms what he did was on a tiny scale, but it was regular and it was real. . . . To a man in his fifties, receiving something less than $150 a week from the government, with negligible property and no job, nor any prospects of improving his position, an extra $20 a week is a matter of real importance. He was quite literally dependent on Mr. Burton for the ability to grow and sell the vegetables and make what may have appeared to counsel to be pin money but which must have been to him money necessary for his daily life.

Further evidence of the neglect of evidence and the appropriation of stories is available in the Maegher dissenting judgment on these issues:

> Insofar as vegetables were sold to the public, *there is no evidence* of how many times this happened, or what the proceeds of sale were. Moreover, in cross-examination Mr. McKenzie said that the growing of vegetables was a hobby rather than a business. The Master was clearly entitled to, and did, believe this evidence. (My emphasis)

Had the Master been trained to take the proceedings in his own courtroom rather less at face value, he might not have neglected the evidence so readily. Priestley does not see these proceedings as transparent, indeed reads them as evidence "which in the circumstances of the appellant seems to me to warrant more consideration than the Master gave it." He offers *as evidence* the cross-examination of the appellant in the earlier trial, thereby putting into practice what Douzinas and co-workers (1994, 23) described as "critical legal scholarship moving to place the law of the institution on trial in the court of ethics":

> Q. How much a week are you allowed to earn, as a pensioner?
> A. Twenty dollars and fifty cents.
> Q. And you earned some of this money by growing vegetables?
> A. Yes.
> Q. At the time you were living with Mr. Burton?
> A. Yes.
> Q. You grew vegetables?
> A. Yes.
> Q. And he provided eggs and poultry?

A. Yes.

Q. Did you have any signs up outside the house that you were selling vegetables?

A. No.

Q. It was purely by word of mouth?

A. Yes.

Q. So it wasn't business?

A. No.

Q. It was more in the lines of a hobby but earned some pin money?

A. Yes.

Whatever the appellant may have understood by the last two questions or intended by his answer to them, there was plenty of other evidence, all on affidavit.

What Priestley does here is to allow the appellant a voice, to let him who comes before the law be heard, and simultaneously to let the power of the institution to silence and appropriate that voice be heard and recognised. What he demonstrates is the asymmetrical distribution of access to talk in the genre of the cross-examination which enacts and performs institutional domination by, in this case, rewriting "business" as "hobby" and "pin money," and, once again, recuperating unruly private stories, eye-witness accounts, into the norms of public or middle-class white male discourse. Priestley changes the genre of the judgement by using the voice of the appellant in cross-examination, subject to cross-examination, as his authority and evidence. In the structure of his judgement this replaces the usual quotation of precedent and contrasts strongly with Maegher's subservience to the usual authorities in the corresponding section of his judgment:

> Nonetheless I find his Honour's (Master Windeyer's) analysis both relevant and helpful in the present context. His Honour said: 'In Kauri Timber Co. (Tas.) Pty. Ltd. v. Rieman (1973), 128 C.L.R. 177, at pp.188–189, and etc..

This quotation, mostly deciding the question of the appellant's dependency in relation to Kauri Timber, is two-thirds of an A4 page in length. What we have in Priestley's judgment is evidence of a change of habit in process, of a subject acting for change within a system that has not changed, of the politics of change in local sites, of the kind of resistance and change that matters.

My final example is an academic paper on the Leigh Leigh Rape Murder Case (Carrington and Johnson, 1994) recently published in *The Australian Feminist Law Journal*. The paper itself constitutes a very troubling and upsetting account of the deafness of the system, when allowed to work unmediated (to evolve in the liberal humanist fashion suggested in some of the papers discussed at the outset of this chapter), in relation to sexual difference. The case the paper discusses is one in which a fourteen-year-old girl was sexually assaulted, raped, and brutally murdered by a group of ten or more boys, as it were in public, at a party. But it is not just the murder that is the focus of the paper. It is the legal process which subsequently occludes the matter of multiple instances of sexual assault, rewrites a case of brutal rape as murder, colludes in the neglect of crucial evidence, reverses the roles of victim and offender by displacing guilt for the murder onto the bad parent and the promiscuous girl (both narratives that are easy targets for this kind of public recuperative work), and condones and approves the violence of young masculinity on these same grounds. The murderer misunderstood: he thought she consented. It is an extraordinary story of the blurring of the boundaries between public and private in the intersections and collusions between local community, police, the judiciary, the court system, and the media.

It is a feminist story, a poststructuralist story, a story that shows just how relentlessly and violently the system of gender hierarchy perpetuates itself, and it is a postmodernist story constructed with the aid of modes of reading and theorising that are capable, just as relentlessly, of showing how a system that constructs itself as modernist, bounded, autonomous, justice, truth, objectivity, is anything but these things. It is academic theoretical work of a very political kind, work which contra Fish, Norris, and others, does not argue that "truth" is nothing but existing consensus beliefs (Norris, 1993, 22–23). It argues rather that that consensus masquerades as "truth"—the truth of the law, the community, the family, the judiciary, and the media—to conceal the "truth" of Leigh Leigh's story, her femininity, her rape, her violation. The system of consensus is able to do this because of the recuperative powers of intertextuality, narrative, and discursive constructions of realities, figural representations, and the emotional and symbolic dimensions of the crime. I want to quote now from the paper itself:

> Our research has a number of theoretical purposes. One of these has been to analyse some of the complex social aspects of punishment by examining the deeply felt emotional responses to and symbolic dimensions of the crime. . . . We have added to this an

analysis which interrogates a remarkable continuity between and blurring of the public and private symbolic dimensions of the crime. Our argument displaces the false dichotomisations often posited between the public and the private, the state and civil society, the local and structural effects of discourse and social power. This is most evident in our analysis of the constructions of adolescent female sexuality generated at the local level in Stockton's youth culture, reproduced in the shape of the police investigation, transformed into juridical discourse and re-presented in public culture through the print and electronic media coverage of the crime. (p. 5)

Here the work is acknowledged as being Foucauldian and feminist in inspiration and method. Later after examination of many of the texts (oral and written) produced through the original and their own investigations the following analysis occurs:

In this passage, Leigh's deep distress about this sexual assault upon her is constructed as the fanciful imaginings of a hysterical virgin who having consented to her first sexual encounter, later felt guilt and fear that she may be pregnant. Given the eye-witness testimony of the deep distress and relentless complaints by the victim, the sighting of blood on her crotch and in between her legs and the forensic evidence of serious injuries to the vagina, *this account of what happened is hardly plausible*. This is evidence more consistent with having been violently sexually assaulted than with "having had sex," implying consent. This problematic reconstruction of Leigh's sexuality intensified when it intersected with the psychological constructions of Matthew Webster as having engaged in an act of misrecognition and not an act of sexual violence. (p. 15; my emphasis)

And yet it is this problematic reconstruction of Leigh Leigh's sexuality which becomes "doxa" and on which the case is judged. The authors of this paper offer a different story as a result of their own investigations:

We have been told it was during this time she sustained most of the injuries to her genital organs as a result of a beer bottle being thrust inside her. We have reason to suspect this was "punishment" for refusing the "invitation" to "root." In sociological terms there has to be some collective responsibility for a murder which follows a sequence of violent assaults involving as many as ten boys. The murder was the fourth and final assault upon the victim. It was the ultimate silence. (p. 29)

The paper concludes with a call for the reopening of the investigation into Leigh's murder. The following report was published in the first issue of the *Australian Feminist Law Foundation Newsletter*, late in 1994:

Since publication, the Royal Commission into Police Corruption has undertaken to examine the various issues raised by Carrington and Johnson in the article. Ironically, the Royal Commissioner is Justice Wood, the judge who presided over the trial of Matthew Webster, who was convicted of Leigh Leigh's murder and sentenced to 14 years goal. A representative of the Royal Commissioner's office has assured Carrington that nothing arising out of Justice Wood's involvement in the trial will affect his consideration of the circumstances of the police investigation. (1994, 2)

This then is a piece of poststructuralist, feminist, and postmodernist research which is radically political in its implications and which, through the *Feminist Law Journal* and Foundation has had and will have political effects of a more than textual kind, even with, and despite, the potential systemic "restoration" hinted at in the above passage. Theory here produces an ethically and politically motivated "close reading" of a "text" which is all too real even if constituted of simulacra and narrative differends. The work is concerned precisely with the absolute normality of the complex system of narrative recuperation it uncovers, the rewriting of a horrific violence into the normality and neutrality of the stereotyped narratives of public and private discourse, and the power of those narratives to conceal and silence even the forensic evidence. What Carrington and Johnson describe is a legal system enmeshed, embodied, incorporated if you like, into everyday life and they do this as part of everyday life in the academy.

There is a real politics in all these examples. And it is both postmodern and poststructuralist in its refusal to go back to earlier categories without recognising the epistemological need to rewrite them constantly, to be ever vigilant of their recuperative tendencies. It is poststructuralist, deconstructive, and postcolonial too in avoiding at all costs the seductions of incorporating or "embracing the other" in liberal humanist, democratic, or socialist unreflective mode. Postmodernist critique and deconstruction, feminist or otherwise, are concerned precisely with making that move problematic, difficult, enigmatic. Multiple realities, poststructuralist subjectivities, and the recognition of irrecon-cilable differences—the recognition of the *differend* and learning to hear its silences in order to let them be heard—will do better with that enigma than those who want to incorporate it and make it the same, or those who want to return to the mirage of earlier decidabilities and determinacies.

REFERENCES

Althusser, L. (1971). *Lenin and philosophy and other essays*. Trans. Ben Brewster. London: New Left Books.

Australian Feminist Law Foundation Newsletter, 1 (December 1994).

Bennington, G. (1994). *Legislations: The politics of deconstruction*. London: Verso.

Butler, J. (1992). Contingent foundations: Feminism and the question of "post-modernism." In J. Butler and J. W. Scott (Eds.), *Feminists theorise the polit-ical*. New York: Routledge.

Carrington, K. & Johnson, A. (1994). Representations of crime, guilt and sexu-ality in the Leigh Liegh rape muder case. *The Australian Feminist Law Jour-nal*, 3, 3–29.

Cornell, D. (1991). *Beyond accommodation: Ethical feminism, deconstruction and the law*. New York/London: Routledge.

——— (1992). The philosophy of the limit: Systems theory and feminist legal reform. In Cornell et al., 1992, 68–94.

——— (1993). *Transformations: Recollective imagination and sexual difference*. New York/London: Routledge.

Cornell, D., Rosenfeld, M., & D. G. Carlson (Eds.) (1992). *Deconstruction and the possibility of justice*. London: Routledge.

Derrida, J. (1976). *Of grammatology*. Baltimore: Johns Hopkins University Press.

——— (1988). *Limited inc*. Evanston, IL: Northwestern University Press.

Douzinas, C., Goodrich, P. & Hachamovitch, Y. (1994). *Politics, postmodernity and critical legal studies: The legality of the contingent*. London/New York: Routledge.

Dworkin, R. (1982). Law as interpretation. *Critical Inquiry*, 9, 179.

Eagleton, T. (1985). Capitalism, modernism and postmodernism. *New Left Review*, 152, 60–73.

Eco, U. (1976). *A theory of semiotics*. Bloomington: University of Indiana Press.

Elam, D. (1994). *Feminism and deconstruction: Ms. en abyme*. London: Routledge.

Fish, S. (1989/1992). *Doing what comes naturally: Change, rhetoric, and the practice of theory in literary and legal studies*. Durham: Duke University Press.

Foucault, M. (1971). Orders of discourse: Inaugural lecture delivered at the College de France. *Social Science Information*, 10(2), 7–30.

Goddard, C. (1993). Daniel's day in court. *The Age*, 22 November, p. 13.

Goodrich, P. & Hachamovitch, Y. (1991). The semiotics of the common law. In P. Fitzpatrick (Ed.), *Dangerous supplements*. Pluto Press: London.

Haraway, D. (1991). *Simians, cyborgs and women: The reinvention of nature*. London: Free Association Books.

Howe, A. (1994). *Punish and critique: Towards a feminist analysis of penalty*. London: Routledge.

Hutcheon, L. (1989). *The politics of postmodernism*. London/New York: Routledge.

Jacobson, A. J. (1992). The idolatry of rules: Writing law according to Moses, with reference to other jurisprudences. In Cornell et al., 1992, 95–151.

Jameson, F. (1983). Postmodernism and consumer society. In H. Foster, *The anti-aesthetic: Essays on postmodern culture*, (pp. 11–25). Washington: Bay Press, 1983.

——— (1984). The politics of theory: Ideological positions in the postmodernism debate. *New German Critique*, 33, 33–65.

de Lauretis, T. (1984). *Alice doesn't: Feminism, semiotics, cinema*. Bloomington: Indiana University Press.

Lyotard, J.-F. (1988). *The differend: Phrases in dispute*. Manchester: Manchester University Press.

Luke, A. (1993). Genres of power? Literacy education and the production of power. In R. Hasan and G. Williams (Eds.), *Literacy in society*. London: Longman.

MacKinnon, C. A. (1987). *Feminism unmodified: Discourses on life and law*. Cambridge, MA: Harvard University Press.

——— (1989). *Towards a feminist theory of the state*. Cambridge, MA: Harvard University Press.

de Man, P. (1986). The resistance to theory. In *The Resistance to Theory*. Minneapolis: University of Minnesota Press.

Matoesian, G. M. (1993). *Reproducing rape: Domination through talk in the courtroom*. Chicago: University of Chicago Press.

Narogin, M. (1988). *Doin wildcat: A novel koori script*. Melbourne: Hyland House.

————— (1990). *Writing from the fringe: A study of modern aboriginal literature*. Melbourne: Hyland House.

Norris, C. (1989). *Deconstruction and the interests of theory*. Norman: University of Oklahoma.

————— (1992). *Uncritical theory: Postmodernism, intellectuals and the Gulf War*. Amherst: The University of Massachussetts Press.

————— (1993). *The truth about postmodernism*. Oxford: Basil Blackwell.

O'Shane, P. (1993). Launch of *The Australian Feminist Law Journal*, speech. *The Australian Feminist Law Journal*, 2 (1994), 3–12.

Probyn, E. (1993). *Sexing the self: Gendered positions in cultural studies*. London/New York: Routledge.

Rorty, R. (1991). Feminism and pragmatism. *Michigan Quarterly Review*, Winter 1991, 231.

Rosenfeld, M. (1992). Deconstruction and legal interpretation: Conflict, indeterminacy and the temptations of the new legal formalism. In Cornell et al., 1992, 152–210.

Scott, J. W. (1988). *Gender and the politics of history*. New York: Columbia University Press.

Smith, D. E. (1990). *Texts, facts and femininity: Exploring the relations of ruling*. London/New York: Routledge.

Spivak, G. (1983). Displacement and the discourse of woman. In M. Krupnick (Ed.), *Displacement: Derrida and after*. Bloomington: Indiana University Press.

————— (1989). Feminism and deconstruction, again: Negotiations. In Spivak (Ed.), *Outside in the teaching machine*, (pp. 121–140). New York/London: Routledge, 1993.

Stephens, J. (1992). The HSC examination committee: A view from 1991. *The Teaching of English*, 2, 22–26.

Thornton, M. (1994). Discord in the legal academy: The case of the feminist scholar. *The Australian Feminist Law Journal*, 3 (1994), 53–71.

Threadgold, T. (1993). Critical theory, feminisms, the judiciary and rape. *The Australian Feminist Law Journal*, 1 (1993), 7–26.

———— (1994). Re-writing law as postmodern fiction: The poetics of child abuse. In J. N. Turner and P. Williams (Eds.), *The happy couple: Law and Literature,* pp. 322–341. Sydney: The Federation Press.

Weedon, C. (1987). *Feminist practice and poststructuralist theory.* Oxford: Basil Blackwell.

Yeatman, A. (1990). *Bureaucrats, technocrats, femocrats: Essays on the contemporary Australian state.* Sydney: Allen & Unwin.

CONTRIBUTORS

SANDRA LEE BARTKY is Professor of Philosophy and Women's Studies at the University of Illinois at Chicago. Her interest in feminist philosophy is tied to commitments to feminist politics in which she has been involved since the Civil Rights Movement of the late 1950s. Her fields of specialization, apart from feminist theory, are existentialism and phenomenology, critical theory, poststructuralism, ethics, political and social philosophy, Marxism and neo-Marxism. She has published widely in these areas over the last three decades, and her most recent book is *Femininity and Domination* (Routledge, 1990).

ANNA BENNETT is an honours student in the Department of Sociology and Anthropology at the University of Newcastle, Australia. Her research interests are in feminism and popular culture, and she has worked as a research assistant with Kerry Carrington on a project titled *Representations of Adolescence & Femininity in Popular Culture*.

SUSAN BORDO is Professor of Philosophy and Otis A. Singletary Chair in the Humanities, Department of Philosophy, at the University of Kentucky. Her areas of specialization are philosophy of culture, feminist thory, and philosophy of the body. Her most recent book, *Unbearable Weight: Feminism, Western Culture and the Body* (University of California Press, 1993) was nominated for a Pulitzer prize, and was selected one of the "Notable Books of 1993" by *The New York Times*. She is currently working on a book on masculinity.

KERRY CARRINGTON is Senior Lecturer in Gender Studies at the University of Western Sydney (Hawkesbury). In 1991 she won the Jean Martin Award for her doctoral studies. She is the author of *Offending Girls: Sex, Youth & Justice* (Allen & Unwin, 1993), and co-editor with M. Dever, R.

Hogg, A. Lohrey, and J. Bargen of *Travesty! Miscarriages of Justice* (Pluto Press, 1991); with S. Cook and J. Bessant of *Cultures of Crime & Violence* (La Trobe University Press, 1994); and with B. Morris of *Politics, Prisons and Punishment* (La Trobe University Press, 1994). She has published widely in a range of journals on diverse topics such as girls' graffiti, feminist criminology, and postmodernism.

REY CHOW is Professor of Comparative Literature at the University of California at Irvine. She is author of *Woman and Chinese Modernity* (University of Minnesota Press, 1991), *Writing Diaspora* (Indiana University Press, 1993), and *Primitive Passions: Visuality, Sexuality, Ethnography, and Contemporary Chinese Cinema* (Columbia University Press, 1995).

PATRICIA DUDGEON is Head of the Centre for Aboriginal Studies at Curtin University in Western Australia. She has worked closely with Aboriginal communities throughout Australia, and has been instrumental in developing the Centre into a full-fledged academic department. She is a qualified psychologist and currently a member of the Parole Board of Western Australia. She has published numerous articles on Aboriginal education and related issues in Australian monographs and journals.

ZILLAH EISENSTEIN is Professor of Politics at Ithaca College, New York. Her most recent books are *The Female Body and the Law* (University of California Press, 1988) and *The Color of Gender: Reimaging Democracy* (University of California Press, 1994). She is presently at work on *Nationalizing Identities and New-Old Hatreds* (Routledge).

GLENIS GROGAN is Coordinator of the Aboriginal Health Unit, Centre for Aboriginal Studies at Curtin University of Technology in Perth, Australia. Her background is general nursing and midwifery. She has many years of experience in rural and remote-area nursing within outback Australia, and has been involved in the establishment of several independent Aboriginal organizations. In her current academic role she has managed and directed the development of current courses in indigenous community health.

ANNELIESE KRAMER-DAHL is a Senior Lecturer at the School of Arts at the National Institute of Education in Singapore. She has taught discourse analysis, and composition in Canada, the United States, and Singapore. Her publications have appeared in *Social Semiotics, South East*

Asian Studies of Social Science, Discourse and other journals, and include analyses of academic discourse and critical readings of contemporary composition theories and pedagogy. Her most recent work attempts a re-vision of writing-across-the-curriculum pedagogy from a feminist perspective.

CARMEN LUKE is Associate Professor in Education at the University of Queensland in Australia. She is the author of *Pedagogy, Printing, and Protestantism: The Discourse on Childhood* (SUNY Press, 1989), *Constructing the Child Viewer: A History of the Discourse on Children and TV* (Praeger, 1990), and co-editor with Jennifer Gore of *Feminisms and Critical Pedagogy* (Routledge, 1992). Her work has focused on feminist theory, media and popular culture, the politics of pedagogy, and women in higher education.

DAVID MORGAN has taught Sociology at the University of Manchester in England for thirty years. His main interests are the sociology of gender with particular reference to men and masculinities and family sociology, and the use of autobiography in social enquiry. He is author of *The Family, Politics and Social Theory* (Routledge, 1985), and *Discovering Men* (Routledge, 1992), and co-authored with Sue Scott *Body Matters* (Falmer, 1993).

DARLENE OXENHAM is an anthropologist currently working as Coordinator of the Centre for Aboriginal Studies at Curtin University of Technology in Perth, Western Australia. She is responsible for the management and development of a degree and diploma course in Aboriginal Community Management and Development. Prior to her current position, she worked for the Department of Aboriginal Sites, Western Australian Museum. Her current research interests are in anthropology, archaeology, and curriculum design.

ANN PHOENIX teaches in the Department of Psychology at Birbeck College, University of London. Her research interests include motherhood, children's development, youth and social identities. She is the author of *Young Mothers* (Polity Press, 1991), and co-edited with Anne Woollett and Eva Lloyd *Motherhood: Meanings, Practices, Ideologies* (Sage, 1991); *Working Out: New Directions for Women's Studies* (Falmer, 1991), with Hilary Hinds and Jackie Stacey; *Black, White or Mixed Race? Race and Racism in the Lives of Young People of Mixed Parentage* (Routlege, 1993) with Barbara Tizard; and *Shifting Identities, Shifting Racisms* (Sage, 1994) with Kum-Kum Bhavnani.

ELISABETH PORTER is lecturer in Sociology at the University of Ulster at Coleraine. She is the author of *Women and Moral Identity* (Allen & Unwin, 1991) and *Good Families* (1995), and has published articles in feminist ethics. Current research interests include contemporary social, political, and feminist theory, ethics, family studies, and caring communities.

TERRY THREADGOLD is Professor of English and Head of the English Department at Monash University in Melbourne. Her research and teaching interests include performance studies, critical legal studies, feminist pedagogy, and critical literacy. She is co-editor with John Tulloch of the *Cultural Studies Series* (Allen & Unwin), with Anne Cranny-Francis of *Feminine/Masculine and Representation* (Allen & Unwin, 1990), and with Penny Perther of *Agitating the Organs of Power: Intersections Between Law & Literature* (Allen & Unwin, forthcoming). Her book *Feminist Poetics* is forthcoming with Routledge.

SUSAN WILLIS teaches courses in minority writing and popular culture at Duke University. She is the author of *Specifying: Black Women Writing the American Experience* (University of Wisconsin Press, 1987) and *A Primer for Daily Life* (Routledge, 1991), and co-authored *Inside the Mouse: Work and Play at Disney World* (Duke University Press, 1995). Her work aims to apprehend the contradictions of capitalism in daily life situations, both intimate and trivial.

ANNE WOOLLETT is Principal Lecturer in Developmental Psychology at the University of East London. Her teaching interests are in the contexts families provide for children's development and her research interests include women's experiences of motherhood and mothering, and women's reproductive health. She is co-author with David White of *Families: A Context for Development* (Falmer Press, 1992), with Naomi Pfeiffer of *Women's Experiences of Infertility* (Virago, 1983), and co-editor with Ann Phoenix and Eva Lloyd of *Motherhood: Meanings, Practices and Ideologies* (Sage, 1991).

INDEX

Aboriginal: education and training, 34, 40, 42, 46, 49, 53; families, 41, 42, 44, 46, 47; health, 33, 42–43; history, 32–35, 51; identity, 12, 44, 48, 49, 50, 51; missions, 37, 39, 41, 47; reserves, 34, 48; women, 12, 33, 37, 38

Adorno, T., 189

Althusser, L., 210, 212, 299

Amusement: and play, 188; culture of, 191–193. *See also* Discovery Zone; Disneyland

Ang, I., 169

Annis, D., 70

Appropriation, 281: of feminist work, 281; of the feminine, 285; American law and, 285–289; of Aboriginality, 299; (re)appropriation, 302

Aristotle, 57, 70, 168

Armstrong, R., 70

Aronowitz, S. and Giroux, H., 247, 249

Authority, 5, 6: of developmental texts, 82–85; fathers as figures of, 61; voices of, 249

Bacon, J., 254

Badhwar, N. Kapur, 68, 69

Baker, C. and Luke, A., 259

Banner, L., 144

Barkley Brown, E., 250

Baron, M., 68

Bartholomae, D., 246, 247

Bartholomae, D. and Petrosky, A., 247, 248

Bartky, S., 20

Baudrillard, J., 170, 171, 284, 292

de Beauvoir, S., 65, 71, 225

Bee, H., 82, 83, 88

Benhabib, S., 60

Benjamin, W., 214

Bennington, G., 288

Berland, J., 196, 197

Berndt, R.M. and Berndt, C.H., 32

Bernstein, B., 251

Besag, V.E., 111

Binge behavior, 129, 137, 140. *See also* Food disorders

Bishop, S., 58

Bizzell, P., 246

Blackstone, W., 268

Bloom, A., 245

Blum, L., 68, 70

Bologh, R.W., 105

Bordo, S., 15, 16

Borges, 198

Boulton, G.M., 87, 96, 97

Bourdieu, P., 168, 281

Bradley, B.S., 95

Bradwell, M., 269

Bradwell v. State, 266–267